JEWISH SALONICA

STANFORD STUDIES IN JEWISH HISTORY AND CULTURE
Edited by David Biale and Sarah Abrevaya Stein

JEWISH SALONICA

Between the Ottoman Empire and Modern Greece

DEVIN E. NAAR

Stanford University Press
Stanford, California

Stanford University Press
Stanford, California

Printed in the United States of America on acid-free, archival-quality paper

Library of Congress Cataloging-in-Publication Data

Names: Naar, Devin E., author.
Title: Jewish Salonica : between the Ottoman Empire and modern Greece / Devin E. Naar.
Description: Stanford, California : Stanford University Press, 2016. |
    Includes bibliographical references and index.
Identifiers: LCCN 2016006659 (print) | LCCN 2016007252 (ebook) |
    ISBN 9780804798877 (cloth : alk. paper) | ISBN 9781503600089 (pbk. : alk. paper) |
    ISBN 9781503600096 (e-book)
Subjects: LCSH: Sephardim—Greece—Thessaloniki—History—19th century. |
    Sephardim—Greece—Thessaloniki—History—20th century. |
    Turkey—History—Ottoman Empire, 1288-1918. | Greece—History—1917-1944.
Classification: LCC DS135.G72 N33 2016 (print) | LCC DS135.G72 (ebook) |
    DDC 949.5/65—dc23
LC record available at http://lccn.loc.gov/2016006659

Typeset by Bruce Lundquist in 10.25/15 Adobe Caslon Pro

In memory of *Nono*
Isidore B. Naar
(1917–2008)

CONTENTS

FIGURES AND MAPS

Maps

Figures

PREFACE

El ijo de mi ijo,
dos vezes mi ijo.

The child of my child
is doubly my child.

—Judeo-Spanish proverb

Salonica is a city that I have heard about since I was a child. I tasted its foods and smelled its aromas; the sounds of at least one of its many languages bounced off my curious yet mostly uncomprehending ears. It was the city where my paternal grandfather, whom I called *Nono*, was born in 1917, the same year that, as he later sang to me from a stanza of a popular folk song, *se kemo Salonik* ("Salonica burned"). A turn-of-the-century picture of his father, my great grandfather, perplexed me: a bearded rabbi wearing an Ottoman fez. How could it be, I wondered, that my befezzed great grandfather, *Haham* Benjamin H. Naar, had been born in a place called "Turkey" (i.e., the Ottoman Empire), whereas his son was born in Greece, without the family having moved? Why did relatives from Greece and Turkey speak neither Greek nor Turkish among themselves but rather a language they called "Spanish," which they also chanted as part of the predominantly Hebrew prayers at their synagogue in New Jersey? In retrospect, my dual sense of intimacy with and estrangement from the distinctive world from which my family came, and the desire to bridge the gap, planted the germ of my evolution as a historian and my interest in the subject of this book.

As I sought to learn more about this world as a college student, I began asking questions of *Nono* and his generation, and they graciously shared their memories with me. My great uncle Leon B. Naar also brought my attention to a family treasure: the remnants of my great grandfather's library, including nineteenth-century editions of classics of Ladino literature, like *Meam Loez* and *Pele Yoes*, in addition to a stack of handwritten correspondence composed in a language identified for me as "Spanish," yet which looked unlike anything I had ever seen before. This correspondence introduced me to the distinctive Sephardic Hebrew cursive, *soletreo*, which I painstakingly taught myself to read. My college-level Spanish and basic knowledge of Hebrew, combined with the few words of "our Spanish" I had learned as a child, enabled me to begin to comprehend the documents. But I wanted to understand more. Soon I found myself asking *Nono* to speak with me on the phone every week in his mother tongue, and he eagerly obliged.

The family correspondence detailed with great emotion the devastating fate of another one of my grandfather's brothers, Salomon (1903–1943), his wife, Esther (née Pinhas, 1902–1943), and their two children, Rachel (1925–1943) and Benjamin (1930–1943), who remained in Salonica and ultimately perished in Auschwitz. A deep curiosity about Salomon's world, not only the devastating circumstances surrounding his and his family's death but also the dynamics that shaped their lives, led me, via a circuitous route, to the specific topic of this book. I became intrigued by what Jewish life might have looked like in Salonica—once a "city full of Jews," I was told—in the wake of the transition from Ottoman to Greek sovereignty, the same Salonica that my grandfather had left in 1924 but where Uncle Salomon and his family remained.

In search of Uncle Salomon, I entered the lost world of Jewish Salonica. My investigations into the history of Salonica's Jews over the past fourteen years brought me across the globe in pursuit of the dispersed and largely forgotten Jewish community's archives—Salonica, Athens, Jerusalem, Moscow, New York, and Washington, DC. I always kept an eye out for references to Salomon and his family. As I uncovered scattered references to these long-lost cousins in Greece, I began to reconstruct their world and was struck by the multiple strains of affiliation—religious, political, cultural, socioeconomic—that intertwined in their experience and seemed to offer a counterexample to the prevalent scholarly representation of Jews in interwar Salonica as embattled, excluded, and obstinate in the face of pressures from the state to Hellenize.

Rather than being removed from the center of the city and suffer economic hardship, as the general picture of life for Salonica's Jews during the interwar years would suggest, Salomon and his family ascended the socio-economic ladder, moving from the family's humble residence at the time of the fire of 1917 in the impoverished Jewish quarter, Vardar, to a flat on an upscale pedestrian street adjacent to the Aghia Sophia church in the heart of the city. As an accountant for the local branch of a New York-based company, Salomon benefitted from upward social mobility. But professional success did not prevent Salomon from trying to arrange for his family's immigration to the United States throughout the 1930s—a fruitless effort due to strict American immigration quotas. Remaining in Salonica, Salomon nonetheless engaged in Jewish communal and Greek cultural domains.

Fragmentary records of the Jewish community reveal that Salomon actively participated in Jewish religious, political, and institutional life in Salonica. From 1923 to 1932, he numbered among the city's *mezamerim*, officials who assisted in the performance of the prayer services in the synagogues—a position he inherited from his father, the rabbi, at the Mayor Sheni congregation. As recorded in accounting ledgers from 1929, Salomon also made a financial transaction with the Salonica-Palestine Company, a Zionist enterprise that promoted the development of Jewish business in Palestine, especially through the acquisition of real estate in Tel Aviv. Later, during the German occupation, Salomon was appointed to the committee of the Matanoth Laevionim, the Jewish soup kitchen, as noted by the historian Joseph Nehama in a volume dedicated to the Jews of Greece, *In Memoriam* (1948). The family letters reveal that Salomon was charged with distributing milk and yogurt to the sick and elderly as they boarded the trains to Auschwitz in 1943, before he and his family met the same fate.

When I uncovered the fragmentary records of the Matanoth Laevionim, I was amazed to discover a letter from 1942 inviting Salomon to serve as a member of the organizing committee. And then I found Salomon's response, in which he gladly accepted the appointment. Notably, both documents were penned in fluent, flowing Greek. This seemed to indicate that Salomon and the committee members of the Matanoth Laevionim had not only successfully learned Greek but preferred that language, even for intra-Jewish matters, over the presumably more familiar Judeo-Spanish or even French.

Although born in the Ottoman Empire, to what extent had Salomon embraced his new status as a Greek citizen while maintaining connections to

the Jewish community? The educational decisions that he and Esther made
for their children throw some light on the question. They did not send Shelly
and Benny to the Jewish communal schools or to a foreign school but rather
to a Greek private school, Valagianni. Operating according to the Montes-
sori model, Valagianni included classes in Greek language, literature, and
history, with emphases on the humanities, sciences, music, and art. French
and English were compulsory foreign languages, whereas German and Hebrew—yes, Hebrew—were electives. Mostly bourgeois families, merchants,
white-collar employees, lawyers, and doctors sent their children there. As
many as a third of the students were Jewish at any given point during the
interwar years.

    I was amazed to discover among the records of the Valagianni school,
preserved in private hands, that Salomon's daughter not only numbered
among the best students in her class but was also involved in the school's
patriotic festivities. The program for the annual celebration of Greek independence in March 1938 included Rachel's name at the top of a list of
students called upon to present the Greek flag in conjunction with the performance of a patriotic play *Hail, Hail Liberty!* The title alludes to a famous
verse in the Greek national anthem composed by the celebrated nineteenth-
century revolutionary poet, Dionysios Solomos. Rachel participated in the
patriotic celebration without, it seems, compromising her status as a Jew and
despite her father's apparent affiliation with Zionism.

    It appeared that Salomon and his children could successfully blend their
Jewish, Hellenic, and Zionist affiliations. How common was it for Jews in
interwar Salonica to combine these allegiances? What did it say about the
possibilities of Jewish participation in the life of Greece in the decades prior
to World War II? While the story of my grandfather planted in me an interest in the history of Salonica's Jews, it was wrestling with the multiple
threads of identity that wove themselves together in the story of his brother,
Salomon, and his family, that inspired me to explore the specific themes of
this book.

    How, in short, did the transition from Ottoman to Greek sovereignty
impact Jewish society, and how did Jews varyingly embrace, resist, and negotiate the process both as individuals and as a collective? What did it mean
for them to be Salonican, Jewish, Ottoman, and subsequently Greek? What

does the Jewish story tell us about the dynamics of the Ottoman and Greek worlds and the ruptures and continuities between them? Were the struggles faced by Salonica's Jews particular to the city or part of broader phenomena impacting Jewish communities or other populations in Europe and the Middle East? What are the aftereffects and enduring legacies of these transformations today?

ACKNOWLEDGMENTS

I owe my first debt of gratitude to my relatives with roots in Salonica for sharing their memories of the city with me, for their patience in answering myriad questions, and for serving as my first informants. I am especially grateful to my late grandfather, Isidore B. Naar, who inspired my research; to his brothers and sisters; and to the extended Naar, Nifoussi (and Nefouse), Fais, Auyash, Pavon, Oziel, and Cohen clans (as well as my Rochkind and Katz relatives). Many friends and mentors helped me early on. Izo Abram, David Sheby, and Brian Berman helped me decode *soletreo*. Gary Schiff kindly invited me to explore the uncatalogued papers of his step-uncle, Isaac Emmanuel, who became a central figure in this book. As an undergraduate at Washington University in St. Louis, I benefitted from my studies with Henry Berger, Martin Jacobs, Louis Fishman, Ahmet Karamustafa, and in particular Hillel Kieval, who supervised my senior thesis and encouraged me to pursue graduate studies.

The year I spent in Salonica as a Fulbright scholar was unforgettable and numbered one of many stays in Greece over the past decade. At the Fulbright offices, I remain grateful to Artemis Zenetou, Nicholas Tourides, and Dimitrios Doutis. A special debt of gratitude goes to the Jewish Community of Salonica and its executive council, under the presidency of David Saltiel, who provided me with access to archival materials and continues to encourage my research. Samuel Josafat, Marcel Hassid, Ida Nahmias, and Lucy Nahmias

provided key administrative support. Rena Molho, a pioneer of Jewish histori-
cal study in Greece, invited me to attend my first academic conference in 2004
and continues to inspire me. Over the years, many friends in Greece helped
me with my research and shared their perspectives: the late Leon (Lelos)
Arouh, Paul Hagouel, the late Andreas Kounio, Heinz Kounio, Davico Saltiel,
Solon Solomon, Mordehai Frizis, and Daniel Ashkenazi-Weise. Evangelos
Hekimoglou pointed me to sources and scholarship. Special thanks go to Aliki
Arouh, Jacky Benmayor, Alexis Menexiadis, Leon Saltiel, Paris Papamichos
Chronakis, Iosif Vaena, and especially Erika Perahia Zemour at the Jewish
Museum of Salonica, and my Greek-language teacher, Nina Molho.

In my hunt for the archives of the Jewish community of Salonica, I
benefitted from the support of many colleagues who enabled me to identify, catalog, and prepare the records for microfilming. With chief archivist
Fruma Mohrer and her colleagues at the YIVO Institute for Jewish Research
in New York, I cataloged the Salonica holdings there and benefitted from
the advice and expertise of Marcia Hadad Ikonomopoulos from the Kehila
Kedosha Janina Museum; Steven Bowman at the University of Cincinnati;
Isaac Benmayor from Salonica, who continued to help me decode documents
in Greek; and David Bunis, the director of Judezmo Studies at Hebrew University in Jerusalem, whom I was pleased to welcome to the University of
Washington a decade later as a visiting scholar. In conjunction with the Jewish Museum of Salonica, I put together a successful documentary exhibition
and bilingual Greek-English catalog. Hadassah Assouline at the Central Archives for the History of the Jewish People in Jerusalem and Anatol Steck,
Vadim Altskan, Radu Ioanid, Leah Wolfson, and the late Isaac Nehama at
the United States Holocaust Memorial Museum in Washington, DC, were
great partners in the process, as was Patricia Grimsted at Harvard, who arranged for me to access Salonica materials in person at the Russian State
Military Archive in Moscow. In New York, I also received assistance from
the American Sephardi Federation librarian, Randall Belinfante, and the
Special Collections curator at Yeshiva University, Shulamith Berger, and had
conversations with Robert Bedford of the Foundation for the Advancement
of Sephardic Studies and Culture.

In Israel, I benefitted from the assistance of Dov Cohen, then at the Ben
Zvi Institute; Yaron Ben-Naeh and Eyal Ginio at Hebrew University; and

Shmuel Refael at the Salti Center for Ladino Studies at Bar Ilan University. Meetings in Tel Aviv with David Recanati (the son of Abraham Recanati); Meir Pinto (the grandson of Rabbi Haim Habib); and a presumed long-lost cousin and Auschwitz survivor, Shmuel Naar (a student of Mercado Covo) shaped my perceptions of the subject. I also learned from conversations with scholars Minna Rozen, Gila Hadar, and Eliezer Papo.

I received crucial feedback at various phases of this project through presentations at conferences and symposia: Modern Greek Studies meetings at Indiana, Yale, Simon Fraser, and Princeton; Association for Jewish Studies meetings in Washington, DC, Chicago, and Los Angeles; conferences on Sephardi Itineraries and on Salonica organized by Esther Benbassa at the Centre Alberto-Benveniste at the Sorbonne; a workshop on Jewish history at Oxford hosted by Christian Wiese, David Rechtor, and Mitchell Hart, and another on Crossing Borders convened by Sarah Abrevaya Stein at UCLA; a symposium on Cultures in Exile at the University of New Mexico-Albuquerque hosted by Eleni Bastéa; the Ruth Gay Seminar at YIVO; a conference convened in Salonica to commemorate the hundredth anniversary of the city's incorporation into Greece, organized by Dimitris Keridis, among others; lectures arranged by Matthias Lehmann at the University of California-Irvine, Liora Halperin and David Shneer at the University of Colorado-Boulder, and Basil Gounaris and Giorgios Antoniou at Aristotle University of Salonica, where I spoke about the history of the Jewish cemetery on the site where it once stood; and, finally, an impactful workshop convened at the International Hellenic University in Salonica that resulted in a marvelous issue of *Jewish History* about Salonica's Jews edited by Anthony Molho, Eyal Ginio, and Paris Papamichos Chronakis.

My debts to teachers, friends, and colleagues at Stanford are innumerable. Special thanks to Charlotte Fonrobert and Vered Karti Shemtov, Zachary Baker, and Mary Felstiner. Keith Baker and Shahzad Bashir offered insights into European and Islamic history that shaped the conceptual framework of this book. I also benefitted tremendously from the friendship of and extended conversions with Binyamin Blum, Olga Borovaya, Julia Phillips Cohen, Dina Danon, Daniel Kupfert Heller, and Uğur Z. Peçe. Steven Zipperstein taught me much about the craft of history and the dynamic nature of the profession, and provided exceptional guidance and feedback along the way. It is my primary mentor, Aron Rodrigue, to whom I owe the greatest debt of gratitude. Our ongoing dialogue, his insightful criticisms, and his vast knowledge of Sephardic Jewry and the Ottoman world shaped this project in countless ways. *Mersi muncho!*

At the University of Washington, I am grateful to Reşat Kasaba and the Jackson School of International Studies for cultivating a lively academic environment, especially in Ottoman studies; Noam Pianko and the Stroum Center for Jewish Studies for fostering dynamic engagement with Jewish history in scholarly and communal forums; and, chaired by Lynn Thomas and Anand Yang, the Department of History, which most importantly invited me to lecture about World War I to a broad audience and compelled me to highlight the broader ramifications of my research. I am also grateful to these three units for their financial support to help bring this book to fruition. Elena Campbell, Purnima Dhavan, Susan Glenn, Maureen Jackson, Reşat Kasaba, Nektaria Klapaki, Joel Migdal, Noam Pianko, Vince Rafael, Shalom Sabar, Charity Urbanski, Adam Warren, and Glennys Young provided feedback at various stages. Sarah Stroup and Mika Ahuvia helped decipher tombstone inscriptions in Latin and Hebrew, respectively, while Katja Schatte helped me interpret sources in German.

As home to one of the largest Sephardic Jewish populations in the country, Seattle and its community serve as an inspiring resource. Many families with roots in Salonica—Abravanel, Almosnino, Altchech, Azous, Ezratty, Handaly, Hanokh, Matalon, Shaloum, and others—shared their memories with me; others helped galvanize our new Sephardic Studies program. Ty Alhadeff, Isaac Azose, Aryeh Greenberg, Albert S. Maimon, and many others offered insights into the Sephardic world. Congregation Ezra Bessaroth, Sephardic Bikor Holim, and the St. Demetrios Greek Orthodox Church—named after the patron saint of Salonica—have taken a keen interested in my work. I am indebted to the Sephardic Studies Founders Circle—Eli and Rebecca Almo, Joel and Maureen Benoliel, Harley and Lela Franco, Richard and Barrie Galanti, and Sharon and Marty Lott—and especially to the Isaac Alhadeff Foundation for making Sephardic Studies a permanent fixture at the University of Washington.

Izo Abram, Jacky Benmayor, Daniel Bessner, Olga Borovaya, Julia Phillips Cohen, Paula Daccarett, Doxis Doxiadis, Katherine Fleming, Daniel

Kupfert Heller, Paris Papamichos Chronakis, Uğur Z. Peçe, Aron Rodrigue, David Sheby, Sarah Abrevaya Stein, and two anonymous readers provided key feedback at various stages in the development of this manuscript. At Stanford University Press, I am immensely grateful to series editors Sarah Abrevaya Stein and David Biale for supporting my project; to Friederike Sundaram, Nora Spiegel, Anne Fuzellier, Margo Irvin, and the rest of the team for shepherding it along; and to Kate Wahl, the press editor, for seeing its potential and bringing it to fruition. Special thanks to copyeditor Angela Roskop Erisman and to Bill Nelson, who drew the maps.

My in-laws Lori and Howard Soroko and brother-in-law Adam offered constant encouragement as I composed many of these pages under their roof. My late-night conversations and brainstorms with my brother, Aaron, helped me gain a better perspective on the narrative structure of my project—and its present-day ramifications. My father, Harry, transmitted something of Jewish Salonica to me and, as a painter, taught me to think about historical writing as an art.

I owe an extra special thank you to my mother, Barbara, who dedicated countless hours to reviewing drafts of the manuscript and offering critical, detailed feedback over the book's long gestation.

My partner, Andrea, has been living with Salonica for more than a decade; after many visits, she knows the city well. As a skillful teacher and close reader, she provided invaluable feedback at all phases of this project, helping me to articulate some of the foundational concepts for this book. For her sustenance and love, I remain forever grateful. As this book entered its final stages, Andrea and I were thrilled to welcome to this world our first child, Vidal, who, already through his name, carries on the spirit of Jewish Salonica.

NOTES ON TRANSLITERATION

For more than four centuries, Jews in Salonica, as in other parts of the Balkans and the Ottoman Empire, spoke and wrote in a language based on fifteenth- and sixteenth-century Iberian dialects (primarily Castilian but also Aragonese, Leonese, Portuguese, etc.). To this Ibero-Romance base, they integrated linguistic elements from Hebrew and Aramaic, the languages of Jewish tradition; Turkish and Greek, the languages of their neighbors in the Ottoman realm; and, later, Italian and French, the languages of European prestige. Historically printed in various styles of the Hebrew alphabet, both *letras de rashi* (Rashi script, also known as rabbinical type) and *meruba* (block type), it was handwritten in a particular style of Hebrew cursive, known as *soletreo*, until World War II, although some documents appeared in Latin letters earlier.

The language and its different varieties have been identified by several names, including Judeo-Spanish, Ladino, Judezmo, Djudyo, and others. While it is now common practice in English-language scholarship in the United States to refer to all varieties of the language—printed and spoken, calque translations and original compositions—as Ladino, I have opted to call it Judeo-Spanish in an attempt to reproduce the way that my sources identified the language. For a variety of reasons, by the twentieth century, Jewish journalists and communal leaders in Salonica tended to refer to their spoken language as *djudeo-espanyol*, derived from the nineteenth-century

French coinage, *judéo-espagnol*, and subsequently rendered into Greek as *ispanoevraïka*. My sources from Salonica sometimes referred to the spoken language as Judezmo, especially in popular forums, but almost never as Ladino, which was instead used occasionally to describe calque translations from Hebrew and certain literary or liturgical texts. This was not the case in all communities—in the United States, for example, Ladino gained currency as the name for the spoken language during the interwar period—but the term Ladino was seldom used in Salonica to identify the everyday language of the people.

I have adopted a modified version of the *Aki Yerushalayim* transcription system, which represents Judeo-Spanish phonetics and pronunciation in order to facilitate broad comprehension. When original sources were composed in Latin letters, I have preserved the author's orthography. In reproducing common names, I have utilized standard spellings in English and French (e.g., Covo instead of Kovo). In order to preserve the flavor of the pronunciation of Hebrew among the Jews of Salonica, I have omitted the "h" in certain words or expressions of Hebrew origin particular to the locality (e.g., Talmud Tora Agadol, rather than Talmud Torah Ha-gadol), but I have adopted standard English spellings for Hebrew words that are common in English (e.g., Torah rather than Tora to refer to the scrolls of the Five Books of Moses). For Hebrew scholarship and biblical references, and for Modern Greek, I use a simplified version of the Library of Congress system that emphasizes phonetics. For Ottoman Turkish terms known in English, I use the English versions (e.g., pasha rather than paşa).

The name of the city that is the subject of this book has been rendered as Salonica, which, along with Salonika, are the standard English spellings. Jews referred to the city as "Saloniko" (from the Italian Salonicco) in the local Judeo-Spanish press and as "Saloniki" in Hebrew until 1937. That year, the Greek state passed a law compelling the city to be referred to by its Greek name, Thessaloniki, and the post office announced that thereafter it would accept only mail addressed to Thessaloniki. Judeo-Spanish sources after 1937 therefore also referred to the city as "Thesaloniki" or "Tesaloniki" (the latter because it was difficult to represent the *theta* sound of Greek in the Hebrew-lettered Judeo-Spanish of the era). The city is also called "Selânik" in Turkish, "Solun" in Bulgarian, "Salonique" and "Thessalonique" in French, and sometimes "Thessalonica" in English, especially in reference to antiquity. Names of other cities in in the region are identified by their standard, current English names (e.g., Istanbul rather than Constantinople and Izmir rather than Smyrna) unless the sources identify them in other ways.

References to all dates have been preserved in the calendar of the sources. At times in Salonica, as many as four calendars were at play for the city's Jews: Hebrew, Islamic, Gregorian (sometimes identified as *ala franka*, or European), and Julian (sometimes identified as *ala grega*, or Greek). Sometimes multiple dates were used, and I have occasionally noted when that is the case. Sometimes it is not possible to determine whether the Gregorian or Julian calendar was being used. While the Ottoman Empire began using the Gregorian calendar for certain purposes in 1917, Greece did not do so until February 16, 1923, which became March 1. Certainly after that date, the reader can assume that all dates provided, other than those in the Hebrew calendar, are in accordance with the Gregorian calendar.

Belgrade

Sarajevo

ROMANIA

YUGOSLAVIA

BULGARIA

Sofia

Plovdiv

Skopje

BLACK SEA

ADRIATIC SEA

ALBANIA

Edirne

Demotika

Istanbul

Monastir

Serres

Drama

Xanthi

Komotini

Florina

Veria

Kavalla

Salonica

Kastoria

Ioannina

Larissa

Trikkala

Volos

AEGEAN SEA

TURKEY

Preveza

Kerkira (Corfu)

GREECE

Halkis

Izmir

Athens

Piraeus

IOANIAN SEA

Rhodes

CRETE

MEDITERRANEAN SEA

Border of Ottoman Empire (1878)
Borders in 1919

The Consolidation of Greek Territory
Kingdom of Greece, 1832
Ionian Islands, 1864
Thessaly, 1881
Epirus, Macedonia and Crete, 1913
West Thrace, 1923
East Thrace and Ionia, 1920; and lost to Turkey, 1923
Dodecanese to Italy, 1912; to Greece, 1947

0   50   100 mi
0   50   100   150 km

Map 1. Salonica in the context of the Ottoman Empire, the Balkans, and Asia Minor during the consolidation of Greek territory, 1832–1947.

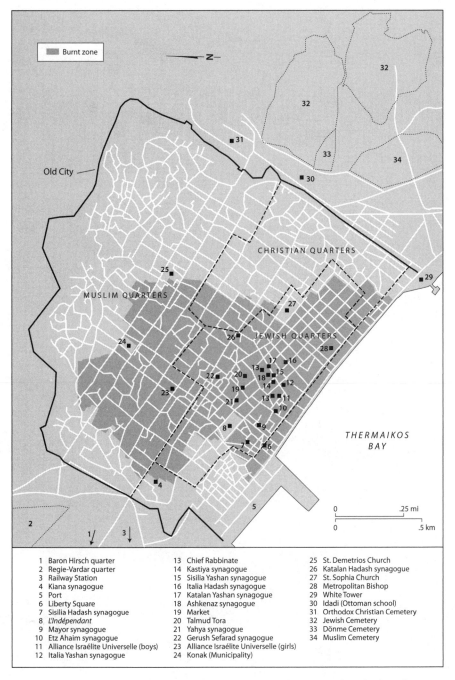

Old City

CHRISTIAN QUARTERS

MUSLIM QUARTERS

JEWISH QUARTERS

THERMAIKOS
BAY

0   .25 mi
0   .5 km

1	Baron Hirsch quarter	13	Chief Rabbinate	25	St. Demetrios Church
2	Regie-Vardar quarter	14	Kastiya synagogue	26	Katalan Hadash synagogue
3	Railway Station	15	Sisilia Yashan synagogue	27	St. Sophia Church
4	Kiana synagogue	16	Italia Hadash synagogue	28	Metropolitan Bishop
5	Port	17	Katalan Yashan synagogue	29	White Tower
6	Liberty Square	18	Ashkenaz synagogue	30	Idadi (Ottoman school)
7	Sisilia Hadash synagogue	19	Market	31	Orthodox Christian Cemetery
8	*L'Indépendant*	20	Talmud Tora	32	Jewish Cemetery
9	Mayor synagogue	21	Yahya synagogue	33	Dönme Cemetery
10	Etz Ahaim synagogue	22	Gerush Sefarad synagogue	34	Muslim Cemetery
11	Alliance Israélite Universelle (boys)	23	Alliance Israélite Universelle (girls)		
12	Italia Yashan synagogue	24	Konak (Municipality)		

Map 2. Approximate locations of sites of Jewish interest in Salonica before the fire of 1917. The boundaries of the Jewish, Christian, and Muslim quarters are not absolute, as members of each community resided elsewhere.

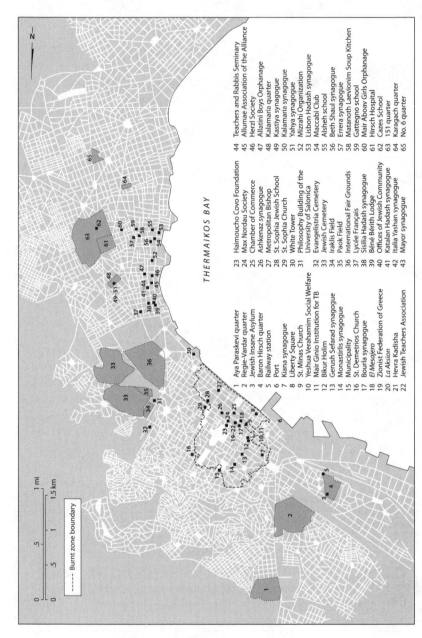

Map 3. Approximate locations of sites of Jewish interest in Salonica on the eve of World War II, c. 1939.

JEWISH SALONICA

IS SALONICA JEWISH?

Boz del puevlo, boz del sielo.
The voice of the people is
the voice of the heavens.

—Judeo-Spanish proverb

"Salonica is neither Greek, nor Bulgarian, nor Turkish; she is Jewish," proclaimed David Florentin, a journalist and the vice president of the Maccabi club of Salonica, amidst the Balkan Wars (1912–1913). After more than four hundred years under Ottoman rule, Salonica (Thessaloniki in Greek)—a strategic Aegean port city at the crossroads of Europe and the Middle East and the gateway to the Balkans—now faced the possibility of being annexed to Greece or Bulgaria. Their armies occupied this "coveted city," and their representatives courted the "Jewish citizens of Salonica," whom they perceived to be influential and whose support they wanted.[1] But Florentin feared that constricting the city to the borders of Bulgaria or Greece would cut ties with markets in the Balkans and devastate the city's economic raison d'être, the port, from which the merchant classes—and much of the urban population as a whole—derived their livelihoods: "Salonica would become a heart that would cease to beat, a head that would be severed from its dismembered body." In petitions to the World Zionist Organization in Berlin, Florentin boldly argued that, if preservation of Ottoman rule could not be assured, Salonica should be transformed into a international city, like Tangiers or Dalian (in Manchuria), guaranteed by the Great Powers and policed by the Swiss or the Belgians but preferably with a Jewish administration—a kind of autonomous Jewish city-state.[2]

Florentin argued that such a seemingly unexpected scenario was the only reasonable fate for Salonica, the "Queen of 'Jewishness' in the Orient." Salonica represented a dynamic Jewish center, where the majority of the population was Jewish—and purportedly had been so since the arrival of Sephardic Jews expelled from Spain in 1492. Jews could be found in all strata of society as bankers, businessmen, retailers, merchants, civil servants, boatmen, and port workers. In laying out his argument, Florentin echoed grand characterizations of his city by visitors to this "Pearl of the Aegean." Right-wing Zionist leader Vladimir Jabotinsky, who visited in 1909, referred to Salonica as "the most Jewish city in the world," the "Jerusalem of Turkey," where even the post office closed on the Jewish Sabbath. Labor Zionist David Ben-Gurion, who sojourned in the city in 1911, remarked that Salonica constituted "a Jewish labor city, the only one in the world." British and French travelers further emphasized the "predominance" of the "chosen people" in this "New Jerusalem," where the Jewish Sabbath was "most vigorously observed," and where, they speculated, the Temple of Solomon might be rebuilt or the messiah would appear.[3]

Amidst a cauldron of competing claims over the future of Salonica made by the Great Powers, international organizations, and major newspapers, the city emerged as the "cockpit of the Eastern Question," the site where, according to political commentators, the fate of all Ottoman territories would be determined.[4] The Austro-Hungarian Empire viewed the city as the "gate to the Mediterranean" and saw the benefits of establishing an independent Jewish statelet that would guarantee the empire's access to a warm water port.[5] The Jewish Territorialist Organization, which advocated for the creation of a Jewish homeland anywhere in the world, similarly supported the plan. The *New York Times* suggested that the creation of an autonomous Jewish Salonica appeared *more* feasible than a future independent Jewish state in Palestine, for the latter would have to be built virtually from scratch.[6] The Alliance Israélite Universelle in Paris and the Anglo-Jewish Association in London also expressed support. In contrast, the World Zionist Organization met the proposition with ambivalence on the grounds that the creation of a Jewish state in Salonica would undermine the establishment of a Jewish state in Palestine. The main Judeo-Spanish newspaper of Istanbul, *El Tiempo*, dismissed the prospect of Jewish autonomy in Salonica as a "fantastical" and "utopian" scheme.[7]

Most strikingly, Salonican non-Jews expressed preference for Jewish rule or internationalization. Local Muslims, Vlachs, Jews, and Dönme (descendants of Jewish converts to Islam who were officially recognized as Muslims) formed the Macedonian Committee to advocate for internationalization, arguing that the "principle of nationalities," which underpinned the concept of "self-determination" championed by US President Woodrow Wilson, should be applied to Salonica like everywhere else—and thus Jews, who formed the predominant "national" demographic element in the city, ought to reign sovereign.[8] A similar constituency of merchants at the city's Chamber of Commerce further contemplated transforming Salonica into a free city and encircling it with barbed wire to minimize smuggling.[9] But none of these proposals was to be. Greece permanently annexed the city in 1913.

The dream of Jewish autonomy, the possibilities of internationalization, and aspirations for a different future for Salonica did not disappear. Following the Balkan Wars, many Salonican Jews dispersed across the globe as "exiled sons" in the wake of the capture of their "motherland," Salonica, by Greece. Some who settled in New York anticipated the arrival of a "cleansing deluge" with World War I that would transform Salonica into the capital of an autonomous Macedonia—and thus precipitate their return from temporary exile.[10] Perhaps Greek statesman Ion Dragoumis' vision for an "Eastern Federation" would unite all the peoples of the region through shared state governance.[11] Or maybe a proposal to the Spanish government by a Salonican Jewish merchant, Alberto Asseo, for the creation of the "United States of Europe" would gain traction.[12]

Again appealing to the principle of nationalities, a well-known Salonican Jewish journalist, Sam Lévy, then residing in Lausanne, submitted a final plea to the Paris Peace Conference in 1919. Only if Salonica were given international recognition and administered by the Jews as a neutral, yet demographically predominant, population ("two-thirds" according to Lévy) would Salonica "enter the great family of the League of Nations," assure "tranquility in the Balkans," and "guarantee European peace." Levy's fashioning of Salonica's Jews as the sovereigns of a distinct Salonican "nation," on a par with other European nations, constituted the most audacious claim about the city's possible status and a creative resolution to the problems generated by the post-imperial world.[13]

One wonders what direction Balkan and European geopolitics might have taken if any of the bold visions for Jewish autonomy or internationalization of Salonica had succeeded. The idea of transforming Salonica into a kind of free city if not a Jewish city-state may strike us in the twenty-first century as quaint, if not absurd, but it emerged from realistic expectations at the time, as evidenced by the creation of similar types of polities in the region: Turkish-speaking Muslims in Gumuldjina (Komotini), in Thrace, established an independent albeit short-lived state in 1913.[14] Why not something similar in Salonica for Jews? The case presents an intriguing counterfactual for a work of fiction along the lines of Philip Roth's *Operation Shylock* or Michael Chabon's *Yiddish Policeman's Union*. It also unsettles our assumptions about the possibilities of Jewish sovereignty in the modern era and the inevitability of the collapse of empire and the triumph of the nation-state.

The alternative proposals for Salonica's future represent only a fraction of the multiple responses to the transition from Ottoman to Greek rule by different segments of the city's Jews, who neither acted as a unit nor resigned themselves to the fortune imposed upon them. Jewish Socialists advocated that the city be incorporated into Greece or Bulgaria or benefit from an international regime—any option other than remaining under Ottoman rule—in order to gain greater "liberty." When it became clear that the city would become part of Greece, Jewish Socialists promptly initiated Greek language courses for their constituents.[15] In reaction to the Greek army's entry into the city in October 1912, a prominent Jewish educator, Joseph Nehama, insisted that the Jewish masses "maintained a most dignified and proper attitude. Certainly they have shown no hostility, but neither have they shown satisfaction. . . . What will be the new conditions created for our fellow Jews . . . ?"[16] While initially sharing the ambivalence of the Jewish masses as identified by Nehama, Chief Rabbi Jacob Meir soon welcomed King George I of Greece to Salonica, affirmed his loyalty to the Greek crown on behalf of the Jewish population, and bestowed a blessing upon the king.[17] But when King George I of Greece was assassinated near the White Tower in 1913, Greek newspapers falsely accused the Jews until it became clear that the assassin was a Greek anarchist; even then, tensions between the two populations did not subside.[18]

The transfer of Salonica to Greece in 1912 became a turning point during more than a decade of war (1911–1923) that facilitated the end of the

Ottoman Empire and resulted in mass carnage. Over two million residents of Asia Minor lost their lives, including nearly a million victims of the Armenian genocide. Millions of refugees fled across crumbling imperial borders and newly drawn national boundaries; others traversed seas and oceans both voluntarily and forcibly in what became one of the largest population movements in human history.[19] In the wake of World War I (1914–1918), the Greco-Turkish War (1919–1922)—which Greece remembers as the "Great Catastrophe" and Turkey designated as the "Turkish War of Independence"—resulted in the Treaty of Lausanne (1923), which formalized a compulsory population exchange between the two countries on the basis of religious affiliation: with some exceptions, a half million Muslims were expelled from Greece and sent to Turkey, whereas one and a half million Orthodox Christians were expelled from Turkey and resettled in Greece. The same religious categories that had underpinned the Ottoman imperial social order were recast anew as the primary markers of national belonging. In the case of Salonica, Muslims (and Dönme) departed, and a hundred thousand Orthodox Christians arrived. Exempted from the population transfers, Jews largely remained in situ. Rather than transporting themselves to a different country, a different country had come to them. From a demographic plurality (or majority, depending on the statistics cited) in Ottoman Salonica, Jews ceased to serve as the sovereigns of the city and instead became a minority confronting unprecedented pressures from the new state and from their neighbors.

During this period of transition, Salonica's Jews developed a repertoire of strategies to negotiate their position and reestablish their moorings in the changing political, cultural, and economic landscape. *Jewish Salonica* tells the stories of a cross-section of Salonica's Jews and situates them as protagonists engaged in an ongoing process of self-fashioning and adaptation amidst the tumultuous passage from the multireligious, multicultural, multinational Ottoman Empire to the homogenizing Greek nation-state. While keeping in mind the devastation wrought by the Holocaust, which decimated Salonica's Jewish population, this book highlights how Jewish actors of varying classes, professions, and political affiliations, speaking as individuals or on behalf of institutions, as official or unofficial representatives of the Jewish collectivity, sought to shape their destiny and secure a place for themselves in the city, the province of Macedonia, the Ottoman Empire and subsequently the Greek state, and the broader Jewish world.

Instead of emphasizing the rupture between the Ottoman and modern Greek worlds that seemed to provoke an inexorable period of decline for Salonica's Jews leading up to World War II, this book also explores the legacies of the cultural, legal, and political practices of the late Ottoman Empire on the consolidating Greek state that reveal the continuing dynamism of Salonican Jewish society. As a tool to govern its diverse populations and maintain order, the Ottoman state recognized its non-Muslim populations (namely Jews and Christians) as distinct, largely self-governing communities (*millets*) protected by imperial privileges. Vestiges of this form of *millet* governance, which imbued religious communities with a modicum of "non-territorial autonomy" within the borders of the state, outlived the empire itself especially as evidenced in the legal and political structures of post-Ottoman states such as Egypt, Lebanon, Israel, and Turkey.[20] Greece should also be included in this list, for it, too, inherited and adapted some of the tools of Ottoman state governance to manage its own diverse populations. As the Ottoman state did for non-Muslims, Greece recognized its non-Christian populations (namely, Jews and Muslims) as distinct religious communities endowed with certain powers of self-government—this time in the name of minority rights.

Jewish Salonica recognizes both the continuities and ruptures between the Ottoman Empire and modern Greece while shifting attention away from the state and toward the people. The book highlights how Salonica's Jews emphasized their sense of local identity during the passage from empire to nation-state and at the crossroads of Ottomanism and Hellenism. During this period of readjustment, Salonica's Jews re-anchored themselves in the city and embraced the city itself—and no greater territory—as a kind of homeland. Salonican Jewish leaders believed that reaffirming their connection to the city and their status as Salonicans would bridge the gulf that separated the world of the receding Ottoman Empire from that of the ascendant Greek nation-state. They localized their sense of citizenship by relying on their rootedness in Salonica to justify their participation in the Ottoman and subsequently Greek polities. The more the demographic predominance of Jews in Salonica diminished under Greek rule, the more Jewish leaders reinvested in their sense of connection to the city, reinventing it either as a distinctly Jewish site and symbol or as an unquestionably Greek topos to which Jews nonetheless belonged. Visions of "Jewish Salonica" (*Saloniko la djudia*), as Judeo-Spanish sources referred to the city, served as surrogates for the dream of Jewish autonomy, as substitutes for lost imperial allegiances, and as inspiration for Jews to reroot themselves in the aftermath of empire, within the context of the new Greek nation-state, and on the new map of twentieth-century Europe. City-based identity in the case of Salonica constituted a legitimate and modern mode of self and collective expression that competed with other categories of belonging, such as nation, religion, class, or ideology, sometimes complementing these latter affiliations, at other times challenging them.

Jewish activists transformed Salonica into a stage for the articulation of a variety of political positions and developed visions of the city in service of their agendas. Salonica's Jewish socialists viewed the city as home to "the most important Jewish community in the Balkans" not only for all of its accomplishments, but also because they still hoped that the Jewish working class would one day triumph in the city as in Jewish institutions.[21] They construed their local activism as rehearsal for a larger class revolution. Zionists also saw the city, after World War I, as a staging ground for a future independent Jewish state. From their perspective, Tel Aviv, the new Hebrew city, was to become a New Salonica, just as Salonica, the "Hebrew City in Exile" par excellence, had become a New Jerusalem. They argued that the city's Jews, once de facto rulers of Salonica, ought to play a central role in building a Jewish state in Palestine.[22] In contrast, Liberals who advocated for integration construed Salonica as the "Macedonian Metropolis" and envisioned the cooperation of Jews and Orthodox Christians within a modern framework of "Hellenic Judaism" as key to the city's prosperity and as a model for intercommunal relations moving forward. From each perspective, the city—as space, idea, and identity—remained central.

The case of Salonica also offers a window into the anxieties and aspirations of an urban Jewish population grappling with the unprecedented challenges that confronted Jews across Europe during the early twentieth century in the context of war and the redrawing of the map. Salonica occupied a central position in the Sephardic orbit in the Balkans and the eastern Mediterranean, with cultural, commercial, political, and familial links to Istanbul and Izmir, Sarajevo and Sofia, Monastir and Rhodes, Jerusalem and Cairo. A Sephardic studies scholar from Turkey, Maír José Benardete even touted Salonica as an "archetype of a Levantine Sephardic community," after which all other Jewish communities in the region patterned themselves.[23] After its incorporation into Greece and the breakdown of the Judeo-Spanish cultural sphere, Salonica played a key role for the country's Jews. The Jewish Community of Salonica imported several tons of flour each year to manufacture *matza* for Passover and organized twenty-three communities—from Athens to Corfu—into the Union of the Jewish Communities of Greece to defend the interests of Hellenic Judaism (1929).[24] A Jewish notable in the town of Demotika encapsulated the reliance of Greece's Jews on Salonica: "In small communities in the provinces where we often live in hopeless situations, we have always had as consolation and hope that in a moment of anguish we can count on the saving graces of the great Jewish agglomeration of Salonica."[25]

Salonica's Jews also cultivated links with Jews beyond their immediate geography that brought them into conversation with broader Jewish and general cultural, political, and social trends that profoundly impacted local dynamics, whether through the Alliance Israélite Universelle in Paris, the Board of Deputies of British Jews in London, the World Zionist Organization in Berlin, or informal connections fostered by Salonican Jewish intellectuals who read and published in Jewish journals in Poland. Unlike the Ashkenazic context, divisions between Reform and Orthodox Judaism never impacted Salonica (nor any of the other former Ottoman locales). Like the Ashkenazic context, however, a wide range of Jewish political movements did develop in Salonica, from various versions of Zionism to Jewish socialism and communism whose organizers created more than ten specifically Jewish political parties during the interwar years—a fraught dynamic that looked more like Warsaw than Istanbul. Across the continent, in Vilna and Bialystok, Prague and Vienna, Sarajevo and Istanbul—as in Salonica—Jews proposed their own solutions to the changing political landscape, grappled with new meanings of "nation" and "state," and reconceptualized their relationship to their city in the context of shifting boundaries and "unmixing of peoples" that accompanied the collapse of the Habsburg, Romanov, and Ottoman empires.[26]

They often reimagined their city as an exceptional "earthly Jerusalem" (*Yerushalayim shel mata*) to which they forged strong attachments without necessarily relinquishing their faith in the "heavenly Jerusalem" (*Yerushalayim shel mala*).[27] Salonican Jews elaborated a set of narratives about their city as a historic Jewish metropolis and a Jewish homeland, a concept ultimately cemented with the designation of the city as the "Jerusalem of the Balkans." By drawing analogies to Jerusalem, Jewish activists sought to render their city relevant and central to the Jewish experience and, during an era of transition, to legitimize their role as meaningful participants in their city, in their country, and in the broader world. If Salonica's Jews saw their city, like Jerusalem, as their "mother city," their *ir va-em be-Israel* (literally, "city and mother in Israel," 2 Samuel 20:19), they were not alone, for the city was also known in Greek as the "mother of refugees" and the "mother of Orthodoxy."[28] All agreed that Salonica was a mother city—but whose mother was she?

Confronting Salonica's Ghosts

The dynamic engagement of Salonica's Jews in the politics, culture, and economics of the city in addition to their devastating destruction during the Holocaust were, for a long time, expunged from the city's history and public memory as part of a nationalizing process that sought to render Salonica exclusively and perpetually "Greek." Such liminal status led one scholar to characterize Jewish Salonica—excised not only from the Greek national narrative but also marginalized in Europe-centered modern Jewish studies—as an "orphan of history."[29] The end of the Cold War and the possibilities of considering "the other" in society in a new light finally spurred greater interest in Jews in Salonica and Greece. The post-Cold War era of the 1990s became the "coming out" phase of Jewish history in Greece. The naming of Salonica as the Cultural Capital of Europe in 1997 introduced discussion of the Jewish presence in the city in a public forum for the first time, and the conversation continues to be informed by a celebratory interest in and nostalgia for the so-called cosmopolitan and multicultural world of Ottoman Salonica. Increased interest—not only in Greece but also among scholars in France, Israel, and the United States—initiated a "post-celebratory," critical phase in the study of Jewish history in Greece, to which this book seeks to contribute.[30]

At the intersection of the coming out and post-celebratory phases, Mark Mazower's *Salonica, City of Ghosts* (2004) offered the first accessible overview in English of the history of Salonica from the Ottoman conquest in 1430 until the end of the World War II. Mazower presented the "cultural and religious co-existence" of the city's multiple residents within "a single encompassing historical narrative" that would not privilege the Jewish, Muslim, or Christian perspectives. Mazower indicated that he found a model for such an inclusive narrative that emphasized the "hybrid spirit" of Salonica in a work composed by a "local historian" in the wake of the Balkan Wars.[31] This local historian was none other than the Jewish educator and banker, Joseph Nehama, who penned *La Ville Convoitée* under the pseudonym P. Risal in 1914.

It is important to note that the author of such an inclusive history was Jewish precisely because, in the wake of the Balkan Wars, only a Jew—unconnected to irredentist nationalisms and not speaking on behalf of any state in the region—could dare to write an inclusive history of such a coveted city. He could do so precisely because he spoke from the margins of political power while drawing upon a sense of confidence and legitimacy derived from his position as a representative of the local voice. Such an endeavor was dangerous and could sow the seeds of nationalist animosity—hence Nehama's decision to publish the book using a discrete pen name. Although not culturally, demographically, or economically marginal in Salonica at the time, Jews lacked political power, did not have an army behind them, and could more readily imagine a story from the margins, one that decentered the state and acknowledged the range of residents inhabiting the city. *Jewish Salonica* seeks to recover the local milieu that produced figures like Nehama, who saw themselves not only as Jews but also as spokesmen for their city, sometimes inclusive of all of its diverse inhabitants, while other times prioritizing Jewish perspectives. Even Nehama moved between both positions: while emphasizing the role that a multiplicity of populations played in the city's history, he drew a clear conclusion about the identity of Salonica: "today it is Jewish and Spanish: it is Sephardic."[32]

Jewish Salonica contributes to the growing post-celebratory scholarship on the city by focusing on the variegated Jewish experiences in and visions of Salonica. While it involves a discussion not only of Jews but also of their interactions with their neighbors and with the state, it does not offer an all-inclusive narrative. Instead, *Jewish Salonica* enters the city's history through a Jewish prism and seeks to reinterpret that history from the vantage point of Salonica's Jewish residents. One of the book's primary goals is to temper the general thrust of existing studies that highlight the downward spiral of Salonica's Jews following the city's incorporation into Greece. According to these interpretations, after Salonica comes under Greek rule, Jews—like Muslims—are considered "doomed." The failed plans for internationalization and Jewish autonomy amidst the Balkan Wars emerge, if mentioned at all, as the last hurrah, a final stand of a Jewish population whose incorporation into the Greek nation-state signifies the beginning of the end.[33] Jews in Greek Salonica, especially during the tenures of Eleftherius Venizelos as prime minister, are characterized as "the most intractable and alien element" in Greece, "unwanted compatriots," and "under siege."[34] As these narratives unfold, Jews experience an inexorable period of decline as the objects of nationalizing, anti-Jewish policies and popular actions.[35]

According to these accounts, very few opportunities emerged for Greek-Jewish rapprochement during the interwar years, and the categories of "Greek" and "Jew" remained fixed along ethnic lines, the former identified as the true nation, and the latter largely considered alien. Only during the dictatorship of Ioannis Metaxas (1936–1941), so these studies suggest, did Salonica's Jews experience a short respite from the animosity directed against them by their neighbors and by the state prior to World War II. These narratives end with the decisive trauma of Nazi occupation and genocide. In 1943, the Nazis rounded up and deported more than forty-five thousand of Salonica's Jews—nearly 20 percent of the city's residents—to their deaths at Auschwitz-Birkenau. Nazis unwittingly solidified the Hellenization of the city by transforming multiethnic Ottoman and Jewish Salonica into a "city of ghosts." The story most often told of Salonica's Jews thus ends in destruction, erasure, and the suppression of memory. In these tales, which reinforce a lachrymose conception of Jewish history, Jews in Salonica become objects of nationalist ambition and victims of Greek antisemites or Nazis and their collaborators rather than historical actors in their own right.

These narratives of decline echo interpretations offered by Salonica's Jewish intellectuals writing in the immediate wake of the war who viewed the period prior to World War II as a prelude to the destruction of the city's

Jews. Still mourning the agonizing annihilation of the city's Jews during the German occupation, the rabbi and historian Michael Molho in 1948 solidified the perception of the three decades prior to World War II as a period of decline that culminated with the Holocaust: "[T]he Balkan Wars and the First World War gradually decrease the importance of this Sephardic center [Salonica] that declines and is annihilated at the hands of the Nazis, in the terrible year 1943."[36] In search of a more dynamic and complex understanding of the pre–World War II period that avoids a teleological approach, *Jewish Salonica* disentangles the interwar years from the period of the German occupation and does not interpret them as a staging ground for the Nazi genocide, thereby allowing the story prior to the war to be understood on its own terms.

Some of the available scholarship attributes the decline of Salonica's Jews to their purported resistance to Hellenization measures that prevented them from *really* becoming Greek prior to World War II; such an explanation must be reconsidered. Without taking into account the alternative perspectives that permeate this book, recent studies argue that Salonica's Jews established a "nascent but inchoate" Greek Jewish identity through the 1930s and only came to identify themselves and be identified by others as fully Greek once they left—either in Auschwitz, Israel, or New York.[37] Some scholars have even suggested a causal link between Salonican Jews' alleged failure to become Greek—assuming their own obstinacy was the barrier—and their eradication during World War II. If only Jews in Salonica had learned the Greek language better and assimilated more completely, the argument goes, they could have hidden more easily and more of their Orthodox Christian neighbors would have come to their aid during the German occupation.[38]

When scholars and commentators argue that Jews in Salonica never really became Greek prior to World War II, they presuppose that the parameters of Greek national and political identity had already been fixed by the interwar years. *Jewish Salonica* joins a small but growing body of scholarship that argues that the boundaries of national belonging in Greece and the meanings of citizenship were by no means set but rather in the making throughout the nineteenth century and into the twentieth. Like other national identities in the region, Greek national identity had to be learned, coerced, courted, and chosen. As evidenced by the opposition mounted by the Orthodox Christian

Patriarchate in Istanbul to the Greek War of Independence in the 1820s and the refusal of peasants near Salonica in the early twentieth century to identify with any nation at all, instead insisting on their status as Christians alone, Greek national identity continued to develop over a long period.[39]

The ensuing state-led project to Hellenize Salonica after 1912 must be conceptualized as part of this protracted process that involved not only force but also dialogue and compromise between the state and the city's Jews as well as a variety of other populations in the wider region: Slavic-speaking Orthodox Christians, Orthodox Christian refugees from Asia Minor and the Black Sea region—many of whom spoke Turkish as their primary language (the Karamanlis) or the distinctive Pontic dialect of Greek—as well as a variety of other culturally diverse populations, including Vlachs, Roma, and Slavic-, Albanian-, and Turkish-speaking Muslims in Thrace and Epirus.[40] Among these varied populations, only Orthodox Christians, who had constituted the *Rum millet* in the Ottoman Empire, became the standard bearers of the consolidating Greek nation.[41] Salonica's Jews played an active role in the process, not only as the objects of Hellenizing measures imposed by the state but also as agents who shaped the contours of the enterprise. They argued that even if they could never become full-fledged members of the Greek nation—unless, perhaps, they ceased being Jews—they nonetheless could become Greek patriots, legitimate "Hellenic citizens" (*sivdadinos elenos*) with shared civic commitments.

A new and expanded source base makes it possible to hear an additional range of voices from Salonica's Jews that reveal the active role they played during an era of rupture and transition. Until now, the tale of Salonica's Jews has been told largely from the outside looking in: state records privilege the top-down perspective and prerogatives of bureaucrats and policy makers; travelers' accounts and consular reports highlight the gaze of the foreigner; and correspondence with international organizations, such as the Alliance Israélite Universelle, reveals observations of a select Jewish elite writing for a European audience. While integrating these invaluable viewpoints, *Jewish Salonica* offers an unprecedented insider's view by reference to the heretofore largely unstudied official archives of the Jewish Community of Salonica and the extensive outpouring of the local periodical press. These primary sources reveal Salonican Jews' perspectives regarding their own experiences, articulated principally in the Jewish vernacular and intended for a local Jewish readership. These sources help us understand how Salonican Jews—primarily but not exclusively the elites—explained their world to themselves. They offer additional narratives to the standard one of decline by revealing the previously unrecognized extent to which Jews and their institutions, as well as the Jewish press, not only struggled but also flourished during the interwar years.

Written mostly in Judeo-Spanish but also in Greek, Hebrew, and French, the surviving archives of the Jewish Community of Salonica date from 1917 to 1941 and record the actions of the Jewish Community, its administrators, and its members. Confiscated by the Nazis during the German occupation, they miraculously survived over the past seventy-five years, largely inaccessible, uncatalogued, and dispersed across the globe: in New York (YIVO Institute for Jewish Research), Moscow (the former Osobyi Secret Military Archive), Jerusalem (Central Archives for the History of the Jewish People), and Salonica, where I literally dug materials out of a storage room and transferred them to the city's Jewish museum.[42] While several scholars in Israel have begun to explore some of these archives, *Jewish Salonica* is the first study to draw on all four repositories.

The communal archives illuminate the interactions of the city's Jewish institutional body with everyday Jews. While the perspectives of the Jewish literate, male, middle, and leadership classes—journalists, rabbis, teachers, politicians, merchants, and communal functionaries—predominate, *Jewish Salonica*'s reference to the archives also provides glimpses into the worlds of stevedores, soldiers, prisoners, converts, women, and the impoverished masses who, if illiterate, sometimes commissioned scribes to compose petitions on their behalf or offered oral testimony recorded by the rabbinical court. The archives also document the relations between the Jewish Community and local, regional, and state governmental bodies and with organizations and individuals across the globe. The archives detail the structure and extensive governance of the Jewish Community—its Communal Council, General Assembly, chief rabbinate, school network, Jewish neighborhood administrations, and twenty Jewish philanthropic institutions, including a hospital, a medical dispensary, a soup kitchen, an old age home, orphanages for girls and boys, and an insane asylum. In short, more Jewish institutions operated in Salonica during the interwar years than ever before.

The archives reveal that the Jewish Community of Salonica retained considerable power during the interwar years. Recognized by the Greek state as "a legal entity of public law" (according to Law 2456 of 1920), the Jewish Community functioned in parallel to and in some cases in competition with the municipality of Salonica. The Jewish Community managed its own Office of Statistics and Civil Status modeled explicitly on the *Lixiarhio*, or the civil registry office, of the municipality. But the Jewish Community benefitted from one additional power not available to the municipality: the right to issue certificates of identity to its members for both domestic and international use.[43] The very structure of the Jewish Community represented in the communal archives permitted—in fact compelled—Salonican Jews to retain connections with the communal body throughout the interwar years. The extensive bureaucratic powers of the Community demonstrate that Ottoman imperial practices continued to mold the experiences of Salonica's Jews once the city became part of Greece.

The local press constitutes the other major source base to help us comprehend how Salonica's Jews understood their world, responded to it, and reshaped it. Despite a scholarly consensus that Judeo-Spanish print culture experienced a precipitous decline following the collapse of the Ottoman Empire, this was not the case in Salonica, where more newspapers and magazines appeared in Judeo-Spanish than in the other major publishing centers combined (105 in Salonica compared to 45 in Istanbul, 30 in Sofia, and 23 in Izmir).[44] In Salonica, the period *after* 1912 constituted the height of Judeo-Spanish publishing. The circulation of the city's only Judeo-Spanish newspaper in 1898, *La Epoka*, reached 750. By 1927, the French consul estimated that more than 25,000 copies of Judeo-Spanish newspapers circulated in the city, with 5,000 each of the daily *El Puevlo* and the Zionist weekly *La Renasensia Djudia*.[45] A visitor in 1929 counted fourteen Jewish periodicals, including seven dailies, and observed that "the Jewish press in Salonica is exceedingly well-developed."[46] Even if illiteracy continued to plague segments of the population, those without direct access to the written word often learned of the latest headlines from relatives or acquaintances. An older style of communal reading continued after 1912, as evidenced by a photograph in *National Geographic* (1916) of fourteen Jewish men gathered around a man reading a newspaper aloud in one of Salonica's public squares, suggesting that more individuals gained access to the discussions in the newspapers than subscription figures would suggest.[47] The newspapers nonetheless must be understood as primarily representing the voices of literate elites.

Despite the Hellenizing pressures of the interwar years, the majority of Jewish printed matter in Salonica continued to appear in Judeo-Spanish (in Rashi typeface) until World War II, including the last newspaper, *El Mesajero*, which the German occupation forces closed down in 1941. But Hellenizing pressures and aspirations also transformed Jewish print culture in interwar Salonica. The mouthpiece of the so-called assimilationists, *Evraïkon Vima tis Ellados* (*Jewish Tribune of Greece*), established in 1925, appeared in bilingual Greek and French editions. Rather than obstinately resist the acquisition of the Greek language, Zionists had proposed creating a Jewish daily in Greek even earlier, in 1923.[48] The organ of the Zionist Federation of Greece, *La Renasenia Djudia* (*The Jewish Renaissance*), introduced a Greek section in 1932 in order to appeal to Jews throughout Greece, a portion of whom knew only Greek; to Jewish youth in Salonica, who increasingly gained fluency in Greek; and to the wider Greek-reading public, to elicit support for the Zionist enterprise.[49] Although not assimilationists, Zionists favored accommodating the new realties of life in Greece. Some Jewish newspapers even published multilingual lexicons that highlighted the "four languages of our city"—Judeo-Spanish, Hebrew, Greek, and French—and which local Greek newspapers praised as a "unique work in the world."[50] In interwar Salonica, Greek became a Jewish language—used by Jews—and Judeo-Spanish a Greek one—used in Greece and occasionally by Orthodox Christians: a Greek public notary, for example, printed his business cards in Judeo-Spanish, in Rashi script, to attract a Jewish clientele.[51]

With reference to the archives and the local press, *Jewish Salonica* demonstrates how Jews in Salonica harnessed their multiple affiliations—to the city, community, and state, as well as to differing ideological postures and linguistic and cultural expressions—at the intersection of empire and nation-state, as the last generation of the city's Ottoman Jews sought to transform themselves and their children into the first generation of Salonica's Hellenic Jews. The sources offer glimpses into the multiple ways in which Salonica's Jews understood and interpreted the complexities and contradictions imbedded in their

Figure o.r. A quadrilingual Judeo-Spanish, Greek, Hebrew, French dictionary published serially in the newspaper *El Puevlo*, 1932. Source: National Library of Israel.

experiences. In effect, this book begins to restore the voices of Salonica's Jews and to tell their stories in their own words.

Salonica's Jews between City, Community, and State

Jewish Salonica focuses on how Salonica's Jews sought to secure a place for themselves amidst the transition from the Ottoman Empire to modern Greece in three domains: as Salonicans, as members of the Jewish Community, and as citizens of the state. While Jews—like their Muslim and Christian neighbors—had expressed connections to their city, to their community, and to their state for many generations, the nature and character of those affiliations dramatically transformed beginning in the nineteenth century due to the implementation of centralizing administrative reforms by the Ottoman state, known as the *Tanzimat* ("reorganization," 1839–1876). These reforms brought into existence new institutions and new modes of political belonging through the creation of municipalities (in Salonica in 1869); by formalizing the self-governing structures of non-Muslim communities, known as *millets* (for the Jewish Community of Salonica, in 1870); and by officially transforming the empire's Muslim, Christian, and Jewish subjects into citizens (introduced in 1856 and formalized by the Ottoman Nationality Law of 1869). Jews in Salonica simultaneously gained three layers of citizenship as they ascertained certain rights and obligations vis-à-vis not only the state but also their community and the municipality. As *Jewish Salonica* will illustrate, Jews in Salonica continued to renegotiate the relationships between these three affiliations from the late nineteenth century until World War II.

Although the concept of citizenship was new in the nineteenth century, the practice of proclaiming loyalty to the sovereign was not. Jews in the Ottoman Empire had introduced a prayer for the government, *Noten teshua lamelakhim* ("He who gives salvation to the kings," Psalm 144:10), into their liturgy in the sixteenth century. The prayer formed part of a long-standing formula in support of the so-called vertical alliance according to which Jews across Europe entrusted their fate to their sovereign.[52] The difference is that, while most Jewish communities discarded the *Noten teshua* in the nineteenth century during the era of emancipation, it continued to be invoked in Salonica until World War II.[53] In the context of both the Ottoman Empire and Greece—where the separation of church and state was not introduced—the process of embracing the new responsibilities of citizenship involved the incorporation of religious metaphors. In the wake of World War I, a Jewish notable in Salonica emphasized to his constituency that their future success in Salonica would be contingent upon their embrace of two religions: the religion of Judaism and the religion of patriotism, the latter defined as "the religion of love for the homeland."[54] By invoking allegiances to both religions simultaneously and localizing them in the city, Jewish elite continually sought to fashion themselves and the Jewish masses into local patriots, conscientious Jews, and devoted citizens—ultimately, to transform their "country of residence" (*paiz*) into their "homeland" (*patria*).

Beginning in the late nineteenth century, the local Judeo-Spanish press developed a new vocabulary for Salonica's Jews to describe their evolving relationships with their city, community, and state. The Judeo-Spanish press tethered Jewish residents of Salonica to the city by identifying them as Salonicans: *Selaniklis* (from Turkish), *Salonisianos* (from French), and *[Te]salonikiotas* (from Greek). Salonica's Jews also described themselves as *sivdadinos*, as "citizens" of their city, to which they felt a sense of allegiance and where they engaged in political activism (all municipal councils included Jewish members until the 1930s). The status of citizen of Salonica was not reserved for Jews alone; the term *konsivdadino* ("fellow citizen") referred to their Muslim and Christian neighbors. In contrast to Orthodox Christian *resfuyidos* ("refugees") who arrived from Asia Minor in the 1920s, Jews insisted on referring to themselves until World War II as *yerlis* ("indigenous," from Turkish), a further indication of their self-perception as native to the city.

The Judeo-Spanish press also oriented its readers toward the formal institution of the Jewish Community and referred to it simply as "the Community" (*la komunita*). Throughout the pages that follow, the Jewish Community refers to the formal institution and its official spokesmen, such as the Communal Council or the chief rabbinate. Other times, Judeo-Spanish sources invoked the term *komunita* to construct an imagined community, a sense of collective belonging among local Jews despite their socially stratified, disunited, heterogeneous composition. Competing individuals or groups, often via the press or voluntary associations and clubs, spoke in the name of the community, often without authorization from the Jewish Community or in opposition to it. The ubiquity of voluntary associations and the defining role they played in shaping public debate led a local newspaper to quip: "Each city has a characteristic that endows it with its particular seal. Paris has its boulevards and *bon vivants*, Istanbul has its ships and ferries, Naples has its street mobs reaching out to the sun, and Salonica has its clubs."[55] Political, literary, and social clubs along with the local press cultivated broader conceptions of community—focused on the people rather than the institution, on Jewish civil society rather than the governing body— and designated as the "Jewish collectivity" (*la kolektivita djudia* or *la djuderia*, literally "Jewry"), the "Jewish population" (*populasion djudia*), the "Jewish people" (*puevlo djidio*), the "Jewish element" (*elemento djidio*), and the "Jewish public" (*puvliko djidio*). There was considerable slippage among these interrelated concepts and competing visions of what they entailed.

At the level of the state, the *Tanzimat* sought to win the allegiance of the empire's residents—inclusive of Muslims, Christians, and Jews—by transforming them from subjects into citizens and promising them equality with regard to property rights, education, government appointments, and the administration of justice. Encouraging their constituents to embrace the new status introduced by the reforms, Judeo-Spanish publications began to invoke the term *Otomano* (the translation of the Turkish *Osmanlı*) as an over-arching designation that referred to all the empire's citizens. Synonymous with *Otomano*, a new term, *turkino*, also entered the Judeo-Spanish lexicon and further captured the transformation of the sultan's subjects into Otto-man citizens. In the Judeo-Spanish translation of the 1858 Ottoman penal code, the Ottoman Turkish phrase *teba-yı devlet-ı âliyye* ("subjects of the Sublime State," i.e., the Ottoman Empire) was rendered as *suditos turkinos* ("subjects of Turkey" or "citizens of Turkey") and referred to *turkos, gregos,* and *djidios* alike.[56] When Sultan Abdülmecid I visited Salonica in 1859, for example, Saadi a-Levi composed songs in his honor that fused the language of the centuries-old prayer for the government by calling upon God to grant the sultan "everlasting salvation" with the new rhetoric that referred to the sultan's arrival as a "festive day" for "every *turkino*," in other words, all Otto-man citizens in the city.[57]

The diffusion of terms in the Judeo-Spanish press such as *turkinos* and *Otomanos* to describe all Ottoman citizens formed part of the broader process through which Jews engaged with and embraced the Ottoman state-promoted ideology of Ottomanism (*Osmanlıcılık*). The Ottoman state developed the political framework of Ottomanism to try to resolve the ten-sion involved in the expectation that non-Muslims simultaneously express allegiance to their respective communities (*millets*) and to the Ottoman state, a dualism accentuated by the *Tanzimat* reforms.[58] Ottomanism involved the promotion of political allegiance to the empire among all citizens by empha-sizing a supracommunal civic nationalism, according to which non-Muslims could identify with their specific communities while simultaneously demon-strating their loyalty as Ottoman citizens. Scholars disagree over the sincerity of the project of Ottomanism on the part of state elites and whether it was doomed to fail from the start. But Ottoman Jewish leaders, who did not pro-pose an alternative to empire, committed to the promise of Ottomanism.[59]

Unlike Greeks, Bulgarians, and Armenians, some of whom strove at varying points for national liberation, Ottoman Jews did not seek politi-cal independence and increasingly gained status throughout the nineteenth century as *en sadık millet* ("the most loyal community"). In an attempt to demonstrate their loyalty to the empire and to ensure their place as Jews and as Ottomans, Jewish leaders in Salonica, Istanbul, and Izmir orchestrated a remarkable celebration in 1892 to commemorate the four hundredth anniversary not of the expulsion of the Jews from Spain, but rather of their welcome in the Ottoman Empire. During this period, Sultan Abdul Hamid II (r. 1876–1909) abolished the recently promulgated constitution (1876–1878), imposed press censorship, narrowed the frame of Ottomanism by emphasizing Islamism, and perpetrated mass violence against Armenians (1894–1896). Fearing the fate of other non-Muslim populations, Jews emphasized their allegiance to the Ottoman state both out of sincerity and self-defense.[60]

Initiated from Salonica, the restoration of the Ottoman constitution and ultimate overthrow of Sultan Abdul Hamid II in 1909 provoked renewed enthusiasm for the promise of Ottomanism that sought to bind the various residents of the empire to each other and to the state. Only the shared Ottoman homeland, according to this formulation of civic nationalism, could safeguard the interests and aspirations of each "element" (*unsur*) that constituted the new Ottoman "nation." Salonica's Jews met the promulgation of the constitution with cries of *biva la patria* ("long live the homeland") and *yaşasın millet!* (in Turkish, "long live the nation!" referring now to the Ottoman nation of which they saw themselves a part), which they integrated into their anthem, *La Marseillaise Salonicienne*. The Jewish poet, Jacob Yona, similarly encouraged all Ottomans to serve the "homeland" (*patria*): "All of the *turkinos* [must] be well informed: / our strength depends on being well united / great glory will [come to us] united as brothers."[61]

Jewish elites continued to promote a consciousness as *sivdadinos Otomanos* among the Jewish masses. Jewish leaders in Salonica agreed on their support of the Ottoman state but disagreed over how it should be expressed and how to negotiate their status as citizens and as Jews. Should the Jewish Community continue to play a role in the lives of Jews? Should they preserve their communal autonomy, rely on their own courts and the chief rabbi, and participate in Jewish communal schools and philanthropies? Or should they integrate into the general institutions of the city and the state? Could and should they participate in both? Which language(s) should Jews prioritize: Judeo-Spanish, Hebrew, French, or the language of the state? Jews continued to ask these questions even after Salonica passed into Greek jurisdiction. Three principal positions emerged: integrationism, socialism, and nationalism.

Animated by Enlightenment ideals, the more secularized middle classes and supporters of the Alliance Israélite Universelle, a Paris-based educational enterprise that sought to uplift the Jews of the East and established its first boys' school in Salonica in 1873, advocated that Jews should integrate into the surrounding society, prioritize their status as citizens, and relegate Judaism to the private sphere of religion in order to achieve full emancipation. A Judeo-Spanish expression captured this stance: *djidio en kaza, ombre ala plasa* ("a Jew at home, a man in public"). Self-proclaimed liberals, they advocated for the abolition of Jewish communal autonomy and separate legal status, conceived of themselves as "Jewish Ottomans," and envisioned the Ottoman Empire as a suprareligious structure capacious enough to accommodate religious differences among its constituent populations. While a major influence in Jewish communal politics from the late nineteenth century through World War I, the power of the Alliance in Salonica waned during the interwar years.

The introduction of freedoms of assembly and of the press following the Young Turk Revolution in 1908 galvanized new political movements such as socialism and nationalism that activated additional segments of Jewish society.[62] Accustomed to the concept of the *millet*, Ottoman Jews easily grasped the new vocabulary of nationalism, as the Judeo-Spanish term for "*millet*" and for "nation" was the same: *nasion*.[63] For Jewish socialists and nationalists alike, Ottomanism did not signify a supra *religious* ideology that sought to accommodate Jews, Muslims, and Christians under its umbrella but rather a supra *national* framework to accommodate Jews, Turks, Greeks, Bulgarians, and Armenians. Blending socialism and nationalism, the city's Socialist Workers' Federation—the largest socialist organization in the Ottoman Empire—sought to unionize all the city's workers across national lines, including Jews, Bulgarians, Greeks, and Turks. The Federation boasted a significant Jewish membership and leadership. As a defender of the working class, the Federation also promoted Judeo-Spanish as the language of the people. It quickly became clear during the Second Constitutional period, however, that liberation had not yet come for the working classes as evidenced by numerous strikes and the persistent domination of the bourgeoisie, including representatives of the Alliance, in Jewish communal governance.[64]

Esther Benbassa and Aron Rodrigue emphasize that a "variety of Zion-isms" took hold in Salonica, the most prominent form of which initially focused not on the building of a Jewish homeland in Palestine, but rather on the strengthening of Jewish communal identity in Salonica itself.[65] Al-though drawn from the middle classes like the supporters of the Alliance, Zionists opposed assimilation and the conceptualization of Jewishness as a question of private religious conscience. Zionists understood themselves as Jewish nationalists with the right to express their voice as Jews in both the public and private domains. Although embracing their status as Ottoman citizens—despite claims to the contrary by detractors, including representa-tives of the Alliance—they saw themselves as "Ottoman Jews" rather than "Jewish Ottomans." They believed that Jews should preserve their communal autonomy while gaining full rights as citizens of their country. Leaders of the first Zionist club in Salonica, Bene Sion ("Sons of Zion") initially argued that their vision of Zionism entailed Jewish cultural and national regeneration at the local level and saw the new rights introduced with the Young Turk Revo-lution as applying to themselves not as individuals, but rather as a collective that aimed "to develop their moral qualities, their nationality, in the world."[66]

Distinguishing between political allegiance (to the state) and cultural and religious allegiance (to the Jewish nation), the Bene Sion also advocated that other Jews suffering persecution in Romania and the Russian Empire be permitted to settle in Ottoman Palestine. They argued that, by admitting Jewish migrants, Palestine would flourish economically, remain Ottoman "by sovereignty," and become Jewish "by religion and culture." "Our beloved homeland"—the Ottoman Empire—would again provide a safe haven for Jews as it had in the wake of the Spanish expulsion.[67] But the end of Otto-man rule over Salonica in 1912 curtailed this dream. Salonican Zionists later concentrated more attention on promoting immigration to Palestine and the project of building a Jewish state there while continuing to defend local Jew-ish interests.

Variations of the three primary, competing Jewish ideological postures articulated on the cusp of Salonica's incorporation into Greece—integrationism (the Alliance), socialism (the Workers' Federation), and nationalism (Zionists)—shaped Jewish politics until World War II. New dynamics during the interwar years only compounded class divisions and

cleavages between the secular and the religious. Fissures multiplied as political affiliations were overlaid upon older networks of power based on
kinship and profession. Each group sought to promote its own agenda in
local, communal, and statewide politics by seeking to speak on behalf of the
Jewish collective. Jewish nationalists splintered into diaspora nationalists,
liberal Zionists, religious Zionists (the Mizrahi), and Revisionist Zionists
and battled for influence against integrationists (who referred to themselves
as the Moderates) and with Jewish socialists and communists. Many Jews,
meanwhile, remained politically disengaged or disenfranchised. Political differences bred animosities: Zionists denounced communists as "traitors" and
the latter portrayed the former as "devils."[68] Sometimes Jewish Moderates
agreed with Greek state officials that Zionists obstinately resisted Hellenization. Other times disagreements turned violent, with fistfights erupting
between Jewish communists and Zionists, and with tensions spilling into
nearby towns. During one Passover Sabbath in Kastoria, Revisionist Zionists and General Zionists brawled in the synagogue and choked the cantor;
a hundred criminal charges were filed.[69] The different political positions
developed by Jews in Salonica advocated for different solutions to the pre-
dicament they confronted as they sought to accommodate their status as
Salonicans, as members of the Jewish Community, and as citizens of the
Ottoman Empire and subsequently of Greece.

From Ottomanism to Hellenism

With Salonica's incorporation into Greece (1912), an ascendant vision of Hellenism displaced the established Ottomanism, further politicized dynamics
among Jews and between them and their neighbors, and required Jews to
reimagine their position not only within the city but also in the consolidating
Greek state. Salonica had figured prominently in the Greek state's expansionist vision, the *Megali Idea* ("The Great Idea"), an irredentist program that
aimed to extend the boundaries of the Greek state (est. 1830) to encompass
and redeem all the potential members of the Greek nation—namely, Orthodox Christians. Aspiring for imperial grandeur, the *Megali Idea* imagined
the formation of a Greater Greece, the revival of the Byzantine Empire,
and the recreation of the Greece of Five Seas.[70] As the former co-capital
of Byzantium and a strategic commercial node, Salonica emerged as a key

stepping-stone en route to Asia Minor and ultimately Constantinople, the historical center of the Orthodox Christian Patriarchate and former capital of the Byzantine Empire. The fundamentally Greek Salonica envisioned by the promoters of the *Megali Idea*, however, diverged greatly from the Jewish city that they ultimately annexed. Salonica's Jews found themselves in an unusual position as their city became central to the expansionist aspirations of Greek nationalism, whereas they themselves, by virtue of not being Orthodox Christians, were not part of that vision.

The pervasiveness of religious vocabulary in the dominant vision of Greek nationalism emerged with the war of independence itself (1821–1830). The revolutionary slogan—"fight for faith and fatherland!"—and the first constitution of independent Greece in 1822 enshrined the connection between religion and nation: "those indigenous inhabitants of the state of Greece who believe in Christ are Greeks."[71] Perhaps most dramatically, Greek Independence Day was fixed as March 25 to correspond not with any particular battle during the revolution, but with the Annunciation of the Virgin Mary. A myth of Greek national annunciation was now overlaid upon the foundational tale of Christianity.[72] The intertwining of religion and national identity persisted as a key feature in the development of Greek nationalism. In the interwar years, during the Fourth of August Regime (1936–1941) that sought to fuse the values of classical Greece with Byzantine Orthodoxy, Prime Minister Ioannis Metaxas appealed to already-established tropes when he promoted his slogan of Greek nationalism: "Fatherland, religion, family."[73] This kind of message remains powerful today for, as one scholar notes, "Orthodoxy is still considered to be the keystone of Greek national identity."[74]

While a smaller Jewish population had inhabited largely Orthodox Christian Greece prior to 1912, their numbers increased exponentially, from fewer than ten thousand to closer to ninety thousand with the annexation of Salonica. Jews elsewhere in Greece were few, not very concentrated, and internally diverse. In 1913, for example, only 140 Jewish families lived in Athens, 100 of whom the press identified as "native," whereas 40 were "immigrants."[75] While partly comprised of Greek-speaking Romaniote Jews, the Jews of Athens also included Ashkenazim and Sephardim. (All chief rabbis of Athens during the first half of the twentieth century were native Judeo-Spanish speakers from Izmir, Salonica, and Hebron.)[76] Although the capital

of Greece, Athens would remain of secondary importance in comparison to
Salonica from a Jewish perspective.

Once Salonica became part of Greece, tensions between Jews and Orthodox Christians intensified due not only to their differing languages but also
to enduring prejudices as reflected in continuing allegations that Jews killed
Christ, periodic blood libel accusations, and economic competition. In addition, resentment lingered due to the alleged role that Istanbul's Jews played
in the execution of the Orthodox Christian Patriarch during the Greek
Revolution (1821), which led to retaliatory massacres against Jews across the
Peloponnese.[77] Slanderous allegations that a Jew had served as the sultan's
executioner in Salonica and murdered Greek rebels during the revolution in
the 1820s circulated more than a century later, in 1931, and contributed to
anti-Jewish outbursts. Only when a Jewish teacher and several Orthodox
Christian students at the university spoke out against the rumor was it put
to rest.[78] The popularity of the *Protocols of the Elders of Zion*, translated into
Greek by *Makedonia* in 1928, reinforced deep-seated antisemitic sentiments in
Greece and provoked Jewish leaders to protest to the president of the Greek
government and the Departments of Interior, Justice, and Foreign Affairs.[79]

In addition to the thread of Orthodox Christianity, another aspect of
Greek national identity drew on the mythologies of classical Hellenism and
introduced another set of tensions into the prospect of harmonious relations
between Jews and Greeks. In the philosophies of the Enlightenment and romanticism, Hellenism had been imagined as the antithesis of Judaism (or
Hebraism), as a world of knowledge in contest with a world of faith. In a
well-known example, the nineteenth-century German poet Heinrich Heine
damningly concluded that, by nature, "all people are either Jews or Hellenes,"
the former tending toward "asceticism, excessive spiritualization, and image-
hating," whereas the latter "rejoices in life, is proud of display, and is realistic.[80]

Within the European Jewish framework, these interpretations were
superimposed over other long-remembered frictions. The Jewish holiday of
Hanukkah, for example, commemorates the victory of the Maccabees over
their Hellenic oppressors who sought to Hellenize the Jews and forcibly assimilate them by stamping out their religious practices. In Hebrew, the verb
lehityaven, "to assimilate," literally means "to become Greek," Yavan being the
biblical toponym applied to Greece. For Jewish intellectuals inspired by the

Enlightenment, Judaism and Hellenism served in modern times as ciphers for the conflict between those Jews who sought to preserve Jewish difference versus those who favored integration. Classical Greece symbolized the allure and challenge of secularism and modern culture.[81]

But in twentieth-century Greece, the encounter with the mythic notions of Judaism and Hellenism took on an entirely different layer of meaning initially quite removed from the European narratives. Orthodox Christian leaders in Greece preoccupied themselves not only with ideals of classical Greece but also with medieval and modern conceptions rooted in Byzantium and in Christian Orthodoxy. In fact, for much of the Ottoman period, Orthodox Christians had rejected the designation "Hellene" altogether, for they associated it with pre-Christian paganism. By appropriating European philhellenic sentiment, Greek Enlightenment thinkers developed a Greek national narrative that sought to wed the world of ancient Athens to Orthodox Christianity, Byzantium, and the Greek language in a contiguous thread of Hellenic history. The embrace of the Hellenic past also legitimized the designation of the citizens of modern Greece as "Hellenes."[82] Due to its pagan, classical antecedents linked less to Christianity than to Europe and the Enlightenment, the more secular framework of Hellenism seemed more appealing to Jewish intellectuals in Salonica seeking to carve out a place for themselves and their community in modern Greece. The task at hand would be to discover ways to reconcile Judaism and Hellenism, both the mythologies and the twentieth-century realities.

Because the *Megali Idea* aspired to transform Greece into a new empire, Greek statesmen incorporated imperial sensibilities into their brand of Hellenism that, for practical reasons, relied on legal structures and categories bequeathed by the Ottomans. In effect, Hellenism incorporated elements of Ottomanism in order to accommodate Judaism. At the height of the hope for continued Greek expansion into Asia Minor in 1920, the Greek state recognized the Jews as a religious minority and reconfirmed the status and structure of the Jewish Community of Salonica as it had existed in the late Ottoman era. Jews gained recognition as a kind of neo-*millet*, along with the Muslims in Thrace—a status now legitimized by reference to Hellenism and minority rights as promoted by the League of Nations.[83] That status did not go away with the end of Greek imperial aspirations following the expulsion of the Greeks from Asia Minor in 1922 and the concomitant dissolution of the *Megali Idea*. Especially following the establishment of the Hellenic Republic in 1924, the Greek state embarked on a more thorough and forceful nation-building project to Hellenize Salonica and all the New Lands acquired since 1912. But this nationalizing process coexisted with imperial-style dynamics as the Greek state continued to recognize the separate legal status of the Jewish Community.[84] Hellenization emerged as a prolonged process that involved continued negotiation between the state and the city's Jews—and the formal Jewish Community—as well as a variety of other populations in the region.

Administrative echoes of the Ottoman Empire persisted in the manner in which the Greek state simultaneously preserved the differentiated, collective, legal status of the Jewish Community while also seeking, however haltingly, to transform individual Jews into citizens. Tensions abounded. Although asked to serve in the military and increasingly to speak Greek, Jews were compelled to vote in a separate electoral college (1923–1933) in order to minimize their influence on Greek elections, were not permitted to marry non-Jews except through a ceremony abroad or following conversion (civil marriage did not exist until 1982), and remained under the surveillance of the Ministry of Foreign Affairs. Although the Greek foreign minister endorsed the creation of a Jewish national home in Palestine, the Greek state recognized its own Jewish citizens as a religious minority. Such processes of differentiation implemented by the Greek state did not prevent the Judeo-Spanish press from imagining Salonica's Jews as an integral part of the "Hellenic people" (*puevlo eleno*) bound by shared territory and citizenship if not religion or ethnicity.[85] This vision of Jewish Hellenism in interwar Salonica, reflected throughout this book, defined Hellenic citizenship according to the principle of jus soli (based on residence) rather than jus sanguinis (based on descent or national/ethnic membership).[86]

The adjustment from the Ottoman to Greek frameworks, from the world of Ottomanism to that of Hellenism, therefore not only presented Salonica's Jews with an immense, unprecedented set of challenges but also offered them unexpected opportunities. Scholars typically identify three demoralizing turning points amidst this transition. First, a crippling fire in 1917 left seventy thousand of the city's residents homeless, including fifty thousand

Jews, and destroyed thirty-two synagogues, as well as numerous Jewish clubs and associations, schools, libraries, and communal archives. Regarding the fire as "providential" in order to impose a new, modern, European, and Greek urban plan, the state prevented the fire victims from rebuilding their homes and institutions in the city center, which had served as the heart of Jewish life for centuries.[87]

Second, under pressure from Orthodox Christian refugees from Asia Minor, the Hellenic Republic introduced a Sunday closing law in 1924 allegedly to level the economic playing field. The law overturned the long-standing custom not only among Jews but the entire city to rest on Saturday in observance of the Jewish Sabbath. Finally, in the context of the depres-

Figure 0.2. Cadastral document for the New Catalan synagogue. Issued to the Jewish Community of Salonica in 1922, after the synagogue had been destroyed by the fire of 1917. Source: The Jewish Museum of Thessaloniki. Published with permission.

sion in 1931 and spurred by accusations made by a major Greek newspaper (*Makedonia*) that Jews were disloyal to the state and enemies of the Greek nation, a mob led by the right-wing National Union of Greece perpetrated the first major anti-Jewish attack in Salonica's history, the Campbell pogrom, which resulted in a Jewish neighborhood being burnt down. The perpetrators were never convicted, and the series of events eviscerated the widely held image of Salonica as a Jewish safe haven.

Although each of these events undermined the status of the city's Jews and provoked waves of emigration, they did not entail the inevitable dissolution of Jewish life in Salonica. Rather, each event compelled Salonica's Jews to develop new forms of political and cultural engagement in order to retain a sense of Jewish collectivity, to solidify their connection to the city, and to foster a sense of belonging to the Greek polity. In the wake of the fire of 1917, the editors of *El Puevlo*, which became the most important Judeo-Spanish newspaper in the city, launched their first issue in order to "return our great community to its flourishing state as it had been" prior to the fire and to "assure the future of the Jewish people" in the city.[88] *El Puevlo* argued that the fire, although disastrous, would provide an opportunity to create a "new Community," more democratic and more efficiently run.[89]

While the Sunday closing law of 1924 overturned the legendary status of Salonica as the *Shabatopolis*, or city of the Sabbath, Jewish leaders did not resign themselves to the imposition of the new law. The Interclub Israélite, an umbrella group representing thirteen of the most prominent Jewish associations in Salonica, submitted a petition to the League of Nations, via the Board of Deputies of British Jews in London, arguing that the Sunday closing law violated their minority rights protections.[90] But their efforts were not successful. Back in Salonica, the Shomre Shabat ("Guardians of the Sabbath") organized two thousand members to convince many Jewish shop owners to observe the Sabbath by choice. The rabbinical court further brokered compromises with Jewish merchants that permitted, for example, a Jewish butcher to open his shop on Saturday mornings to sell to Christian clients and initiated what the press referred to as "modern Shabbat," which promoted more harmonious relations with non-Jewish neighbors.[91]

Finally, despite—or perhaps because of—the anti-Jewish Campbell attacks in 1931, representatives of the Jewish Community, the Zionist Federation of Greece, and the Club of Liberal Jews joined rallies at St. Minas Church in support of the "union" (*enosis*) of Cyprus to Greece later the same year. "In our quality as Hellenes," the Jewish representatives proclaimed, "we have, with all of Hellenism, protested to the Nations to recognize the sacred will of the Cypriotes." In response, the National Organization of Greek Army Veterans praised the declarations of Salonica's Jews, who "revealed their Hellenic soul."[92] Were these expressions of genuine patriotism or artificial, self-defensive loyalty—or both?

The most prominent Greek statesman of the twentieth century, Prime Minister Eleftherius Venizelos, urged Salonica's Jews to go beyond pledges of political loyalty and follow the example of their Romaniote coreligionists if they were to guarantee a place for themselves in Greek society. A few thousand Romaniote Jews had resided in Greek-speaking lands—most notably Ioannina, in Epirus—since antiquity (since the Roman era, hence their name), spoke Greek fluently, gave their children Greek names, and, as Venizelos saw it, expressed their Judaism exclusively as religious (rather than national) difference.[93] Venizelos offered an ostensibly liberal promise that echoed features of Greek Enlightenment thinker Rhigas Velistinlis' unrealized eighteenth-century vision for a pluralistic Hellenic Republic inclusive of Greeks, Serbs, Bulgarians, Vlachs, Armenians, Jews, and Turks—all bound together by shared Greek language and civic responsibilities.[94] If Jews adjusted their cultural and political orientation, Venizelos suggested, they would become Hellenes and be accepted as such. In this regard, Salonican Jewish Ottomanism and Hellenism diverged concerning the role of language: while Turkish never assumed the role of the dominant Jewish language prior to 1912 within the framework of Ottomanism, once the city came under Greek rule, Greek moved to the center stage and challenged the position of Judeo-Spanish, Hebrew, and French. This language, it was hoped, would provide the glue to bind Jews to their Christian neighbors—many of whom, including refugees from Asia Minor, were also learning Greek—and to the state.

Seeking to carve out a space for themselves in Greece, Salonica's Jewish elite appealed to a definition of Hellenism modeled on their understanding of ancient Athens, its proverbial liberalism, and emphasis on civic belonging. In place of the Ottoman-Jewish romance that revolved around 1492, Jewish leaders developed new narratives about the centrality of Salonica to

Hellenic history and the key role played by Jews in that history, dating back
to the first century, when the apostle Paul preached at the Romaniote synagogue in Salonica. They emphasized the complementarity—rather than the
antagonism—between Hellenism and Judaism, philosophy and monotheism,
which they construed as the dual founts of modern civilization. Endorsing nationalist narratives, they fashioned present-day Jews and Greeks as
the cultural heirs and genealogical descendants of Moses and Plato. The
Judeo-Spanish press even claimed, by reference to the fourth-century Greek
historian Diodore, that Jewish presence in Greece dated to the era of Moses:
those Jews who did not follow him to the Promised Land settled in Greece.[95]
Zionists patterned their own efforts for Jewish national liberation in Palestine on Greek nationalism, the success of which they viewed as a model and
inspiration for their own aspirations, a project they referred to as their own
"great idea" (*la grande idea*). Salonican Zionists did not consider their desire
to create a Jewish state in Palestine to negate their simultaneous pledges of
allegiance to Greece.[96]

The well-known journalist, member of Greek Parliament, and leading figure in Salonica's Zionist movement, Mentesh Bensanchi, insisted that there
was no contradiction between being a Hellene and a Jew. This was because
he envisioned the Hellenic polity "as truly liberal"—a country that, if true to
the ancient liberal Hellenic spirit, would recognize and respect cultural and
communal differences among its citizens. In this version of Hellenism, Jews
and Orthodox Christians equally warranted their status as Hellenes, whether
as "Hellenic Jews" (*djidios elenos*), "Jewish Hellenes" (*elenos djidios*), or "Hellenic citizens of the Israelite confession" (*citoyens hellènes de confession israélite*).
Ultimately, visions of civic Hellenism, just as Ottomanism before it, sought
to resolve the tensions embedded in the preservation of Jews' dual legal status as citizens of the country and members of the Jewish Community. After
Greece annexed Salonica, rather than abolish the Jewish Community, the
state reconfirmed its legal status and ironically incorporated it into the process of Hellenization. In essence, the challenge posed by Jews in interwar
Salonica was not that they unequivocally resisted Hellenization, as scholars
often suggest; rather, they articulated a different vision of what Hellenization could become. Was it in vain that, referring to mother Greece and her
Christian and Jewish citizens, Bensanchi asked: "Can a mother not love her

many children?"[97] Even if the state appeared willing to embrace its varied citizenry—if the mother could embrace her Jewish and Christian children— would those children be willing to accept each other as siblings?

The chapters that follow trace key dilemmas confronted by Salonica's Jews that reflect their attempts to navigate the transition from the Ottoman Empire to modern Greece, from the 1880s until World War II. The first chapter explores the creation and development of the institution of the Jewish Community of Salonica. Due to the largely self-governing status of the Jewish Community, everyday Jews relied upon it—as if it were a municipality or a state, as one commentator observed—to endure the tumultuous transition from Ottoman to Greek jurisdiction, including war, fire, and economic crisis. Sometimes in conflict and other times in partnership with the state, the Jewish Community defined its members, subjected them to Jewish marriage law, managed Jewish popular neighborhoods for the impoverished, and facilitated the induction of Jewish men into the army. Allegiance to the Jewish Community and to the state sometimes complemented each other, whereas other times they stood in opposition.

The ongoing debates over the role and nature of the spiritual and political leader of the Jewish Community, the chief rabbi, forms the heart of the second chapter. Deliberations among competing Jewish political factions over the nature of the position of the chief rabbi reflected their differing values and contested visions for the future of Salonica and its Jewish residents from the late Ottoman era until World War II. While Jewish political groups largely agreed that the chief rabbi ought to represent the city's Jews to their neighbors, the state, international organizations, and Jewish communities abroad, they often disagreed over who the chief rabbi ought to be and what kind of image he should project to the world about the status of the Jews of Salonica.

Jewish leaders also believed that the future of Jewish life in Salonica would be forged at school, a site that acquired a sacred aura for its crucial role in educating the youth. The third chapter argues that schools became sites in which to transform the children of the last generation of Ottoman Jews into the first generation of Hellenic Jews, conscious of their status as Jews and as citizens of their country. Focusing on the contested role of language and its relationship to questions of identity and belonging, the chapter also emphasizes the unexpected ways in which the Jewish Community and the state partnered to develop new Jewish educational opportunities.

The fourth chapter charts how Salonican Jews' interest in their own history migrated from the margins of public awareness during the late Ottoman era to the very center of public attention during the interwar years. During this period, Jewish intellectuals created narratives of their own community's past to unify themselves in the context of fragmentation and crisis, to imbed themselves in the Ottoman context, and, by rewriting their story, to advocate for a place within the Greek context. In the process, local Jewish historians varyingly envisioned their city as Jewish ("Jerusalem of the Balkans"), Sephardic ("Citadel of Sephardism"), or Greek ("Macedonian Metropolis"), and agreed that greater knowledge of their past would help them secure their future.

The final chapter interrogates the place of the Jewish cemetery of Salonica—once the largest in Europe—within the spatial, political, and cultural landscapes of the city from the late Ottoman era until World War II. It focuses on the tactics that representatives of the Jewish population deployed to safeguard their burial ground in the context of nineteenth-century Ottoman urban reforms and then in the face of expropriation measures endorsed by the Greek state and the local university. Could a Jewish necropolis remain in the center of what was supposed to be a Greek metropolis? The participants in the ensuing campaign sought to demonstrate that the tombstones spoke, that the inscriptions narrated the integral role played by Jews—as indigenous Salonicans—in their city, and by extension, in the broader Greek world. The attempt to safeguard the spaces of the Jewish dead constituted an effort to secure the place of the Jewish living in Salonica and all of Greece—and reveals the ultimate fragility of the effort.

Jewish Salonica uses these thematic cases to explore not only how the city's Jews saw themselves as rooted in the city and connected to their community, but also how they experienced triumphs and vicissitudes across the divide between the Ottoman Empire and modern Greece. It investigates what it meant to be not only a Saloncian Jew and a Sephardic Jew, but also an Ottoman and a Hellene. By studying how Salonica's Jews confronted the transition from the Ottoman Empire to the Greek nation-state, *Jewish Salonica* highlights the dilemmas confronting minority populations in general and the arsenal of creative survival strategies and mechanisms of adaption they developed as the world of multicultural empires gave way—haltingly, incompletely—to one of homogeneous nation-states. On the cusp of this transition in the wake of World War I, a Judeo-Spanish novelist characterized Salonica as a "perpetual gateway" and "the most hospitable center on earth," due to its location between East and West. "All peoples passed through this city, occupied it, stopped by, or visited; it can be called a hotel open to the nations. Since Babel, one can say, God never created anything better."[98] As the twentieth century progressed, the open and hospitable posture of the city increasingly gave way to exclusivity. Salonica—like Greece, Europe, and the Middle East more broadly—continues to wrestle with the legacy of that transformation today.

⟨ CHAPTER 1 ⟩

LIKE A MUNICIPALITY AND A STATE
The Community

Dos djidios, tres keiloth.

Two Jews, three synagogues.

—Judeo-Spanish expression

In the wake of World War I, the Judeo-Spanish newspaper *El Puevlo* strikingly depicted the existence not of one but "two Salonicas" (*las dos Salonikos*). "Greek Salonica" offered a model of self-sufficiency, self-sacrifice, and compassion as evidenced in its extensive network of philanthropic institutions, like the esteemed Papafio Orphanage. In contrast, "Jewish Salonica," embodied in the array of institutions and philanthropies run by the official Jewish Community, continued to struggle from the demoralizing impact of the fire of 1917 and lagged behind its Greek counterpart—a dynamic that the newspaper hoped would change. Part of the difference stemmed from the backing that Greek Salonica received from the municipality and the state, whereas Jewish Salonica materialized through the largely independent efforts of the Jewish Community. Each produced parallel and competing, sometimes intersecting and cooperating, versions of the city.[1] The editor of *El Puevlo*, Mentesh Bensanchi, went further by idealizing and personifying the Jewish Community as nourishing the city's Jews: "If the Community could speak, she would say: 'I am the embodiment of the Jews, and everything that could interest the Jews commands my attention.'"[2] The sway that the Jewish Community held over the city's Jews even led Abraham Benaroya, the leader of the Socialist Workers' Federation, to observe, in a less celebratory manner, that the Jewish Community "imposes itself on its members like a country does on its residents."[3]

The descriptions of such a separate, robust, and autonomous Jewish community in twentieth-century Salonica was both unusual and anything but preordained. Largely self-governing Jewish communities, running their own affairs according to their own laws, once existed across Europe in the medieval and early modern eras. Ensconced in political and social environments defined by classes or estates (nobility, clergy, peasantry, townspeople, etc.), each of which operated according to different codes of law, the Jewish communities received special dispensations from the ruling authority, whether kings or noblemen in Europe or the sultan in the Ottoman Empire; there was nothing unusual about this. Beginning with the French Revolution, however, the established structures, including the estates and Jewish communities, were largely abolished as the old order of empires and privileges gave way to a new order of nation-states, rights, and duties that sought to transform, at least in theory, Jews and all the other residents of a given state into active citizens. Within the new framework, in which the new states demanded full and exclusive loyalty, there was increasingly less space for other entities to demand allegiance or to mediate the relationship between the individual citizen and the state. There was no room for "a state within a state."[4] During the French Revolution in 1789, Count Stanislas of Clermont Tonnerre, a deputy in the French National Assembly, portended the dissolution of the formal, self-governing Jewish communities first in France and subsequently across the continent: "The Jews should be denied everything as a nation, but granted everything as individuals. They must be citizens."[5] Even in the Russian Empire, home to the largest Jewish population in the world, the czar abolished the *kahal*, the executive council of the Jewish community, in 1844, although it continued to operate without official sanction.

The dynamics in the Ottoman Empire and Greece played out differently. During the period of Ottoman imperial reform in the nineteenth century, the *Tanzimat*, the status of non-Muslim communities (*millets*) was formalized and their institutions of self-governance, while limited by the state, were not abolished but rather modernized and codified. Simultaneously, the Ottoman state sought to transform all of its residents, Muslims and non-Muslims alike, into citizens with rights and duties. The competing demands for allegiance made by the new communal structures and the state existed in a precarious balance until World War I. At the conclusion of World War I, following extensive advocacy on the part of Jewish notables and despite serious disagreement among them, the Greek state renewed key aspects of the self-governing status of the Jewish Community of Salonica (Law 2456 of 1920). The perpetuation of the Jewish Community in Salonica signified the unexpected legacy of *millet*-style imperial structures, recast in the language of minority rights, in the context of the Greek nation-state.

Situated within the broader transition from Ottoman to Greek sovereignty in Salonica, the sui generis character of the Jewish Community of Salonica becomes clear. Rena Molho emphasizes the unusual situation, as Greece became the "only country in the world that recognizes its Jewish communities as legal persons of public law."[6] As certain aspects of the authority of the Jewish Community endured due to its legal recognition and the power derived from it—despite continual contestation among Jewish representatives and with the state—Jews in Salonica found themselves classified as both members of the Jewish Community and citizens of Greece in a dynamic that replicated that of the late Ottoman era. Despite, or perhaps because of, the tenuous balance that the dual affiliations provoked—and in spite of economic problems, political fragmentation, increased Hellenizing pressures, and greater social interactions between Jews and Orthodox Christians—the Jewish Community provided a sense of stability during a period of rupture and remarkably played a role for the Jewish masses that, in other countries, the municipality or the state would have provided. Indeed, the Greek state utilized the term *koinotita* to identify the Jewish Community—a term that also signified an autonomous "township."[7] It was precisely the dependence of the Jewish masses on the Jewish Community that led to *El Puevlo*'s description of "two Salonicas": to what extent did the Jewish Community generate a parallel version of the city that protected the interests or limited the options of local Jews?

The archives of the Jewish Community of Salonica as well as the local press reveal the multiple ways in which Jews of all varieties, sometimes willingly and other times begrudgingly, continued to interact with the Jewish Community, relied on the Jewish Community to intervene with local or state authorities, or requested that the Jewish Community serve as a surrogate for the latter two institutions. On other occasions, Jews advocated for the reform—or the abolition—of Jewish communal institutions or sought to escape their authority. After elucidating how the Jewish Community, its institutions, and its functions crystalized during the *Tanzimat*, this chapter turns to the debates following Salonica's incorporation into Greece that resulted in the state reluctantly granting legal standing to the Jewish Community in 1920 and then reflects on the status of Jews in comparison to other minorities in Greece and to Jews in Turkey. The remainder of the chapter highlights the defining roles played by the Jewish Community of Salonica, which reserved the power to determine and manage its membership, to operate a rabbinic tribunal (*beth din*) to impose rabbinic marriage law and enforce communal boundaries, to administer public housing projects for the Jewish masses, and to negotiate with the state regarding Jewish military service. Each domain tested the limit to which the Jewish Community in Salonica could bridge the gulf between the Ottoman Empire and the Greek nation-state for the city's Jews.

From Congregations to Community

When the German occupation forces in December 1941 compelled the long-time chancellor of the Jewish Community, Daout Levy, to compose a history of the Jewish Community of Salonica, Levy selected a telling starting point. He did not begin in the first century, with the Romaniote Jewish presence in the city during the apostle Paul's visit; nor did he begin in 1492, another obvious possible starting point that marked the mass arrival of Sephardic Jews fleeing from Spain. Instead, he began in 1870, the year that the Communal Council was formed as the supreme governing body of the Jewish institutions in the city, and thus the year the Jewish Community of Salonica, as he knew it, was born.[8]

Prior to the formal institutionalization of the Jewish Community with the creation of the Communal Council during the nineteenth-century era of reform, the *Tanzimat*, the Ottoman state had developed a complex set of practices to manage its relationships with the diverse non-Muslim populations granted permission to reside within the imperial realm. Jews, Armenians, and Orthodox Christians benefitted from extensive opportunities or privileges of self-government in exchange for a pledge of loyalty and for a special tax (*cizye*). Within this framework, *kehalim* or "congregations" reigned supreme among Ottoman Jews from the sixteenth through the eighteenth centuries. The *kehalim* constituted the primary, largely autonomous Jewish governing bodies that managed their own affairs independently, as if each were "a city unto itself."[9] Each *kahal* (or *kal*, as pronounced among Sephardic Jews) served as a synagogue, court of law, school, charity, and burial society, and appointed one of its members as *kahya* or *vekil*, an intermediary responsible for negotiating taxes with the Ottoman state.[10] In order to better represent their collective interests to the state, the congregations in Salonica agreed to form the *kolel de la sivdad*, the "(Jewish) collectivity of the city."[11]

During the nineteenth century, the primary legislation of the *Tanzimat* aimed to transform its Muslim, Christian, and Jewish populations into Ottoman citizens, but at the heart of the project lay a tension. In seeking to create an inclusive Ottoman identity irrespective of religious affiliation, the Ottoman state also officially recognized and formalized the structures of the Jewish, Greek Orthodox, and Armenian *millets*, which reminded the various populations of their duties not only as citizens but also as members of their communities. While the Ottoman state limited the judicial powers of the non-Muslim courts, which were no longer sanctioned to try criminal cases or to adjudicate commercial disputes, it also codified previously informal non-Muslim representative and organizational bodies through the promulgation of statutes to govern the inner workings of each community. The statutes called for the establishment of elected councils to govern the affairs of each of the newly and formally recognized Communities.[12]

The Communal Council (Konsilio Komunal) served as the executive branch of the Jewish Community of Salonica's self-government and was overseen by the president. The members of the Communal Council were drawn from the General Assembly (Asamblea Djenerala), a legislative body and miniature Jewish parliament to which representatives were elected. These governing bodies also operated in conjunction with the Rabbinical Council (Konsilio Ruhani, literally, "spiritual council"), overseen by the chief rabbi who also supervised the Beth Din (rabbinical court).[13]

Initially, only those Jewish men in the city who were wealthy enough to pay the *pecha*, a 2 percent capital tax assessed and collected by the Community, could vote or run in communal elections. From an initial 300 *pecheros* (those capable of paying the *pecha*), 1,300 men qualified in 1913. On the eve of World War II, the number of *pecheros* had increased dramatically to 3,733.[14]

The *pecha* provided key revenue for the Jewish Community to run its various institutions and accounted for about 15 percent of the total budget in 1929 and about one quarter in 1934.[15] Despite the greater numbers of those capable of paying the *pecha*—and the greater income derived from it—the Judeo-Spanish press complained about the sometimes mendacious manner in which the wealthy and their "cliques" continued to find their way into leadership roles by exchanging political "favors" (*hatires*) in the "shadows."[16]

A major, democratizing reform instituted in 1921 partly transformed the established dynamics. Zionists, Jewish Socialists, and Jewish liberals pressured the General Assembly to introduce universal male suffrage in communal elections by granting Jewish men aged twenty-one and over the right to vote regardless of their ability to pay the *pecha*. The number of registered voters therefore increased exponentially, from those select few who could pay the *pecha*—300 in the late nineteenth century and 1,300 in 1913—to more than 7,000 in 1934. The remarkable increase in the number of voters—although still only a minority of the city's Jews—demonstrated that more Jews had become actively involved in the Jewish communal political process than ever before. The irony was that, even as the total membership of the Jewish Community of Salonica decreased during the first four decades of the twentieth century due to emigration, the number of those enfranchised and participating in communal politics swelled. But since the number of seats in the General Assembly was contingent on the size of the Jewish population in the city, as the Jewish population decreased, so, too, did the number of seats on the General Assembly: from eighty-five elected members in 1918, to seventy in 1930, to fifty in 1934.[17] The paradox was that increased enfranchisement transpired simultaneously with demographic diminution.

A sampling of registered voters preserved in the files of the Communal Electoral Commission of 1934 indicates that, in addition to a small number of successful merchants, middle-class professionals and small businessmen predominated among the voters, who also included a wide range of unskilled laborers, impoverished and unemployed, who did not pay the *pecha*. The following loose categories offer a sense of the diversity: Merchants included the fabric merchant, paper merchant, coffee vendor, grocer, lemonade vendor, leather merchant, fruit seller, vegetable vendor, book dealer, second-hand clothing dealer, lumber merchant, bicycle seller, traveling salesman, sandal merchant, cheese vendor, shirt vendor, photography supplies vendor, *halva* vendor, mirror seller, broom seller, poultry seller, glass merchant, wood seller, exporter, and construction supplier. Manual laborers and those in service industries included the fisherman, ferryman, boatman, stevedore, port worker, barber, shoemaker, carriage driver, tram worker, railway worker, chauffeur, milkman, winemaker, wall painter, haberdasher, waiter, domestic, handyman, baker, confectioner, soldier, tobacco laborer, machinist, linoleum worker, sack maker, coal worker, sawyer, box maker, butcher, slaughterhouse worker, gravedigger, miller, and iron worker. Artisans included the electrician, jeweler, tinsmith, tailor, goldsmith, musician, stonemason, furrier, glazier, cloth maker, typographer, quilt maker, cobbler, and carpenter. White collar employees included the clerk, lawyer, journalist, pharmacist, druggist, banker, money changer, realtor, accountant, communal employee, lithographer, engineer, rent collector, tax collector, notary, agronomist, nurse, cashier, forwarding agent, student, and teacher.[18]

Elected by increasingly democratic-style means, the governing councils of the Jewish Community (the Communal Council and General Assembly) appropriated many of the functions previously performed by the *kehalim*. Reflecting on the period from the 1870s until 1913, *El Liberal* viewed these centralizing administrative reforms as a major achievement, a sign of the progress of the Jews of the city, and a symbol of their successful self-governance. From the *kehalim* and the Talmud Tora (the Jewish religious school), the Communal Council gradually arrogated to itself the powers to collect special taxes (*gabelas*) on kosher meat, wine, and cheese and assigned the income to support a wide array of religious, educational, and philanthropic institutions. *El Liberal* hoped that, within the new context of the Greek state, the Communal Council would continue its effort to unify the administration of the Jewish Community.[19] But intense resistance to centralization persisted: following the fire of 1917, the rabbis objected to attempts by the Communal Council to intervene in the internal functioning of the synagogues on the grounds that, since 1492, they had been governed exclusively by their own members (*yehidim*).[20]

The centralization of the Jewish Community also precipitated the expansion of Jewish institutions under the aegis of the Communal Council, often times in conjunction with the chief rabbinate, during the late Ottoman period and beyond. New institutions included the Beth Yosef rabbinical seminary (1897); Matanoth Laevionim (soup kitchen) (1901); Hirsch Hospital (1908); the Carlos Allatini Orphanage for Boys (1908); and the Jewish Insane Asylum (1908). Other institutions included the long-standing Bikur Holim (medical dispensary, established in the sixteenth century but rebuilt, 1922), the Mair Aboav Orphanage for Girls (1925), the Benosiglio Maternity Ward (1936), the Saul Modiano Old Age Home, the Meir Ginio Institution for Tuberculosis, Bene Avram (medical assistance), Union Mutual (Jewish mutual aid federation), the Malbish Aroumim (to supply clothing to needy students, 1920), and Tora Umeleha (to provide school supplies to students, 1917). The reach of these institutions was extensive. In 1938, for example, the Hirsch Hospital admitted 2,216 patients to the pathology, surgery, dermatology, neurology, gynecology, physiology, and ear, nose, and throat departments; received 9,568 outpatient visits; and placed 19,780 pharmaceutical orders.[21]

From the offices of the Jewish Community on Sarandaporou Street and under the aegis of the Communal Council, the director supervised an extensive series of other commissions, including those for funerary services, education, housing, neighborhood administration, real estate, synagogues (which coordinated the committees for fifty-six recognized congregations and study halls, or *batei midrash*), taxation (for the *pecha* and *gabela*), accounting, civil status, elections, and *matza* distribution. During the 1930s, the Communal Council also subsidized the Béné Bérith Lodge, the Alliance Israélite Universelle, the Maccabi Society, Devora (a women's philanthropy), and Halel ve-Zimra (religious choir), in addition to the Jewish newspapers in Judeo-Spanish (*La Aksion, La Renasensia Djudia, El Mesajero,* and *El Tiempo*) and French (*Le Progrès, L'Indépendant,* and *La Volonté*).[22] By the 1930s, the Jewish Community employed an extensive bureaucracy of a hundred functionaries, an additional fifty teachers, plus six judges on the Beth Din (rabbinical court), ten *shohatim* (ritual slaughterers), six *moalim* (ritual circumcisers), and more than twenty *hazanim* (who performed weddings), while also regulating close to fifty kosher butchers.[23]

The writer and teacher Mercado Covo lamented in 1911 that Salonica had not yet reached the status of those "Jewish cities" in Galicia, Russia, and Lithuania that constituted "great Jewish centers."[24] Salonica, Covo asserted, could only reach the heights of a true "Citadel of Jews," like Vilna or Lodz, when "she [Salonica] will shine" for her schools, rabbinical seminaries,

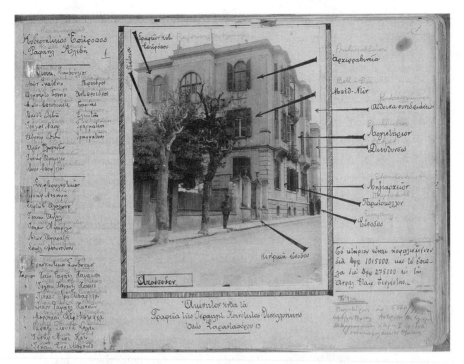

Figure 1.1. The building of the Jewish Community of Salonica, 1939. The main offices on Sarandaporou Street, including those of the Beth Din and chief rabbinate, are labeled in Greek, and the names of the members of the Communal Councils are listed to the left. Part of an album of the Jewish Community's assets confiscated by the Nazis during World War II, it bears notations in German. Source: The Jewish Museum of Thessaloniki. Published with permission.

normal school, hospitals, old-age homes, orphanages, great philanthropic institutions, scholars, artists, literati, doctors, and rabbis. Ironically, by the time Covo died in 1940, as World War II first began to impact Greece, the Jewish Community of Salonica had established all of the institutions that Covo had imagined as desiderata thirty years before.

From Communal Privileges to Minority Rights

In order for the Jewish Community to be perpetuated across the Ottoman-Greek divide, the strategies of legitimization changed. The initial period of Salonica's transition from Ottoman to Greek rule witnessed the devastation of World War I and the National Schism that split Greek society over whether to enter the conflict, a massive fire in 1917 that destroyed the center of Salonica, and international events such as the Russian Revolution and the Balfour Declaration. During this period, Zionists, Jewish socialists, and Jewish integrationists disagreed over whether the Jewish Community of Salonica should continue to exist as it had in the late Ottoman era. When those in favor of its perpetuation succeeded in imposing their will and convinced the Greek state to recognize the Jewish Community in Salonica—as well as Jewish Communities throughout the country—they appealed not to the antiquated vocabulary of imperial privileges but rather to the ascendant discourse of minority rights in vogue at the conclusion of World War I and endorsed by the League of Nations. The framework of minority rights ultimately permitted the Jewish Community in Salonica to persist, but it impacted other minorities in Greece (such as Muslims and Slav-speaking Orthodox Christians) as well as Jews in Turkey differently.

From the perspective of Zionists during World War I, only the official recognition of the Jewish Community by the state would enable the Jews of Salonica to bridge the chasm that separated their Ottoman past from their Greek present and enable them to build a future for themselves as Jews in Greece. Precisely for this reason, Mentesh Bensanchi, the editor of *El Puevlo*, lamented that, without official recognition from the Greek state, it was as if the Communal Council, the executive administrative body of the Jewish Community, was "impotent" or, even worse, did not exist at all. Only if officially recognized by the state, Bensanchi argued, could the Jewish Community continue to operate its own schools and philanthropic organizations, as well as meet the needs of its members and benefit from the rights that Jews, as a "national minority," deserved.[25]

According to their Judeo-Spanish mouthpiece, *Avanti*, Jewish Socialists in 1913 were initially divided over whether the Jewish Community should continue to exist in the new context of the Greek state and, if so, whether members of the Socialist Workers' Federation should participate in it. One faction argued that the Federation should engage with the Community but only temporarily, until the municipality and the state wrested control of mutual aid and education away from the Jewish Community. Another faction argued that the Federation ought to work to dissolve the Jewish Community and focus on advocacy vis-à-vis the municipality and the state. But Abraham

Benaroya, the leader of the Federation, articulated the position ultimately adopted by the Federation. He characterized the Jewish Community as a "national institution" that "imposes itself on its members *like a country* does on its residents." He further compared the Community to a *municipality* and a *state*, indicating that these entities derived their political and civic value by virtue of their influence over a considerable population. The Federation therefore decided to organize the struggle for class equality within the Jewish Community and to empower Jewish workers to "conquer" the Community and to "liberate" it from "bourgeois oppression." Such a victory would be accomplished, *Avanti* explained, by the introduction of universal suffrage in the Jewish Community so that port workers, coach drivers, and bootblacks could finally share in institutional governance along with the wealthy, who could afford to pay the communal tax (*pecha*), a prerequisite until 1921 for voting in communal elections.[26]

But throughout World War I, some Jewish socialists feared that rabbis and Jewish merchants in leadership positions in the Jewish Community would be unwilling to introduce the desired reforms—especially universal suffrage. They were joined in their skepticism by Jewish liberals who were drawn from the Jewish middle classes like the Jewish nationalists but who advanced the integrationist ideology of the Alliance Israélite Universelle. For Jewish liberals, the Jewish Community perpetuated antiquated imperial privileges, bolstered the anachronistic notion of Jews forming a state within a state—a status obliterated in France after the Revolution of 1789—and offered protection for the "leading plutocratic and theocratic section of the community."[27] Jewish liberals advocated that Jews exercise their individual rights as citizens rather than their collective rights as a minority. They feared that the Jewish Community, if preserved, would promote the wishes of rabbis and impose religious formalities on Jews—in terms of marriage practices, diet, or Sabbath observance—regardless of conviction.

Seeking to reconcile the competing demands made by representatives of the various Jewish factions, the long-time president of the Jewish Community of Salonica, Jacob Cazes, who was part of the merchant elite, undertook negotiations with state officials during the final years of World War I. Although ostensibly in favor of integration—he ran in the 1915 Greek state elections on the ticket of Venizelos' Liberal Party—Cazes recognized the increasing sway of Zionists within local Jewish politics. Despite the grave distress provoked by the fire of 1917, pronouncements later that year by the Greek foreign minister in favor of the creation of a Jewish home in Palestine—even prior to the Balfour Declaration—galvanized local Zionism. Jewish leaders convened a Panhellenic Jewish Congress in Salonica in 1919 to advocate for their own civil, political, religious, and national rights in Greece and for the recognition of a Jewish homeland in Palestine, which they considered a necessary refuge not for themselves but for Jews suffering persecution elsewhere, namely Russia and Romania.[28] Participation in the Congress on the part of official spokesmen for the Jewish Community and the former director of the local Alliance—despite the Alliance's official opposition to Jewish nationalism—signified the triumph of the agenda of national rights among Jewish elite in Salonica.

Jacob Cazes built on the momentum from the Panhellenic Jewish Congress to request that the Greek state endorse the national rights of the country's Jews. Claiming to speak in the name of the Jews of Salonica and all of Hellenic Jewry, Cazes petitioned the governor general of Macedonia to recognize the Jewish Community in Salonica and others across the country in locales with Jewish populations. Cazes demanded that each be granted the right to operate Jewish schools and to teach Jewish languages, in addition to that of the state, and to administer Jewish hospitals and other philanthropic institutions; he also demanded that the members of each Jewish Community be exempt from observing Sunday as the day of rest. Anticipating reservations on the part of the governor general, Cazes remarkably argued that the capacity of Jews to live in Greece as a distinct nation would not damage the interests of the state. Instead, he concluded, "if the Jews enjoy these rights, they will be happy citizens who contribute to the welfare of the state."[29] He saw no contradiction in proclaiming the status of Jews as a distinct nation and as citizens of Greece. Rather than rely on a dated vocabulary of privileges and dispensations that had shaped the place of Jews in the old regimes of Europe, Cazes hoped that the Greek state, motivated by its proverbial liberalism and sympathetic to the new formulation of minority rights due to the presence of large Greek Orthodox populations in Turkey and Bulgaria also in search of protections, would grant his demand for Jewish national autonomy within the borders of Greece.

Greek state representatives initially opposed the existence of self-governing communal bodies within its borders. For many countries in Europe, the granting of minority rights in any capacity represented the perpetuation of the old system of privileges and dispensations that a truly sovereign nation-state should not accept, especially in the former Ottoman realm, where capitulation treaties had permitted European powers to protect their protégés by granting them extraterritorial status. The Greek ambassador in London, Ioannis Gennadius, confirmed his opposition to special treatment for certain populations in 1914 to Lucien Wolf, a leading British Jewish figure who advocated for Jewish interests during the war and at the Paris Peace Conference: "To ask us to make special distinctions or grant special privileges would be to upset the very principle of equality which is on the other hand demanded of us. . . . You cannot ask us fairly or consistently to consider our Jewish fellow citizens differently than they are considered in England, nor has any other creed or nationality thought of requesting . . . a system of capitulations in Greece."[30] As late as the spring of 1919, the British consul in Salonica suspected that Jewish leaders would not get their way: "The abolition of all official recognition of the Jewish Community and their rights to manage their internal affairs . . . combined to make the Jews (and not the Jews only) long for the return of the Turks."[31]

A number of factors, however, remarkably shifted the balance in favor of the perpetuation of the Jewish Community of Salonica: continued lobbying on the part of Jewish leaders in Salonica, such as Jacob Cazes; extended discussions at the Paris Peace Conference, where Lucien Wolf, the secretary of the Board of Deputies of British Jews, supported the cause of Salonican Jews; the introduction of the Minorities Treaties guaranteed by the newly-established League of Nations including the Treaty of Sèvres, which Greece signed in 1920; the aspirations of Greek state officials to demonstrate their good will toward minorities in order to improve their international reputation and advance their own expansionist goals in Asia Minor; the desire of the Greek state to streamline its interactions with its Jewish citizens through a centralized channel—much as the Ottoman state had done with its diverse populations—rather than undertake negotiations separately with different Jewish interest groups; and, finally, the ouster of Venizelos and the Liberal Party in the 1920 elections and the return of the monarchy. Under the ensuing reign of King Alexander, in 1920, the Greek state passed Law 2456, "Concerning Jewish Communities," which formally established Jewish Communities in Salonica and in locales across the country, and endowed each with its own statutes (Salonica's were ratified in 1923 but Corfu's not until 1932).[32]

Paradoxically, the 1920 law met virtually all of the requests that Jewish leaders and the Panhellenic Jewish Congress had outlined in their petitions to the Greek authorities but did so in the name of religious rather than national rights. With the rise of the nation-state as the ideal political framework in post-World War I Europe, most European states refused to recognize national populations within their borders in order to prevent territorial succession in the name of national self-determination. Nations, not religions, deserved states. Within a framework that granted Jews rights as a religious minority, the Greek state law recognized Jewish Communities as legal entities under public law in Salonica and in each locale in the country where at least twenty Jewish families resided. All Jews in each of those locations were subject to the authority of the Community in matters of religion. The definition of "religion," however, was broad and included the right of the Jewish Community to collect the *pecha* (communal tax), to maintain rabbinical courts to adjudicate marriage and questions of civil status, to operate philanthropies and schools, to permit its members to rest on Saturday, and to elect the General Assembly and Communal Council to govern its affairs.

At first glance it may not seem surprising that the Greek state—struggling to consolidate its hold on new territories conquered during the Balkan Wars, involved in a decade of nearly continuous war, inundated with refugees, and plagued by political instability and economic woes—allowed the preservation of the Jewish Community. But the Greek state did intervene extensively in the dynamics of its other populations by creating new Muslim Communities, abolishing Orthodox Christian Communities, and suppressing the language of Slavic-speakers. Only the structure of the Jewish Community survived the transition from Ottoman to Greek rule largely intact.

The Greek state treated its Muslims (and those who were not Orthodox Christians, more generally) analogously to the Ottoman state's treatment of Orthodox Christians (and non-Muslims, more generally). The close proximity of the passage of the Greek state laws governing Muslim and Jewish

communal entities—July 3, 1920, and July 29, 1920, respectively—demonstrates that the Greek state thought about these two populations together.[33]
Through the creation of the Muslim Community, a new *millet*-style, corporate entity emerged within the context of the Greek nation-state. The state
granted certain rights of self-government to the Muslim Community that
paralleled those granted to the Jewish Community, including a council to
manage houses of worship, benevolent institutions, and schools. Despite
recognizing Muslims as a religious minority, the Greek state continued to
imagine them as prospective subversive agents of neighboring states, whether
Turkey in the case of the Turkish-speaking Muslims in Thrace, or Albania in
the case of the Chams (Albanian-speaking Muslims) in Epirus.[34]

The Greek state also intervened actively in the governance and institutions of Orthodox Christian populations. The year after the formalization
of the Jewish and Muslim Communities, the Greek state promulgated Law
2508 (April 1, 1921), which dismantled the Orthodox Christian Community
of Salonica (as well as those throughout the country) that had been operative
since the Ottoman era. Since 1913, new state functionaries had arrived in Salonica from Athens and other provinces of Old Greece and gradually wrested
power away from local Orthodox Christian elite. Now, with the 1921 law, the
state definitively dissolved the Orthodox Christian Community and redis-
tributed its assets: its schools went to the state, charities became independent
legal entities, church properties came under the management of the churches
themselves, and other property was arrogated to the state.[35] The Greek state,
in short, ensured that no institutions would mediate the relationship between
its Orthodox Christian citizens—deemed "real Greeks"—and the state.

The Greek state intervened even more extensively in the lives of Slavic-
speaking Orthodox Christians in the region of Macedonia. The Greek state
conceived of Slavic-speakers, due to their Orthodox Christian religious affiliation, as "Greeks by descent" who had been forcibly Slavicized, while still
preserving their national consciousness as Greeks. Shared religion became the
primary factor for justifying shared descent. So as to not cultivate Bulgarian nationalist sentiment among Slavic-speakers, the Greek state denied them
rights of self-administration and suppressed their Old Calendar religious
practices, their agricultural-based social organization (*zadruga*), and their language. Most dramatically, Greek state laws in the 1930s prohibited the use of

the Slavic idiom "in streets, coffee-houses, and anywhere that it can be possibly spoken." Those who violated these measures faced severe penalties, including fines, the forced drinking of castor oil, prison time, and exile.[36] In contrast to Jews and Muslims, Slavic-speakers remained illegible to the Greek state.

Situated in the broader context of the post-Ottoman world, Greece followed a different path from neighboring Turkey. Turkey adopted more radical, secularizing reforms that abolished many Ottoman-style structures, which, ironically, the Greek state perpetuated (with regard to Jews and Muslims). Greece retained Orthodox Christianity as the state religion and preserved the national language in the Greek alphabet despite the establishment of the Hellenic Republic (1924). In contrast, the Republic of Turkey (1923) disestablished Islam as the state religion, abolished the sultanate and the caliphate, substituted the European hat for the fez, and implemented an alphabet reform that transformed Turkish from a language written in Arabic to one written in a modified Latin script. The legal status of Jews (and other non-Muslims) became part of the discussion regarding the reforms of the Republic of Turkey.

The Treaty of Lausanne (1923), which formalized the exchange of populations between Greece and Turkey, stipulated in article 42 that the Turkish government permit "non-Muslim minorities" to maintain their own courts to settle questions of family law and personal status "in accordance with the customs of those minorities." The leadership of the Jewish Community of Istanbul believed that the treaty would guarantee Jews in Turkey rights as full Turkish citizens without compelling them to relinquish their corporate identity. But the new Civil Law Code (1926) overturned these expectations. The authors of the code opposed granting minorities privileges, which they viewed as an embarrassment to national sovereignty. Privileges were construed exclusively as relics of the old order that no longer had a place in the new Republic of Turkey.[37]

Unlike Greece, the Turkish state and the public did not compromise. Turkish newspapers cajoled minority populations to forsake article 42 of the Treaty of Lausanne. With the consent of the chief rabbinate in Istanbul, the Jewish Community became the first non-Muslim Community in Turkey to repudiate the privileges outlined in article 42 and in so doing emerged as a model minority, whose example the Armenian and Greek Communities soon followed. The Turkish state viewed Jews as a model minority not only for relinquishing their privileges but also because their leadership maintained a low profile by promoting *kayadez* ("silence"), not protesting, and not making trouble for themselves.[38]

Jews in Turkey provide a foil to those in Salonica. The president of Salonica's Communal Council, Jacob Cazes, and other leading Jewish representatives had loudly and brazenly negotiated for the reinstitution of official recognition of the Jewish Community by the Greek state and continued to negotiate with the state over many other matters throughout the interwar years. Jewish leaders in Salonica remained unwilling to relinquish claims to self-government in certain domains and by no means subscribed to a policy of *kayadez*.

Who We Are and Where We Are Going: Delimiting Communal Membership

Like many observers during the interwar years and since, a Jewish notable in Athens characterized Salonica as home to "99.99 percent Sephardic Jews."[39] The reality, however, was much more complex and diverse. Michael Molho dramatically referred to Salonica as a center of *kibbutz galuyot*—"the ingathering of the exiles" (Deuteronomy 30:1–5)—where Jews scattered across the world found refuge and solace.[40] Salonica therefore stood out from other Jewish centers in the region not so much because of its alleged homogeneity but, to the contrary, because of the extent to which membership in the Jewish Community was open to all Jews regardless of their place of birth, sex, native language, citizenship, cultural background, religious customs, level of observance, or financial standing—so long as, according to the 1923 statutes, they resided in the city for at least six months. The Jewish Community reserved the right to determine, classify, and enumerate—in other words, to know—the population subject to its authority. As the Judeo-Spanish newspaper, *El Liberal*, observed, the possession, quantification, and analysis of information about its members served as a tool of governance: "We will see, as in a mirror, our entire Community and we will know who we are and where we are going."[41]

Serving as a safe haven not only for Sephardic Jews escaping from the Iberian Peninsula but also for a variety of Jews fleeing from elsewhere, Salonica developed a reputation as a Jewish refuge. The names of the city's synagogues recalled the diverse geographic origins and cultural back-grounds of their founders. Many synagogues bore names referring to places in Spain (six) and Portugal (four), as well as Italy (nine); others referred to France, Germany and Hungary, and North Africa; and the oldest congrega-tion in the city, Ets Ahaim, nicknamed "Congregation of the Greeks," was established by Romaniote Jews in the first century.[42]

Again in the nineteenth and twentieth centuries, Salonica served as a refuge for Jews of different backgrounds who sought physical security and new economic opportunities that contributed to the dramatic increase in the city's Jewish population. They participated in broader population movements facilitated by the advent of the steamship and the railroad that accompanied industrialization and contributed to the unusual demographic composition of Salonica. At the turn of the century, more than twenty million residents lived in the Ottoman Empire, of whom no more than a half million were Jews (2.5 percent). More than 15 percent of the empire's Jews thus lived in Salonica, where they comprised around half of the city's residents. Popula-tion registers from 1884 and 1905 indicate that Jews settled in Salonica from across the region—Athens, Corfu, Dardanelles, Drama, Edirne, Gallipoli, Ioannina, Istanbul, Izmir, Ishtip, Kastoria, Kavalla, Larissa, Monastir, Serres, and Trikkala—thereby contributing to the demographic weight.[43] The several thousand Monastirlis who settled in Salonica erected their own synagogue in the city center in 1927.[44] By the 1930s, according to Jewish communal birth registers, the fathers of 10 to 15 percent of Jews born in Salonica were from other locales.[45] Jews fluent in both Greek and Judeo-Spanish from Trikkala, such as Asher Moisis, Yomtov Yacoel, and Haimaki Cohen, played leading roles in the Jewish Community of Salonica during these years. They served as lawyers, council members, and politicians and as a bridge to the Greek cultural environment.[46]

Several thousand Ashkenazic Jews, fleeing eastern Europe in the 1890s as well as pogroms in Kishinev in 1903 and Odessa in 1905, settled in Salonica. In the wake of World War I, a local newspaper reported: "A week does not pass without young Jews from Poland, Ukraine, Romania or other countries of Eastern Europe arriving in our city."[47] In Judeo-Spanish, these Yiddish-speaking Jews became known as Lehlis ("Poles" in Turkish) or Mashemehas, derived from an apocryphal story about Ashkenazim who arrived at the port asking, in Hebrew, *Ma shemeha?* ("What is your name?"). Yiddish was known as *Mashemehesko*.[48] As refugees suffering from poverty, eastern European Jewish women came to be associated with prostitution. *El Puevlo* characterized Salonica's red-light district as "filled with *mashemehas*," for whom Russian Jewish men served as pimps. Such status did not prevent the Jewish Community from housing Russian Jews in the Hirsch district.[49]

In contrast to the lowly reputation of eastern European Jews in Salonica, wealthy Jewish merchants from Italy, especially Livorno, known as *Francos*, numbered among the city's most prominent residents. Benefitting from capitulation treaties due to their French or Austrian consular protection and, later, Italian citizenship, families such as Allatini, Morpurgo, Fernandez, and Modiano played key roles in developing Jewish communal institutions in Salonica in the nineteenth century.[50] Their influence contributed to the standardization of Italianisms in local Judeo-Spanish, such as *komunita* for "community" (from *comunità*) and the name of the city itself, *Saloniko* (from Salonicco).[51] Due to the Italo-Ottoman War over Libya (1911–1912), however, the Ottoman authorities expelled those individuals protected by Italy, including the famous Allatini family—a blow to the Jewish communal leadership.[52] A small but influential cadre of Salonican Jews acquired Spanish, Portuguese, and Austro-Hungarian protection in 1912–1913 amidst the transition from Ottoman to Greek rule in hope of evading local tax burdens.[53] Joseph Nehama noted that, at the time, merely 5 percent of the city's Jews benefitted from foreign protection.[54]

While the Greek state tried, in 1923, to exclude Jews holding foreign citizenship from the Jewish Community of Salonica, Jewish leaders successfully lobbied to prevent the imposition of the new regulation and to retain ecumenical membership criteria. This was a major concession that demonstrated the continued power of Jewish leaders to negotiate with the Greek state. The Greek state continued to encourage, and in some cases forced, Jews in Salonica holding foreign passports to acquire Greek citizenship, but *all* remained members of the Jewish Community. From the perspective of the Jewish Community, the citizenship of its members did not gain relevance until the reign of Metaxas, when, in 1936, Jewish communal birth registers began recording the citizenship of newborns in the column marked *keila* ("congregation"), previously used to identify the father's synagogue affiliation.[55] German Foreign Ministry records indicate that the number of Jews in Salonica holding foreign citizenship had been reduced from several thousand at the time of the Balkan Wars to 864 individuals by the time of the Nazi occupation, including 511 with Spanish and 281 with Italian citizenship—an indication that the vast majority of Jews who remained in the city had acquired Hellenic citizenship.[56]

Accurate statistics on the city's Jewish population remain difficult to ascertain. The 1830 Ottoman population registers, for example, suggest that, due to persecution by the Ottoman state during the Greek War of Independence (1821–1830), Salonica's Orthodox Christian population decreased, thereby enabling Jews to became the largest constituency in the city (44 percent of adult males).[57] Although it was commonly understood that Jews constituted the plurality, if not the majority, of the population of Salonica, Ottoman population registers of 1830, 1884, and 1905 were notoriously inaccurate. As population figures became tools of nationalist ambition in the twentieth century, Salonica entered a battlefield of "ethnological statistics" with Greece and Bulgaria, each claiming that Greeks or Bulgarians constituted the predominant demographic group in the region.[58] The Judeo-Spanish press conceded in 1913 that the precise number of Jews in Salonica, if considerable, remained unknown: "Some say 60 thousand, others 70 thousand. Some go up to calculating our number at 90 thousand or even more." The lack of statistics "approximating the truth," the press concluded, prevented Jewish leaders from substantiating the claim that Jews predominated in the city and impeded their ability to defend their collective rights.[59]

The fire of 1917 provided an opportunity for the Jewish Community of Salonica to undertake its own "complete census" (*resansiman komplido*). The use of a French-derived term, *recensement*, signified that the model was to be found not in the earlier Ottoman population registers but in the modern methods of the European census. Since the fire destroyed the Jewish communal schools, the director of the Jewish Community, Daout Levy, dispatched Jewish teachers to all the neighborhoods and to temporary encampments that housed fire victims in order to record the names of the Jewish residents of the city according to family unit, including men, women, and children, and indicating sex, age, address, and occupation; whether they were victims of the fire or not and, if so, whether their home or place of work sustained damage; whether their property had been insured and, if so, for how much; and whether they were in need of bread, coal, clothes, or milk. The *resansiman* also classified each family as "poor," "middle class," or "not needy." A new Judeo-Spanish bulletin, *El Sinistrado* ("The Fire Victim"), encouraged readers to cooperate with the census takers so that all Jews and especially victims of the fire could "defend their rights."[60]

Cooperation was forthcoming. The resulting twenty-four volumes of census registers, arranged by family name in quasi-alphabetical order and penned in flowing Judeo-Spanish *soletreo* in purple ink, recorded personal data for 75,062 Jews in Salonica—likely one of the most reliable figures for city's Jewish population. The census, which served as the basis for the Office of Statistics and Civil Status that operated under the auspices of the chief rabbinate, continued to be updated—albeit incompletely—until 1941, registering new births, deaths, marriages, divorces, emigrations, conversions, or appearances before the Beth Din. Documents issued by the Jewish Community, including birth, marriage, or death certificates and other affidavits, referred to relevant entries in the census which doubled as a central population registration.[61] Recognition of membership in the Jewish Community resulted from an essentially bureaucratic process of having one's name and other personal data inscribed in these documents, referred to as *los rejistros de la Komunita* ("registers of the Community").

As outlined in article 24 of Law 2456, the recorded number of Jews residing in the city became tied to the level of financial assistance the municipality and the Greek state provided to Jewish institution. Special incentive therefore emerged to ensure that as many Jews as possible could be counted (in 1934, for example, the municipality and state ministries provided approximately 20 percent of the operating budget of the Jewish Community).[62] The significance of the Jewish Community's own count became ever more clear, according to Judeo-Spanish newspapers, precisely because the censuses of Salonica undertaken by the Greek state in 1913 and 1928 were conducted haphazardly, did not involve enough census takers proficient in Judeo-Spanish, and distinguished residents according to citizenship so that Jews holding foreign passports were counted not as Jews but in a separate category, as foreigners.[63] Such grievances, however, could not overturn the consensus that the Jewish population was decreasing due to emigration. *La Aksion* lamented as early as 1930 that, "like a mirror," statistics now reflected the demographic "decline" and "lamentable situation" of the Jewish collectivity.[64] While estimates of the Jewish population of Salonica had ranged from 60,000 to more than 100,000, by 1934 estimates ranged from 35,000 to 60,000.[65] In the absence of reliable figures, a controversy erupted in the press in 1938 when Joseph Nehama argued that, due to emigration, only 40,000 Jews remained in Salonica. In response, Daout Levy evaluated the data available from the distribution of *matza* at Passover to estimate the total at 58,300.[66] *La Aksion* settled on the figure of "at least 55 thousand."[67]

Until World War II, the archive of the Jewish Community—and especially the Office of Statistics and Civil Status, of which the 1917 census served as the centerpiece—sought to bind members of the Jewish Community of Salonica together, regardless of their citizenship, through the act of registration. The counting and classification of the Jews of Salonica enabled the Jewish Community administration to know its members in unprecedented albeit imperfect ways, to provide social services, and to extract taxes from them. The resulting archive of the Jewish Community, as the repository and record of these links, became the source of the Jewish Community's authority. It is therefore not surprising that, when Nazi forces arrived in Salonica in 1941, their first act was to confiscate the archive, in order to cripple the Jewish Community and undermine its ability to function effectively.[68]

The Authority of Rabbinic Tribunals and the Boundaries of Community

On the eve of the World War II, leading educator Joseph Nehama believed that Greece gradually approached a legal system that would be more uniform for all citizens and on a par with that of other European countries. Across nineteenth-century Europe, states had imposed uniform legal systems that applied equally in all domains to all citizens of a given country, regardless of religious or communal affiliation. Greece lagged behind as a degree of "legal pluralism"—the usage of differing codes of law for different populations typical of imperial settings—prevailed with regard to both Muslims and Jews. Law 147 of 1914 and Law 2456 of 1920 continued to grant official juridical autonomy to the Beth Din, or rabbinical court, with regard to the regulation of Jewish civil status, namely marriages, divorces, and other aspects of family

law (chapter 3, article 12).[69] But Nehama expressed satisfaction that the jurisdiction of the rabbis continued to be reduced (e.g., Law 5549 of 1933):

> The Hellenic regime dissolves a range of archaic privileges that placed Jews
> in a separate legal status and excluded them from the [Greek] national family
> into which they have an interest and desire to integrate, without repentance
> or regret. Old barriers fall, and increasingly, the Hellenic family is preparing
> to welcome into its bosom the fraction of [the people of] Israel who live on
> the lands reconquered by the Greek people, resurrected to a free and inde-
> pendent existence.[70]

Despite Nehama's wishes, his clear integrationist ideology, and his embrace of Greek nationalist rhetoric, his vision remained far from reality.
During the first half of the twentieth century, crucial tensions continued to
shape the legal status of Jews in Salonica—as both members of the Jewish
Community and as citizens of Greece—that perpetuated Ottoman *millet*-
style structures in Greece.[71] Jews in Salonica continued to rely upon the
Beth Din to mete out justice and to provide them with a sense of relative
stability across the chasm that separated the Ottoman world and the Greek
nation-state. In some domains, such as Jewish marriage law, the Beth Din
reserved exclusive jurisdiction even though an increasing number of Jews
sought to circumvent rabbinical authority by converting out of Judaism and
traversing communal boundaries. In other realms, those who considered
themselves to be "good Jews" (*buenos djidios*) continued to submit themselves voluntarily to the judgment of the *dayanim* ("rabbinical judges") even
with regard to issues over which the Beth Din had no official jurisdiction.

Until the nineteenth century, rabbis in the Ottoman Empire wielded
considerable authority to impose their will on their flock. Often with the
backing of the Ottoman authorities, rabbis and *dayanim* who served on
the Beth Din in Salonica meted out punishments to those who violated their
rulings, including the *falaka*, or bastinado (caning the soles of the feet); the
herem, a form of censure that cuts off an individual from social and economic
relations with the Jewish collectivity; and, more distinctive to Salonica, a
prison, where those convicted could be locked up at the discretion of the
rabbis.[72] When, in 1874, a member of a prominent family of Jewish printers
was accused of smoking a cigarette on Saturday—and thus of desecrating

the Sabbath—the rabbis appealed to Jewish notables of the city to intervene with the Ottoman governor of the city, who dispatched the gendarmerie to capture and imprison the convicted party, whom the rabbis placed under *herem*. But the following year, in 1875, the same family established a successful Judeo-Spanish newspaper—a sign that punishments meted out by the rabbis, including the *herem*, had lost much of their enduring power.[73] In 1885, the infamous rabbinic prison was finally abolished.

While the extensive powers of rabbis in Salonica to police and punish the behaviors of the Jewish masses symbolized the once legendary autonomy of the city's Jews, the reforms of the *Tanzimat* severely curtailed the authority of the Beth Din, although without abolishing it. *La Epoka* reported in 1888 that as many as 150 cases came before the rabbinical judges *each day* and advocated that certain reforms be instituted to expedite the adjudication process.[74] An article in 1909 ridiculed the *dayanim*, who lounged comfortably on a sofa enveloped by swirls of cigarette smoke, as litigants stood before them, yelling at each other as their supporters cheered them on. In the twentieth century, an era of enlightenment and progress, the newspaper wondered, could the sessions of this "court of Jewish justice" be conducted in a more orderly manner so as to restore its prestige?[75]

While the purview of the Beth Din had been curtailed to focus largely on questions of civil status during the *Tanzimat* and continuing through interwar Greece, we must not underestimate the extent to which family law played a central role in dictating the everyday lives of Greece's Jews and their interactions with not only each other but also their non-Jewish neighbors. The Greek state granted the Beth Din the exclusive right to determine whom Jews could marry and, in effect, with whom they could constitute a legal family unit. The Greek state passed another law in 1932, indicating that it would enforce rabbinical decisions concerning marriage and divorce and prosecute those in violation of rabbinic rulings who, if convicted, could face up to two years in prison.[76] Remarkably, within the context of interwar Greece, the *dayanim* gained a new level of legitimacy, benefitted from the official imprimatur of the government with regard to marriage and civil status, and could appeal to the Greek State Court of First Instance to enforce its rulings. The backing that the Beth Din continued to receive from the state with regard to promoting marriage among Jews explains why its proceedings, as late as 1938, began by evoking the sovereign: "In the name of the King of the Hellenes, George II, the religious tribunal of the Jewish Community of Salonica . . . is convened."[77] The absolute majority of Jews continued to marry other Jews not only due to social custom, preference, or the expectations of the rabbinical elite but also in accordance with Greek state law.

Until World War II, the Jewish Community certified more than twenty *hazanim* ("religious functionaries") to perform weddings, inscribe them in the Office of Statistics and Civil Status within the Community, and then register them with the municipality in exchange for a tax for the service.[78] The Jewish Community also required prospective couples to submit an official request for permission to marry and to pay the annual capital tax (*pecha*) prior to granting permission to wed. Even Jews acculturated into Greek society—as evidenced by their signatures in Greek appended to the court proceedings (written in Judeo-Spanish and Hebrew)—continued to depend on the Beth Din not only to certify marriages and divorces but also to adjudicate marriage disputes.[79]

Jewish women also required a dowry in order to marry. The taxation records of the Jewish Community of Salonica from as late as 1940 include the files of the *presiadores*, communal functionaries who assessed the dowries of Jewish couples as they prepared to wed.[80] Bouena Sarfatty railed against the custom of the dowry in her poems and hoped it would be abandoned.[81] As early as 1900, *La Epoka* explained that Jewish women who opted to convert did so in order to avoid assembling the dowry.[82] A popular Judeo-Spanish song released in 1924, *El mal de las dotas*, similarly decried the "evils" of the custom, which became increasingly burdensome during the depression in the 1930s, and inspired a proposal for a "League Against Marrying with a Dowry."[83] The Jewish Community in nearby Serres even came into conflict with the chief rabbinate in Salonica when the former invited Jews to Serres to marry without requiring dowries or the payment of the marriage tax.[84] In another instance, in 1938, the rabbi in Trikkala agreed to marry a Jewish couple even after having received explicit orders from the chief rabbinate in Salonica not to do so. In response, the Rabbinical Council in Salonica proposed that a chief rabbi for all of Greece be established, with its seat in Salonica, in order to intervene in the decisions of rabbis across the country when necessary.[85] The onset of World War II prevented the proposal from being pursued.

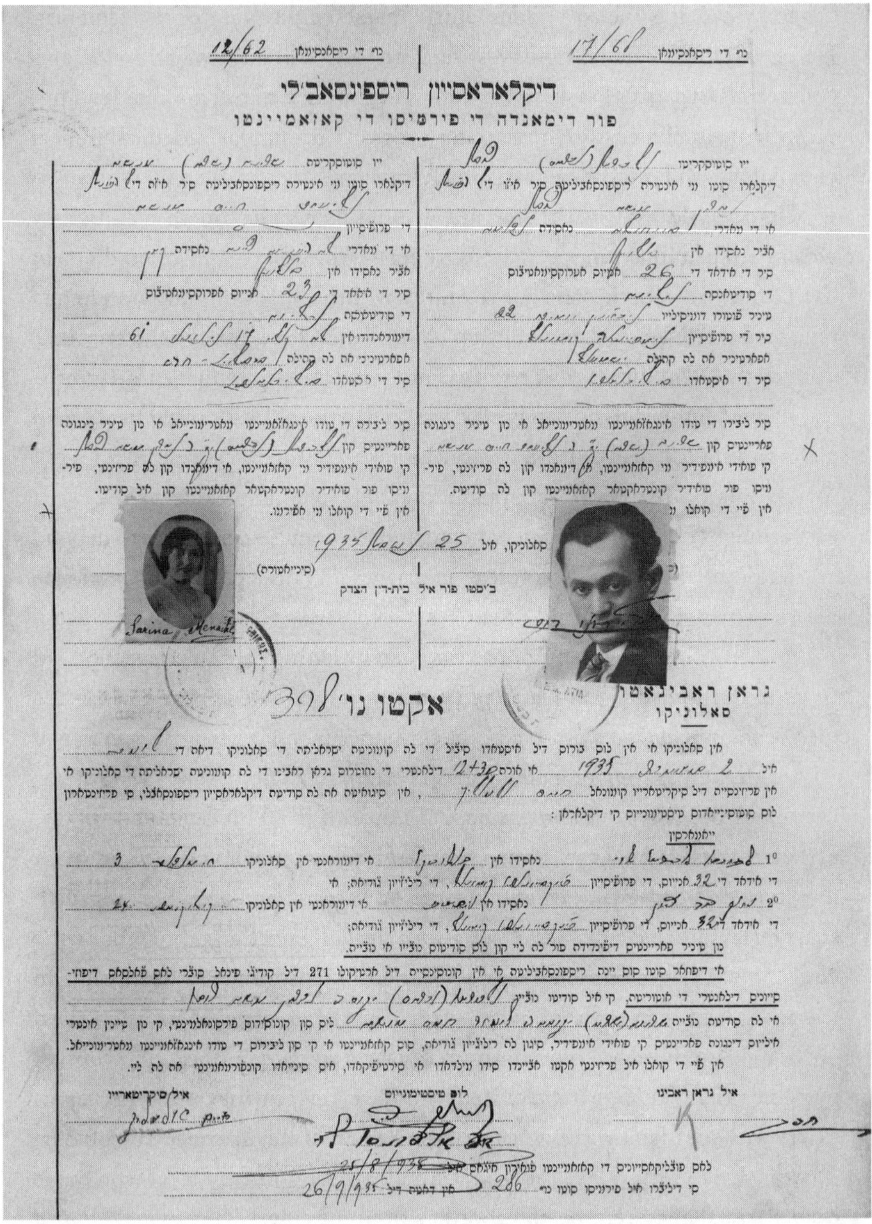

דיקלאראסיון ריספינסאב'לי

פור דימאנדה די פירמיסו די קאזאמיינטו

אקטו נו' 398

גראן ראבינאטו

סאלוניקו

Figure 1.2. A request for permission to marry by Alberto Rousso and Sarina Menashe, 1935. Submitted to the Office of Civil Status of the Jewish Community of Salonica. Source: The Jewish Museum of Thessaloniki. Published with permission.

As debate over the status of the dowry continued, discussion over the legalization of civil marriage, which would permit the union of a Jew and a Christian (or Muslim) without one converting to the other's religion, began in the early 1930s in the context of deliberations about a new Greek civil code. When the press misquoted the president of the Jewish Community of Athens as embracing the idea of "mixed families of Jews and Orthodox [Christians]," Greek and Judeo-Spanish newspapers vehemently objected and instead promoted the status quo.[86] In protest, a young Jewish man, Gedalia Alaluf, who fell in love with his Orthodox Christian coworker, Nitsa, wrote a Judeo-Spanish novella describing the pain they experienced due to their inability to marry without one sacrificing his or her religion. The story ends with a fictitious scene of them committing suicide. In the Greek preface to the novella, Alaluf advocated for the introduction of civil marriage to save the increasing numbers of Jews and Christians who wished to marry while maintaining their religions. Unable to do so, Alaluf fled to Serres where he was baptized as Vassilis and married.[87] Ultimately, civil marriage was implemented in Greece in 1982.[88]

Even though the Jewish Community, with the backing of the Greek state, enforced legal structures to prevent marriages between Jews and Christians, social boundaries between them were increasingly transgressed, as evidenced by a rise in so-called mixed marriages—possible only if one of the partners converted to the other's religion (as Alaluf did) or if the couple married abroad in a civil ceremony. Conversion in Salonica remained marginal, involved more women than men, and never reached the rate experienced in other European countries.[89] In 1930, for example, a total of eleven women converted out of Judaism—a concerning number for the rabbis.[90] The increase in social and marital relations between Jews and Orthodox Christians (and others) in Salonica during the interwar years nonetheless indicates an increase in the possibilities of transgressing communal boundaries and the extent to which individual Jews began to challenge the expectations of the Jewish Community and to undermine social convention, which favored endogamous marriage among "good Jews" (*buenos djidios*). Such transgressions—made possible through new sites of socialization for men and women regardless of their religion, sites like movie theaters, parks, cafes, workplaces, and the tramway—provoked alarm in the local press, which increasingly decried the new "epidemic" of conversions, first "diagnosed" in the 1920s and which gained greater proportions in the 1930s.[91] The phenomenon also introduced new questions about the very boundaries and meaning of "community."

Jewish conversion to other religions was not a new phenomenon in interwar Salonica. Conversos fleeing the Inquisition in Spain and Portugal settled in the Ottoman realm in the sixteenth and seventeenth centuries where they embraced the practice of normative Judaism. Given that they had converted to Christianity on the Iberian Peninsula under duress, rabbis in the Ottoman Empire viewed them as never having stopped being Jews according to the principle that "a Jew, though he or she sins, remains a Jew" and thus did not impose obstacles (such as a requirement that they formally convert to Judaism) to their smooth integration into the established Jewish communities.[92] Another exceptional set of circumstances that involved the transgression of communal boundaries resulted in the seventeenth-century conversion of the messianic figure, Sabbetai Sevi, to Islam. A group of his faithful followed suit, converted to Islam, and established their own distinct sect of self-described "believers" (*maminim*) to whom outsiders referred, in Turkish, as Dönme ("turncoats"). While some of the Jews who converted at the time did so out of conviction, others, especially those from wealthy families, likely did so in order to evade high taxes demanded of them. By the twentieth century, they were recognized officially as Muslims and included in the exchange of population (1923) that sent almost all of Greece's Muslims to Turkey.[93]

Significantly, until the era of the *Tanzimat*, the Ottoman authorities permitted non-Muslims to convert only to Islam and prohibited the conversion of Muslims out of their faith. Conversion also required the permission of religious authorities. Jewish conversion to Islam continued to function largely as a mechanism for Jewish men to enhance their status and for Jewish women to escape power dynamics or economic obligations in their community. A Judeo-Spanish folk song captures (and mocks) the latter motivation for conversion. It tells the story of a "girl from Salonica" who burns her stuffed grape leaves. So disappointed by the culinary failure, the mother prepares to beat her daughter. To escape her punishment, the daughter runs to a *dayan* to request permission to convert to Islam and receives it.[94] The local press reported several instances of Jewish women who converted to Islam:

of the thirty-one converts registered in the province in 1890, eight were Jews (seven of whom were women).[95]

Once conversion to religions other than Islam became possible, Jewish women occasionally converted to Catholicism or Protestantism due to contact with missionary schools. These schools actively, although generally unsuccessfully, sought new recruits among Ottoman Jews and translated texts such as the New Testament into Judeo-Spanish in order to make their religion more appealing. The prospect of the conversion of Jewish girls to Christianity increased the motivation for the Jewish Community of Salonica to develop Jewish schools for girls to educate them and keep them in the fold.[96] Conversions to Protestantism could be attributed in part to conviction. But, as Michael Molho recalled, a well-educated cousin revealed himself to be a "traitor" and "hypocrite" for his decision to convert to Protestantism.[97]

Once Salonica came under Greek rule, social and sexual boundaries between Jews and non-Jews were traversed even as the practice of relying on Jewish courts persisted. One case involved an unmarried Jewish woman who confessed to having relations with both a Jewish man and a Muslim man, and became pregnant without knowing who the father was. A Jewish woman declared her intention to run off with a Greek officer and appeared before the Beth Din to divorce her Jewish husband.[98] Some instances leaked to the press, as when a Jewish girl asked her father for permission to convert to Christianity to marry her Greek lover. When the father denied the request, the daughter attempted suicide before stealing some of her family's savings, running away with her lover, writing a letter of apology to her relatives for dishonoring them, and converting to Christianity to marry.[99] Some Jewish women who converted to Orthodox Christianity in order to wed later changed their minds and, with the consent of the chief rabbinate and the bishop and following ritual immersion (*tevila*), the Jewish Community accepted them back as members.[100]

The Judeo-Spanish press increasingly reported on scandals that erupted over intercommunal relations and conversions. When Esterina Mizrahi converted and took the name Maria, and Florika Sheby was baptized as Evangelia in order to marry, the news resulted in front-page headlines.[101] *El Mesajero* highlighted a case of a poor Jewish girl from the Regie district whose parents had arranged her marriage. The week before the engagement ceremony, the girl ran away in the middle of the night with a Greek milkman with whom she had been in a secret relationship for three years. Presumably, as the article concluded, the couple fled to a village where the girl would convert to Christianity and the couple would be married.[102]

Local newspapers presented the act of conversion as threatening the very communal boundaries upon which Salonican society had been founded for generations. *El Puevlo* referred to those who converted out of Judaism as "traitors to the people." The newspaper viewed conversion as stemming from a lack of Jewish education, lack of Shabbat observance, lack of Jewish solidarity, and the pressures of antisemitism.[103] The Greek newspaper *Apoyevmatini* similarly decried "Greek-Jewish marriages" on the grounds that they constituted signs of "moral decline" and "dishonor" for the Greek people.[104] Others argued that the phenomenon had to do not with religious beliefs but rather, as in the late Ottoman era, with socioeconomic concerns. *Akropolis* in Athens reported that Jewish women, especially the poor, converted to avoid assembling the dowry, which Jewish men continued to require but which Greek Christian men did not.[105]

The rabbis developed creative methods to manage and interrupt intercommunal relationships. Sometimes they coerced Jewish women to disavow non-Jewish lovers and confirm their dedication to the Jewish Community in official, signed affidavits like this one:

> I declare that four months ago I stopped having relations with a non-Jew who I was seeing, that I will not engage in any more relations with him, that from now on I will only engage in honorable conduct worthy of proper daughters of Israel, that in the case that I give birth to a boy, I promise to circumcise him according to the prescriptions of our holy law, and that whether a boy or a girl, I promise to care for it and raise it.[106]

In this context, "honorable conduct" signified engaging in relations only after marriage and only with a Jewish husband. In another case, rabbis consulted lawyers and permitted the son born to a Jewish man and a Orthodox Christian woman to be circumcised and inscribed in the communal registers, even though, technically speaking, the boy was not born Jewish according to rabbinic law.[107] In yet another case, the rabbis, following the law of matrilineal descent, inscribed in the registers a boy born to a Jewish woman and an Orthodox Christian man but with the condition that the newborn be given the mother's Jewish surname.[108]

Conversion and intermarriage during the interwar years emerged as phenomena at the extremes of the socioeconomic spectrum. While poor Jewish women seem to have been more likely to convert to marry a Christian suitor, the local press reported on several cases of wealthy Jewish men marrying Orthodox Christian women. Among wealthy couples, the man tended to be Jewish and neither partner converted; rather, they traveled abroad—to Belgium, for example—registered their civil marriage, and returned to Greece, where the state recognized their union. In the early 1920s, Chief Rabbi Bension Uziel made an important ruling regarding how the Beth Din should proceed if the non-Jewish partner in a civil marriage performed abroad should seek to convert to Judaism.[109] In the 1930s, several mixed marriages within aristocratic circles in the city took place abroad without any of the spouses converting. Two of the cases involved Jewish notables: Albert Nehama, the director of the Banque Union, the Consul of Poland, and the brother of the well-known writer and teacher, Joseph Nehama; and Albert Amariglio, another prominent member of the Jewish Community who had served on the Communal Council.[110]

That such leading figures within the Jewish Community married Orthodox Christians—something unthinkable in previous eras—demonstrates the extent to which the very concept of "community" itself was transformed in the context of the Greek nation-state as Jews and Christians increasingly blurred and transgressed the boundaries that had for so long separated them. In the aftermath of the Ottoman Empire, the persistent legal categories that continued to demarcate the boundaries of the Community for Jewish residents of Greece, as enforced by the Beth Din and with the backing of the state, came increasingly in conflict with more fluid social realities and their new status as citizens of Greece.

Even though the Beth Din retained official authority to adjudicate only questions of civil status and a small but increasing number of Jews sought to circumvent the rabbis altogether, others remarkably continued to rely on the Beth Din to adjudicate cases over which it did not have official sanction. Two thousand cases of the Beth Din from 1919 to 1940 indicate that Jews appealed to the *dayanim* with regard to not only civil status but also personal disputes and defamation; settlement of wills, testaments, bequests, and inheritance; and commercial disputes, business partnerships, and debts. During the 1930s, the Beth Din also reprimanded drunkards, gamblers, and unfaithful spouses, as well as merchants who violated the Jewish Sabbath, bakers who baked leavened bread during Passover, and butchers who sold non-kosher meat, and it extracted from them promises, signed by witnesses, not to repeat their reprehensible actions.[111] A husband even took his wife to the Beth Din to have her reprimanded for previously seeking recourse to a state court to preside over their marital dispute.[112] Bouena Sarfatty recalled the situation in the interwar years: "The Jews of Salonika don't go to court. / They go to the Community that has a Beth Din. / The rabbis have the final word."[113]

More directly pinpointing the reasons for continued reliance on the Beth Din, a Jewish man who appealed to the rabbinical court to resolve a dispute with his uncle explained his rationale in 1938: "Although the power to enforce, that is, the legal validity, of the Beth Din has been reduced today to that which pertains to marriage law, each and every good Jew [*kada uno i uno buen djidio*] nonetheless obliges himself to follow the recommendations [of the *dayanim*]."[114] The desire to preserve one's reputation as a "good Jew" in Salonica notably contributed to the operation of a kind of shadow court system in Greece as the Beth Din of Salonica ruled in a wide array of areas over which it had neither official sanction nor recourse to enforce its rulings other than through the will of those who chose to submit themselves to the judgment of the *dayanim* combined with social and familial pressures.

But when two prominent Jews decided to appeal to the civil courts of the Greek state in the 1930s to mete out justice, their behavior—which flew in the face of the expectations of the *buen djidio* ("good Jew")—provoked major controversy. Although there were many instances in the Ottoman period when Jews brought their claims to the state (Islamic) courts or to consular tribunals, clearly against the wishes of the rabbinical elite, in the hope of receiving a more favorable ruling, these instances during the interwar years provoked the Jewish public to denounce the complainants as *malshinim* ("informers") overly eager to publicize intracommunal tensions to non-Jewish authorities for their own benefit. Moreover, the episodes introduced the question as to whether the Beth Din ought to be reformed, if not abolished.

The first case, in 1932, involved a dispute between the leader of the Mizrahi party of the religious Zionists, Abraham Recanati, and the organ of the General Zionists, *La Renasensia Djudia*, which insulted Recanati in its columns.

Seeking to teach his adversaries a lesson, Recanati brought a libel case against the newspaper to Greek civil court. In the interim, another Judeo-Spanish newspaper, *El Puevlo*, accused Recanati of desecrating the Sabbath. As the head of a religious Jewish organization, widely perceived to be pious, and thus appalled by the latest accusation, Recanati sought the intervention of the Beth Din in the hope that the *dayanim* would clear his name. But the rabbis of the Beth Din argued that, by taking the first case to civil court, Recanati had sacrificed his status as a *buen djidio*, insulted the Jewish people, and thus lost his right to seek justice from the *dayanim*. The humiliating controversy likely contributed to Recanati's decision to leave Salonica for Palestine shortly thereafter, where he allegedly insulted the rabbis back in Salonica (thereby producing another scandal).[115]

In the second case, in 1934, the new chief rabbi of Salonica, Sevi Koretz, brought another Judeo-Spanish newspaper to Greek civil court for defamation. *El Tiempo*'s criticism of Koretz's high salary had devolved into ad hominem attacks that Koretz found intolerable. This time, however—perhaps due to Koretz's stature as the chief rabbi—the *dayanim* did not condemn Koretz as they had Recanati. *El Puevlo* now argued that both Koretz and Recanati were justified in taking their cases to civil court, which would impose actual fines and punish those convicted, and which, except in the realm of family law, the Beth Din could not do.[116]

The Recanati and Koretz court controversies provoked a debate in the Judeo-Spanish press over the role and function of the Beth Din in Salonica. A five-part expose in *La Aksion* in 1936 entitled "Shouldn't the Beth Din be reformed?" began with a disclaimer aimed at pacifying those who might be offended by the suggestion. While accepting that the Beth Din numbered among "the most glorious institutions inherited from our ancestors," the newspaper wondered if it would be possible to preserve the essence of rabbinic law but implement rulings in a way that would resonate more with the modern spirit and increase the prestige and relevance of the institution.[117] An episode that provoked another controversy in 1937–1938 made the question of Beth Din reform more acute as it focused on the adjudication of family law—a domain over which the *dayanim* had official jurisdiction.

The case involved a Jewish woman whose husband had moved abroad for ten years, never to return and never to grant his wife a divorce: a classic example of *aguna* (the status, according to rabbinic law, of a woman "chained" to her husband against her will). In the interim, the woman began a relationship with another Jewish man and bore a child by him. Once news arrived that the husband had died abroad, the new partner and the woman, now a widow, sought permission from the Beth Din to marry. Not only did the *dayanim* categorically refuse the request, but they also categorized the child as a *mamzer* ("bastard" born via an adulterous relationship between a married woman and a man not her husband), who, according to rabbinical law, would be permitted to marry only another *mamzer*. The father of this child retained a lawyer, who threatened to bring the case to the civil authorities. But the *dayanim* remained fixed in their position and reminded the complainant that the state could not overturn the decision of the Beth Din because, according to Law 2456 of 1920, all responsibility to adjudicate questions of Jewish family law devolved to the Jewish tribunals, which ruled in accordance with rabbinic law.[118] According to this law, the Greek state could determine only whether the issue adjudicated by the Beth Din fell within its competency, not whether it had ruled fairly.

The incident produced public outcry that momentarily transformed the meaning of *buen djidio*. Even the new president of the Mizrahi, the religious Zionist party, agreed that the *dayanim* had overreached. A group of Jewish lawyers and members of the local Béné Bérith Lodge—whom *La Aksion* also characterized as *buenos djidios*—initially proposed that the Beth Din be dissolved and all family law be adjudicated in the future exclusively by Greek state civil courts. A "good Jew" could now mean one who sought justice for a Jewish woman and her new family. Remarkably, however, this notion of *buen djidio* was short-lived, as the proposal to suppress the Beth Din created even greater public rebuke. The Jewish lawyers and the Béné Bérith backtracked and explained that they intended for the Beth Din to be preserved but also reformed and modernized.[119]

The meaning of *buen djidio* now entailed one who "considers the existence of the Beth Din indispensable either because it renders rulings based on the Talmud or because it conserves Jewish life in the diaspora." *La Aksion* outlined three positions on the future of the Beth Din. Religious Jews wanted the rabbinic tribunal to continue to operate as it had, according to the letter of the rabbinic law. A second group wanted to modernize the Beth Din by establishing a formal office, appointment schedule, procedural code, and published decisions; gaining legal validity for the *ketuba* (as Jewish marriage contracts were valid at this point only after being notarized); establishing a court of appeals also under the auspices of the *dayanim*; and training a new cohort of Jewish judges. A third position not only favored these modernizing reforms but also advocated for the expansion of the jurisdiction of the Beth Din to encompass questions such as the death of a spouse, alimony, and inheritance, which the *dayanim* often adjudicated in practice but not always with official sanction to do so. This group also advocated that the text of the *ketuba* be reformed to accommodate questions pertaining to *agunot* and *mamzerim* to avoid the above-mentioned situation.[120]

The talk of reform, however, offended the president of the Beth Din, Isaac Hassid. He agreed that, while the purview of the *dayanim* could be expanded, no changes to either Jewish law or its implementation would be accepted. Displeased by the extent to which his colleagues on the Rabbinical Council seemed ready to cave to outside pressure, Hassid resigned and died three months later. As two of the other main *dayanim* of the Beth Din, Pinhas Barzilai and Jacob Hagouel, all died within a few years of Hassid, the new generation of rabbis may have been more open to entertain changes.[121] The start of World War II, however, appears to have forestalled reforms from being introduced. It is nonetheless remarkable that, by that time, the discussion had moved away from the prospect of dissolving the Beth Din to a focus on modernizing its administration, expanding its purview, and increasing its power.

The formal and informal influence of the Beth Din ensured that the Jewish Community continued to exercise a degree of autonomy through the interwar years and an ability to shape the lives of its members in continuity with late Ottoman practice and to provide a bridge to the new context of the Greek state. The fact that Jews and Christians could not easily marry each other meant that social distance persisted between the two populations even as boundaries began to blur. Remarkably, the German Foreign Office envoy in Greece in 1937 viewed the absence of civil marriage and the separation of Jews from Christians as a model for Nazi Germany:

> No racial mingling between Jews and the Greek host nation takes place in
> Salonika because of its special position. The Greek state is de facto, if not
> in the legal sense, inclined toward anti-Semitism. The Orthodox Church

plays a major role in this true anti-Semitic inclination by forbidding inter-marriage with Jews. With this, the Salonikan Jews cling strongly to their religion: conversions to the Orthodox Church are rare. A feeling of foreign-ness exists between the Jews and the Greeks that [is similar to that which] National Socialist Germany aims to achieve through its Jewish policy.[122]

In most parts of German occupied Europe, when the Nazis introduced the Nuremberg Laws, which made it illegal for Jews to marry Christians, it sparked a major controversy. But the introduction of these laws in Salonica, in 1943, remarkably did not cause great alarm because intermarriage was, practically speaking, already illegal, and the Beth Din continued to impose its rulings on the Jewish masses.

A Purely Jewish Atmosphere?
Public Housing Projects and the Jewish Masses

As the Beth Din retained its power to determine whom Salonica's Jews could marry, other administrative arms of the Jewish Community shaped the everyday lives of the Jewish masses through the management of Jewish public housing projects. As Leon Saady recalled: "Housing? How did we live there [Salonica]? Housing was built by the Community for the poor. A rich man could very well go out and build his own house, but the poor needed the help of the Community."[123] These districts were where, as the Judeo-Spanish poetess Bouena Sarfatty recalled, those Jewish families "without a cent" resided.[124] While wealthy Jews benefitted from greater financial inde-pendence, the impoverished Jewish masses relied on the Jewish Community which, when it came to public housing, served as an intermediary with and occasionally as a surrogate for the municipality and the state and eased the transition from Ottoman to Greek rule.

Despite the efforts of the Jewish Community, the Jewish housing projects evoked painful images of Jewish poverty and destitution. A Judeo-Spanish novel that appeared in 1930, *La Socheta Podrida: Shenas dela vida reala de Saloniko* ("The lost society: scenes from real-life Salonica") presented the tragic tale of a young Jewish girl in the Teneke Maale (Turkish for "tin district") where, according to the local press, 380 indigent Jewish families lived in tin shacks (*kulibas*) in conditions described as "living hell" (*gehinom en vida*).[125]

Figure 1.3. Residents in an impoverished Jewish neighborhood in Salonica, 1941. Photographed for the Institute for the Study of the Jewish Question, a Nazi-party institution devised for propaganda purposes. Source: Institut Der NSDAP zur Erforschung Der Judenfrage, YIVO Institute for Jewish Research, RG-222. Published with permission.

With her mother deceased and a brother on his deathbed, adolescent Sarah becomes the object of abuse by her alcoholic father. Although seeking to preserve her sense of dignity, Sarah cannot prevent her father from selling her to a sex slave trafficker for a "bottle of *raki* and a few coins." Forced into a life of prostitution, she contracts syphilis and dies.[126] A scathing commentary on poverty, alcoholism, prostitution, and the ills of Jewish life in the interwar years, *La Socheta Podrida* also offered a harsh critique of the Jewish Community for its failure to ensure the well-being of the impoverished Jewish masses living in the Jewish districts. By administering an extensive network of Jewish neighborhoods, the Jewish Community nonetheless sought to improve the situation amidst the transition from Ottoman to Greek jurisdiction over the city.

Beginning after a fire in 1890, which destroyed the city center where Jews had resided in Ottoman Salonica for generations, new Jewish neighborhoods began to form to house the victims of the fire, especially to the west of downtown, such as Regie Vardar and Baron Hirsch (the latter made possible by donations from the German-Jewish philanthropist Maurice de Hirsch). While wealthy Jews built mansions to the east of the city, along the sea in *Las Kampanyas*, the new neighborhoods to the west housed not only fire victims but also new Jewish arrivals from towns and cities in the region, as well as those fleeing persecution in the Russian Empire, and emerged as part of broader Ottoman urban renewal projects initiated during the latter part of the nineteenth century.[127]

More than the fire of 1890, the fire of 1917 definitively dissolved the centrally located compact Jewish quarter and resulted in the creation of temporary and permanent dwellings for the more than seventy thousand victims of the fire, including more than fifty thousand Jews. The municipality and state prioritized solving the housing crisis for Orthodox Christians that was compounded with the arrival of masses of refugees in the 1920s. Largely in parallel, the Jewish Community aimed to resolve the housing question (*la kestion de las moradas*) for Jews. In order to house homeless Jews, the Jewish Community acquired military barracks and hospitals on the eastern outskirts of the city that Allied troops had utilized during World War I, such as Campbell, 151 (renamed Benosiglio in 1934), and No. 6, and converted them into Jewish housing projects. The Jewish Community also took over the administration of several neighborhoods established and owned by the municipality and the state to cater to another segment of the Jewish population left homeless by the fire.[128]

During the interwar years, a substantial proportion of the Jewish residents of the city dwelt in the Jewish housing projects, especially the poor. Each neighborhood developed a particular reputation. Although redesigned as a "garden city," Regie to the west became the site of the resettlement of the city's poor and homeless Jews; as many as twelve residents slept in a single room.[129] Characterized by its street names that evoked Greek mythology— Irinis, Safo, Afroditi—Vardar became the red light and entertainment district. Robert Campbell, a Levantine Brit who sold the eponymous neighborhood to the Jewish Community after World War I, complained that the poorest Jews dwelt in "his" district when he had expected "second class" Jews, not those at the bottom, to reside there.[130] In contrast to Regie, Vardar, and Campbell, Baron Hirsch domiciles were deemed more "prestigious."[131]

Cut off from middle and upper class Jews who returned after the fire of 1917 to live in the city center or along Queen Olgas Street by the sea, the residents of the popular neighborhoods lived in a different world. *El Puevlo* reported that, despite not having been affected by the fire, the "dirtiness in the quarters of Vardar and Kalamaria surpass the limits of belief and imagination."[132] As Yaacov Handali recalled in his memoir, only during the German occupation, when assigned by the Nazis to conduct a Jewish census, did he discover Jews living in "wretched poverty" in "neighborhoods that I either did not know existed or had never been to before."[133] Indeed, 70 percent of all "indigent" Jews resided in the Jewish popular neighborhoods in 1939. These impoverished families, who accounted for around half of the city's total Jewish population, contributed to the general pauperism among Salonican Jews on the eve of World War II.[134] The Judeo-Spanish press lamented that the "vast misery" of Salonica's impoverished Jews made the poorest Jews in Poland look like Rothschilds.[135]

Referred to in Judeo-Spanish as *kuartieres populares* or *foburgos* (from the French *faubourg*, which displaced the Ottoman term, *maale*), the new neighborhoods or suburbs on the outskirts of the city represented the first exclusively Jewish districts in Salonica whose residents shared class as well as communal affiliations.[136] The creation of explicitly Jewish neighborhoods

Neighborhood	Families	Individuals
Angelaki	180	665
Eliaou Benosiglio (151)	1145	3997
Kalamaria	461	1656
Baron Hirsch	760	2590
Teneke Maale	438	1689
Aya Paraskevi	452	1577
Regie (Vardar)	1753	6376
No. 6-Karagatch	374	1437
Neighborhood Subtotal	5563	19967
City Center	2177	8378
Total	7740	28345

Figure 1.4. Jews registered as "indigent" with the Jewish Community, 1939. Source: "Tableau sovre el numero de posserrores de carnetos de indigenza y las almas," March 28, 1939, USHMM, r. 690, d. 122.

after 1917 challenged both the purportedly class-based plan of the new city and what was supposed to be its unquestionable Hellenic character. With Jewish residents now scattered across the city, albeit in relative concentration, each neighborhood formed a self-sufficient Jewish social unit, complete with a neighborhood administration, synagogue, and Jewish communal school all under the aegis of the Communal Council. A union of residents as well as cultural, religious, and political associations enriched Jewish society in each neighborhood.

Neighborhood organizations and interest groups, notably those comprised of women, frequently called upon the Jewish Community to meet their needs, whether philanthropic, educational, or religious.[137] While formally excluded from the governance of the Jewish Community and not permitted to vote in communal elections, Jewish women nonetheless organized their own spheres of civic and religious engagement in the city's popular quarters and successfully negotiated with communal leaders to meet their demands. The 151 neighborhood (also referred to as a district or quarter) became home to a number of Jewish women's organizations, most notably the mutual aid society, Devora, named in honor of the biblical heroine and founded in 1920 to provide medical assistance to members and to distribute coal to the needy.[138] By 1921, it counted more than 350 members: exclusively Jewish women who lived in the 151 neighborhood.[139] The steering committee expressed pride in its members' middle-class status and the sacrifices they made in order to promote the organization which, as one of its advertisements read, served as a model for "aristocratic" Jewish women who otherwise wasted their time with luxuries and entertainment.[140] The organization also came to the aid of the victims of the Campbell attacks in 1931.[141] But even Devora relied on the Jewish Community. In 1933, for example, the organization requested permission from the Superior Commission for Jewish Instruction to erect a booth in the courtyard of the neighborhood school in order to distribute coal to the needy.[142]

Ad hoc groups of Jewish women in the 151 neighborhood made additional demands of the Jewish Community. Eighteen Jewish women, for example, requested that the chief rabbinate install a *mikve* ("ritual bath") in their neighborhood so that they and other Jewish women could perform the obligation of *tevila*, or ritual immersion, and thus avoid violating religious

laws of ritual purity.[143] At the other end of the city, Jewish women who convened under the name Feminist Society for the Rights of Women in the
Regie quarter requested that the Communal Council pay for teachers to
provide them with Judeo-Spanish and Greek lessons to advance their level
of literacy. The Council met part of the demand by hiring a student at the
University of Salonica to instruct the women four hours a week in Greek
language, literature, writing, and arithmetic—a sign that the state language
took priority.[144]

While catering to the demands of numerous interest groups in the various districts, the Jewish Community further shaped the lives of the Jewish
masses by developing a network of neighborhood administrative commissions
that had not existed during the late Ottoman period. The centralization of
the administration of the neighborhoods materialized in 1926 through the
establishment of the overarching Commission of Jewish Quarters under the
direction of David Matalon. An influential Zionist and one-time deputy in
the Greek Parliament, Matalon sought to alleviate the financial burden placed
on the poor residents of the quarters by assuring that their district functioned
smoothly by collecting rents and determining which families, due to their
poverty, would be permitted to reside in their apartments rent free. He also
hoped that the neighborhoods would "provide the population in question
moral nourishment necessary to maintain a healthy, purely Jewish atmosphere, [and advance] sentiments of love and devotion for the Community on
which they rely in all domains of housing, instruction, and philanthropy."[145]
Matalon sought to cultivate an attachment among Jewish residents of these
quarters not to the city or the state but to the Jewish Community.

The extensive responsibilities granted to the Commission of Jewish Quarters symbolized the increasing role that Jewish communal institutions played
in the daily lives of Jews residing in the *foburgos*. Hundreds of Jews petitioned
the offices of the Commission for housing (*demandas por morada*) and expected
their rights to be protected.[146] In each quarter an administrative commission
answered to the Communal Council, while residents established their own
unions (*union de moradores*) to advocate for their interests, which sometimes
conflicted with the Community or the neighborhood commissions. Some of
the unions, such as the one in the Hirsch quarter, formally incorporated.[147] In
one instance, 140 residents signed a petition on behalf of the 600 families in

that district to demand that certain members of the quarter's administrative commission be removed and others be appointed.[148]

The activities of the residents of various popular quarters became highly politicized. They soon formed their own political party, the Foburgistas, which generally appealed to people with left-leaning sentiments and often battled for members with the Communist party, which was also active in neighborhoods to the west—Baron Hirsch, Regie, Aya Paraskevi, and Teneke Maale.[149] Together they opposed the efforts of Zionist associations to spread their messages among the working classes. Most successful in the 151 district, Zionists saw in the popular neighborhoods both an opportunity to promote their ideology and a challenge due to the large concentration of impoverished Jews attracted to communism.[150]

In 1924, representatives of seven principal Jewish neighborhoods convened a congress, established their own central committee, and published a manifesto that sought to cut across political divides and advocated for unity among all Jewish residents of the popular quarters. The vision of the First Congress of the Federation of all the Residents of the Popular Quarters confirmed the renewed role of the Community as the primary resource to which Salonica's impoverished Jews turned for their well-being in the context of interwar Greece. The Federation demanded that the Community protect the interests of the Jewish residents of the neighborhoods not only by maintaining the living conditions but also by intervening with the municipality and the state so that the latter "no longer completely ignore the fate of the thousands of unfortunate residents who live in misery in the neighborhoods."[151]

The criteria according to which the Federation of all the Residents of the Popular Quarters distinguished the responsibilities of the Jewish Community from those of the municipality and the state are remarkable. From the perspective of the Federation of all the Residents of the Popular Quarters, the exclusive responsibilities of the Community involved providing public education, hygienic care for the youth, financial aid to those residents in need, and public meeting spaces; maintaining public works; and distributing coal.[152] The responsibilities to be shared by the Community and the municipality and/or the state, from the perspective of the Federation, included supplying general medical care, water, and lighting. The exclusive responsibilities of the municipality and the state were limited to removing refugees illegally occupying Jewish schools, supplying new homes for those in danger of losing theirs due to the new city plan, and maintaining roads leading up the neighborhoods—but not necessarily those inside.[153] When it soon became clear that the state could not guarantee housing for those Jewish families faced with the possibility of becoming homeless due to the implementation of the new city plan, the responsibility fell upon the Jewish Community, which established the Construction Committee to erect additional Jewish housing developments.[154] Furthermore, even though the municipality may have been responsible for cleaning the streets, it delegated to the Jewish Community the task of clearing away sewage.[155] With the goal of providing additional public housing, the Jewish Community expanded the 151 quarter by erecting new, modest houses and apartments (*kazetikas* and *apartamentikos*) for Jews in search of dwelling; some were sold for half the cost while other tenants were not required to pay rent.[156]

The limit of state involvement in the roadwork of the Jewish neighborhoods—up to the entrances but not necessarily inside—symbolizes the extent to which neither the state nor the municipality seemed to express broader interest in the neighborhoods. To fill the void, residents of the Jewish neighborhoods turned to the Jewish Community, which thereby retained and even expanded aspects of self-government and served as a surrogate for the municipality, as well as a mediator between and advocate for Jewish residents of Salonica vis-à-vis the state. By depending on the Jewish Community in the midst of rupture and dislocation provoked by a series of wars, a major fire, population transfers, rising Hellenizing pressures, and increased economic difficulties, Jews in Salonica sought to manage the protracted and tumultuous transition from the Ottoman Empire to the Greek national state and re-anchor themselves in their city and in their new country.

During the tenure of Prime Minister Metaxas, the leaders of the Jewish Community cast the hands-off approach of the state with regard to Jewish housing in a positive light and as a sign of the state's magnanimity for permitting them to undertake a new building project without any obstructions. In order to make way for the new central train station, the city plan for Salonica in 1939 called for the leveling of Teneke Maale, the impoverished Jewish quarter that had served as the scandalous setting for the aforementioned novel, *Socheta Podrida*. As the district faced destruction, the Jewish Community relocated the residents to the Aya Paraskevi neighborhood and temporarily housed 120 families in Jewish schools and synagogues.[157] Supplemented by financial contributions from the Salonican Jewish public, the Jewish Community erected a new and modern apartment building (the Greek term *polikatikia* now used in Judeo-Spanish) not only to accommodate the displaced but also to improve their living conditions. At the entrance of the building, a commemorative plaque recognized King George II and Metaxas; the governor general of Macedonia, Georgios Kirimis; Chief Rabbi Koretz; the Jewish Community's Construction Committee; and the "generous contributions of the Jewish element" that made the *polikatikia* possible.[158]

The ceremony for the installation of the plaque began with the recitation of a passage from the book of Psalms followed by the singing of the hymn of Metaxas' Fourth of August Regime. Koretz and Jewish notable Albert Ginio gave energetic speeches that provoked "frenetic applause" in favor of the king, Metaxas, and Kirimis. In attendance, Kirimis thanked the wealthy who had alleviated the suffering of the poor by funding the *polikatikia*, and emphasized the "excellent disposition" of the government of Metaxas toward the "Jewish element," against whom, he emphasized, the state would not tolerate either discrimination or malevolence.[159] Due to the intervention of the Jewish Community, the state would now, finally, acknowledge the plight of the Jews in the city's impoverished quarters and give its blessing to the improvement of their living conditions like all residents of Salonica.

The Jewish neighborhoods of Salonica evoke powerful emotions about the history of Jews in Salonica—especially regarding the poor, whose stories are often overlooked or inaccessible. These Jewish neighborhoods often conjure images of Jewish persecution: the Campbell neighborhood served as the site of the first and only major anti-Jewish violence perpetrated by Orthodox Christians in Salonica, in 1931. The image of the Baron Hirsch quarter similarly remains forever tarnished by its final use, during World War II, as a main Jewish ghetto near the railway station where the Nazi occupation forces rounded up Jews prior to their deportation to Auschwitz. But neighborhoods also became key sites of pride and identification for Jews in Salonica that could be folded into a kind of multilevel sense of belonging. A survivor of Auschwitz, Jacob Levy, seamlessly interwove his neighborhood connection with his status as a Salonican, a Jew, and a Greek in a poem he composed in Greek. It concludes:

> From the old neighborhood of Regie Vardar I come,
> Strong Jewish young men
> There have seen the light!
> I shout it loudly and I am proud of it
> I am a Salonican!
> And I will be 'til the end
> A true and faithful Greek![160]

This geography of memory thus became linked to locality, not only at the city and state levels but also at the microlevel of the neighborhood that carried with it significant symbolism as another site of belonging.

The Most Holy Duty of a Citizen: Military Service

Just as they often relied on the Beth Din to establish the legal parameters of their marriages and on the Commission of Jewish Quarters to house their families, Jewish men also depended on the Jewish Community to determine their eligibility for military service and to induct them into the Greek army. While the popular quarters of Salonica provided Jewish masses with a sense of neighborhood identification to which they appealed in order to advocate for their rights, the experience of military service for Jewish men introduced them to the world beyond their city and initiated them into their duties as citizens. Conscription into the army became a hallmark of the modern state, and, for Jews, a sign of their emancipation and status as citizens.[161] But the authority of the chief rabbinate to mediate the relationship between Jews and the state with regard to military service also reflected the afterlife of the Ottoman Empire and the continuing power of the Jewish Community to shape the experiences of its members and to serve as a partner with the state, which depended on the Jewish Community to conscript Jewish men into the Greek armed forces. While Jews in Salonica became eligible for military service like all other citizens of Greece, they became part of the Greek army specifically as Jews.[162]

Since the 1869 Ottoman citizenship law enacted during the *Tanzimat*, Jews, like all non-Muslims, were no longer required to pay the tax for non-

Muslims (*cizye*) but rather became subject to the *bedel-i askeri*, a tax that exempted them collectively from military service.[163] Beginning in 1909, during the Second Constitutional period, Jews throughout the Ottoman Empire became eligible for compulsory military service for the first time when the state abolished the *bedel* in order for all citizens, regardless of religion, to fulfill the same duties vis-à-vis the state. But Joseph Nehama identified a continuing Jewish hesitance to engage in armed conflict by asserting that "we had long ago changed our instruments of war into ploughshares and our ploughshares into strongboxes," indicating a continued aversion to military service and the preference to pay for exemption.[164] Moving away from this position by 1911, and motivated by their support for Ottomanism, Jewish intellectuals such as Mercado Covo began emphasizing the necessity of Jews to serve in the Ottoman army—and the long-standing precedents of Jewish heroes fighting valiantly since ancient times.[165] While many Jews aided the Ottoman home front and contributed financially to the Red Crescent during the Balkan Wars, some Jewish men from Salonica served in the Ottoman military as evidenced by reports about their exploits or the locations where some were being held captive (e.g., in Belgrade by the Serbian military).[166]

Once Salonica came under Greek rule in 1913, due to the negotiation of Chief Rabbi Jacob Meir, the new sovereigns postponed compulsory military service for Jews, in part to demonstrate to the European powers Greece's capacity to treat non-Christians favorably. When Princess Alice came to Salonica in 1915 seeking support for Greek soldiers through the Hellenic Red Cross, Jewish clubs encouraged the Jewish public to fulfill their "holy duty" by contributing to the campaign and demonstrating their "sentiments as good Hellenes."[167] Conscription began only during World War I, amidst the National Schism that divided Greece's citizenry over the question of whether or not to join the war and, if so, on which side. Once Venizelos' government entered the war in 1916 on the side of the Allies, Jews were gradually conscripted into the Greek military. While this call provoked a wave of emigration among Jewish men who sought to evade military service, the 1917 census of the Jewish Community in the wake of the fire that year included entries for a few Jewish men listed as *askyer* (the Turkish term for soldier still in use in Judeo-Spanish). Communal registrations from 1923 also include entries for Jewish men who served in the Asia Minor campaign with photographs of them in Greek military uniform.[168]

The service of Jews from Salonica in the Greek military during these two wars provided a major turning point. As Joseph N. Nehama argued in *La Aksion*, the participation of Jews such as himself in major battles during World War I (such as Skra di Legen, which involved the first successful deployment of Greek troops against the Bulgarians) provided evidence that Salonican Jews had embraced their new Greek homeland. Nehama's experience was unusual in that he enlisted. Although a civil employee for the French army stationed in Salonica, he joined the national defense of Greece. Along with three other Jews—a stevedore and a railway worker from Salonica as well as an oud player from Drama—Nehama served on the front lines with his Orthodox Christian compatriots (despite being occasionally mocked for his "Jewish" accent when speaking Greek). He recalled that "since the liberation of Macedonia, this was the first time that the Jewish collectivity gave true proof—written in blood—of their love for the Hellenic homeland."[169] Wounded in battle, Nehama was crippled for the rest of his life.

As Jews began to serve in the Greek military and sought to demonstrate their dedication to their new homeland, the Jewish Community negotiated for its employees to be exempted in order for Jewish institutions and synagogues to continue to function without interruption. The question of who would receive the coveted exemption in exchange for payment—a renewed *bedel* system from Ottoman times—provoked heated debate. A primary way to secure exemption was to be classified by the chief rabbinate as "Jewish clergy," such as a *mezamer*, a synagogue functionary charged with assisting in the performance of prayers at a given synagogue.[170] But complaints of "flagrant injustice" abounded when those who could pay, rather than those who could perform the liturgy, gained exemptions.[171]

The chief rabbinate centralized the registration of all of the synagogue's *mezamerim* in 1916.[172] While the Greek state initially granted exemptions to 250 *mezamerim*, the number was later reduced to 200, then to 60, and then elevated to 72 by 1941; competition for the spots remained fierce.[173] Synagogue committees petitioned the chief rabbinate to demand that their candidates be listed as *mezamerim*.[174] The Judeo-Spanish press published lists of those *mezamerim* required to pay the *bedel* (this Ottoman Turkish term continued to be used in Judeo-Spanish through the interwar years).[175] The Jewish Community also corresponded with the military recruitment office to ensure that exemptions were recognized or payment reduced.[176]

While negotiating exemptions for *mezamerim*, the chief rabbinate also inducted new Jewish conscripts into the Greek military. The governor general of Macedonia, the metropolitan bishop, military generals, the director of the police, municipal officials, the chief rabbi, and members of the Jewish Communal Council participated in ceremonies for the swearing in of new military classes. In 1932, for example, the bishop recited prayers, led the soldiers in an oath, and gave a speech. Rabbi Haim Habib next spoke, also notably in Greek, emphasizing that the soldier's purpose was to accomplish "the most holy duty of a citizen toward his fatherland, the duty of military service." Habib then drew on a passage from Jeremiah (29:7) invoked by Jews across the ages to justify their support for the regime in power: "Look after the well-being of the city in which you dwell . . . since your well-being is its." Through an appeal to the Hebrew Bible, and specifically a passage that formed the core of the *Noten teshua* (the prayer for the government), Habib legitimized Greek military service for Salonican Jews, whom he instructed to conceive of their country as an extension of their beloved city.[177] He expressed his hope that the Jewish recruits would fulfill their duty and gain the affection of the state and of the entire "Hellenic nation."[178] Habib helped incorporate Jewish soldiers, as Jews, into the broader Hellenic national project.

The swearing-in ceremony gained an extra layer of meaning in 1938, during the reign of Metaxas, when the number of Jewish officers in the Greek army tripled, from two to six.[179] In his patriotic induction speech, Chief Rabbi Koretz declared: "The homeland is our common mother. She cares for us since our tender youth, looks after our physical and spiritual growth and grants her material protection to all of her children without distinction. And you, worthy children of our beloved homeland, should be proud of the highest service that she confirms upon you today."[180] The image of Greece as the mother and of Jews as children equal to their Christian brothers justified their sacrifices on behalf of their country. Registrations in the archive of the Jewish Community recorded, for example, an entry for Raphael Presiado, born in 1919 in Salonica to parents from Kastoria and Preveza, whose "soul went to heaven for the homeland, 21 November 1940" (*n[ishmato] e[den] por la patria*).[181] Presiado numbered one of the hundreds of Jewish soldiers from Salonica—as well as elsewhere in Greece, most famously Colonel Mordehai Frizis of Halkis—who not only fought for the Greek army against Italy in 1940–1941, often in the Fiftieth Regiment, nicknamed the "Koen Battalion," but who also lost their lives on the battlefield.[182]

Relying on the chief rabbinate both to evade military conscription and to be sworn in as new soldiers, Jewish men serving in the Greek military also depended on the intervention of the chief rabbi in order to observe Jewish holidays. During World War I, however, such a mechanism had not yet been formalized. The previously mentioned Joseph N. Nehama therefore lobbied his commanding officer to receive permission to return from the front lines to Salonica for Passover in 1917 on the grounds that, since he would not be eating bread for a week, he would not be able to maintain his strength or fulfill his military duties. Expecting that he would not receive permission, and while on guard duty less than a kilometer away from the opposing Bulgarian troops, he began to recite silently the Haggadah in Judeo-Spanish, from memory—an act that evoked fond memories of his family gathered for the festive meal. As he concluded the recitation from memory, he said aloud, in Hebrew, as is customary, "Next year in Jerusalem!" in response to which he heard someone shout, "Amen!" Out of the shadows, a fellow Greek solider emerged, also Jewish, who had come to inform Nehama that his request for leave had finally been granted.[183]

In times of peace, during the interwar years, Jewish soldiers relied increasingly on the chief rabbinate to intervene with the military authorities on their behalf to accommodate holiday observance. As the Greek military regularly posted new soldiers far away from their hometowns to familiarize them with the idea of the broader homeland and inculcate in them nationalist ideals, Jewish recruits often found themselves at great distances from the nearest Jewish community. A Jewish sailor posted in Kefalonia therefore begged the chief rabbinate to secure him leave from the Greek navy for the upcoming High Holidays.[184] Nine Jewish soldiers from Salonica stationed in Piraeus similarly requested that the chief rabbi intervene with the military authorities so that they might return home for Passover.[185] By 1939, Chief Rabbi Koretz sought to standardize the process of securing leave for Jewish soldiers during Jewish holidays and also proposed sending a rabbi to Florina, near the Yugoslav border, to hold services at the military camp there.[186]

While Jewish men relied on the chief rabbinate to negotiate their military service, they could also leverage their status as Greek veterans by appealing to veterans' organizations to advocate on their behalf vis-à-vis the Jewish Community. Socializing with Orthodox Christians in the military, Jewish men cultivated new bonds that continued after their service. In one instance, a Jewish employee of the Jewish Community who had served in the Greek army during the Asia Minor campaign took advantage of military connections to request a raise. As a guard of the Jewish cemetery, he complained that his shirt was in tatters and he could afford to feed his family only dark bread and olives. While the Jewish Community initially rejected his request for a raise, he appealed to the Union of Veterans and Soldiers of Macedonia, of which he was a member. The Union petitioned the Jewish Community requesting that the employee receive the deserved raise that "will provide comfort to a suffering comrade, whose family will bless you."[187] Even as the Jewish Community retained the power to mediate between its members and the state with regard to military service, Jews who participated in the Greek army could leverage that experience in their interactions with the Jewish Community in a further example that illustrates the tensions pulling Jews in Salonica between their status as members of the Jewish Community and citizens of the Greek state.

Conclusion: Putting Things in Their Place

The authority of the Beth Din, the administrative reach of the Jewish neighborhoods, and the mediation of military service show that the Jewish Community of Salonica continued to play an expansive role in the lives of the city's Jewish masses until World War II. Bound together by social convention and certain legal structures and despite class, ideological, professional, and other differences, Jews in Salonica relied on the Jewish Community for multiple purposes. The Jewish Community provided a stabilizing force for the city's Jews as they reestablished their footing in the aftermath of the Ottoman Empire, in the wake of war, fire, population transfers, economic downturn, anti-Jewish activism, increased state pressures, and political fragmentation. Sometimes they relied on the Community because they wanted to; other times, they had no choice.

Within the context of a relatively weak state, the Jewish Community served as the "protector" of its members, especially the destitute masses.[188] The Jewish Community was supposed to "put things in their place" (*meter las kozas en sus lugar*): to ensure that the needs of the city's Jews were met and their interests protected.[189] Even oppositional Jewish political groups, including right-wing Revisionist Zionists, continued to recognize the Communal Council, the executive branch of the Jewish Community, as the "supreme authority of Salonican Judaism."[190] As late as 1939, when Jews appealed for aid to branches of the Greek government, such as the governor general of Macedonia, they received replies that the Jewish Community, not the state, was apparently responsible for dispensing assistance to Jews.[191] The same recourse applied to Jewish felons: thirty-two male and female Jewish prisoners in Salonica's New Prison requested assistance from the Jewish Community as Passover approached and received *matza*, cheese, olives, and twenty-five drachmae each.[192] Although they had violated state law, these convicts retained rights as members of the Jewish Community. Even the notorious Jewish smuggler Samuel Nefussy had received free milk from the Jewish Community prior to being gunned down by Salonica's police in 1930.[193]

While the Jewish Community remained the primary focus for Salonica's Jewish masses, the municipality and the state increasingly contributed to Jewish philanthropic endeavors. On the eve of the war, for example, a modest but noteworthy 13 percent of the budget of the Matanoth Laevionim (Jewish soup kitchen), which provided daily lunch to more than a thousand Jewish youth, derived from government subsidies. The introduction of additional social service assistance by the Metaxas government also explained why the membership of Adassa, a Jewish mutual aid society in the No. 6 neighborhood, decreased from 250 to 200 in 1939: because some members could now rely on the state to meet their needs. Furthermore, Adassa benefited from a subvention from the municipality.[194]

The victory of the modern rhetoric of minority rights over the antiquated concept of imperial privileges breathed new life into the Jewish Community of Salonica, invested it with certain aspects of self-government, and empowered it to serve alternatively as a substitute for and a partner with the municipality and the Greek state, as well as a mediator between branches of government and the Jewish residents of Salonica. While, as Joseph Nehama saw it, old barriers were indeed falling and Jews increasingly became integrated into the life and politics of Greek society, some of the old structures remained intact—although reframed—that encouraged and other times forced Jews to conceive of themselves not as Hellenic citizens identical to their Christian neighbors but specifically as Hellenic Jews. Jews' multiple formal and informal connections to the Jewish Community continued to bind them—especially the impoverished—to each other and to Jewish institutions. The tension between their status as members of the Jewish Community and as ostensible citizens of Greece still persisted on the eve of World War II.

CHAPTER 2

WHO WILL SAVE SEPHARDIC JUDAISM?
The Chief Rabbi

Pipino yerli, haham ajeno.

Local cucumber and a foreign rabbi (are preferable).

—Judeo-Spanish expression[1]

·

Writing in *The Jewish Chronicle* of London in 1932, the Salonica correspondent bemoaned the nearly decade-long absence of a permanent chief rabbi in his city:

> It is a lamentable spectacle to see on the one hand the most compact Sefardic Community in the world, with such a glorious past, reduced to searching the four corners of the earth to find a pastor, a Community that once had so exuberant a Jewish life that it was deservedly styled "a mother town in Israel," and which, in the sixteenth and seventeenth centuries, provided galaxies of Rabbis of world fame; and, on the other hand, Sefardic world Judaism reduced to such a state of spiritual decadence that all of its springs are dried up and it is powerless to provide from its own resources a guide for the Community. Is this the complete desiccation of this branch of the thousand-year-old stem of Israel, formerly so full of sap?[2]

Under the headline "Who Will Save Sefardic Judaism?" *The Jewish Chronicle* presented the quest abroad for a chief rabbi of Salonica as an effort to counter the "decadence" of the once great Jewish center struggling to reestablish its prestige in the wake of the Ottoman Empire's dissolution and within the context of interwar Greece.

The "rabbis of world fame" that once populated Salonica included some of the most eminent sages of the early modern era who presided over prestigious rabbinical academies and introduced the printing press to the city in 1515. During the 1530s, Rabbi Joseph Caro resided in Salonica where he consulted the city's famed rabbinical libraries as he prepared his monumental work, *Beth Yosef*, the forerunner of his code of Jewish law, the *Shulhan Arukh*, which Jewish communities across the globe adopted and still consult today. A native of Salonica and a renowned kabbalist, Salomon Alkabetz composed the famous Sabbath hymn *Leha Dodi*, still sung in synagogues on Friday evenings across the world. An author of biblical commentaries, treatises on natural physics and astronomy, and a homiletic work in Judeo-Spanish on the origins of good and evil, Moses Almosnino numbered among the dozens of other sages who transformed sixteenth-century Salonica into "a mother town in Israel."

But, as *The Jewish Chronicle* lamented, the reputation of Salonica's rabbis during the interwar years had been reduced to a shadow of its former glory. The newspaper expressed the hope that Salonica's Jews could regain their prestige by crowning themselves with a new and worthy rabbi. *The Jewish Chronicle* focused on the newest candidate for the position: born in Poland and educated in German universities, Sevi (Hirsch) Koretz was favored to become the next chief rabbi and, in effect, "save Sephardic Judaism" as represented by its most populous center, Salonica. But could a foreign-born Ashkenazic Jew fulfill the role of spiritual leader of the Sephardic metropolis now inundated with the new pressures of Hellenization?

The proposal to crown Salonican Jews with a modern, western-educated chief rabbi was not new in the interwar years, as scholars have assumed, but rather formed part of more than a fifty-year-long saga regarding the nature of Jewish leadership in the city, in the Ottoman Empire, and in Greece. The Jewish notable Moise Allatini had already recommended in 1875 that Salonica's most promising rabbinical students be sent not only to Istanbul to study but also to Paris or London, so they might return home to enlighten the "darkened East."[3] Allatini's proposal paved the way for the position of the so-called progressives who, over the subsequent decades, increasingly demanded a European, modern, cultured rabbi to serve at the helm. Even appearance—dress and the style of facial hair—symbolized the stature, ideology, and religiosity of a given candidate.

From the 1880s through the 1930s, debates over prospective candidates for chief rabbi focused on whether they could be considered *dinyo* ("worthy"), *konvenivle* ("suitable"), or *mahsus* (a Turkish-derived term signifying "intentional" or "particular") for the great Jewish collectivity of Salonica. But what counted as *dinyo, konvenivle,* or *mahsus* differed for various Jewish elite and changed over time, between the Ottoman and Greek frameworks and as Jewish political factions multiplied and battled for power. The debates over the most suitable characteristics of the chief rabbi often invoked a series of value-laden dichotomies: modern/traditional, foreign/native, European/Oriental, Ashkenazic/Sephardic, university educated/yeshiva educated, democratic/authoritarian, political figurehead/Talmudic scholar.

Disputes over the character of the chief rabbi served as a microcosm of the broader conflicts among Jewish interest groups—Zionists, the Mizrahi, the Alliance, Socialists, the rabbinical corps, communal administrators, journalists—that revealed deep-seated anxieties about the social, cultural, and political position of and aspirations for the city's Jews and their institutions, which increased amidst the transition from Ottoman rule to the Greek nation-state. The various interest groups invested considerable effort in the debates over the chief rabbi position, for its holder symbolized the status of the Jewish collectivity and would determine, as *La Epoka* noted, the very "future of our community": its role in the city, in the country, and on the world stage.[4]

The Model Chief Rabbi: Jacob Covo (r. 1887–1907)

From the 1680s until 1887, Salonica's Jews did not recognize a single rabbinic authority for the entire city. Instead, a triumvirate of rabbis managed the so-called internal affairs of the Jewish collectivity (referred to as the *kolel*). Each of the three rabbis bore the title *rav akolel* and served for life; some became famed Talmudic scholars compared to the likes of Maimonides.[5] Despite the creation of the citywide Jewish Community and the Communal Council in the 1870s to manage its administration, the triumvirate continued to operate until 1887. During that time, as Joseph Nehama reflected, Salonica's rabbis benefitted from "veritable autonomy" with regard to the governance of Jewish religious practices and formed a kind of "theocratic republic."[6] The so-called external affairs of the *kolel*, however, were not in the hands of the rabbinic authorities. Rather, as in medieval Europe where a merchant or other lay leader served as the *shtadlan* ("intercessor") who interfaced with the authorities, so too in Salonica and in other cities across the empire did merchants serve as the *kahya* or *vekil*, as this representative was known in the Ottoman context. Often an ad hoc position, the *kahya* or *vekil* negotiated taxes to be paid to the Ottoman coffers on behalf of each city's Jewish congregations.[7]

The dynamics changed when the Ottoman state created a new position in 1835: the *haham bashi* ("chief rabbi"). Designated as the official representative of Jews across the empire, the *haham bashi*, with its seat in Istanbul, was modeled on the Orthodox Christian and Armenian patriarchates. Each position provided a set conduit through which the state could interface with non-Muslim populations. The Organic Statutes of the Jewish Community (1865) specified that "the chief rabbi is the leader of the entire Jewish nation that resides in the Ottoman Empire; he is the one who puts into practice the orders of the imperial state. As a consequence, he must enjoy the confidence and the credit of the state and of the nation."[8] The chief rabbi represented the Jewish *millet* vis-à-vis the government and served, in effect, as a state functionary. As a way to ensure state control, the Ottoman authorities often recognized the *haham bashi* as *kaymakam* ("acting" chief rabbi) and dismissed him as needed.[9] The new position in Istanbul was replicated at the local level as the state appointed a *haham bashi* as the official Jewish representative in cities across the empire. In Salonica, the Ottoman state designated one of the rabbis in the triumvirate as the *haham bashi*, whose position rendered obsolete the earlier ad hoc *kahya* or *vekil*. But discrepancies between how the state and the Jews viewed rabbis remained. While Ottoman state yearbooks only identified the single *haham bashi* in Salonica, Jewish sources continued to refer to the triumvirate.[10]

Eulogies for the last two members of the final triumvirate, *Haham Bashi* Samuel Arditti (1812–1887) and *Haham* Meir Nahmias (1804–1888, the alleged creator of *Raki de Haham Nahmias*, the city's most famous *ouzo*[11]), emphasized their status as sages, rabbinical judges, Talmudic scholars, sustainers of Jewish law, and enforcers of religious observance. Eulogies praised both rabbis as respected elders, advisors, and pastors animated by sentiments of justice, honesty, and morality that contributed to "harmony among the Jews of Salonica."[12] The eulogies alluded to the limited impact of these rabbis beyond the Jewish domain. One speaker referred to the "friendly relations" cultivated by Arditti, as *haham bashi*, with Orthodox Christian leaders, Ottoman authorities, and European consuls. Thus all of Salonica—not just Jews—suffered a great loss with Arditti's death: "Poor you, city of Salonica! How you've been left desolate!"[13] But Arditti's death was rationalized as divine punishment of the city's Jews for their lax observance of Jewish law. The deaths of Arditti and Nahmias formed part of a major "disaster" resulting from an epidemic that killed the last triumvirate rabbis, the head of the Beth Din, and then his successor. These losses contributed to the dissolution of the triumvirate.[14]

The discussion regarding the successor to the post of *haham bashi* revolved around a new set of criteria. The Communal Council and the city's rabbis nominated Jacob Covo (nicknamed Yakovachi, 1825–1907) to the position in 1887 in part because of his status as a rabbinical scholar and a belief in his capacity to improve the moral and material standing of the Jewish masses. Covo indeed became the last Salonican-born rabbi whose rabbinical rulings were published (posthumously, in 1915, as *Kohav mi-Yakov*). But they also believed he would serve as a "worthy" public representative of the city's Jews as an "enlightened," "liberal," "tolerant," and "young" rabbi (sixty-three at the time)[15]—terms not previously associated with such a position. A grandson of a previous *haham bashi* (Asher Covo, d. 1874), Jacob Covo also played a role in broader municipal politics. As a member of the Commission of Public Instruction, he reorganized the Talmud Tora, a feat later touted as the most important improvement made to a Jewish institution in the city since 1492.[16] He also brokered an agreement between the previous rabbinical triumvirate and Jewish notables regarding the establishment of an Alliance Israélite Universelle school in Salonica. While some of his rabbinical predecessors had despised—and cursed—the Alliance and its main proponent, Moise Allatini, Covo praised them—another sign of his purportedly progressive attitude.[17] As the first *haham bashi* in Ottoman Salonica to speak Turkish—the language of the state—Covo was poised to initiate a new era of Jewish civic engagement.

Jacob Covo became the first and only Salonican-born rabbi to exercise authority as the *haham bashi* and exclusive *rav akolel*. During his two decades in office as *kaymakam* ("acting" chief rabbi)—a title given as a precaution by the state—Covo injected displays of Ottoman imperial patriotism into Jewish communal institutions and celebrations. Upon reception of the imperial *berat* ("patent") to serve as *haham bashi*, Covo met with the governor general of Salonica and praised the sultan—in Hebrew—by expressing the devotion of the city's Jews to the empire and emphasizing their sense of gratitude for the protection and liberty from which they benefitted.[18] Seeking to prepare the city's Jewish youth for participation in Ottoman public life, Covo introduced Turkish classes into the Talmud Tora, the Jewish school for boys, for the first time (1889).[19] He also helped to orchestrate empire-wide celebrations in 1892 to commemorate the arrival of Jews in Ottoman lands four centuries earlier. Covo further renewed Jewish institutional life in the city. He founded the Beth Yosef seminary to educate "modern rabbis"—knowledgeable in Turkish and French—to serve as "guides of our communities."[20] He promoted the Ets Ahaim mutual aid society and publishing house, which endorsed the observance of traditional Judaism. Finally, he rebuilt Jewish institutions in the city following the disastrous fire of 1890 and managed several financial crises at the turn of the century. The sultan awarded Covo a number of high honors (second and third class *osmaniye* and *mecidiye*) for his efforts.[21]

When Covo died in 1907, *La Epoka* in Salonica and *El Tiempo* in Istanbul mourned the loss on behalf of Jews across the "entire East."[22] Both newspapers confirmed the image of Covo as an enlightened, tolerant, and respected pastor who, imbued with a "modern spirit," placed the city's Jews on "the path of progress" and represented them vis-à-vis the Ottoman authorities in a "worthy manner." A crowd of five thousand filled the Talmud Tora to listen to the eulogies, including Ottoman officials; representatives of the Greek, Bulgarian, and Armenian communities; and European consuls. Special prayers of mourning were recited in the Italian synagogue in Istanbul. *La Epoka* assured its readers that Covo would be remembered as the "ideal pastor," a model chief rabbi who mastered the domains of both internal and external affairs.[23] Decades later, Joseph Nehama praised Covo for overseeing a "golden age" for Salonica's Jews, an idealized era in which, according to Isaac Emmanuel, the city operated as a "Jewish republic" and a *Shabatopolis*.[24] But a challenging question emerged in the local press immediately following Covo's death: could an equally venerated, capable, and intelligent successor be found locally?

From the Ottoman Sultan to the Greek King: Chief Rabbi Jacob Meir (r. 1908–1919)

The nomination of Covo to the position of *haham bashi* following the dissolution of the rabbinical triumvirate in 1887 transpired immediately, with little public debate and with the cooperation of the Ottoman authorities. In the wake of his death in 1907, the process was completely different and a successor was not immediately selected. Debates in local Jewish circles and those in Istanbul and Izmir, compounded by the dramatic impact of the Young Turk Revolution (1908), transformed into an empire-wide affair the question of who Salonica's next chief rabbi ought to be, what his functions should be, and even if there should be one at all. As the Judeo-Spanish press declared, the Jewish Community of Salonica, now lacking not only a chief rabbi but also a spokesman and a vision for the twentieth century, faced "one of the most important points in its history."[25]

The Judeo-Spanish press agreed that a "worthy" chief rabbi had to be located for Salonica, but disagreed over the merits and liabilities of "modern" and "European" candidates versus those considered "traditional" and "eastern." Rather than settle for one of the many local "famed theologians," *La Epoka* argued that Salonica's Jews needed a "suitable" representative to protect their interests and dignity vis-à-vis the authorities, especially as violent clashes in the region between Bulgarian and Greek nationalists contributed to a sense of insecurity. Moreover, such a leader would need to be a "democrat"—a new concept in the discussion—who could adapt to the exigencies of modern life and abide by the "will of the people." These aspirations left *La Epoka* in a quandary. Since the Beth Yosef seminary, according to the newspaper, had not yet produced "modern rabbis," it was unlikely that a desirable local candidate could be found. But *La Epoka* also surmised that "our Jews" would *never* accept a leader from elsewhere, neither an *Izmirli* nor an *Estambuli*, and certainly not a European.[26]

As an alternative, *La Epoka* proposed dissolving the position of *haham bashi* altogether—a move that threatened the established imperial order. *La Epoka* recommended that the rabbinical triumvirate be revived to deal with religious questions and the *kahya*, a lay representative, to interface with the authorities. *El Tiempo* in Istanbul, backed by *El Komersial* in Izmir, denounced the proposal to abolish the chief rabbi as "absolutely incompatible with the interests and prestige of the great community of Salonica."[27] The Istanbul newspaper criticized the editors of *La Epoka* as "free thinkers" and "immature youngsters" ignorant of the purpose of the chief rabbi.[28]

But this was exactly the point: what was a chief rabbi supposed to be? *El Tiempo* argued that it would make no sense for a "religious community" to exist without a "religious leader" because the "tolerance" that the Otto-man authorities had granted to the empire's Jews and other non-Muslims was predicated on their status as "religious groupings" headed by "religious magistrates." The abolition of the chief rabbi, the newspaper warned, would make Salonica's Jews look like "radicals" by disrupting the established order and bringing them dishonor—even danger. *La Epoka* angrily demanded that *El Tiempo* and *El Komersial* extricate themselves from Salonica's affairs.[29]

But *El Tiempo* raised a critical question: If Salonica's Jews would be will-ing to abolish their highest-ranking office, would they support the abolition of other high-ranking positions perceived to be out of sync with modern life—perhaps even the sultan himself? If such a radical phenomenon were to transpire, *El Tiempo* implied that it could be attributed to the initiative of Salonica's Jews—and by extension all Ottoman Jews—and thus bring about grave consequences. Given that, less than a year later, in 1908, the Young Turks launched the revolution that ultimately led to the deposition of Sul-tan Abdul Hamid II (in 1909); that the revolution began in Salonica; that a number of prominent local Jews figured among its supporters, including *La Epoka*'s editor, Sam Lévy; and that in certain circles the revolution was at-tributed to a Jewish-Freemason conspiracy, the fears articulated by *El Tiempo* appeared to be founded.

The Jewish Communal Council in Salonica ultimately agreed with *El Tiempo* that the city still required a chief rabbi. Four candidates emerged. The famed rabbi and historian Abraham Danon, from Edirne, withdrew from consideration. Instead, factions initially supported two Salonican-born rab-bis living abroad: David Pipano, chief rabbi of Sofia, and Hezekiah Yeoshua Shabbetay, chief rabbi of Tripoli. *La Epoka* explained that, as "our own" (*los muestros*), both candidates were "worthy" of the position, especially Shab-betay, who knew Turkish.[30] But doubts were raised over whether either was "modern" enough; neither spoke French. Self-styled progressive Salonican Jews living in Egypt argued that a candidate must be sought among non-Salonicans: "The words 'modern chief rabbi' should not scare the masses."[31]

A controversy regarding the chief rabbinate in Jerusalem brought a fourth candidate into the discussion and enabled Salonican Jewish leaders to im-port a rabbi who satisfied both the traditionalists and the progressives: Rabbi Jacob Meir (1856–1939), the *haham bashi* of Jerusalem whose appointment there was being contested by opposing factions.[32] Within this heated context, the president of Salonica's Jewish Communal Council, Jacob Cazes, invited Meir to consider the position in Salonica. Born in Jerusalem to parents from Rhodes, Meir benefitted from previous contact with Salonica: he had visited and befriended the previous *haham bashi*, Jacob Covo. Moreover, the family of Meir's wife, Rachel née Yitzhaki, had come from Salonica to Palestine.[33]

Beyond his links to Salonica, Meir appeared to be ideally suited for the position. As a renowned rabbinical scholar, relatively young, and imbued with the "spirit of modernity," Meir had served on the Beth Din in Jerusalem and helped to found a Jewish hospital. In addition to Judeo-Spanish, he also spoke modern Hebrew, French (which contributed to his modern status), and Arabic, the sacred language of Islam that enabled him to build links to the Ottoman authorities. He also developed good rapport with both Sephardim and Ashkenazim. Unusual at the time, he promoted the Alliance and the Zionist movement. As the established Jewish leadership and the Ottoman authorities in Jerusalem saw the Alliance and Zionism as threats, they wished to remove Meir. Undeterred by the controversy, the Judeo-Spanish press in Salonica viewed Meir as a suitable representative of the city's Jews.[34] The only criticism was that he did not know Turkish.[35]

Honored to serve as the "head of the most important and most enlightened Jewish community in the East," Meir agreed to become the *haham bashi* of Salonica only if he were elected unanimously.[36] Initially thirty-three members of the General Assembly voted for Meir and three for Shabbetay, but the latter's supporters agreed to switch their votes. Following Meir's "unanimous" victory, the Assembly sent lawyer Joseph Naar to Istanbul to ensure that the Ottoman authorities confirmed the appointment.[37] The Ottoman authorities in Istanbul, however, did not immediately follow through. Rumors circulated that Meir would be barred from Salonica; perhaps he would become chief rabbi of Cairo. The sense of distress at the local level stemming from the absence of a chief rabbi and the inability of Jewish leaders to sway the Ottoman authorities reverberated across the empire.[38] *El Tiempo* characterized the issue as seriously impacting all "Ottoman Judaism."[39]

The episode demonstrated how contingent Jewish authority was on the endorsement of the Ottoman state. The *kaymakam* in Istanbul, Moshe Halevi, finally intervened successfully with the grand vizier, and the Ottoman government sanctioned Meir's installation as the new *haham bashi* of Salonica.[40] Meir arrived in Istanbul and visited the imperial palace at Yildiz where Sultan Abdul Hamid II decorated him with honors (*mecidiye*, second class).[41] *La Epoka* published poems in Meir's honor in anticipation of his arrival in Salonica.[42]

The Jewish Community of Salonica orchestrated an elaborate investiture ceremony for Meir that reinforced dual allegiances to Judaism and to the Ottoman Empire. An overflowing crowd of fifteen thousand gathered at the Talmud Tora. As Meir entered the sanctuary, wearing his uniform and imperial decoration, a band played the "Hamidian March" (the Ottoman imperial anthem during the era of Sultan Abdul Hamid II). Meir saluted the crowd and bowed before the Holy Ark (*ehal*) before taking his seat next to a cadre of Ottoman officials with whom he spoke in Arabic and French. A chorus of students from the Talmud Tora school next sang a song composed for the occasion to the tune of the "Hamidian March." Rounds of applause followed with cries, in Turkish, of "Long live the sultan!" Meir then ascended to the pulpit (*teva*), where he enveloped himself in his prayer shawl (*tallet*) and pronounced the *sheheheyanu* (a Hebrew prayer for special occasions). For the first time in his thirty-five-year career, he delivered a public address in Judeo-Spanish.[43]

In his speech, which fused religious and political rhetoric, Meir sought to demonstrate the devotion of the city's Jews to the empire, their commitment to Judaism, and their increased prestige in the Jewish world. He expressed his gratitude for attaining the "highest position in the rabbinate"—more important, he implied, than even the *haham bashi* in Istanbul. He then articulated his goals, beginning with "Torah": to strengthen Jewish religious observance, to preserve the unique status of the Jewish Sabbath in the city, and to improve Jewish education—all so that the grand statement "For from Salonica shall go forth Torah" (an allusion to Isaiah 2:3 in which Salonica was substituted for Jerusalem) would again ring true. Notably, he also included the obligation of Jews to study Turkish: acquisition of the state language, while an expression of devotion to the empire, also constituted a vehicle through which Jews could improve their status.

Meir next focused on "kingship" (*malhut*, in Hebrew): strengthening the commitment of the city's Jews to their sultan and their empire by regularly reciting prayers for the government, defending the empire in word and act (though not sword, given the exemption of non-Muslims from military service), and expressing gratitude to the sovereign for his protection. Since Ottoman authorities had voiced concerns about him in Palestine, Meir likely conveyed his sense of allegiance to the empire out of both genuine belief and self-defense to provide clarity on the matter. Following Meir's speech, a chorus intoned the *Noten teshua* (the prayer for the government, in Hebrew), which was followed by cheers of "Long live the sultan!" Meir then retired to his new residence, where he received Jewish notables, who welcomed him to their city and kissed his hand.[44]

The news of Meir's arrival attracted attention from afar and elevated the reputation of Salonica. The famed promoter of modern Hebrew, Eliezer Ben-Yehuda, praised Meir's appointment from Jerusalem.[45] *The Jewish Chronicle* in London argued that, with Meir at its head, only Salonica benefitted from a worthy and modern pastor in the Ottoman realm, whereas those rabbis elsewhere in the empire "are not cultured, and are imbued with ideas of the past."[46] When a controversy erupted over the appointment of the new empire-wide *haham bashi* in 1908, rumors circulated that Meir would be nominated to the position.[47] Instead, a conflict ensued over the appointment of the Alliance's candidate, Haim Nahum.[48]

Amidst the fray, a Judeo-Spanish newspaper in the capital, *La Bos*, solicited the intervention of Salonica's Jews by appealing to their past grandeur now confirmed with Meir at the helm: "The city of Salonica was always City and Mother in Israel [*ir va-em be-Israel*], city full of rabbis; the [rabbinical] works . . . that shine and enlighten the entire universe come forth from there. The city of Salonica still sustains the Jewish religion; and among all of her efforts to maintain national prestige number not working on the day of Shabbat."[49] The role of the city—and its Jews—on the world political stage, as the headquarters of the Young Turk movement, and as home to a loyal Ottoman Jewish population also rendered Salonica great in the view of *La Bos*: "[T]he city of Salonica was the city of salvation" where the Young Turks reintroduced the constitution and brought "liberty" to the empire.[50] *La Bos* argued that Salonica's Jews must now help resolve the *haham bashi* controversy. While the imperial capital and the empire-wide *haham bashi* sat in Istanbul, the newspaper intimated, the real Ottoman Jewish heart lay in

Salonica. Meir projected this image by becoming the first *haham bashi* of Salonica to refer to the city as "City and Mother in Israel" on his official printed stationary (*rosh ha-rabanut be-i[r] v[a-em] b[e]-I[srael] Saloniki*).[51]

Meir served as chief rabbi of Salonica through eleven years of transformations for the city's Jews. As a leader during the Young Turk Revolution, Meir retained his position when so many others were ousted, including the *kaymakan haham bashi* in Istanbul. He also faced the challenging task of navigating the Balkan Wars, the transition from Ottoman to Greek rule over the city, and World War I. Perhaps most devastatingly, Meir confronted the dramatic losses of the fire of 1917, which left thousands homeless and destroyed many institutions and priceless libraries—including Meir's personal collection. Meir also witnessed the proliferation of Jewish political factions as Zionist and socialist associations formed and multiplied. Worn out from a decade of struggle, Meir decided to return to Jerusalem in 1919. The Judeo-Spanish press reported that Meir left for "personal reasons" but also hinted that conflicts with the Communal Council stood at the heart of the issue.[52] Moreover, since the Greek state did not officially recognize the legal status of the Jewish Community until 1920, the office of the *haham bashi* lacked de jure authority during this period.

After his departure from Salonica, Meir became a potent symbol for his successors and hagiographers. They emphasized neither his immersion in Ottoman politics nor the obstacles he confronted during the Balkan Wars or following the fire of 1917, but rather the cordial relations he cultivated among Jews, Orthodox Christians, and the Greek state for, during Meir's tenure, Salonica experienced its so-called liberation. Commemorations of October 26, the anniversary of the city's capture by the Greek army, featured stories in the Judeo-Spanish press, accompanied by photos of Meir, that recounted his legendary leadership during the transition and his embrace of the new sovereign.[53] A Judeo-Spanish booklet published by *La Aksion* in 1931, *The Liberation of Salonica*, similarly celebrated Meir's role in successfully navigating the transition of Salonica to Greek jurisdiction (1912–1913), gaining the favor of the king, and defending the honor of the city's Jews.[54]

This kind of image also emerged in a homage at Salonica's Beth Shaul synagogue following Meir's death in 1939. At the memorial service, Chief Rabbi Sevi Koretz touted Meir for his service to "our community, to our

רבינו יעקב מאיר
סאלוניק

S. E. le Grand Rabbin
Jacob Meïr
de Salonique-~~Turquie~~.
Grèce

Figure 2.1. The chief rabbi of Salonica, Jacob Meir, dressed in his official uniform. Source: Author's private collection.

homeland, and to our nation . . . whose memory will be etched eternally in gold in the history of our renowned community, the ancient City and Mother in Israel." Koretz emphasized that Meir skillfully managed the transition from Ottoman to Greek rule and paved the way for those Jewish leaders who followed him: "In 1912, [Meir] knew how to attach our community to the new homeland, to its new historic destiny, finding the path to the hearts of the beloved royal family and the governments of our beloved homeland as well as the sympathy of the entire Hellenic people."[55] In effect, Meir's memory was retrospectively harnessed to promote a model of a patriotic chief rabbi in the new Greek framework, just as Covo before him had been in the Ottoman context. But at the time of Meir's departure from Salonica in 1919, the status of the city's Jews, their relationship with the new regime, and who would serve as the next chief rabbi remained uncertain.

A Constitutional Crisis and a Cultural Conflict: Bension Uziel (r. 1921–1923)

The divisiveness among Jewish communal administrators that contributed to Meir's resignation paralleled the larger scene of Greek politics during World War I. The National Schism (*Ethnikos Dihasmos*) divided the country over the question of whether to enter the war and, if so, on which side. Two governments with two armies each commanded half of Greece. King Constantine of Greece advocated neutrality from his base in Athens. Pitted against him, Venizelos established an opposition government in Salonica and invited the Entente armies into the city.[56] In 1917, threatened by Allied forces, Constantine abdicated in favor of a son, Alexander. Following the conclusion of the war and Alexander's death, Greece held a referendum to decide between establishing a republic under Venizelos or bringing King Constantine back from exile. Readers of the local Judeo-Spanish press in Salonica therefore encountered daily headlines—"The Question of the King," "Republic or Monarchy?" and, satirically, "King or Republic? It's the Same *Halva*"—that appeared beside others, such as "The Question of the Chief Rabbi."[57] Jewish elite reevaluated their own communal constitution in parallel to that of the Greek state.

The citizens of Greece ultimately voted for the return of the monarchy—a result conveniently blamed by republicans on Salonica's Jews, a new electoral constituency in the country falsely accused of swaying the vote and betraying the nationalist cause.[58] Within this tense context, protracted debates emerged in Jewish circles over Meir's successor, which took advantage of the crisis to chart a course for the future: would an academic rabbi with a rabbinical ordination, vast culture, and a PhD from a European university be appropriate for the city, or would a traditionally educated *haham* from the East be preferred? Who would lead the greatest Sephardic center in the post-Ottoman world, especially as it recast itself in Hellenic and European molds?

Unlike the debates in 1907, which had provoked the intervention of Jews in Istanbul and Izmir, this time, with Salonica now constricted within the borders of Greece, the discussion remained a local affair. Some Jewish groups—such as the Mizrahi, a new religious-nationalist party that splintered off from the more secular Zionists—asserted that the recognition of minority rights for Jewish communal organization could not be guaranteed without the strong authority figure of the chief rabbi.[59] The Mizrahi joined an unsuccessful demonstration of Zionists to convince Meir to remain in Salonica, at least until a new chief rabbi could be found.[60]

Once Meir's departure from Salonica became a fait accompli, the debate again revolved around pinpointing a worthy and suitable candidate—and determining precisely what these terms meant in the new context of Greece. Traditionalists argued that a rabbi from the East would be the preferred successor due to his knowledge of Judeo-Spanish; his familiarity with "our customs"; and because it was not necessary for Salonica to look anywhere else.[61] The Mizrahi and rabbinical corps nonetheless rejected the candidacy of Haim Nahum, the *haham bashi* in Istanbul, even though he fit several criteria, because they objected to his opposition to Zionism and his ties to the assimilationist Alliance.[62]

More progressive activists criticized what they perceived to be the antiquated, Ottoman, oriental, and authoritarian manner of conducting politics, which they attributed to the traditional educations acquired by rabbis in the East. *El Puevlo* ridiculed the demonstrations to keep Meir in Salonica and argued that fear surrounding his departure stemmed from the "false belief among the masses that all that the Jewish Community has obtained from organizations abroad, the authorities, etc., is through the *hatir* ["favor," "respect," or "influence"] of the chief rabbi and because of his personal authority."[63]

From the journalist's perspective, Meir's departure was not to be lamented. *El Liberal*, the successor to *La Epoka*, thanked Meir for leaving and ridiculed him for having acted as "sovereign dictator" animated by a spirit of "absolutism" and an unwillingness to collaborate with the Communal Council.[64]

Offering an antidote to the purportedly eastern and backward notion of *hatir* (notably, a Turkish term), Mentesh Bensanchi, co-editor of *El Puevlo* and one of the most dominant voices in interwar Jewish journalism in Salonica, emphasized the European notion of "culture" (*kultura*). This term had not been invoked during the previous debates over rabbinical succession. "Culture" revolved around upbringing, education, language competency, demeanor, and worldview. Bensanchi concluded that "true" (or "secular," "vast" or "general") culture could be acquired only at universities in the West and insisted that no candidates with the necessary culture could be found in Salonica. Of the 265 Jewish clergy affiliated with the 55 synagogues in Salonica, only 20 of them were deemed "true rabbis" and, of those, only 2 were considered "somewhat modern" because of their acquaintance with French.[65]

The Judeo-Spanish press lamented that the rabbinical seminary, Beth Yosef, remained unsuccessful in creating spiritual leaders with the necessary culture.[66] Although the fire of 1917 had left the institution in ashes, the students continued their studies at an Alliance school, but the results were unsatisfactory.[67] Despite their exposure to "general studies," including natural science, physics, geometry, algebra, and Jewish history, graduates continued to "lack proficiency in French"—a sign that they were not acquiring the desired culture. The Communal Council threatened to shut it down.[68] Others defended the Beth Yosef and insisted that, even if it did not produce eminent European rabbis like Zadoc Kahn or Joseph Bloch, "its students can very well become the kinds of rabbis that our community requires."[69]

The purportedly poor education attained by local rabbis drove the progressive camp to advocate that the next chief rabbi be imported from abroad: not necessarily from Palestine, for that territory was in the East, but rather from Europe. Bensanchi reminded his readers that "Sephardi Judaism . . . can count in its bosom Talmudists full of erudition and religiosity, but not rabbis like those of the West" who "exert influence" on "all classes of society" (including the middle and upper classes and not just the devout) because of their "vast culture" and education in languages, history, literature, philosophy and sciences.[70] *El Liberal* drew the damning conclusion that there was no choice but to hire "an Ashkenazi rabbi."[71]

Even if shocked by the suggestion to import an Ashkenazic rabbi, those who looked to the West for potential candidates developed a creative argument to support their position and to allay the objections of their opponents. Bensanchi explained that a European chief rabbi would be suitable for Salonica's Jews not because they needed to be uplifted from their backward, eastern condition but precisely the opposite: in order to confirm their justified position as an authentically modern and European Jewish collectivity. "Our community," he assured his readers, "is advanced enough today to require a [modern] pastor."[72] He elaborated further: "A chief rabbi from the East cannot adapt himself to Salonica, which can be considered a European city, and there is a great chance that such a[n Eastern] spiritual leader will not exercise any influence on the spirits [of the people], limiting himself to occupying his post in form alone. . . . Do not be afraid of the word European."[73] The concept of a "modern" chief rabbi now signified geographic and cultural ties to Europe.

Bensanchi developed another creative way to frame Salonica within Europe by remolding Sephardic Jewish identity and emphasizing what he referred to as the shared "Latin mentality." Defining "mentality" according to shared language, Bensanchi characterized Salonica's Jews as "Latin" rather than "Oriental," due to their mother tongue, Judeo-Spanish, a Romance and thus "Latin" language (reinforced by the French spoken by the middle and upper classes). Salonica's Jews therefore required not a Judeo-Spanish speaking rabbi but one fluent in any "Latin" language, such as French or Italian, which resonated with Judeo-Spanish and the local "mentality."[74] While he had deployed the terms "Sephardi" and "Eastern" interchangeably in the past, largely in reference to the former Ottoman Jewish world, Bensanchi now radically altered his definition: "When speaking of Sephardim, surely [we] intend to speak of the Jews of the East, but Sephardim are also Jews of France and Italy where the mentality is reasonably close to ours."[75]

In December 1920, the General Assembly of the Jewish Community of Salonica finally voted on two candidates, who each embodied different visions for the future of Jewish life in the city. Jacob Cazes, the president of the Communal Council, along with Bensanchi and *El Puevlo*, endorsed the "modern" candidate. As a rabbi from Livorno and a native Italian speaker, forty-year-old Dr. Rabbi Alfredo Toaff (1880–1936) possessed the requisite Latin mentality and the appropriate culture due to his education at the University of Pisa. He had studied Hebrew literature and classical languages, including ancient Greek, which would help him to learn modern Greek.[76]

Prior to his departure from Salonica, Meir had recommended the candidacy of one his protégés, Bension Uziel (1880–1953), the chief rabbi of Jaffa.[77] Descended from a famed rabbinical family and experienced as a teacher and rabbinical judge in Palestine, Uziel spoke Judeo-Spanish, Hebrew, Arabic, Turkish, and French—the latter endowing him with "culture." Drawing on orientalist tropes, Bensanchi continued to argue that rabbis like Uziel would be "dangerous" because of their alleged opposition to "democratic" principles and lack of "tolerance." But Uziel demonstrated that, although Eastern and merely educated at a yeshiva, he represented a true "democrat" capable of bringing together traditional and modern constituencies, Sephardim and Ashkenazim, and Zionists and the Alliance. The support that Uziel garnered from the Alliance supplemented his endorsement by the Mizrahi, the rabbinical corps, and influential Zionists, such as the well-respected educator Isaac Alsheh, who warned that the selection of a western rabbi would bring a "veritable revolution to the community." With forty-four votes in favor and sixteen votes in opposition, the General Assembly of the Jewish Community of Salonica decided to invite Uziel for a trial period of three months, at the end of which the final decision would be made.[78]

The satirical Judeo-Spanish newspaper *El Chaketon* ("The Jab") caricatured the two candidates and the anxieties surrounding the issue:

> The two rabbis in sight,
> The professor and the kabbalist,
> The one who wears a turban and the other a hat,
> In the end, the Jerusalemite and the European
> Were put on a plate,
> And everyone looked them up and down.
> The Palestinian is more appetizing
> For the council and for the people . . .[79]

Upon his arrival in 1921, Uziel successfully demonstrated that he could be a model democrat and appeal to all segments of the Jewish population in Salonica.[80] *El Puevlo* conceded that Uziel possessed "general knowledge, however elementary," and appeared open to "modern ideas." In an interview with the newspaper, Uziel appealed to the notions of "tolerance" and "justice" as inspiring his activities as chief rabbi. He praised the "nobility" of Salonica's rabbis and, appealing to constitutional discourse, expressed his hope to "collaborate in perfect harmony with the Communal Council and General Assembly, which are the direct manifestations of the will of the people."[81]

Convinced of his "suitability" to serve as chief rabbi, in March 1921, the General Assembly approved the hiring of Uziel as chief rabbi—by a vote of thirty-three in favor, four opposed, and one abstention—for a term of five years; nearly two years without a chief rabbi thus ended.[82] At the same meeting, the General Assembly brought the discussion regarding democracy to its logical conclusion by introducing universal male suffrage in communal elections.[83] Hesitant to leave Palestine during such a key period for the development of the Zionist movement in the wake of the Balfour Declaration, Uziel justified his decision to answer the "call" from Salonica as a way to "sanctify" himself as a "servant of God's people."[84]

While the arrival of Meir as the chief rabbi of Salonica in 1907 represented a victory for progressive Jewish circles, the appointment of his protégé, Uziel, in 1921 represented a compromise, albeit one that favored the rabbis, the Mizrahi, and the traditionalists. Without knowledge of Greek, not holding Greek citizenship, and new to the country, Uziel did not engage in elaborate demonstrations of patriotism like his predecessors had in the Ottoman context. During an era in which Greece remained at war (with Turkey) and in which state representatives wanted to display their tolerance toward minorities to justify the annexation of parts of Asia Minor, the Greek state did not interfere in the election of the chief rabbi.

With Salonica still decimated by the fire of 1917 and with synagogues still in ashes, Uziel dedicated his tenure as chief rabbi to internal affairs.[85] Among his accomplishments, Uziel convinced Jewish bankers to refrain from business on the Sabbath and tobacco factories to grant Jewish workers Saturdays off.[86] He encouraged Sabbath observance by appealing not to religious justifications—because God commanded it—but to Jewish nationalism—because the Sabbath defines the Jews as a people—and captivated the youth and the middle classes in so doing.[87] He also reorganized aspects of the Beth Yosef seminary.[88] As his final act, he founded the Agudat Hahamim, an association that united all of the city's rabbis in order to reverse "religious and moral decline" and to sustain "our holy traditions."[89]

After completing only two years of his contract, Uziel resigned in 1923 in order to return to Palestine—ostensibly for "family reasons" and to resume his duties as chief rabbi in Jaffa-Tel Aviv.[90] But the same types of constitutional conflicts between the Communal Council and the chief rabbi that had compelled Meir to leave Salonica now affected Uziel. *El Puevlo* argued that Jacob Cazes, the president of the Communal Council, had prevented Uziel from interacting with the government by keeping him "in the shadows."[91] *El Puevlo* now accused the president of the council of displaying an "anti-democratic" and "unconstitutional spirit."[92] Uziel sailed for Jaffa in the summer of 1923—but he did not disappear from Salonican Jewish politics.[93]

With Uziel's departure, Jewish leaders in Salonica began to search for a successor who could reclaim the role of previous chief rabbis as an intermediary with the authorities. Now, however, the *hatir* ("influence") of the lay president was as much a concern as that of any potential chief rabbi. Bensanchi continued to argue that the problem stemmed from the inability of an Eastern rabbi, like Uziel, to captivate the "educated classes."[94] While Uziel named Solomon Tagger, the chief rabbi of Beirut, as his successor, Bensanchi remained adamant about the need for a modern rabbi and argued Tagger was not.[95] With no other suitable candidates in sight, the Communal Council and the General Assembly designated the head of the local Beth Din, Emanuel Isaac Brudo, as the *lokum tenens*, or "acting," chief rabbi (the Latin phrase replacing the Ottoman term, *kaymakam*) to focus on internal, religious matters.[96] But the council continued the search for a worthy candidate imbued with European culture and implemented a new, two-pronged approach by sending a local rabbi abroad to continue his studies in Europe and by placing an ad in *The Jewish Chronicle*: "The Jewish community of Salonica desires Chief Rabbi, with deep religious culture as well as university degree; one with knowledge of French preferred."[97]

Hellenic Judaism, Zionism—and a *Comitadji?*
The Candidacy of Marcus Ehrenpreis

The question of the chief rabbi soon lost its primacy within public Jewish debate in Salonica as other issues, namely the influx of Orthodox Christian refugees from Turkey, produced new tensions. The movement to Hellenize the territories of New Greece acquired during the Balkan Wars coincided with the establishment of the Hellenic Republic (1924). Under pressure from refugees, the new government passed the Compulsory Sunday Closing Law. Moreover, a decade-long period of political instability in Greece ensued during which more than twenty changes of government took place (1924–1935). Paralleling the national context, the Jewish Community of Salonica, also facing increasing political fissures, remained without a permanent chief rabbi (1923–1933).

When the issue of the chief rabbi returned to public discussion, it appeared—for the first time—as a question not only for Jews in Salonica but for those throughout Greece. Following the birth of the Hellenic Republic, a new framework identified as "Hellenic Judaism" or "Judaism of Greece" shaped the dynamics of Jewish politics, including the question of the chief rabbi.[98] Growing pressures to integrate into Greek society and greater interactions between Salonica's Jews and those throughout the country—such as through the Zionist Federation of Greece (est. 1919)—contributed to the development of the notion of Hellenic Judaism. Zionists hoped that Hellenic Judaism would emerge as an internationally recognized category—parallel to French Judaism and German Judaism—and thereby dissolve the disdained category of Eastern Judaism. With the retirement and death of the *lokum tenens* chief rabbi, Emanuel Isaac Brudo (d. 1925), the local Judeo-Spanish press lamented that the post of chief rabbi "remains vacant in critical times for Judaism of Greece."[99]

The emergence of Hellenic Judaism as a category challenged the notion that Salonica's Jews should conceptualize themselves as part of a broader Jewish collective united by Latin mentality and linked to Jews in Italy and France. The terms of discussion now began to change as Hellenic Judaism came to be defined in relation both to political borders and to ideological sentiment. Perhaps 15 percent (about ten thousand) of the country's Jews, mostly those in Ioannina and in towns in Old Greece, spoke only Greek, thereby justifying the shift, at least in part.

Zionists played an important role in developing the category of Hellenic Judaism as they aimed to legitimize their activities in the eyes of the Greek state and increase their involvement in the Europe-wide Zionist movement. With the rise of the Zionists and the waning influence of Alliance supporters, attention turned toward Germany, home to the World Zionist Organization, for prospective candidates. As one of the most prominent Zionists in Greece, Mentesh Bensanchi now completely redefined "mentality" along political rather than linguistic or cultural lines: "Almost all the rabbis who have great value and whose general sentiments would correspond with our own will be found in the German-speaking countries." In France, Bensanchi argued in a loosely veiled attack against the Alliance, "there exists a tendency of pronounced assimilation in which we would not partake."[100]

Negotiating these radical shifts—away from France and toward Germany, and away from Salonican or Sephardic identity in favor of Hellenic Judaism—Jacob Cazes, again serving as president of the Communal Council in 1925, nominated a candidate for the position of chief rabbi whom he hoped would satisfy Zionists and the Alliance. Through Albert Pipano (the son of David Pipano, a candidate for the chief rabbi of Salonica in 1907, then in Sofia), Cazes contacted Mordehai (Marcus) Ehrenpreis (1869–1951), a native of Lviv (Poland) who had graduated from the Hochschule für die Wissenschaft des Judentums in Berlin and served as chief rabbi of Djakovo (Croatia), Sofia, and, since 1914, Stockholm.[101] Ehrenpreis's reputation as a traditional Talmudic scholar combined with the "vast, modern culture" he gained through his German education made him a "suitable" candidate according to *El Puevlo*. The newspaper detailed his accomplishments in the field of Jewish literature and politics. At the request of Herzl, he had translated the invitation to the First Zionist Congress in Basel (1897). A contributor to major Hebrew periodicals, Ehrenpreis also attracted to his Sabbath sermons Jews of all classes—including the young, the educated, and the wealthy—in addition to Christians. His linguistic prowess was equally impressive: Hebrew, German, Polish, Scandinavian languages, Yiddish, French, Italian, and English—as well as Judeo-Spanish, which he had learned in Sofia.[102]

Enthusiastic about the prospect, the General Assembly unanimously decided to invite Ehrenpreis to Salonica for a preliminary visit.[103] The invitation represented an unprecedented shift: "The rapprochement of Sephardi and Ashkenazi Judaism is making new progress. Proof is that for *the first time in history*, the chief rabbinate of Salonica is offered to an Ashkenazi."[104] Ehrenpreis initially hesitated but soon warmed up to the idea of serving "the venerated community of Salonica, without a doubt one of the most respected in the world."[105] He agreed to visit Salonica.

During his visit, Ehrenpreis initially made a positive impression by promoting a grand image of Salonica as a European Jewish center worthy of a "European" rabbi. He applauded the "order" and "cleanliness" of the Matanoth Laevionim (Jewish soup kitchen) and the Mair Aboav Orphanage for Girls, which gave the impression of "a piece of Europe in the East."[106] He praised the administrators for their "organization," "zeal," and "activity"—"even rare in the West."[107] At the Beth Shaul synagogue, Ehrenpreis lectured in Judeo-Spanish in favor of strengthening Jewish communities in the diaspora while also building a "national center in Palestine," which garnered support from Zionist organizations.[108] The General Assembly and the Rabbinical Council agreed to offer the position of chief rabbi to Ehrenpreis, who said he would decide upon his return to Stockholm.[109]

The most significant proposition to emerge from Ehrenpreis' visit was whether, if he were to accept, he would become chief rabbi of Salonica alone or of all of Greece. The possibility of nominating a chief rabbi of Greece had been outlined in state Law 2456 of 1920, "Concerning Jewish Communities." But only in the post-1923 period, with the development of the category of Hellenic Judaism and increased pressures of Hellenization, did the idea receive consideration.[110] Ehrenpreis advocated for the creation of a chief rabbi for the entire country to split his time between Salonica and Athens in order to safeguard the well-being of Salonica's Jews and to ensure close relations with the government, especially during the dictatorship of General Theodoros Pangalos (1925–1926). Ehrenpreis concluded that he would agree to be chief rabbi of all of Greece, not chief rabbi of Salonica alone.[111]

For the first time, Jews across the country—in Salonica, Athens, and elsewhere—debated the prospect of a chief rabbi of Greece.[112] *El Puevlo* proposed that the chief rabbi should reside in Athens to facilitate contact with the government, visit Salonica during important Jewish holidays, and occasionally visit other communities in the provinces, with a secretary remaining in Athens to manage current affairs. Each Jewish Community would cover the expenses of the chief rabbi in proportion to its population: Salonica would pay the most.[113] The organ of the Zionist Federation of Greece, *La Renasensia Djudia*, declared, in contrast:

> The true capital of Hellenic Judaism is the Jewish Community of Salonica. And as a consequence, it is here that the site of the chief rabbinate of our country should be located. . . . The Judaism of Salonica, because of its numerical importance and its moral situation, constitutes a capital factor in the general structure of Judaism of the republic. It is natural, it is logical, that she [Salonica] should not be sacrificed in favor of the small community of Athens, where the chief rabbi of Greece would find a veritable desert from the Jewish point of view. This would place him in the near complete impossibility—for lack of contact with the Jewish masses—of entirely fulfilling his mission.[114]

Regardless of the location of the seat of the countrywide chief rabbi, representatives of most Jewish communities throughout Greece expressed support for the plan.[115]

While debates about a countrywide chief rabbi developed, the religious-nationalist group, the Mizrahi, which had separated from the more secular Zionists, launched a smear campaign against Ehrenpreis in its newspaper, *Pro-Israel*. Abraham Recanati, the leader of the Mizrahi, drew on Saül Mézan's *Les Juifs Espagnols en Bulgarie* (1925), which claimed that Ehrenpreis had been "aligned with the plutocracy of Sofia, relying solely on rich and princely power, but in front of the violent opposition of the Zionist democracy he was obliged to leave the country."[116] Recanati further denounced Ehrenpreis as an enemy of "orthodox" Judaism, a consumer of non-kosher meat, a "freethinker," and a "heretic" who rejected the Jewish national ideal.[117] *El Puevlo* refuted these accusations by asserting that Ehrenpreis was "certainly religious," and that his "experiences" in Sofia were only of local concern.[118] *El Puevlo* concluded that, given his status as an "enlightened rabbi" familiar with the ways of the East and of Judeo-Spanish, Ehrenpreis must be hired "at all costs."[119]

The comparison between Jews in Greece and those in Bulgaria caused further anxiety among Salonican Jewish elite. In *Les Juifs Espagnols en Bulgarie*, Mézan also argued that, in the post-Ottoman world, Bulgarian Jews had emerged as most "advanced" in the region due to their Ashkenazic-style embrace of the Zionist ideal: "The Bulgarian Jew is much less Oriental than his brothers in Salonica and Constantinople. He has the energy of the Ashkenazi, less fanatic and refined. . . . That is why the Bulgarian Jews were among the first Sephardis to understand the national ideas of the Ashkenazi Jews, and why they embraced these ideas with fervor leaving far behind other Spanish Jews in the Balkans."[120] Mézan thus dethroned Salonica from its position as the model community in the region.

Jewish communists posed another challenge by entering the dispute and, by forming an unlikely alliance, supported the Mizrahi's campaign against Ehrenpreis. The Jewish communist organ, *Avanti*, denounced Ehrenpreis as a "plutocrat" and an "instrument of the bourgeois Zionists" interested only in the wealthy and in making a handsome salary. Unlike Recanati, who feared that Ehrenpreis was an opponent of Jewish nationalism, communists feared that he supported Zionism too fervently.[121] What began as a polemic among Jewish nationalists—Bensanchi representing the more secular Zionists and Recanati the religious-nationalist faction—now became a class conflict as Jewish communists continued their efforts to undermine the bourgeois hegemony in Jewish communal politics. Ehrenpreis ultimately rejected the offer to become chief rabbi of Greece and indicated that the campaigns conducted against him (by the Mizrahi and communists) strongly influenced his decision.[122]

Ehrenpreis's rejection seemed to be a victory for the unlikely pair of the Mizrahi and the Jewish communists. But the Greek government also had reasons to oppose Ehrenpreis. In his memoir, *Between East and West*, Ehrenpreis recalled that Pangalos, then the dictator of Greece, "showed interest in the plan" for a chief rabbi of Greece and "promised the support of the government."[123] The Greek Ministry of Foreign Affairs, however, saw Ehrenpreis as a symbolic threat to the country. While chief rabbi of Sofia, Ehrenpreis had embarked on a diplomatic mission on behalf of King Ferdinand during the Balkan Wars in which he sought to promote the irredentist aspirations of Bulgaria that included the annexation of Salonica. Ehrenpreis had planned to visit Salonica in 1913 to promote the idea among Jewish leaders but canceled the trip after Greek nationalists, who viewed him as a Bulgarian *comitadji* ("insurrectionary"), threatened to assassinate him.[124]

Ehrenpreis' efforts on behalf of Bulgaria had not been forgotten, especially as tension between Greece and Bulgaria heightened. The same month Ehrenpreis was invited to visit Salonica, Pangalos nearly started a war with Bulgaria over the killing of a Greek soldier by the Bulgarian border patrol (the so-called Incident at Petrich). The Greek Ministry of Foreign Affairs officially disapproved of Ehrenpreis because he was not a Greek citizen—a new criterion—and implied that the chief rabbi of Greece certainly could not be a Bulgarian *comitadji*. The Ministry demanded that the position of chief rabbi of Greece be given to a Greek citizen, just as Greek Catholics had given their leadership position to one of their own, despite efforts to import a candidate from abroad.[125] Although varied segments of the Jewish communal leadership in Salonica supported Ehrenpreis' candidacy, opposition mounted by the Mizrahi, uncharacteristically supported by the communists and the Ministry of Foreign Affairs, ultimately thwarted his bid for chief rabbi.[126]

In the wake of the Ehrenpreis debacle, the Communal Council appointed Haim Habib, a local, well-respected rabbi, to fill the position of *lokum tenens* chief rabbi. Habib took responsibility for religious matters; the Communal Council managed institutional administration and representation vis-à-vis the authorities.[127] The question remained as to whether an authentic Sephardic, Salonican-born rabbi holding Greek citizenship could be found. Ehrenpreis intimated that if any place were to have a Sephardic chief rabbi at its head, it ought to be Salonica. "This is perhaps the last place in the world," he romantically recalled in *The Soul of the East*, "where the Sephardim, this Judaic group of multiform interest, can hope to survive in their pristine purity."[128] But it remained unclear whether Jewish leaders in Salonica would agree that culling a candidate from among their own was the ultimate goal.

One of Ours: The Candidacy of Isaac Emmanuel

The victory of the Mizrahi in preventing Ehrenpreis from becoming chief rabbi was reinforced in November 1926 with the visit to Salonica of Vladimir Jabotinsky, the controversial right-wing leader of the Revisionist Zionist movement. Advocating for the establishment of a Jewish political state in

Palestine, Jabotinsky excited a crowd of four thousand local Jews by proclaiming that "we are trying to establish in Israel something which is similar to what our eyes see in Salonica."[129] He referred to the perception that Jews in Salonica participated in every aspect of the life of the city and managed their own affairs as if an independent Jewish state. Jabotinsky inspired a segment of the Jewish population of Salonica with a sense of self-confidence that had been eroded over the past years and countered the prevailing notion that salvation in the form of a chief rabbi must come from abroad.

Although some editorials in the Judeo-Spanish press during 1927 continued to lament the "decadence" of the Salonican rabbinate and regretted the failure to hire Ehrenpreis, others now called for a Salonican rabbinical renaissance. *El Puevlo* advocated for the reorganization of the Beth Yosef seminary and the strengthening of a privately run seminary, Or Ahaim, to train rabbis and teachers for Salonica and all of Greece. Editorials begged rabbis who had taken up commerce to return to the rabbinate—and several did.[130] The Communal Council initially rejected an offer from the new rabbinical seminary on the Italian-ruled island of Rhodes to educate aspiring Salonican rabbis—although one Salonican student, Salomon Aelion, ultimately studied there for several years.[131] An atmosphere in which Salonican Jewish leaders, now led by Zionists of various orientations, aimed to develop themselves on their own terms provided the opportunity, however brief, to consider one of Salonica's own for the position of chief rabbi.

The Communal Council funded the studies of an up-and-coming Salonican rabbi, Isaac Emmanuel (1896–1972), who now, in 1927, completed exams at the famed Rabbinical Seminary of Breslau and the University of Berlin, and enrolled for graduate study in history at the University of Lausanne. Moise Allatini's 1875 proposal to send the best local students abroad to complete their rabbinical training was finally coming to fruition. Rather than import an academic rabbi with vast culture from abroad (like Toaff or Ehrenpreis), Emmanuel was sent to Europe in the hope that he would return as the first Sephardic academic rabbi, or "Dr. Rabbi." The decision to send Emmanuel to Breslau, rather than to a seminary in France, confirmed that German-oriented Zionists had displaced the established French-oriented, Alliance-led leadership in Salonican Jewish communal politics. Germany, rather than France, now constituted the model "West."

Embodying the spirit of democracy that permeated discussions about the chief rabbi, Emmanuel seemed suited to continue his studies abroad. Not part of a rabbinical dynasty, Emmanuel represented relatively new blood (although his father was a rabbi). As a parvenu, Emmanuel became one of the first rabbis unrelated to the rabbinical families of Molho, Nahmias, or Stroumsa to acquire the coveted *hazaka* ("right") to perform *shehita* ("ritual slaughter") thanks to the training he received from Chief Rabbi Bension Uziel. Contributing to this democratic image, Emmanuel's reputation as a gifted orator required an expansion of the Ahavat Olam (Yenisherlis) synagogue in the Vardar district in order to accommodate the overflow audience.[132]

Emmanuel's affiliation with the Mizrahi movement sealed his selection for the position. He and Abraham Recanati, the leader of the Mizrahi, met as young men at the Evora synagogue in the Vardar district. Emmanuel joined the Salonica branch of the Mizrahi organization, which Recanati founded (1919), and referred to himself as one of Recanati's *hasidim*.[133] Emmanuel studied at the Or Ahaim rabbinical seminary; Recanati sat on its board. When the Communal Council decided to send the most promising rabbinical students abroad, Recanati endorsed Emmanuel.[134] Emmanuel left for Breslau in 1923, simultaneously with the appointment of Emanuel Isaac Brudo as *lokum tenens* chief rabbi and the publication of the ad in *The Jewish Chronicle* soliciting applications from abroad. The Communal Council kept its options open.

While a *seminarista* in Breslau, Emmanuel participated in the debates over the chief rabbi from afar. Writing in *El Puevlo*, Emmanuel indicated that Salonica was not alone in its quest for a chief rabbi. Communities in Frankfurt and Basel as well as Sephardic congregations in Berlin, Hamburg, and London struggled to find qualified spiritual leaders. He sharply criticized "European" rabbis, whom he viewed as incompatible with the needs in Salonica:

> The rabbis of Europe are extremists. They are orthodox or liberal, the first insupportable, the second intolerable; the orthodox will not get along with the council and the liberal not with the *dayanim*. The Ashkenazi is capricious by nature [and] does not compromise easily. Not knowing [Judeo-]Spanish and

Greek, he will be unable to speak to the vast public and to plead the case of our community before the authorities. As a consequence, a man such as this will not remain among us for very long (as was the case with Dr. Ehrenpreis in Bulgaria) and we will return to the same state as today.[135]

The antagonism that Emmanuel experienced in Breslau between Sephardim and Ashkenazim clearly colored his view. Alleging the incongruity of Ashkenazic and Sephardic Jews and alluding to controversies regarding Ehrenpreis, Emmanuel recommended that, if no other candidates could be found, Bension Uziel be invited to return. Emmanuel also implied that if Uziel declined, Emmanuel himself could fill the role.

Inspired by his immersion in *Wissenschaft des Judentums* (the scholarly study of Judaism), Emmanuel also contributed to the growing sense of Salonican Jewish self-confidence that had been shaken since the fire of 1917. He believed that the high caliber of education he received in Breslau could be replicated in Salonica. In *El Djidio*, the Mizrahi annual, he argued that academic rabbis could be trained at home. The key, Emmanuel argued, was to guarantee them employment. This would be accomplished through the establishment of an "academic seminary" to be recognized by the state as a Jewish theological seminary.[136]

As in Europe, a theological seminary in Salonica would teach students not only the Talmud but also philosophy, homiletics, and Jewish history. Students would have to be fully committed to Judaism and Jewish nationalism so that the seminary would not create—in a jab at the Alliance-supported Ottoman chief rabbi—"some Rabbi Haim Nahums." If a theological seminary were established in Salonica, the "flourishing of our Judaism" would be ensured: "We would deserve, with good reason, to call ourselves the worthy descendants of the wise Sephardim who first established celebrated Jewish seminaries and universities in Europe."[137] Salonica could return to its former glory as the great Jewish capital of the region. Nothing immediately materialized from Emmanuel's proposition.

His appeals to the proud history of Jewish Salonica and his call to restore its former glory made Emmanuel an attractive candidate for the position of chief rabbi. While visiting Salonica during the High Holidays in 1926, Emmanuel sought support from the Alliance and the Greek government. He lectured at a venue that promoted integration, the Béné Bérith Lodge, on the subject of Greeks and Jews in antiquity, emphasizing the historic synergies between the two peoples. Judeo-Spanish and French newspapers praised Emmanuel's explication of the relationship between the theocentric view of Judaism and the anthropocentric view of Hellenism, a relationship which, despite inner opposition, resulted in fruitful synthesis throughout history. *L'Indépendant* reported: "The orator concluded in showing that, in antiquity, Greeks and Jews lived as two brotherly peoples and that it is on these traditions of friendship, based on a vast reciprocal understanding, on a very close philosophical communion, which one should, in the present epoch, base the relations between the two peoples."[138] The Greek Foreign Ministry also commented on Emmanuel's lecture.[139] It appeared that Emmanuel found favor from the government—unlike Ehrenpreis, he was a Greek citizen—and from the Alliance, for whom he presented historical and philosophical precedents for accommodation among Greeks and Jews.

As Emmanuel prepared to graduate, with honors, from the Rabbinical Seminary of Breslau in 1927, he emphasized in letters to the Communal Council the benefits he could bring to Salonica as an academic rabbi. At the graduation ceremony in Breslau, professors, government officials, and religious leaders announced that Emmanuel and the other Sephardic graduate, Asher Hananel from Sofia, would "expand Jewish culture among the Sephardim, who at a certain time held the monopoly on Jewish scholarship and literature."[140] The anticipated rapprochement between Sephardim and Ashkenazim would help Salonican Judaism return to its cherished status as City and Mother in Israel. A German newspaper indicated that "Dr. Emmanuel" was "expected to be Chief Rabbi in Saloniki."[141]

When he was "expected," however, was unclear, as Emmanuel, after graduating from Breslau, enrolled at the University of Lausanne. As his studies progressed in history, philosophy, French literature, and psychology, doubts emerged. While still in Breslau, Emmanuel had recognized that certain political groups back home opposed his candidacy but he had begged that "the honorable council must see past this" and continue to support him for the greater good.[142] Ultimately, it appears that Emmanuel did not garner the support of the secular Zionists, who exerted increasing influence on communal affairs. Local newspapers commended Emmanuel's final lecture at the Beth Shaul synagogue in 1929 as "proof" that he "by no means wasted time during his sojourn in Germany" and begged the Communal Council to keep Emmanuel in Salonica: "We must show Rabbi Emmanuel that his future should be here among his own, among the Jewish family of Salonica whose history he traces for us with so much knowledge." But it was clear that his future lay "under other skies."[143]

In recalling his decision to leave Salonica, Emmanuel explained that he wanted to pursue a master's degree and doctorate in Lausanne before assuming the position of chief rabbi, but the Communal Council rejected the proposal.[144] Recognizing that his future in Salonica was not assured, he had begun inquiring about positions in the Americas (New York and Seattle) in 1928.[145] In London, Emmanuel met with a cousin of Rabbi David de Sola Pool, the reverend of Shearith Israel, the Spanish and Portuguese Synagogue in New York. De Sola Pool mockingly suggested that, in meeting with Emmanuel, his cousin "prepare for the Turko-Tutonic-Swiss invasion."[146] De Sola Pool's cousin reported that Emmanuel had been "offered a position in Salonica (which trained him and to which he owes $1230 to be repayed [sic] out of his salary), but disorganization & economic instability there do not allow of adequate salary." As a result, Emmanuel seemed "somewhat lost and discouraged." Described as "gentle," an "idealist," "academic," and "rather good looking," Emmanuel also struck de Sola Pool's cousin, more damningly, as "a follower rather than leader. Loyal follower. Not a politician. Nor material capable of development."[147]

Zionists appeared to agree that Emmanuel would not be a suitable chief rabbi. They feared that, despite his erudition as a scholar, he did not possess the connections or the political acumen to achieve the desired rapprochement between East and West, Ashkenazic and Sephardic, and to interest international Jewish organizations in the plight of his native community. They insinuated that Emmanuel—perhaps any native son—could not transcend his Oriental birth and reach out to the West in ways that Zionists would have liked. Instead, Emmanuel continued his studies in Lausanne, relying on financial support from relatives, and published his doctorate on the history of the Jews of Salonica in 1936 before accepting a position as chief rabbi of the Caribbean island of Curaçao. A final effort to provide Salonica with a suitable local chief rabbi failed.

A Mission Abroad: The Candidacy of Isaac Herzog

Reflecting on Emmanuel's departure and Ehrenpreis' rejection of the post of chief rabbi, Jewish leaders in Salonica presented the question of the chief rabbi as the main issue to be addressed by a new organization created to unite the country's Jews: the Union of the Jewish Communities of Greece (est. 1929).[148] "Now more than ever," declared David Florentin, an advocate for the Union, "everyone recognizes the absolute need to place at the head of Hellenic Judaism a religious leader capable of responding to all our numerous population." Florentin referred to the continued enforcement of the Compulsory Sunday Closing Law, a threat to expropriate the Jewish cemetery, increased unemployment, and antisemitic campaigns in Greek newspapers.[149] Following the suggestion of Bensanchi, the Communal Council established a "special commission" to find a "suitable" chief rabbi in December 1929.[150] An irony came into focus: while the Communal Council sought a spiritual leader for Hellenic Judaism, they looked exclusively beyond the boundaries of Greece to achieve this goal.

The Communal Council dispatched representatives of the special commission to Europe in search of candidates.[151] In 1930, two prominent Zionists, school director Isaac Alsheh and senator Asher Mallah, traveled to Belgrade, Zagreb, Vienna, Baden, Prague, Franzansbad, Berlin, Geneva, Lyon, Barr, Strasbourg, Paris, London, and Dublin in search of candidates. Meanwhile, the Salonica Press Office observed the "mission" with great apprehension, complained to the Greek Foreign Ministry in Athens that the hiring of a foreign chief rabbi was not permitted, and lamented that the Jewish Community seemed intent on going through with their plan regardless.[152]

Unhampered by the Greek state, Alsheh and Mallah received extensive input from the most prominent Jewish figures in Europe who destabilized their assumptions about the relationship between West and East, Ashkenazim and Sephardim. Heinrich Brody, the chief rabbi of Prague, Samuel Grünberg, a professor at the Rabbinical Seminary of Berlin, and Moritz Freier, a rabbi in Berlin, all indicated that the best candidate for the job would be Bension Uziel, the former chief rabbi of Salonica.[153] These assertions suggested that Jewish leaders in Salonica internalized the superiority of the West—and their own inherent inferiority—more than some of these top representatives of so-called Western Judaism. The comments also suggested that Jewish leaders in Europe did not think a Western rabbi would be appropriate for Salonica.

As the Communal Council in Salonica insisted on the need for a chief rabbi from the West, Alsheh ultimately recommended Isaac Herzog (1888–1959), the chief rabbi of Dublin.[154] One of the most eminent Jewish figures of the day, Herzog later became the Ashkenazic chief rabbi of Palestine (and then the State of Israel). The Communal Council contended that only a European rabbi with great stature—like Herzog and unlike Uziel or Emmanuel—could plead the case of the Jews of Salonica before international Jewish organizations and help secure funding for educational and charitable work. Notably, the goal was not necessarily to locate a candidate who could solidify linkages with the state, but rather to identify one who could strengthen relationships with Jewish philanthropies abroad. Given the Communal Council's requirements, Alsheh concluded his confidential report on the mission by declaring: "The ideal chief rabbi for Salonica is Doctor Herzog."[155]

This was a dramatic conclusion, especially considering that, in the debates over Meir's successor in 1920, Alsheh had argued against the European candidates on the grounds that they would bring an unwanted revolution to Salonica's Jews. But different times required a different outlook. Moreover, how could Herzog, whom Alsheh met in Berlin, resist a community of Jews twenty times larger than his own (sixty thousand as compared to three thousand), a community that "gave to Judaism men of great valor and fame"?[156]

As the Communal Council worked with the Union of the Jewish Communities of Greece to court Herzog and corresponded on the matter with the chief rabbi of the United Kingdom, Joseph Hertz, the vacant position played a central role in polemics during the local Jewish communal elections in 1930.[157] *El Puevlo* blamed the current absence of a permanent chief rabbi on the Mizrahi, whose "shameful" campaigns in *Pro-Israel* in 1926 prevented Ehrenpreis from accepting the position.[158] "New steps have been taken," the editorial explained, referring to the trip by Alsheh and Mallah, "for the acquisition of a chief rabbi, which, when our party [the Zionists] comes to power, will be crowned with success."[159]

For *El Puevlo* and the Zionists, the communal elections in 1930—and the parliamentary elections in 1932—produced startling results and undermined the possibility of hiring Herzog. Since a considerable segment of the Jewish population disapproved of the Zionists, who supported Venizelos despite his association with harsh Hellenization measures, general disillusionment reigned among Jewish voters, and many abstained from the election. In 1932, the Radicals (the Mizrahi and Revisionists combined), led by Recanati on an anti-assimilation platform, strikingly aligned with the Alliance in support of the "anti-Zionist" ticket—a further protest against the hegemony of the Zionists and their association with Venizelism. By the time Herzog declined the invitation to become the chief rabbi of Salonica or Greece in 1932, not only had the elections altered communal dynamics, but the effects of the worldwide economic crisis had taken hold, and Jews in Salonica had—for the first time—become victims of violence perpetrated by their Orthodox Christians neighbors.[160]

A Pogrom, a Philosopher, and an Embrace of Hellenism: Sevi Koretz (r. 1933–1943)

In June of 1931, as the Union of the Jewish Communities of Greece met to discuss the question of the chief rabbi and representatives of Hellenic Judaism left for the Zionist Congress in Basel, the local Greek press, led by *Makedonia*, published rumors that members of Salonica's Maccabi, a Zionist youth sports club, had participated in a meeting in Sofia of Bulgarian irredentists—*comitadjis*—who plotted to capture Salonica. The so-called Campbell riots ensued, in which Orthodox Christian nationalists attacked several Jewish neighborhoods. Judeo-Spanish newspapers compared the events to pogroms in eastern Europe. A tragic irony emerged. While Jewish leaders in Salonica, especially Zionists, sought to import an Ashkenazic, academic rabbi to resolve their problems, they also feared that they were now becoming like their persecuted Ashkenazic brethren of eastern Europe. The issue of the chief rabbi now emerged not as a "question" but as a veritable "problem."[161] Some now viewed the hiring of a chief rabbi as a luxury in times of financial crisis. So many Jews had emigrated from Salonica, one writer argued, that the "question of chief rabbi, which presented itself urgently several years ago, has lost much of its importance and also its raison d'être . . . for whom would we be hiring such a chief rabbi?"[162]

Judeo-Spanish newspapers in the early 1930s reflected deep anxieties about increased emigration and conversion, and, in the context of the economic depression, suicide. They revealed fears of the destruction of Salonica's Jews not only by external violence but also by self-inflicted means. The alleged betrayal of Zionists, who remained supportive of Venizelos despite claims that he was responsible for the Jews' woes, contributed to these concerns. Not convinced of the irrelevance of a chief rabbi or the fatalistic view that Jewish life in Salonica was doomed, the Communal Council inaugurated a new search motivated by Zionists who hoped to redeem themselves in the eyes of the Jewish public. Rather than a new mission to Europe, they requested recommendations for candidates from contacts abroad.[163]

In seeking to locate a suitable chief rabbi, the Communal Council appealed to the glorious past of Jewish Salonica and advertised the position as an opportunity to lead one of the oldest, most prestigious Jewish communities in the world—despite the tumultuous current events described in local Jewish newspapers. With no prospects in sight, A. S. Yahuda, the renowned Jerusalem-born writer and personal friend of Einstein and Freud, observed: "The situation of our brothers in Salonica is not what it used to be, and the attitude of our adversaries makes it [the position of chief rabbi] even more challenging and much less attractive."[164]

But a new candidate emerged in November 1932: Sevi (Hirsch) Koretz. Born and raised in Poland, Koretz studied at the Vienna Rabbinical Seminary, the Hochschule für die Wissenschaft des Judentums in Berlin, and the Hamburg Institute for Oriental Studies; he wrote his dissertation on the concept of hell in the Koran. At age thirty-eight, he served as a rabbi in Berlin, where he distinguished himself for his "idealism" and "attachment to Jewish causes."[165] Given his proficiency in German, Yiddish, French, Hebrew, and ancient Greek, Koretz assured the Communal Council that he would quickly learn Judeo-Spanish and modern Greek. Prominent Jewish personalities in Germany, including Kurt Blumenfeld, president of the Zionist Union of Berlin, the acclaimed Rabbi Leo Baeck, and Ismar Elbogen, a professor at the Hochschule in Berlin, encouraged Koretz to apply.[166] Koretz's wife, Gita, later recalled that Blumenfeld "painted a very rosy picture" of Salonica, a place "with many possibilities" and a "springboard" to something even bigger and better.[167] She did so with good reason: concluding his tenure as chief rabbi of Salonica, Jacob Meir had become Sephardic chief rabbi of Palestine; Bension Uziel would follow the same trajectory.

During Koretz's visit to Salonica in 1933, debates focused on the theoretical need for a chief rabbi and the suitability of Koretz, as an Ashkenazic Jew, to lead a Sephardic flock. The rabbinical corps, the Mizrahi, the Alliance, and Jewish communists all expressed initial reservations. Joseph Nehama, the director of the Alliance, worried about the irreconcilable differences in "mentality" between Sephardim and Ashkenazim and surmised that Koretz, as a non-native Romance-language speaker, could not "engage the great public heart to heart, soul to soul" (although he saw promise in Koretz as he had in Ehrenpreis for both were modern, European rabbis).[168]

Rather than focus on mentality, the strongest proponents argued that a rabbi like Koretz could cement financial and spiritual links between Hellenic Judaism and the West. As Asher Mallah, the president of the Zionist Federation of Greece asserted, "In these dark moments, the chief rabbi will constitute the best and most useful link for us with Western Judaism, which, thanks to him [the chief rabbi] will interest itself more in our collectivity."[169] Such a connection, elaborated David Florentin, another leading Zionist, would spark a renaissance within the local Jewish population and inspire alienated youth and the wealthy to participate in communal affairs.[170] The president of the Communal Council, Eliaou Benosiglio, expressed initial ambivalence but now argued that Koretz could bring "immense material and moral profit" through links to Jewish organizations abroad.[171] On a more fundamental level, since the Greek government recognized the Jews of Greece as a religious minority, Mallah wondered: Could a religious minority exist without a religious leader?[172]

Whether Koretz, if accepted, would be a religious or a political leader provoked additional debate that mirrored the broader political landscape. Holding fast to his liberalism, Albert Broudo, a member of the Communal Council, warned that those who supported the hiring of the chief rabbi desired a political leader, specifically a "dictator" rather than a "diplomat"—an "unrealistic and dangerous dream" prohibited by the communal statutes.[173] During the previous decade, Jewish leaders had moved away from the concepts of *hatir* and authoritarianism and toward culture and democracy. In the wake of the Campbell pogrom and with authoritarianism and fascism on the rise in Greece as throughout Europe, discussion now took place in inverted terms. Asher Moisis, president of the General Assembly of the Jewish Community, favored the previously shunned concepts of authority and prestige conferred upon the chief rabbi solely due to his title. Moisis argued against democracy and advocated that only an "authoritative" leader could accomplish the task of reforming communal institutions because he would "not be susceptible to the capricious influences of universal suffrage."[174] Appeals to democracy, which a decade before had secured Uziel's nomination as chief rabbi, no longer resonated.

During his visit to Salonica in 1933, Koretz succeeded in assuaging the initial opposition and secured his nomination to the post of chief rabbi of Salonica. But it was a challenge. Of the six Jewish representatives who met Koretz at the train station in Salonica, only one initially supported his candidacy.[175] El Puevlo reported that the two groups that mounted the firmest opposition, the Mizrahi and the Alliance, were won over by Koretz's personality, background, and vision. In two lectures—in Hebrew and in French—at the Beth Shaul synagogue, Koretz emphasized his ability to combine traditional Judaism with modern philosophy, to reconcile religion and science as well as his yeshiva education and university degree, to appeal to all segments of the Jewish population, to connect Salonica with Jewish organizations abroad, to bridge the divide between his Ashkenazic origins and the Sephardic culture of Salonica, to secure the favor of the Greek government, and to support Jewish culture in Palestine and in Greece. He argued that Salonica had an important role to play in remedying the "spiritual crisis" affecting Jewish communities across the world: "The Sephardi faction gave to the nation a glorious page in its history, and can return to its former place by becoming a link in the great chain of the Jewish nation."[176] In a final meeting with the Rabbinical Council, Koretz recognized his status as a foreigner before a famed community and ingratiated himself with the established rabbinical leadership: "I am not Sephardi and for this reason I do not know the customs of the community in which I find myself. You will enlighten me, you will guide me."[177]

Before concluding his visit to Salonica, Koretz signed a contract for a five-year term, to begin in May 1933, pending the approval of the General Assembly and the government. He departed with the promise of increasing contacts with Jewish centers abroad to interest them in financially supporting Salonican Judaism.[178] With forty-six votes in favor, two abstentions, and six votes in opposition cast by Jewish communists, who held firm to their principled opposition to the idea of a chief rabbi, the General Assembly approved the nomination of Koretz as chief rabbi of Salonica (not of Greece).[179]

Despite initial resistance, the Ministry of Foreign Affairs in Athens compelled Phillipos Dragoumis, the governor general of Macedonia, to arrange for a special law to accord Koretz Hellenic citizenship (and thus relinquish his Polish passport) with the caveat that, in the future, only Greek nationals would be accepted as chief rabbis in Greece.[180] Dragoumis did so reluctantly, again reminding Jewish leaders that the Greek government had forced the Vatican to appoint Greek citizens as Catholic archbishops in Athens and Corfu. He initially insisted that a foreign chief rabbi would never be recognized by the state, but the fact that Jewish leaders convinced the Ministry of Foreign Affairs to pressure Dragoumis to consent to their demand signified that the Jewish Community retained a degree of power to impose its will on the Greek state and compel the latter to compromise.[181] Underlying the anxiety to approve Koretz was a warning from the Greek Embassy in Berlin, which characterized him as "dangerous" due to his fervent Zionist activities, his "managerial skills," and his "eloquence."[182]

As Koretz prepared to assume his position as chief rabbi of Salonica, Hitler came to power in Germany and thousands of Jews began to flee.[183] As part of this mass exit, Koretz represented the dual image of the Ashkenazic Jew to Salonica's Jews: the western, modern rabbi—a philosopher—and the refugee, escaping a new kind of pogrom in Germany, finding shelter in Salonica, and thus confirming the city's status as a Jewish safe haven, as a City and Mother in Israel. Jewish communal politics in Salonica, after years of stalemate, permitted the selection of a new chief rabbi perhaps precisely because he was a foreigner, not yet enmeshed in local politics, an Ashkenazic Jew in a Sephardic environment, a European who could help solidify the transition of the city and its Jews from the East to the West. Before arriving in Salonica, Koretz visited his native Galicia and reported to a newspaper there how he hoped to "save Sephardic Judaism": "to bridge the chasm between Eastern and Western Jews, and to unite them within the framework of the complete Jewish people, for the sake of its spiritual and material existence both in exile and in the land of Israel."[184] Although donning a beard, the new leader came to Salonica dressed neither in a fez nor in a turban or Ottoman robe, but wearing a top hat and a European suit—all signs that the future of both the community and the country would be with the West. The European attire suited his persona as the local press referred to him as "Dr. Koretz," the title prioritizing his PhD over his rabbinical credentials.

During his decade-long tenure as chief rabbi of Salonica, Koretz experienced major controversies and several successes. Tensions flared over the supposed incompatibility between his mentality and that of the local Jews; power struggles between the chief rabbinate and the Communal Council; polemics over Koretz's salary, perceived by some to be exorbitant (15,000 drachmae per month compared to the next highest-paid employee of the Jewish Community, who earned 6,745 drachmae);[185] and allegations that Koretz aspired for self-aggrandizement and exhibited dictatorial tendencies. Debates over administrative reform, budgetary allocations, and the sale of Jewish communal real estate provoked diatribes in the local press, libel cases brought before Greek civil courts, and controversies over the renewal of his contract in 1938.[186] The poetess, Bouena Sarfatty, accused Koretz of blocking those who opposed him from procuring circumcision certificates for their newborn sons—in effect, preventing them from being registered as members of the Jewish Community.[187]

Accomplishing several of the goals set out for him, Koretz learned Judeo-Spanish and Greek quickly, becoming the first and only permanent chief rabbi in the city to speak the language of the state after 1912. One of his first administrative reforms involved hiring a secretary of the Greek language to ensure smooth communication with the authorities.[188] He also reorganized Jewish institutions by creating the centralized Inspection for Jewish Communal Philanthropic Institutions.[189] He further established a European-style class to train rabbis and Jewish teachers, thereby fulfilling a decades-long desideratum. Koretz promoted educational reform more broadly by strengthening both the Jewish and Hellenic aspects of the Jewish communal school curriculum.

Koretz also placed Salonica on the European Jewish map in new, perhaps unexpected, ways. As promised, he brought the economic plight of Salonica's Jews to the attention of international Jewish organizations: the American Joint Reconstruction Foundation subsidized Salonica's Jewish schools, philanthropies, and housing projects.[190] The chief rabbinate in Salonica also emerged as an important contact for eastern European Jews during the

Jewish holiday of Sukkoth. In 1940, Salonica supplied *lulavim, etrogim,* and *hadas* to Koretz's hometown of Rzeszów, the nearby major Jewish center of Cracow, and the Jews in a small town thirty miles to the west—Oświęcim, recently occupied by the Germans and renamed Auschwitz.[191] The last date palm, citrus, and myrtle the Jews of Auschwitz ever saw likely came to them from Salonica.

Koretz further solidified his relationship with the government in Athens, the royal family (once King George II returned to power in 1935), and Metaxas, who became the prime minister and dictator (1936). While the cultivation of these links have often been interpreted as a ploy by Koretz for personal gain, it is important to recall that those Jewish leaders in Salonica who hired him hoped that he would serve as a strong, authoritarian figurehead and Jewish communal representative vis-à-vis the authorities. According to these criteria, Koretz succeeded in consolidating the internal and external affairs of the Jewish Community, much like Chief Rabbi Jacob Covo had during the reign of Sultan Abdul Hamid II. Koretz also engaged in performances of Jewish loyalty to the sovereign that echoed the style and tone of those from the late Ottoman era.

When King George II visited Salonica in 1936, Koretz sought to demonstrate the allegiance of all the city's Jews to the monarchy through an elaborate reception orchestrated at the Beth Shaul synagogue. The Jewish Community erected triumphal arches in the courtyards of the synagogue emblazoned with the phrase "welcome" in Greek and in Hebrew and adorned with flowers. Prior to the start of the Jewish Sabbath, the king arrived with his motorcade to the boisterous greetings from Jewish notables dressed in their best European garb. Koretz pronounced the *sheheheyanu* in Hebrew and then in Greek translation for the king and the crowd to understand. The press reported that King George II listened attentively to the chief rabbi's benediction.[192] Invited to enter the synagogue and stand in front of the *ehal* (Holy Ark), the king observed a series of songs and prayers chanted in his honor. A communal employee and well-known tenor, Albert Rousso, who had studied at the State Conservatory in Salonica and the National Conservatory in Paris, next intoned the *Noten teshua,* the Hebrew prayer for the sustenance of the king and the government.[193] Koretz translated the prayer

Figure 2.2. Chief Rabbi Sevi Koretz and George II, King of the Hellenes, Salonica, 1936. Source: Yad Vashem. Published with permission.

into Greek and delivered a speech in Greek in which he expressed the Jews' "devotion to their homeland and to the king."[194]

In his speech, Koretz emphasized the synergies between Judaism and Hellenism. He referred to Jewish roots in the city dating back to Hellenistic antiquity and expressed gratitude for the king's recognition of all citizens of the country—both "Christian Hellenes" and "Jewish Hellenes"—as "children of the beloved homeland." He praised the continued efforts of both populations to work together for the "prosperity and progress of the homeland" just as they had in antiquity and during the "era of enslavement"—a reference to more than four centuries of Ottoman rule now framed in Greek nationalist rhetoric. Koretz flattered the king with grand evocations of his "glorious scepter" that bound all of his citizens in an "indelible union" for the sake of the homeland and all of humanity:

> In ancient times, the Greek spirit and the Jewish religious genius showed the way for humanity by proclaiming great and eternal truths. We believe that the descendants of Plato and Aristotle and the heirs of the teachings of the prophets, in collaborating, and in uniting their forces, will offer, under the favorable influence of your majesty, a new contribution toward the regeneration of the spirit and the morale of humanity today.[195]

Koretz concluded by offering a prayer, also in Greek, that God continue to lead the king according to the sublime traditions of ancient Hellenism for the sake and glory of the Hellenic homeland and of world civilization. Lofty rhetoric also characterized how Koretz engaged with Metaxas. Koretz presided over anniversary celebrations of Metaxas' Fourth of August Regime in the Beth Shaul synagogue that echoed in form and style the celebrations orchestrated for the anniversary to the ascension to the throne of Sultan Abdul Hamid II in the Talmud Tora during the late Ottoman era.[196]

Through these celebrations, Koretz attempted to reposition Salonica's Jews, at least on the symbolic level, within the grand narrative of Hellenism, and contributed to a semblance of stability on the eve of World War II. But others perceived Koretz's patriotic statements to be disingenuous. A Greek newspaper in Athens, *Eleftheros Anthropos*, viewed the official representative of the "Jewish Hellenes" as a "foreigner" and "cosmopolitan," despite his acquisition of Greek citizenship, due to his suspiciously extensive knowledge of foreign languages.[197] A "monstrous" rumor even circulated that Koretz sought to obtain Turkish citizenship.[198]

In a tragic irony, rather than represented as the savior of either Hellenic Judaism or Sephardic Judaism, Koretz has been remembered in a negative light, most notoriously as an alleged Nazi collaborator. Detractors claimed that Koretz handed over lists containing the names of Salonica's Jews that facilitated their deportation to Auschwitz (although recent research indicates that Koretz could not have given over the lists, as he was in Athens at the time this act was alleged to have taken place).[199] Outrageous accusations abounded. Bouena Sarfatty claimed that, amidst the destruction of the Jewish cemetery during the German occupation, Koretz looted Jewish tombs and stole jewels to display in his homemade "museum."[200] One survivor even declared that, embittered by the chief rabbi's alleged betrayal, a group of Salonican Jews murdered Koretz in the camps.[201]

Contrary to this revenge fantasy, Koretz actually died of typhus in 1945, just after the liberation of Bergen-Belsen. The survivor's delusional claim indicates the extent to which the chief rabbi's alleged treachery had become entrenched among Salonican survivors. Koretz's name unsurprisingly topped a list of more than fifty so-called privileged Jews accused of collaborating with the Nazis whom the Jewish Community of Salonica brought to the Greek state courts in 1945—a unique war crimes trial and the only one in which a European state imprisoned and executed Jews for their role during the occupation.

The perception of Koretz as collaborator endured because it fulfilled—and continues to fulfill, as Minna Rozen points out—the need to rationalize the tragedy among Salonican Jews themselves, Greek society, and Israeli society. Koretz became a scapegoat within the "official collective memory." Salonican Jews could attribute the destruction of their community to a selfish, foreign, German-speaking rabbi and appeal to pre-war tensions to impute responsibility to a leader who betrayed them in the gravest moment. In Greece, Orthodox Christian leaders and society at large could also attribute the annihilation of their Jewish neighbors to their own leader, the chief rabbi, and in so doing exculpate themselves from any responsibility or wrongdoing as bystanders or collaborators by repeating the refrain that the Jews "did it to themselves." Later, Salonican and Greek Jews in Israel demonized Koretz as a feeble leader who willingly delivered his flock to the Nazis like sheep to the slaughter by appealing to Israeli ideology, which sought to overturn the stereotype of the weak, diasporic Jew.[202]

A previously unknown document in the archive of the Greek Ministry of Foreign Affairs compels us to reexamine the accusations leveled against Koretz. While still imprisoned in Bergen-Belsen, two months before its liberation, Koretz sent a message to the Rabbinical Association of Switzerland (RAS)—likely because that country remained neutral. The RAS then wrote, in German, to the Greek foreign minister in Bern detailing Koretz's request: that after the war, he be given the "opportunity to return to his position as chief rabbi in Salonica" of which he had been the "lawful holder" until the German occupation.[203] Such a plea suggests that Koretz sought to return to Salonica not only for the sake of employment, but also because he likely did not see himself as a traitor, could not imagine that his flock might seek to kill him, and believed he could contribute to the reconstruction of the city's Jewish life.

Two well-known Salonican Jewish intellectuals who denounced Koretz in their post-war writings contributed considerably to the official collective memory that painted the chief rabbi as a traitor. They had personal reasons to demonize him. The first, Michael Molho, who laid out scathing allegations against Koretz in *In Memoriam* (1948), believed that if his own career had developed differently, he would have become the chief rabbi of Salonica instead of Koretz. There is no evidence, however, that Molho was considered as a candidate during the interwar years, although he did become the chief rabbi of Salonica after the war (1947–1950).[204]

Another author of a contemptuous account of Koretz's wartime role was Isaac Emmanuel, the only Salonican Jew considered for the position of permanent chief rabbi during the interwar years. Emmanuel claimed that Salonica's Jews never should have hired a foreign, Ashkenazic rabbi such as Koretz: "The nomination of Dr. Koretz as chief rabbi of Salonica was the biggest mistake that the Communal Council committed in its history."[205] Perhaps more so than Molho, Emmanuel held a grudge despite the decision by the new Central Board of the Jewish Communities of Greece in Athens to invite Emmanuel to serve as chief rabbi of all of Greece in 1949. Despite having desired such a position twenty years before, Emmanuel, later serving as a rabbi in Panama City, declined the offer so he could focus on completing several historical studies on Salonican Jews.[206] Such historical work, Emmanuel believed, would constitute his personal contribution to saving Sephardic Judaism.

Beyond personal animosities, Emmanuel held political resentments. Emmanuel "blamed" the idea of hiring a European, university-educated rabbi like Koretz on the "liberals," the Zionists and the reposition Béné Bérith (an organization associated in Salonica with the Alliance) who represented the more Europeanized, secular, Jewish middle classes.[207] Emmanuel aligned himself with the opposition, the Mizrahi, the religious-nationalist self-proclaimed guardians of Sephardic tradition. After the war, the former head of the Mizrahi, Abraham Recanati, encouraged Emmanuel to "blame" Koretz for the destruction of the Salonica's Jews more than he initially had in his drafts.[208] Accordingly, in the final version of the well-known memorial book, *Zikhron Saloniki: Yerushalayim del Balkan* ("A memorial to Salonica: Jerusalem of the Balkans"), Emmanuel argued that the Communal Council conducted its search for the chief rabbi in a "haphazard" manner and that the entire Jewish population, save the Zionists and Béné Bérith, unequivocally supported the continued tenure of Rabbi Haim Habib, the Salonican-born, *lokum tenens* chief rabbi.[209] Conveniently, Emmanuel omitted from his published account his own candidacy, the fact the he had also courted the support of the Béné Bérith, and his proposal to bring Bension Uziel back from Palestine to serve again as Salonica's chief rabbi (rather than permit Habib to continue in the post).

According to Emmanuel's post-war account, Habib had embodied the ideal Sephardic type, the last link in a 450-year chain of native Salonican rabbis characterized by the qualities of wisdom, honesty, modesty, religiosity, and altruism. On the eve of the war, *La Aksion* had hoped that Habib would become the chief rabbi of Tel Aviv as a step toward becoming the Sephardic chief rabbi of Palestine and as a sign of "the continuation of a very old tradition according to which Thessaloniki, the most important center of rabbinic culture of the Near East, provides great rabbis to almost all of the Sephardic centers."[210] It was not to be. The war began and, once Jacob Toledano (formerly a chief rabbi in Egypt) filled the position in Palestine in 1941, Habib and the rest of Salonica's Jews were under Nazi occupation.[211] After the war, Salonicans in Haifa created the Or Ahaim synagogue in memory of Habib, who perished in Auschwitz.

Conclusion: Saving Sephardic Judaism?

Conceptualized as an issue of central significance for Salonica's Jews from the late nineteenth century through the interwar years, the question of the chief rabbi reflected both real and aspirational relationships between the city's Jewish elite and the state—the Ottoman Empire and, subsequently, Greece—as well as with European Jews. With the introduction of the position of *haham bashi* and the subsequent engagement of the chief rabbi in the political sphere, first exemplified by Jacob Covo, the nature of Jewish leadership in the city was transformed. The ideal rabbi no longer could satisfy his position through erudition and Talmudic knowledge alone but rather required the skills of a worthy representative who could serve as spokesperson for the city's Jews and a partner with the authorities. As much as a teacher, sage, or rabbinic judge, the chief rabbi now needed to be a politician and a diplomat skilled in external affairs. Figures like Covo and Meir, although in different ways, cemented their relationships with the authorities.

The transfer of the city to Greek rule and the resulting instability required Jewish communal leaders, increasingly fragmented along political lines, to reframe the role of the chief rabbi. The brief tenure of Bension Uziel followed by a decade with no permanent chief rabbi revealed the difficulty of the transition to the Greek state and the deep divisions over the future of Jewish life in the city. Only as the political tides in Europe began to turn away from parliamentary politics and toward authoritarianism did Salonica's Jewish leaders agree on a permanent leader in 1933. Koretz's style represented a throwback to the late Ottoman era of elaborate expressions of imperial allegiance now transferred to the Greek royal family and to Metaxas. Koretz also represented the new, for he was an academic rabbi, European, modern— and Ashkenazic. Paradoxically, as an outsider, he learned the Greek language and the rhetoric of Hellenism and projected an image of Jewish loyalty to the Greek crown that mirrored the practices of the late Ottoman era.

As seen through the prism of the chief rabbi, Jewish politics in Salonica served as a barometer of larger political trends. As the first chief rabbi to serve as *haham bashi* and *rav akolel*, Jacob Covo centralized his power to an unprecedented extent; his style, and the duration of his tenure, overlapped with that of the absolutism of Sultan Abdul Hamid II. Jacob Meir arrived in Salonica in 1908 as a progressive force from another province, ushering in a new era for Salonica's Jews that paralleled the ascendance of the Young Turks, who launched their revolution from Salonica (also in 1908) and introduced modernizing reforms. Following the transfer of Salonica to Greek rule and the conclusion of World War I, the same debates over the national constitution in Athens—monarchy versus republic—played out within the Jewish Community as represented in the selection of Bension Uziel as chief rabbi. But just as his tenure was short-lived, concluding in 1923, so too was that of the monarchy, displaced with the proclamation of the Hellenic Republic the following year (1924). The decade of primarily parliamentary politics in Athens that followed corresponded to the decade-long period in which Salonica lacked a chief rabbi. The instability in Athens paralleled that within Jewish communal politics while also contributing to the crystallization of the new category of "Hellenic Judaism." The hiring of Koretz as chief rabbi in 1933, partly on the grounds that he would not be susceptible to the so-called capricious influences of universal suffrage, presaged the restoration of the Greek monarchy and the establishment of Metaxas' dictatorship. The trajectory of the question of the chief rabbi clearly paralleled broader political trends in the Ottoman Empire and in Greece.

The desperation with which some Jewish elite in Salonica sought a chief rabbi from afar, especially during the interwar years, reveals an underlying anxiety about the status and prestige of the city's Jewish collectivity in the post-Ottoman world, a far cry from its previous heights as *ir va-em be-Israel*. Jewish leaders sought to rehabilitate their image and their moral and material situation. Within this context, definitions of "Sephardic" became contested and fungible. Some liberals argued for a broader conceptualization of Sephardim to include European Jews from Italy and France united with their Judeo-Spanish-speaking brethren through shared mentality and Romance languages. Political prerogatives also reshaped the nature of the debate. The definitive split of the liberals into Zionists, who gained power in interwar Jewish communal politics, and supporters of the Alliance, who lost sway, shifted the model of what it meant to be Western away from France and toward Germany.

But Zionists and Alliance-supporters alike feared that it was not possible for one of their native sons to transcend the Oriental milieu of his birth, gain acceptance among European Jews, represent the Jewish collectivity before the authorities, and return Salonica to its rightful place as a celebrated Jewish metropolis. They believed that only an Ashkenazic Jew, by virtue of his European birth and education, could achieve these goals. While Jewish leaders expressed anxiety that they were becoming like Ashkenazim in the aftermath of the 1931 pogrom, they paradoxically emulated the Ashkenazim as they sought to overcome their purportedly retrograde, Oriental origins and become fully European Jews. Especially Zionists, who increasingly shaped the trajectory of interwar Jewish politics, sought to become Hellenic Jews not only because they wanted to be seen as Greek patriots, but also because they desired the respect accorded to all other Jewish collectivities defined within the framework of world Zionism according to national boundaries, whether French Jews, German Jews, or Polish Jews. In the aftermath of the collapse of the Ottoman Empire, the quest for a chief rabbi of Salonica and the appeal to save Sephardic Judaism was ironically addressed by endorsing Ashkenazim to serve as Sephardic rabbis. Activists in Tel Aviv even nominated Koretz as Sephardic chief rabbi of Palestine in 1939.[212]

Although some Jewish notables in Salonica believed that none of their own rabbis were worthy enough to serve as their leader after 1907, in another paradox, Salonican rabbis led Jewish communities across the globe: in Greece (Athens, Hania [Crete], and Larissa), in competing Sephardic centers in Bulgaria (Sofia, Plovdiv, Dupnitsa, and Ruschuk) and Turkey (Izmir), in Palestine and Lebanon (Tel Aviv, Jerusalem, and Tripoli), further westward into Europe (Antwerp, Amsterdam, and Paris), and in the Americas (New York, New Brunswick [New Jersey], and Curaçao). When Isaac Emmanuel became chief rabbi of Curaçao in 1936, he pointed out the fitting precedent: the first chief rabbi of the island, the oldest Jewish community in the western hemisphere dating back to the seventeenth century, had been a Sephardic Jew with family roots in Salonica.[213] For Emmanuel, it appeared as if the gap separating the historic grandeur of sixteenth- and seventeenth-century Salonica from the present was beginning to be filled. The echoes of the City and Mother in Israel continued to be heard, if only by Salonica's rabbinical sons, who brought a piece of their mother city with them wherever they went.

Back home, Salonica's Jews had looked to non-Salonican rabbis since 1907 to guide them across the divide between the Ottoman Empire and the Greek nation-state. The week that the Germans occupied Salonica in

April 1941, just before Passover, the synagogues offered a special *Ashkava* ("memorial prayer") for those great rabbis of recent memory—including Jacob Covo and Jacob Meir—who "maintained the fame of our community" and "brought glory to our collectivity."[214] The chief rabbi, in other words, became a symbol of the status of the city's Jews as a whole: "A good leader is everything; he personifies all."[215]

CHAPTER 3

MORE SACRED THAN SYNAGOGUE

The School

De la kuna saliras
Ala eskola entraras,
I tu ayi mi kerido ijiko
A meldar te ambezaras.

From the cradle
To school you'll go,
And there my darling son
You'll learn to read.

—Judeo-Spanish lullaby[1]

The editors of a Judeo-Spanish textbook published in Salonica in 1880 recognized that education played a key role in cultivating allegiances among
the youth and instituting in them a sense of their national identity: "The re-
formation of a nation must begin with children . . . as that which is planted
in their hearts bears fruit that does not cease but with life itself."[2] From the
late Ottoman era into the interwar years in Greece, Jewish leaders, school
directors, teachers, parents, and journalists in Salonica, as well as government
officials, contested the aims of elementary education: Were Jewish youth—
especially boys but later girls, too—to construe their nation as Jewish or as
Ottoman and subsequently Greek? How would they learn to conceive of the
relationship between their status as members of the Jewish Community and
as citizens of the Ottoman Empire and later of Greece?

Schools served as the primary sites for shaping and inculcating a sense
of national identification and of literacy among citizens throughout Europe
during the nineteenth century. In the region surrounding Salonica, schools
spread nationalist messages and transformed the children of Orthodox

Christian peasants into Bulgarian or Greek ideologues intent on achieving national liberation from the Ottoman Empire, and they also contributed to a series of violent conflicts during the late nineteenth and early twentieth centuries.[3] In the nineteenth century, the Ottoman Empire sought to position itself on a par with European states while simultaneously combating secessionist nationalist sentiment developing in non-Muslim schools as well as the rising influence of missionary schools. The Ottoman Empire looked to France as its model for state educational reform, the establishment of public schools, the training of teachers, and the development of textbooks.[4] Despite holding up France as the model, neither the Ottoman nor the Greek state introduced the principle of *laïcité*, the separation of church and state, into the political systems. A single government ministry in Greece retained responsibility for education and religion, which explains, in part, why educational practices in Salonica did not follow the same trajectory as elsewhere in Europe.[5]

Jewish leaders in Salonica sought to preserve their sense of communal autonomy and considered the self-administration of their own schools to be the cornerstone of their privileges in the late Ottoman era and, later, of their minority rights in Greece after World War I. They greeted Greek Law 2456 of 1920, which granted the Jewish Community the power to run its own schools, as a victory—one that faced continuous challenges over the subsequent two decades. More interventionist than the late Ottoman state, the Greek state, especially during the interwar years, sought to Hellenize its new territories in the north inhabited by Turkish and Albanian-speaking Muslims, Slavic-speaking Orthodox Christians, newly arriving Turkish-speaking Orthodox Christian refugees from Asia Minor, and Judeo-Spanish-speaking Jews. While complete religious homogeneity could not be achieved, perhaps linguistic uniformity could. But this goal was not simple, as debates over which form of Greek should be adopted as the national language—the archaic *katharevousa* or the vernacular *demotiki*—caused extensive controversy, including riots in Athens.[6]

The Greek state viewed the linguistic Hellenization of Salonica's Jews as the key to their incorporation into Greek society. For this reason, the director of the Salonica Press Bureau argued in 1926: "The question of education is the most important issue concerning the Jews."[7] Through education, Jews could learn "to speak Greek like Greeks," to "learn the language of Homer."[8] But different Jewish factions sought to shape the curriculum to suit their own interests and aspirations, which often conflicted with each other or with the state, whereas others sought to achieve a tenuous balance. The issue of language instruction—Judeo-Spanish, Hebrew, French, and Greek—became particularly embattled. The school became the laboratory in which to test and contest the possibilities and processes of transforming the children of the last generation of Ottoman Jews into the first generation of Hellenic Jews, proficient in the Greek language and loyal Greek citizens.

The multiple allegiances at play in the contest over Jewish education and identity are embodied in a postcard circulated for the Jewish New Year in 1926 by the Mair Aboav Orphanage for Girls, established at the initiative of Athehia (a Jewish women's society) and the Mizrahi (the Jewish religious-nationalist party).[9] Sitting in uniform at their desks, with closely cropped hair, the girls and their classroom project a European air. The name of the orphanage—displayed at the top left in Judeo-Spanish and on the banner at the bottom, in larger font, in Greek and French—highlights the Jewish

Figure 3.1. Students and instructor of the Mair Aboav Orphanage for Girls, Salonica, 1926. Source: Jewish Museum of Thessaloniki. Published with permission.

(and specifically Sephardic), Greek, and European layers of identity. The chalkboard in the back of the classroom, displaying the words "teacher" and "student" in Greek and in Judeo-Spanish (in the *soletreo* Hebrew script), reinforce these dual identities. At the back right, the teacher stands before a map of Greece, still with parts of Asia Minor included within the country's borders in fulfillment of the *Megali Idea,* and points to the city of Salonica. Above her is a Hebrew greeting for the Jewish New Year. A Star of David at the top center encapsulates the word Zion, referring to the Land of Israel—a geography removed from Salonica and Greece—and is flanked by the year according to the Hebrew calendar (5687). The multiple languages, geographies, and iconographies on display in this image, although a seemingly dissonant and contradictory constellation of symbols, represent the complexities of Jewish identity in Salonica and the role of the school in reconciling them. It is not surprising that the Judeo-Spanish press claimed that "school is more sacred than the synagogue" due to its unmatched role in shaping the religious, communal, and political identities of future generations of Jews as they traversed the divide from the Ottoman Empire to the Greek nation-state.[10]

Civilizing Missions: Missionaries, the Ottoman State, and the Alliance Israélite Universelle

During the nineteenth century, several intellectual and ideological currents that entered the Ottoman Jewish world transformed the nature of education and the development of Ottoman imperial citizenship. Protestant missionaries, French Jewish educators, and, to a lesser extent, the Ottoman state each promoted their own civilizing mission that sought the allegiance of Salonican Jews. The school became a key locus of contestation. Lay and religious Jewish leaders grappled with and appropriated aspects of the civilizing missions, sometimes reformulating them to suit their own needs. All players recognized the field of education as intimately tied to questions of loyalty and to a sense of belonging.

Similarly, the nature of Jewish education in Salonica evolved over the nineteenth century. As in the Ottoman Empire more generally, teachers initially focused on religious instruction at the elementary level and taught Jewish boys to read Judeo-Spanish and Hebrew in order to recite synagogue prayers, the weekly portion of the Bible (*parasha*), and selections from the

Prophets (*aftara*). While some Jewish youth met with private teachers (*mela-medim*) for lessons at the *meldar* (a small Jewish religious primary school similar to the *heder* in eastern Europe), the Talmud Tora Agadol served as the main institution that catered to Jewish religious instruction and also functioned as a synagogue, religious court (*beth din*), and communal meeting place. Operational since 1520 and located in the center of Salonica, the Talmud Tora had served as the site of high-level rabbinic and scholarly exchange. Although less renowned as a rabbinical academy in the nineteenth century, it continued to unite Jewish youth regardless of their synagogue affiliation or class and remained a symbol of the long-standing Jewish presence in the city.[11]

Some students, however, viewed their experience at the Talmud Tora as detrimental to their educational progress. Saadi a-Levi, who became an important printer in Salonica, despised his "cruel teachers," who implemented the *falaka* (bastinado, or caning of the soles of the feet) to punish recalcitrant students by appealing to a Judeo-Spanish proverb: "It takes blood to learn every letter" (*la letra kon sangre entra*). Saadi, as he was popularly known, also attributed his status as an "ignoramus" to the cruelty and inefficiency of his teachers. His description dovetails with other depictions of Ottoman religious teachers as "physically abusive" and "pedagogically primitive" by those who sought to reform the system.[12]

The arrival of Protestant missionaries to the Ottoman Empire from countries such as the United States and Britain during the early nineteenth century opened new avenues for education in the name of civilization and humanity. The arrival of missionaries in Ottoman society also provoked conflict with local religious leaders—Jewish, Orthodox Christian, Armenian, and Muslim—and the state. The Ottoman state saw missionaries as a conversionist threat and as provocateurs of nationalist and secessionist movements, especially among Christians. While missionaries initially sought to convert Jews by educating them in the truth of Christianity and "restoring" them to Jesus and to Palestine in order to bring about the messianic age, ultimately they received a warmer welcome among certain Armenian circles in search of spiritual and political liberation that contributed to the establishment of the Protestant *millet* in 1846.[13]

Ottoman Jews interfaced with missionaries primarily in regard to education. William Schauffler of the American Board of Commissioners for

Foreign Missions, for example, published translations into Judeo-Spanish of the Hebrew Bible and New Testament and distributed them in Istanbul and Salonica.[14] Saadi a-Levi viewed missionaries as a source of greater insight into Judaism than his teachers at the Talmud Tora.[15] Missionaries also established schools that promoted proselytism but also provided students—including girls—with a modicum of practical or secular knowledge: geography, history, handicrafts, and foreign languages. Missionary reports indicated that while some Jewish parents sent their children to missionary schools, they were mostly attracted to these "practical" skills, especially foreign language instruction; few converted.[16]

In response to missionary activities, the rabbinical elite in Salonica expanded efforts to ensure that Jewish youth remained within the fold by increasing publications in Judeo-Spanish—including school primers—that offered Jewish interpretations of holy texts to arm literate Jews with the necessary knowledge to refute Christian perspectives.[17] The missionary threat also provoked Jewish leaders in Salonica to establish their own Jewish schools for Jewish students, in particular, a girls' school following an announcement that eight Jewish girls attending a Protestant school were going to convert.[18] The new Jewish communal schools aimed to compete with the missionary schools by offering traditional religious instruction and secular subjects, practical skills, and foreign languages. The educational measures enacted by Jewish communal elite to minimize the influence of missionaries paralleled the initiatives undertaken by the Ottoman state over the course of the nineteenth century.

Recognizing the dangers posed by missionary schools and seeking to combat the deleterious effects of European ideological trends, such as nationalism, the Ottoman state included educational reform as a part of the broader project of imperial reorganization, the *Tanzimat* (1839–1876). A decree in 1856 sought to position the Ottoman Empire "among civilized nations" by designating all residents of the empire, Muslims and non-Muslims alike, equal before the law, while granting non-Muslims the "privilege" to shape their own educational programs: "Every community is authorized to establish public schools of science, art and industry."[19] Each community could teach religious subjects and utilize its own language—and not necessarily Turkish—for classroom instruction. The 1869 Ottoman Education Regulation further codified these policies.[20]

Embedded in the *Tanzimat* was an essential tension with which Otto-man Jews—as well as the other non-Muslims—grappled: exercising their privileges that granted them powers of self-government, including with regard to education, while simultaneously becoming patriotic Ottoman citi-zens. The Ottoman state offered a vision of imperial citizenship that did not initially require non-Muslims to learn Turkish to the exclusion of their own languages. The resulting civic nationalism theoretically enabled non-Muslims to express their political loyalty in their own languages while professing their own religions. According to this model of supra-communal Ottomanism, one could become a loyal Ottoman by supporting the continued territorial integrity of the empire without necessarily knowing Turkish. Knowledge of Turkish was required only for those who sought positions in the govern-ment.[21] The Jewish case further demonstrates that linguistic and political allegiances were not identical. The Ottoman state developed an image of the empire's Jews as *en sadık millet* ("most loyal community"), as supporters of the sultan and opponents of secessionist nationalism. Ottoman Jewish elite cultivated this image even as Jews engaged with the Turkish language less than any other non-Muslim population.[22] Not one publication in Ottoman Turkish by Jews in Salonica has come to light.

Jewish elite in Salonica and other Ottoman cities nonetheless advocated that Jews learn Turkish to demonstrate their fidelity to the state and their status as modern, Ottoman citizens. In 1840, the chief rabbi in Istanbul en-couraged Jewish parents across the empire to hire teachers to instruct their children in the Turkish language so as to "earn the respect of the govern-ment."[23] Several Judeo-Spanish newspapers, especially *El Tiempo* in Istanbul, promoted Turkish among the Jewish masses.[24] But proficiency in the lan-guage remained far from a reality for most Ottoman Jews, including those in Salonica. Only in 1895 did a cohort of Jews in Salonica, inspired by the estab-lishment of *Asir*, the first Ottoman Turkish newspaper in the city, form the Committee for the Study of the Turkish Language, which organized night classes; enrollment never totaled more than a few dozen.[25] According to *La Epoka*, three-quarters of the Jews in the city still did not know Turkish in 1900.[26] *El Avenir* explained that even if Ottoman Jews did not know Turkish well, their Judeo-Spanish had already undergone a process of Ottomaniza-tion: "Finding ourselves in continual contact with the Ottomans, we have mixed into our language various words and ideas drawn from the Turkish language, and we have begun to explain all our sentiments, all our thoughts, as if they had come from the heart of an Ottoman."[27] The editorial concluded with the hope that Jews would continue to improve their knowledge of Turkish but conceded that the imprint already made by Turkish on Judeo-Spanish provided evidence of the Ottomanization of the city's Jews.

The prospect that Ottoman citizens could express their patriotism legitimately in a language other than Turkish became clear in Ottoman Jewish schoolbooks. In 1902, Isaac Yeoshua, a Salonican Jew employed by the Ottoman state, published a didactic 112-page Judeo-Spanish textbook entitled *An Overview of the History of the Ottoman Empire: Lessons and Reflections.* Mehmed Reşad, the Ottoman Minister of Public Education, endorsed the publication.[28] The book provided Jewish students with an awareness of Ottoman history (especially the exploits of the sultans) and promoted their identification with the state. The booklet demonstrates that neither Jews nor state officials perceived linguistic and political allegiance to be synonymous within an idealized vision of Ottomanism. Jews could promote Ottoman patriotism without relinquishing their identification as Jews or their Jewish language. After the reintroduction of the constitution in 1908 and the overthrow of Sultan Abdul Hamid II, however, the Young Turk regime enforced Turkish language instruction in schools across the empire, but Salonica did not remain within Ottoman territory long enough to see the demands play out and missed the aggressive "Citizen, speak Turkish!" campaigns of the late 1920s and 1930s in the Republic of Turkey.[29]

Faced with the Ottoman state's relatively hands-off approach during the nineteenth century, seeking to improve the level of Jewish education at the Talmud Tora, to embrace the new sentiment of Ottomanism, and to fend off advances by missionaries, Jewish elite in cities like Salonica initially looked to fellow Jews, especially those in the West—France and Italy, in particular—for assistance. In 1859, leading Jewish merchant families from Italy living in Salonica, known as *Francos*, experimented with new educational practices in Jewish schools. At the invitation of Salonica's most famous *Franco*, Moise Allatini, a teacher named Dr. Lippman from Strasbourg arrived to establish a European-style Jewish school. But after five years of tensions with local rabbis, Lippman left.[30]

Soon Allatini and other Jewish elite turned their attention to Paris, where a new organization, the Alliance Israélite Universelle (est. 1860), promoted educational goals that resonated with their own. Motivated by its own civilizing mission, the leaders of the Alliance sought to uplift their fellow Jews in the Orient whom they viewed as suffering in a state of poverty and ignorance under the yoke of the sultan. The Alliance established schools to provide students with practical skills and knowledge of secular subjects, especially the French language, in order to transform them into productive, loyal, and modern citizens modeled on emancipated French Jewry.[31] The approach of the Alliance was infused with the spirit of nineteenth-century liberalism (and paternalism) that emphasized the capacity of humans to change through education and resonated with the state ideology of Ottomanism: both encouraged Ottoman Jews to consider themselves not only Jews but also citizens.

Allatini proudly declared that the first Alliance schools in Salonica, established in 1873, brought great "honor" to the city's Jews. The new educational institutions—which, in 1880, catered to 662 boys and girls and made special provisions for impoverished children—emerged as models for the rest of the city's residents. The Alliance schools trained a new generation of Jewish elite in Salonica, familiar with Jewish religious texts and endowed with a taste for European literature.[32] Non-Jews sent their children to Alliance schools because they provided a good education according to European standards. Supporters fondly remembered Allatini for having "consecrated his life to the good of humanity and particularly to the moral and material improvement of his fellow coreligionists, whom he brought out of ignorance and misery."[33] As Salonica entered Greek jurisdiction, *El Liberal* celebrated the successes of the civilizing mission of the Alliance that contributed to the creation of new generations of skilled craftsmen and a professional Jewish class. The newspaper indicated that the Alliance operated eight private schools in the city in 1913, including kindergartens and elementary schools for boys and girls as well as professional schools (the central school named in honor of Allatini); they enrolled 3,180 students.[34]

Similar to the paradox at the center of the program of Ottomanism, which sought to balance non-Muslims' religious and cultural commitments to their own communities while promoting their political loyalty to the state, a tension sat at the core of the mission of the Alliance, which orga-nized its curriculum around French despite the vast distance from Paris. By the end of the nineteenth century, an influential, upwardly mobile swath of Salonica's Jews (as well as Orthodox Christians and Muslims) possessed sufficient proficiency in the language to warrant the creation of a French-language newspaper, *Journal de Salonique* (est. 1895), the first local publication to appear in an "occidental language."[35] The acquisition of fluency in French on the part of middle- and upper-class Jews did not, however, cause immediate alarm on the part of the Ottoman state. Added to Judeo-Spanish as the mother tongue, French was folded into Jewish bourgeois identity in Salonica and other urban centers without imped-ing claims to Ottoman loyalty.[36] But rather than guide Jews toward the Ottoman capital in Istanbul and Turkish culture, the Alliance directed stu-dents toward French culture and Paris—the capital of modernity—thereby creating dissonance between the drive to emulate the West and enter the European cultural world, on the one hand, and to activate their status as Ottoman citizens, on the other.[37]

With the support of the governor of the city, the Alliance schools eventually offered Turkish lessons that supplemented the main, French curriculum. The Ottoman state began to send Turkish language instructors to Alliance schools in 1894.[38] In 1900, *El Avenir* celebrated the Alliance's hiring as its advanced Turkish instructor a certain Osman Effendi, a secre-tary for the Oriental Railway who had taught at a local Greek school. The newspaper applauded the new addition to the Alliance's teaching staff but encouraged Jewish notables to promote the Turkish language further by offering awards to those Jewish students most successful in learning the state language.[39]

Motivated by the ideology of integration, the advancement of Turk-ish language acquisition, and the promotion of Ottomanism, the Alliance schools became the first in Salonica to send Jewish graduates to the local Ottoman imperial lycée (*idadi*) built in 1887. As the *idadi* trained civil ser-vants, the enrollment of Jews was interpreted as a sign of their regeneration, their fitness for participation in Ottoman society, their successful acquisition of the state language, and their embrace of Ottoman citizenship. Among the first Salonican Jews enrolled at the *idadi* was the son of the aforementioned

Saadi a-Levi, Sam Lévy (1870–1959), who followed in his father's footsteps and became a major journalist.

In his French-language memoir, Lévy reflected on his experiences at the *idadi* and the preparation he received at the Alliance. His knowledge of Hebrew helped him learn Arabic, as both languages have similar grammatical structures; his knowledge of Judeo-Spanish, which he saw as a composite language due to influences from Italian and French, prepared him for his studies of Ottoman Turkish, similarly shaped by other languages like Arabic and Persian. Lévy arrived at the *idadi* as a Jew but as one who had embraced his identities as Ottoman and as Turkish, evidenced by his chosen name, Kemal. His case illustrates the endpoint of the educational platform of the Alliance, which sought to transform Jews into loyal and engaged citizens of their state.

Although Lévy faced demands from peers and teachers at the *idadi* to convert to Islam, he refused the overtures on the grounds that "Judaism was older and superior to all other religions and even it could not hold me captive." The secularizing influence of the Alliance was on display. A lack of interest in Islam, however, did not interfere with Lévy's embrace of his Ottoman homeland or its language. When an inspector from the Ottoman Ministry of Public Education visited his class and demanded that a student translate an Arabic phrase into Turkish, Lévy produced the translation: "I love pacifists and I am one myself because Allah nourishes me with peace." The inspector responded:

"Wonderful! What is your name, my son?"

"Kemal, sir."

"Kemal what?"

"Kemal Levi, sir."

"Are you Turkish?"

"Yes, sir."

"Muslim?"

"No, sir. I am from the Jewish *millet*."

"Are there other Jews here?"

"Among the boarders no, but there are five day students."[40]

"Do they know Turkish as well as you?"

"I don't think so, sir."

"Where have you learned our national language?"

"At the Alliance Israélite school, sir."

"Thank you my son."

The inspector, Lévy recalled, turned to the other students in the class and said: "I urge you to pursue your studies as your classmate Kemal Levi does."[41]

Through this vignette, Lévy succeeded in presenting himself as both a Jew (although not necessarily a believer) and a model Ottoman conversant in both Arabic and Ottoman Turkish, the national language. His case illustrates the possibility—however tenuous—of disentangling Turkish or Ottoman identity from Islam. While relatively few Salonican Jews studied at the Ottoman state schools, their presence symbolized their transformation into Ottoman citizens. By the Balkan Wars (1912–1913), fifty-six Salonican Jews were attending Ottoman state schools: forty in law school, twelve at the *idadi*, and four at the Teachers College.[42]

Not all graduates of the Alliance in Salonica followed the same path. Many became members of the alumni associations, Association des Anciens Élèves de l'Alliance Israélite Universelle, established for boys in 1897 and for girls in 1909;[43] many promoted the ideals of liberalism and integration inculcated in them as students at the Alliance and formed a formidable political group, known as the Alliancists, who gained considerable power in Jewish communal governance. Others, however, rejected their alma mater's emphasis on assimilation and instead endorsed Jewish nationalism. Eighteen years younger than Sam Lévy, Abraham Recanati, also a graduate of the Alliance, numbered among the most ardent Zionists in Salonica. From a religiously observant home, Recanati revolted against his Alliance training when, at the conclusion of World War I, he established a branch of the Mizrahi party, an organization that endorsed Jewish nationalism and strict adherence to Jewish religious practices.

Recanati became the voice of the Jewish religious-nationalists in the city. The primary purpose of his version of Zionism initially had little to do with Palestine. Rather, he sought to combat "assimilation" and return Jewish youth to the concerted practice of Judaism: "our little westerners" who "barely stutter a few words in French" and who distanced themselves from Judaism. These "so-called westernizers," Recanati continued, "pulled their westernization out of their ass."[44] In order to counter the trend toward secularization, the Mizrahi also entered the battlefield for the allegiances of Jewish youth: the Jewish school.

The Talmud Tora: Between Traditionalism and Ottomanism, Hebraism and Zionism

Recognizing that Alliance schools equipped Jewish students with practical skills and promoted social and economic mobility, the Jewish Community of Salonica appropriated the Alliance's teaching methodologies to restructure the Talmud Tora to accord with the standards of modern education. While Alliance schools promoted the French language and a sense of European belonging to cultivate Jewish middle-class artisans, merchants, and professionals loyal to the state, the Talmud Tora refashioned itself as a school for the Jewish masses that couched its secular studies and Ottoman civic engagement in the language and symbolism of Jewish religious tradition. Whereas the Alliance emphasized individual Jews acting as Ottoman citizens, the Talmud Tora reinforced the status of Jews as constituting a community. By the end of Ottoman rule over Salonica (1912), the Talmud Tora had gained considerable ground in elementary Jewish education and emerged as a competitor to the Alliance.

The reorganization of the Talmud Tora began in 1880 when the Jewish Communal Council of Salonica, relying on the connections of Moise Allatini and other *Francos*, invited Rabbi Moshe Ottolenghi from Livorno to serve as the new school director. Over the next twenty years, Ottolenghi improved Hebrew language instruction and introduced modern Hebrew poetry and literature into the curriculum. At his funeral in 1900, his former students celebrated his contributions to the renewal of the Talmud Tora and led the procession to the cemetery.[45] Among Ottolenghi's most significant legacies was the creation, in 1898, of the first Hebraist association in Salonica, Kadima, whose membership included former students dedicated to the study of Hebrew language and literature, as well as Jewish history. Kadima established an extensive library and produced some of the first intellectuals in the city later drawn to the Zionist movement; it served as a counterpoint to the Association des Anciens Élèves de l'Alliance Israélite Universelle.[46]

With the Alliance ascendant, the Talmud Tora faced an uphill battle for legitimacy and clout among Jewish elite in Salonica. Sympathizing with the

Alliance, *La Epoka* frequently noted throughout the 1890s that the Talmud Tora suffered from insufficient funding and poor hygienic conditions.[47] Fires in 1890 and 1898 left the Talmud Tora largely in ashes. As reconstruction began, *La Epoka* complained that students received "modest religious instruction" that lagged far behind the Alliance.[48] While *La Epoka* conceded that the rebuilt Talmud Tora constituted the "largest instructional establishment" for Jewish youth in the Ottoman Empire, it questioned: "is it the most useful?"[49]

While the curriculum of the Talmud Tora and its annexes in the Kalamaria (est. 1892) and Vardar (est. 1894) districts varyingly included French, Italian, Turkish, geography, and Ottoman history, the centerpiece remained Hebrew—both biblical and now modern. Students used the language at graduation speeches and other ceremonies as a sign of the "revival of our language."[50] Moreover, secular subjects in the curriculum needed to be cast in religious language to make them more palatable to the rabbinic elite and the Jewish masses. Drawing on the ideals of the Haskalah (Jewish Enlightenment), Moshe Ottolenghi argued in 1888 that since the tractates of the Talmud are filled with accounts of Jewish theologians, physicists, doctors, and enlightened men familiar with the sciences, so must the Jews embark upon the study of science, the holy tongue (Hebrew), and foreign languages, in order to "show ourselves deserving of the creator."[51]

Rooted in the urban fabric of Salonica, the Talmud Tora projected an image of an Ottoman Jewish institution with local symbolic power that exceeded that of the Alliance, which continued to be seen as a foreign school. Recast as a modern, European institution, the Talmud Tora also introduced Jewish expressions of Ottomanism to a variety of public ceremonies, including the *albasha*. The *albasha* was a ceremony where communal leaders and the Jewish masses traditionally gathered at the Talmud Tora on the Sabbath before the start of Passover to distribute donated clothing to poor Jewish children. The *albasha* provided an opportunity for middle and upper classes to join with the Jewish poor, reconfirm their sense of religious and communal solidarity, and reflect on the progress of the institution. During the *albasha* in 1890, Chief Rabbi Jacob Covo praised the school for operating "in the European style" and serving as the "source of life" for the city's Jewish masses.[52] In 1900, *El Avenir* again emphasized the key role that the Talmud Tora played in providing Jewish youth, especially the poor, with an education centered on Hebrew and lauded the publication of a new Hebrew grammar book by one of the teachers.[53] This *albasha* in 1900, however, introduced an innovation shaped by the climate of greater engagement with Ottomanism: students performed a play in both Hebrew and Turkish "in order to prove that in the opinion of the directors of the Talmud Tora Hebrew and Turkish have the same importance—and demonstrated the great need to learn the language of the country well."[54] The promoters of the Talmud Tora recognized that, by emphasizing Hebrew and Turkish, they could demonstrate their status as Jews and as Ottoman citizens.

The twenty-fifth anniversary of the ascension to the throne of Sultan Abdul Hamid II in 1900 provided Jewish communal leaders with another opportunity to transform the Talmud Tora from a Jewish prayer and educational center into a space for the expression of Ottoman patriotism. At a ceremony at the Talmud Tora, Torah scrolls were paraded around as a song in honor of the sultan, composed for the occasion, was sung, after which cries rang out: "Long live our beloved sultan!" Cantors then chanted Psalm 21— regarding King David—and dedicated it to their sultan. Chief Rabbi Covo also composed a special prayer in honor of the sultan to be read in the Talmud Tora and the city's synagogues during Sabbath morning services. Upon the opening of the ark, the cantors in each synagogue were to provide the following introduction: "The best sign of love that we can offer to our powerful and philanthropic sovereign is to pray continually for the prolongation of his precious days. And our prayers, which are the present of the humble, are esteemed more than all of the gifts of riches, more than artistic works, which amount to nothing before our sovereign."[55] From the perspective of the religious Jewish leadership and the directors of the Talmud Tora, patriotic prayer, recited in Hebrew in the synagogue, emerged as the best way for them to demonstrate to themselves and to the state their dedication, as Jews and as Ottomans, to their sultan. In honor of the occasion, *La Epoka* published an elaborate masthead adorned by the *tughra* (the sultan's seal) and the text of a special prayer for the sultan—in Hebrew—that lauded the Ottoman Empire as the "kosher kingdom."[56]

Jewish leaders brought their expressions of Ottomanism from the Talmud Tora into public spaces as part of the citywide celebration. Muslim clerics invited Jacques Pasha, a Jewish doctor in the Ottoman military, to supervise the circumcision ceremony for 150 Muslim boys at the municipality. Although still the Sabbath, Chief Rabbi Covo then led a delegation of eighty Talmud Tora students, dressed in special uniforms, to the municipality where they sang songs in honor of the sultan.[57] Songs of praise in Hebrew that flowed from the Talmud Tora to the streets expressed Jews' dedication to the state.

The inauguration of the new Talmud Tora building in 1904 confirmed its status as both an Ottoman and a Jewish institution. The building embodied Ottoman and Jewish affiliations: the Moorish-style archways resonated with Ottoman Islamic architectural vocabulary, while the inclusion of twenty-six pillars, which symbolized the numerical value of one of the Hebrew names for God (according to *gematria*), reflected its decidedly Jewish nature.[58] At the inauguration ceremony, with 1,500 attendees, Chief Rabbi Covo lauded the Talmud Tora as the Salonican *mishkan*, the dwelling place for the divine presence, a sacred site in the city. As the president of the Communal Council, Jacob Modiano, proudly proclaimed, the Talmud Tora constituted "the symbol of the faith of the Jews of Salonica."[59]

As a symbol of Jewish faith, the new Talmud Tora also engaged with Ottoman politics. The inauguration ceremony concluded with a Jewish band playing the "Hamidian March."[60] At that year's *albasha* ceremony, more than two thousand Jews gathered in celebration of their renewed educational and religious center and applauded enthusiastically as a Jewish orphan gave a speech—in Turkish—praising the Talmud Tora for ameliorating his circumstances.[61] Through the performance of the Ottoman imperial march and the speech in Turkish, elements of Ottoman patriotism and praise entered the institutional heart of Jewish communal educational and religious life.

Jewish leaders debated who the new school director of the reconstructed Talmud Tora ought to be. Rather than turn to France or Italy as in the past, the Jewish Community hired Dr. Isaac Epstein, a Lithuanian-born, Swiss-educated pedagogue based in Ottoman Palestine who had gained wide repute, along with the Jerusalem-born, Alliance-educated Hebraist David Yellin, for developing the natural method for the instruction of the Hebrew language, according to which, in the classroom, the teacher speaks only the language students are learning.[62] Epstein was attractive to Jewish leaders in Salonica not only because he could strengthen and modernize the Jewish curriculum of the Talmud Tora, but also because he could preserve the dominant place of Hebrew—rather than French, as preferred by the Alliance.[63]

Bringing his own civilizing message as a Hebraist, modernist, and Zionist, Epstein dedicated his tenure at the Talmud Tora to regenerating education for the Jewish masses in Salonica and placing the institution on the so-called path of progress. The Talmud Tora began to compete with the Alliance for students. The one-teacher private Jewish schools and *meldares* folded as parents placed greater trust in the Talmud Tora and as Jewish socialists criticized private teachers, who allegedly exploited their students by charging too much money and providing little instruction in return.[64]

Epstein's presence also provoked controversy because some Jewish elites perceived his Zionist ideology to be at odds with the prevailing Ottomanist consensus. With Epstein's arrival, oppositional camps in Jewish educational politics clarified their positions: promoters of the Alliance advocated for a modern, European education to shape Jewish youth into good Ottoman citizens and saw French as the pillar of the curriculum. In contrast, those with a more traditional orientation wanted Hebrew and Jewish instruction to remain at the heart of the curriculum while also providing Jewish youth at the Talmud Tora with a sense of Ottoman patriotism and European education. Even though Epstein criticized a number of local Jewish practices as "backwards," his emphasis on Hebrew and strong Jewish identification gained him the support of the traditional camp.[65]

Epstein, the Talmud Tora, and the new chief rabbi, Jacob Meir, gained an ally with the creation of a Salonica branch of the Hilfsverein der Deutschen Juden (est. 1901), the German-Jewish educational and philanthropic rival of the Alliance. Supporting Zionism and focusing on Hebrew and German instruction, the Hilfsverein aimed to build a "strong bulwark against the influence of assimilation." A teacher at the Hilfsverein boasted that its Hebrew kindergarten, despite initial resistance from parents, became the "most popular institution" in this "city of the Jews." He lauded Epstein, the "uncrowned king" of Jewish Salonica, for paving the way for modern Hebrew instruction in the city.[66] Like the Alliance, the Talmud Tora and the Hilfsverein agreed that Salonican Jewish youth ought to become good Jews and good citizens. But the very meaning of "good Jew" and "good citizen," and the prioritization between the two, remained contested.

These dynamics continued to reverberate after the transfer of Salonica from Ottoman to Greek jurisdiction, especially since the primary Jewish

communal educators after 1912 carried with them the legacies of Ottomanism, Hebraism, and Zionism. With the endorsement of Chief Rabbi Jacob
Meir in 1913, Epstein arranged for a dozen promising students to travel to
Palestine to complete their studies at the Hebrew Teachers College in Jerusalem directed by David Yellin. Once trained in the latest pedagogical
methods, with strengthened knowledge of modern Hebrew and familiarity
with the Zionist project, these teachers would return to Salonica to educate
future generations. But just as the graduates of the Alliance followed different trajectories (seen above in the cases of Sam Lévy and Abraham Recanati),
Epstein's protégés opted for different paths. One of his students defended
the Ottoman Empire during World War I and died on the battlefield as an
Ottoman soldier. Others took the opposite stance, joined the British military,
and fought against the Ottomans for the "liberation" of Palestine. Among
those who joined the British Legion, several later became important educators, politicians, and lawyers in Palestine.[67]

Some of Epstein's students, however, returned to Salonica after studying at the Hebrew Teachers College in Jerusalem. After World War I, they
formed the new teaching corps at the Jewish communal schools in Salonica.[68] But the Salonica to which they returned was very different from
the one they had left. No longer under Ottoman rule and now part of the
Greek state, the city was also in ashes—including the Talmud Tora—due
to the fire of 1917. They could no longer depend on their mentor, as Epstein
had returned to Palestine. Imbued with Jewish, Ottomanist, Hebraist, and
Zionist sentiments but now in a city targeted by the Greek state for Hellenization, they faced the daunting challenge of educating a new generation
of Jewish youth, to become not good Jews and good Ottomans but good Jews
and good Hellenes.

To Speak Greek Like Greeks:
Educating Hellenic Jews after the Fire of 1917

Despite the transfer of Salonica from Ottoman to Greek control, a number
of key provisions concerning educational legislation persisted, namely the
ability of the Jewish Community to administer its own schools. In 1920 and
1921, the Greek state passed laws granting Jews and Muslims the power to
operate their own schools by reconfiguring the special privileges for non-

Muslims in the Ottoman Empire as minority rights for non-Christians in Greece. But Law 2456 of 1920, which established the new regulations for Jewish communal education in Greece, introduced a major departure from Ottoman practice by more forcefully imposing the instruction of the state language, Greek, which was to be taught "adequately." The law continued: "Apart from the teaching of Greek as a language, the teaching of history, geography, and science is to be conducted in Greek. The staff to teach the Greek classes will be appointed in the same manner as the staff of Greek state schools. All the other lessons on the curriculum drawn up by each community may be taught in whichever language the community may wish."[69] The law implied that if Jews dedicated adequate attention to Greek language instruction in their schools, they could continue to teach their religion in other languages they deemed necessary, whether Judeo-Spanish, Hebrew, or French. Multilingualism in the curriculum and its implications for national loyalty became hotly contested issues in Jewish education.

Representatives of the Jewish Community never fully acquiesced, nor did they unequivocally resist pressures from the state in the realm of education and language instruction. Rather, they regularly negotiated the implementation of Jewish educational practices and policies. The Communal Council established a new Superior Commission for Jewish Instruction (Komision Superiora de Instruksion Djudia) to centralize the administration of the Talmud Tora and the other Jewish communal schools and to implement the new educational program. The resulting Jewish communal public elementary education system, which relied in part on subsidies from the Greek state, operated in parallel with the state public education provided to Orthodox Christian children while simultaneously serving as a partner—albeit a reluctant one—with the state in integrating Jewish students and Jewish teachers into state educational structures. The eventual participation of Jewish students and teachers in the state educational enterprise contributed to the recasting of Jewish collective identity in a Hellenic mold, one that Jewish leaders hoped would be broad enough for Jews to remain Jews while also becoming Hellenes.

The 1917 fire obliterated the educational system in Salonica by destroying eight Jewish communal schools, the private schools run by the Alliance, and numerous other institutions in the city. Just a few years before, amidst the

Balkan Wars, Jewish communal schools had been requisitioned for Greek military needs or occupied by refugees fleeing the war zone and thus temporarily stopped functioning.[70] The situation was then compounded by the fire. The case of the Talmud Tora is instructive. More than a year after the fire, the institution offered classes for only three hundred of its one thousand students; most of the other seven hundred students lacked formal education during this period.[71] To accommodate some of them, the local Mission Laïque Française, funded by the French state, together with the Jewish Community, established the Franco-Israelite school for fire victims in 1919. Classes were given in French, although the committee of the Talmud Tora ensured that students attended after-school classes in Hebrew; Greek was not included in the curriculum.[72] In another instance, the Alliance offered to take over the Jewish communal school in the Regie district, inundated with Jewish refugees from the fire, but a hundred of the neighborhood's residents petitioned the Communal Council opposing the proposal and preferring that their school remain in the hands of the Jewish Community.[73] Other Jewish youth remained on the streets and received no formal schooling in the years following the fire, a fact that may explain why approximately 20 percent remained illiterate and left their thumbprint on birth registrations they filed with the Jewish Community in the 1930s.[74]

The Greek government's policy regarding the reconstruction of the city following the fire of 1917 caused additional delays in educating Jewish youth. Following the fire of 1890, the Ottoman state had permitted residents of the city to rebuild on their plots. In contrast, the Greek state saw the 1917 fire as an opportunity to remake the urban landscape, erase the centuries-long Ottoman imprint on the city, and transform it into a modern, European, Greek city. According to the reconstruction plan, the lots of the burnt district were auctioned off to the highest bidder rather than returned to the previous owners. The National Bank of Greece outbid the Jewish Community for the plot of the Talmud Tora. When the half-burnt building was demolished to make way for new construction, some students were relocated to the 151 district, where the Cazes School was founded (named after the long-time president of the Jewish Community, Jacob Cazes).[75] Other students were transferred to the nearby *matza* factory but, due to the terrible odor emitted from the adjacent tobacco factory, they were relocated again.[76] A teacher posted at a synagogue utilized as a makeshift school complained about the conditions persisting in 1923: "The location is anti-pedagogical and anti-hygienic. . . . Since the roof has holes in many places and there isn't a ceiling, we've often been forced to have class with rain and snow falling on our heads."[77]

As the reconstruction of the city progressed slowly into the 1920s, a new Talmud Tora remained absent from the cityscape. The Rabbinic Council passionately appealed to the Communal Council in 1924 to rebuild the "heart of all Salonican Judaism," the Talmud Tora, starting with its synagogue: "The Talmud Tora should not remain in ashes any longer. This great synagogue that belongs to the entire Jewish population here should be reconstructed without delay, this great temple of the Talmud Tora, [which] brought us much honor during its existence and represented us with dignity on all solemn occasions."[78] While the Rabbinic Council saw the synagogue as the center of the Talmud Tora, the Communal Council prioritized the rebuilding of the school and, in an unprecedented move, separated the religious and educational functions that together had shaped the institution for generations.[79]

A commission established to rebuild the Talmud Tora school worked with architects to design plans for the new edifice in line with the architectural aesthetics of new Greek Salonica emerging from the ashes. Jewish architects and engineers (Jacques Moche, Elie Hassid, and Elie Modiano) collaborated with the well-known city planner Joseph Pleyber, who had been stationed with the French troops in Salonica during World War I and whom the Greek government commissioned to draw up plans for the new city. Pleyber and the Jewish representatives designed a new Talmud Tora school, which was built in the neo-classical style in the Aya Sophia district, east of where it had previously stood.[80] Just as the reconstructed Talmud Tora in 1904 had engaged with Ottoman architectural styles, the new Talmud Tora in the 1920s resonated with modern Greek aesthetics—evidence of the broader transition from the Ottoman to Greek contexts.

The new Talmud Tora ironically began to be known as the "St. Sophia Jewish school" due to the nearby presence of the eponymous eighth-century Byzantine church. Taking on a seemingly Christian name, and having been designed in a neo-classical style, the new Talmud Tora demonstrated that Jews could contribute to, rather than merely resist, the Hellenization of the cityscape. Pleyber worked with Hassid to build more than a dozen other key buildings in Salonica that gave it its new Hellenic feel—a Greek army memorial and several hotels—further suggesting that Jews participated in process of Hellenization rather than serving only as its target.

By 1928, the new Talmud Tora in the Aya Sophia district was now fully functional, but it was no longer the largest Jewish communal school, the main synagogue, the primary communal meeting place, or the site of the annual *albasha* ceremony. The latter three roles were now assumed by the Beth Shaul synagogue, built in 1890 outside of the old city, beyond the reach of the fire and closer to the new Jewish Community offices on Sarandaporou Street. *El Puevlo* used the past tense in noting: "The Talmud Tora was the glory of our community."[81] The uprooting and disorientation caused by the disappearance of the Talmud Tora had a profound impact on the city's Jews that was only partly mitigated by the rebirth of the school. An era spanning generations during which the Talmud Tora had served as the central synagogue, school, and communal center had come to an end.

When the Aya Sophia school began to function in 1928, it numbered among the eight schools operated by the Jewish Community that catered to 3,365 students. The Alliance instructed an additional 1,287 Jewish pupils, whereas fifteen other private Jewish schools, such as Alsheh, Gattegno, and Pinto, catered to 2,115 students.[82] Approximately 2,000 additional Jewish youth attended a third category of educational institutions: foreign schools, both secular (e.g., Mission Laïque Française) and missionary (e.g., Frères de la Salle).[83] The plurality of Jewish students in Salonica depended on the Jewish communal school system, which faced a challenging path toward the implementation of the state curriculum.

The lack of stable and hygienic settings for Jewish education into the 1920s was not the only reason that Greek language instruction developed gradually in Jewish communal schools. The inability of the state to provide the necessary instructors, despite legal requirements, became a perennial problem. In 1922, when the teachers did not arrive at the beginning of the school year, the fourteen hours per week intended for Greek instruction were instead dedicated to the study of Hebrew liturgy.[84] The following year, one of the Jewish communal school directors complained that the woman appointed by the state to teach Greek arrived late and could not manage the 230 students in her 4 classes, which became so chaotic that they "felt like a real

I. Schools operated by the Jewish Community

School	Boys	Girls	Total	Teachers
Cazes (151)	351	340	691	24
Regie	365	234	599	14
Hirsch	355	237	592	13
Talmud Tora (Aya Sophia)	382	172	554	19
Kalamaria	270	159	429	14
No. 6	128	132	260	7
Campbell	70	60	130	3
Aya Paraskevi	57	53	110	2
Sub-Total	1978	1387	3365	96

II. Private Jewish Schools

School	Boys	Girls	Total	Teachers
Alliance Israélite Universelle (en ville)	539	376	915	26
Alliance Israélite Universelle (Campagnes)	126	246	372	14
Alsheh	404	120	524	32
Gattegno	240	102	342	22
Pinto - Vardar	122	67	189	17
Pinto - Antigonidou	90	55	145	
Achinouh - central	105	74	179	8
Achinouh - annex	38	35	73	4
Ana Varsano	89	61	150	8
Benardut	45	48	93	5
Gabriel Amar	45	35	80	3
Attias	45	35	80	3
Barouch	56	14	70	5
Matarasso	43	24	67	3
Hasson	34	22	56	3
Aelion	30	15	45	2
Ovadia Varsano	15	17	32	?
Sub-Total	2066	1346	3412	155
Total	4044	2733	6777	251

Figure 3.2. Statistics of the Jewish Schools of Salonica, 1928. Source: Reports submitted to the Superior Commission of Jewish Instruction, Salonica, December 1928, JMTh, f. 138.

mental institution."[85] The Commission for Jewish Instruction complained annually from 1928 to 1933 to the inspector general of public education about the absence of qualified teachers of Greek and demanded a "radical solution."[86] These examples show that the Jewish communal leadership tried to ensure that Jewish students adequately learned the language of the state in the face of adverse circumstances.

Contributing to the dilemma, as the Greek newspaper *Taxydromos* observed in 1931, instructors preferred not to teach Greek more than twenty-four hours per week because they "get tired teaching non-Greeks" (presumably referring to non-Orthodox Christians).[87] The challenges that the Jewish Community faced in teaching students Greek therefore paralleled those plaguing Muslim communal schools in Thrace. Despite mandates to fund instructors of Greek at Muslim communal schools in accordance with the Treaty of Lausanne, the Greek state hesitated to do so, especially during a period of economic difficulties in which the state prioritized the integration of Orthodox Christian refugees from Asia Minor.[88]

Despite challenges, the Commission for Jewish Instruction made considerable strides in educating Salonica's first generation of Greek Jews. Known in Greek government circles for his "pro-assimilation views," Jacques Kohn became the new inspector of the Commission for Jewish Instruction.[89] Like Epstein, Kohn was an Ashkenazic Jew. Born in Romania and educated in France, Kohn played a key role in founding the Béné Bérith Lodge in Salonica.[90] This organization's ideology dovetailed with that of the Alliance by promoting integration and shaped the trajectory of Jewish education in interwar Salonica. Part of a Jewish fraternal order founded in New York in 1843, the Béné Bérith in Salonica outlined its goals for "Social Education" in 1925: to strengthen relations between Jews and Christians—or, in Béné Bérith's language, "Christian Hellenes" and "Jewish Hellenes."[91] According to this key discursive framework, Jews and Orthodox Christians were to be understood as two kinds of Hellenes. Such a formulation notably echoed the framework of Ottomanism according to which Jews, Christians, and Muslims theoretically could all be considered Ottomans.

Motivated by the same spirit, the Béné Bérith mobilized the Alumni of the Alliance Israélite Universelle, the New Zionist Club, the Theodor Herzl Club, and the Jewish Community itself to work for the benefit of

all of the city's residents, including through the distribution of clothing
to Orthodox Christian refugee children.[92] This expression of goodwill was
recognized in the public sphere at the same time that tensions mounted.
A group of 650 Christian refugees inaugurated a new "anti-Semitic movement" on the grounds that the city's Jews were disloyal to the country due
to their anti-Venizelist vote in a recent election.[93] Yet simultaneously, *To Fos*,
an anti-Venizelist newspaper, celebrated the foundation of the Greek-Jewish
League at the Chamber of Commerce, which expressed gratitude to the Jews
for their goodwill toward the refugees. A certain Dr. Papazoglou even proclaimed: "The Jews are our brothers. They have lived in this city for more
than two thousand years. Salonica is as much theirs as it is ours."[94]

With a similar spirit of rapprochement, the Béné Bérith established the
first Greek-language Jewish newspaper in Salonica, *La Tribune Juive de Grèce/
Evraïkon Vima tis Ellados* (*The Jewish Tribune of Greece*), which promoted the
good of the Jews of Greece for the good of Hellenism. Notably, the newspaper also appeared partly in French, a sign that Europeanization—represented
through the acquisition of French—served as a conduit for Hellenization.[95]
Evraïkon Vima tis Ellados also collaborated with a major Greek Christian
intellectual to endorse a vision of Jews and Christians as partners in the
project of Hellenism. A professor of linguistics at Athens University, G. P.
Anagnostopoulos, produced major Greek-language dictionaries in the 1930s.[96]
For an authority like Anagnostopoulos, the Greek language constituted the
core of Greek national identity, a claim that *Evraïkon Vima tis Ellados* endorsed. If language, rather than Orthodox Christianity, was the key to Greek
national identity, then Jews could learn Greek and thus become legitimate
Greeks. Anagnostopoulos addressed Jewish readers in Greek: "[B]ecause I
consider the sincere collaboration and brotherly coexistence between the Jews
living in Hellas and the rest of their Hellenic fellow citizens necessary for the
. . . interests of the Greek state, I consider every activity that contributes to this
cordial collaboration and coexistence an urgent duty of every patriotic Hellenic citizen." He characterized the ancient Greek people as worshippers of
Zeus Xenion, the patron of hospitality, as a way of explaining why Jews should
be welcomed as "fellow citizens" (while ironically indicating that Jews should
properly be understood as foreigners and guests). Noting that Jews in other
countries in Europe and in the United States balanced their "national

identity"—as Jews—with the obligations of citizenship, Anagnostopoulos anticipated that Jews in Greece, by "learning perfectly the official language of the
state," could also become "perfect Hellenic citizens and valuable members of
the Hellenic family." He encouraged Jews to make literary and scientific contributions in Greek to "enrich the Hellenic university, and honor their noble
race and Hellenic fatherland."[97] Anagnostopoulos thus distinguished between
the status of Jews as a distinct "nation" and "race," and their status as Hellenic
citizens; he saw no tension between the two. He viewed Jews and Orthodox Christians as two separate peoples who could nonetheless form part of a
shared political and cultural "family" bound not by bonds of blood or religion
but rather by shared territory, language, and intellectual pursuits. For him, the
school, and especially the state public school, became the site through which
ideal Hellenic Jews would be formed.

As a model for Jews in Salonica to emulate, Anagnostopoulos likely had
in mind intellectuals such as Joseph Eliya (d. 1931), a Romaniote Jewish poet
and lyricist from Ioannina. Although attracted to Zionism, he advocated that
Jews embrace Hellenism. He published Greek-language poems in literary
reviews in the 1920s and settled in Athens, where he became a teacher, a
contributor to the *Great Greek Encyclopedia*, and part of left-leaning Greek
intellectual circles. Following his untimely death, a Jewish notable in Ioannina emphasized that Eliya "wanted the Jews of Greece to be Greeks first
and Jews second." An Orthodox Christian colleague characterized Eliya as
"a great intellectual link between the Greek and the Jewish people" with two
mothers: "Judaea and Hellas."[98] Published as a memorial volume in Greek
by the Béné Bérith Lodge in Salonica, *The First Modern Hellenic-Jewish
[elenoevraios] Poet* (1934) lauded Eliya for fusing Hellenism and Judaism and
recapturing the spirit of Hellenistic Jewish writers of antiquity like Josephus
and Philo. The Romaniote Jew thus became the idealized Greek Jew whom
Anagnostopoulos, the Béné Bérith, and even Prime Minister Venizelos,
hoped would also emerge in Salonica.[99]

Animated by the prospect of Jewish-Hellenic rapprochement as promised by Anagnostopoulos and the Béné Bérith, and as symbolized by Eliya,
Jacques Kohn utilized the Jewish communal schools as a vehicle for Jewish
integration into the state educational institutions of Greece. While graduates
of Jewish communal schools were entitled to attend state schools according

to Law 2456 of 1920, only in 1925 did the first five Jewish students do so.[100] Kohn incentivized graduates of Jewish communal schools to attend Greek state secondary schools through scholarships sponsored by the Béné Bérith and backed by the Communal Council.[101] While the Commission for Jewish Instruction discouraged Jewish students from attending foreign schools, especially the Mission Laïque Française (est. 1906), which held classes on Saturday, it supported Jewish attendance at Greek state schools and participation in the project of Hellenism.[102]

The gradual integration of Jews into Greek state schools formed part of the policies voluntarily initiated by the Commission for Jewish Instruction to accommodate the new realities of the Greek context. In 1921, the Commission decided that the language of instruction for arithmetic, left to the discretion of the Jewish Community according to Law 2456, would be Greek.[103] The Commission also decided that teachers would be paid not according to the Western (Gregorian) or Hebrew calendars but rather the Greek (Julian) one.[104] In celebration of the centennial of Greek independence in 1930, Kohn directed teachers to recall the "great and beautiful accomplishments of the Greek heroes" and to inspire in students "sentiments of patriotism."[105] With these initiatives, the administrators of the Jewish communal schools sought to align their practices with those of the state schools.

Some Jewish leaders accepted the integration of Jewish students into state secondary schools or sent their children to private schools, such as the Valagianni Educational Institutes or Anatolia College (where Chief Rabbi Sevi Koretz eventually sent his son). Still others advocated for the creation of a Jewish communal high school. Although the idea of a Jewish gymnasium in Salonica had emerged in the late Ottoman era (1909), it became the subject of serious discussion in the mid-1920s.[106] While figures like Kohn initially encouraged graduates of Jewish communal elementary schools to enroll at Greek state schools, Zionists like Mentesh Bensanchi and Baruch Shiby advocated for the establishment a Jewish communal high school—a Helleno-Jewish gymnasium—to be accredited by the state but with a curriculum overseen by the Jewish Community.[107] The Commission for Jewish Instruction established a few post-elementary classes by 1930 but could not gain state recognition.[108] In the end, no Jewish communal high school emerged in Salonica.

Instead, the Alsheh Commercial and Practical Institute, a prestigious Jewish private school, partly filled this role. Founded in 1880, it sought to educate students as "devoted citizens and good Jews."[109] During the interwar years, the curriculum focused on language instruction—Greek, Hebrew, and French (with optional English and German)—in addition to commercial subjects and sciences. The only Jewish school in Greece with all grade levels accredited by the state, Alsheh encouraged graduates to sit for baccalaureate exams and enroll in universities in Greece and abroad. Alsheh also offered a special curriculum for girls, to train them in commerce and languages, but ultimately with the bourgeois expectation that they would become good housewives. While immersed in the project of Hellenism and endowing graduates with a "deep" knowledge of Greek, the school directors, brothers Isaac and Albert Alsheh, were also noted Zionists. Students learned Jewish history and Hebrew as "a living language"—enough, apparently, for graduates to transition smoothly to life in Palestine.[110] One student even recalled learning "Hatikvah" (the Zionist anthem) "in a class with closed doors and closed windows and being requested not to sing too loudly."[111] The Jewish, Zionist, Hellenic, and European aspects of the curriculum—which administrators, students, and observers sought to reconcile—impressed figures like Bensanchi, who hoped that Alsheh would "become the Jewish gymnasium in the city."[112] It closed in 1938 after training several generations of Jewish businessmen and professionals.[113]

But throughout its existence, as a private school, Alsheh remained an option for only a select few and could not accommodate the general Jewish student population that wanted access to secondary education during the interwar years. At a well-publicized lecture at the Béné Bérith Lodge in 1927, Jacques Kohn boasted that Jewish communal schools—not private schools like the Alliance or Alsheh—provided the most direct pathway for Jewish students to participate in state educational institutions. Of the forty-six Jewish students enrolled in Greek secondary schools, forty-one—nearly 90 percent—had graduated from Jewish communal schools. Successfully learning the language of the country, graduates of the Jewish communal schools first enrolled in the University of Salonica in 1928.[114]

The question of languages remained key to the educational enterprise and to building a sense of cultural and political loyalty among Jewish youth.

Kohn conceived of the language question as a juggling act that sought to satisfy the government with regard to Greek; Zionists with regard to Hebrew; and parents, who saw French as key to their children's future success in the European economy.[115] Rather than elide the instruction of Greek, the Jewish communal school curriculum marginalized Judeo-Spanish despite its support from intellectuals like Sam Lévy and Jewish communists. Kohn ironically made his declarations about the future of all of these languages in Judeo-Spanish, a sign that it remained the lingua franca of Salonica's Jews.

Rather than focus on Judeo-Spanish, Hebrew, or French, Kohn announced that the dedication of the greatest portion of classroom hours to Greek would satisfy the "most intransigent of our assimilationists."[116] Increased hours of Greek language instruction in Jewish communal schools appeased the state and some Jewish parents, who wanted their children to learn the language of the country. Kohn further proclaimed that "the day is not far when there will not be any [Jewish] youth who will not have assimilated the Greek language to the point of speaking it like someone of the Greek race."[117] By speaking Greek like Greeks, Kohn believed that Jews could become legitimate Hellenes just as professor Anagnostopoulos had envisioned. In contrast to previous generations under Ottoman rule, among whom knowledge of Turkish was not widespread, the acquisition of the state language among Jews, especially the youth, reached unprecedented levels once the city came under Greek rule.

The number of Jewish students in Salonica at Greek state secondary schools—especially those from poor families—increased due to their knowledge of Greek and the scholarships offered by the Béné Bérith. El Puevlo congratulated Jewish students and the Jewish communal schools for this accomplishment but noted that integration also produced social isolation. The first Jewish students attending Greek state schools went to the First Gymnasium of Salonica. They often studied together after school in Judeo-Spanish. Most importantly, the Jewish students remained apart because their classmates were Christians from well-to-do families and their poverty stood out more than their Jewishness.[118] This also explains why the Commission for Jewish Instruction transformed the custom of the albasha, which had served as a central communal gathering at the Talmud Tora prior to the fire of 1917. In the interwar years, the albasha, the annual ceremony that had involved the distribution

1921	Hebrew	Greek	French	Judeo-Spanish	Gym	Design
Asile 1	15	15	0	3		
Asile 2	15	15	0	3		
Elementary 1	9	14	8	2		
Elementary 2	9	14	8	2		
Elementary 3	8	14	9	2		
Elementary 4	8	14	10	1		
Elementary 5	9	14	9	1		
1927						
Asile 1	14	14	0	0	0	0
Asile 2	14	14	0	0	0	0
Elementary 1	9	14	7	1	1	1
Elementary 2	9	14	7	1	1	1
Elementary 3	8	14	8	1	1	1
Elementary 4	8	15	8	1	1	1
Elementary 5	8	16	8	0	1	1

Figure 3.3. Curriculum of the Jewish Communal Schools (Hours), 1921 and 1927. Sources: "Prochesos verbales dela komision superior de instruksion," January 3, 1921 (109), CAHJP, Gr/Sa 8; and *Las Eskolas Komunalas de Saloniko—Loke eyos son loke eyos deven ser* (1927), 15.

of clothes to poor Jewish students attending the Talmud Tora, now became an occasion for poor Jewish students to receive appropriate clothing to attend state gymnasia.[119] The *albasha* was repurposed as a tool of integration.

In addition to Jewish communal schools and the Alsheh Institute, Pinto—another private Jewish school—also prioritized Greek language instruction. When the national census took place in 1928, the Pinto School provided thirty Jewish students to serve as interpreters in the Vardar district, home to many impoverished Jews, especially women who spoke only Judeo-Spanish. The Greek census takers, so impressed by the knowledge of Greek among the Jewish students, wrote a flattering letter to the Greek press, quickly reproduced in *El Puevlo*, which congratulated the Pinto School for advancing Greek education and thereby decreasing the divide between Jewish and Christian youth in Salonica.[120] Committed to displays of Greek patriotism, the Pinto School graduation ceremonies later included the formal presentation of the Greek flag and featured Jewish students performing Greek national dances, including the *syrtos* and the *karagouna*, and theater productions in Greek.[121]

As the discussion of the Pinto School in the Greek press demonstrates, the infamous anti-Jewish proclamations of *Makedonia*, a popular newspaper published in Salonica that catered to the Orthodox Christian refugee population from Asia Minor and sometimes supported Venizelism, did not represent the totality of public opinion expressed in the local Greek press. While *Makedonia* regularly charged the Jews with antipathy toward the Greek language—and, by extension, the Greek nation as a whole—other Greek newspapers were more sympathetic. In 1928, *To Fos*, an anti-Venizelist newspaper, defended Salonica's Jews by proclaiming that they did not disparage the Greek language; rather, they continued to study and improve their knowledge of it. *To Fos* further explained that relatively few Jews attended Greek schools not because Jewish youth did not know Greek but because those schools did not accommodate Jewish religious instruction or the Hebrew language. If these aspects of Jewish difference were respected within the context of Greek schooling, *To Fos* surmised that more Jewish students would attend state schools for the betterment of both communities.[122]

To Fos proposed a model for the education of non-Christians—religious minorities—that the Greek state had already implemented for Chams, the Albanian-speaking Muslim population in Epirus. Rather than permit the Muslim Community in Epirus to run its own schools beyond those offering traditional religious education (for fear that modern schooling would foment anti-Greek sentiment and an Albanian national consciousness among the students), the Greek state encouraged Chams to send their children to Greek state schools where the state would provide Muslim instructors to teach Islam and Arabic.[123] Two years after *To Fos* made its parallel suggestion for Jewish education, the Greek state established five special government schools that followed the general state curriculum and employed Jewish instructors to teach Jewish pupils the fundamentals of Judaism and Hebrew modeled on the blueprint of state schools for Chams.[124]

The creation of new government schools for Jewish students (public schools 44 to 48) revolutionized educational practices in Salonica. The number of Jewish students at Greek state schools, in general, had increased over a few years: from the first 5 students in 1925 to 412 at state elementary and 67 at state secondary schools in 1929.[125] With a new law passed by the Greek state in 1930 that forbade Greek citizens from attending foreign-run elementary schools, the approximately two thousand Jewish students enrolled in those schools required alternative options. Since the Jewish communal schools could not absorb them, new government schools for Jewish students sought to do so.

The state therefore intervened extensively in Jewish education while seeking to accommodate Jewish difference in state schools. The government schools for Jewish students, which opened in autumn 1930, followed the state curriculum and apparently enrolled several Christian students.[126] By the early 1930s, more than one quarter of the Jewish students in Salonica attended some kind of Greek state school: of the 2,271 Jewish students enrolled in Greek state schools, 1,440 attended the five government schools for Jewish pupils;[127] and 831 attended fifteen general Greek state schools,[128] nearly 100 of whom received scholarships from the Béné Bérith (up from 18 in 1930, 36 in 1931, and 58 in 1934).[129] In 1934, of those Salonican Jews receiving scholarships, four studied medicine, painting, pharmacology, and midwifery in Athens; forty-eight attended gymnasia in Salonica; and six others studied in Salonica at the University (law), the Teachers College, the Commercial School (two), and the Music Conservatory (two, violin and piano). That year, Bella Yacar, another scholarship recipient, completed her studies at the Teachers College and became one of the first—notably a woman—to teach Jewish history courses, in Greek, at the Alsheh Practical and Commercial Institute in Salonica. These numbers and accomplishments are staggering in comparison to the initial five Jewish students sent to Greek state gymnasia in 1925.

Unlike existing state schools in Salonica, the new schools dedicated specific class periods to Jewish religion and Hebrew language instruction for Jewish pupils. To accommodate these additional classes, the inspector of public instruction requested that the Commission for Jewish Instruction provide fifteen teachers; eight were ultimately assigned.[130] Some, such as Michael Molho, initially refused.[131] Ironically, the Commission considered importing Hebrew teachers from Palestine to meet the demand and ultimately relied on Jewish parliamentarians Mentesh Bensanchi and Asher Mallah to in-

tervene with the Ministry of Education and Religion in Athens to resolve
the issue.[132] Through the inclusion of Hebrew in the curriculum at the new
government schools, the state endorsed the instruction of a language other
than Greek, although not to its exclusion. The key to the Greek government
schools for Jewish students, like those for Chams, was that the instruction of
an additional language be construed as a *religious*—rather than national—
accommodation, hence Hebrew (rather than Judeo-Spanish or another
language) for Jews and Arabic (rather than Albanian) for Chams. Such a
characterization of the languages bolstered the Greek state framework that
recognized Jews and Muslims as religious rather than national minorities.

The University of Salonica also emerged as a key forum for Christian-
Jewish cooperation and tested the limits of multilingualism in the curriculum.
While the first four Jewish students had enrolled at the university in 1928,
Jewish parliamentarians, such as Mentesh Bensanchi, negotiated the following year for the creation of a new and unprecedented chair in Hebrew
language and literature.[133] The Hebraic scholar and Corfu native, Lazarus
(Menahem) Belleli, assumed the position. Fluent in Greek, Belleli had attended the University of Athens and represented Greece at a congress of
Orientalists in Rome.[134] *Makedonia* insisted that the purpose of the chair
was not for the benefit of the city's Jews but to equip students with a classical education inclusive of Hebrew as an ancient language.[135] *El Puevlo*, in
contrast, hailed the inauguration of the chair as a "beautiful manifestation of
Greek-Jewish rapprochement."[136] The university rector similarly envisioned
the goal of the chair to "work toward reciprocal appreciation between Greeks
and Jews in order to enhance their relations . . . for the common good and the
greatest benefit of the shared homeland."[137] Belleli assured his audience that
Jews in Salonica already fulfilled their obligations toward their homeland
and, with deepened knowledge of Greek, their "profound love" for Greece
would only expand. Although *El Puevlo* and *La Verdad* complained about the
low attendance at Belelli's courses and public lectures, the position became a
symbol of the developing category of "Hellenic Judaism."[138] The rhetoric of
Hellenic Judaism emphasized long-standing Hellenic-Jewish symbiosis since
the era of Apostle Paul and recast Salonican Jewish identity in a Hellenic
mold. The rhetoric of Hellenic Judaism envisioned an inclusive framework
for both Jews and Christians to be considered Hellenes.

While state educational institutions in Salonica, both the university and the public schools, accepted the introduction of the Hebrew language into the curriculum, they elided Judeo-Spanish. The question of Judeo-Spanish was not raised for the state elementary and secondary schools. At the University of Salonica, however, the prospect of creating an additional chair of Spanish language and literature, to be funded by the Spanish government, emerged in 1930. The effort to promote Spanish interests in Salonica had begun at the turn of the century, in the wake of the loss of the Spanish colonies in 1898, and as political circles in Spain sought new economic outlets. Seeking to achieve rapprochement with the descendants of those Sephardic Jews expelled from Spain in 1492, whom they characterized as "Spaniards without a homeland," the Spanish government offered Spanish consular protection to some of the most prominent Jewish merchants in Salonica and, in 1924, offered the possibility of acquiring Spanish citizenship.[139]

As another step in this process, the Spanish Embassy in Athens requested the creation of the Spanish chair at the University of Salonica in 1930 in order to "satisfy the needs of the seventy thousand Spanish-speaking Sephardim in the city." Clearly, the aim would have been to teach Jews Castilian rather than their traditional Hebrew-scripted Judeo-Spanish. Since a chair in Hellenic studies had been established at the University of Barcelona since 1928, the creation of a chair of Spanish in Salonica, the Spanish Embassy argued, would be a welcomed act of diplomatic reciprocity. While neither the Greek Ministry of Education and Religion nor the Ministry of Foreign Affairs objected, the University of Salonica itself responded that the creation of such a chair would "perniciously counter the work of Hellenizing the Jewish element of the city."[140]

The Spanish chair never materialized. A language with the backing of a foreign state, Spanish (or at least a language related to it, namely Judeo-Spanish) was actively used by Jews in Salonica as the everyday vernacular and appeared to be a threat to the Greek nationalizing project. In contrast, Hebrew did not benefit from the backing of a foreign state and could be perceived by the Greek state as a language of religious difference. Moreover, since very few Jews in Salonica actually spoke Hebrew, it did not overtly challenge the state program of Hellenization. Even though Zionist organizations in Salonica insisted that the instruction of Hebrew formed part of Jewish *na-*

tional education and requested space in the Jewish communal schools to hold supplementary Hebrew language classes, the Greek state and Jewish elite who advocated for integration construed the language as a marker of religious difference.[141] Using this argument, the Commission for Jewish Instruction negotiated with the inspector of public instruction in 1928 to reduce the hours dedicated to Greek from twenty to seventeen or eighteen (depending on the grade level) and reassigned the additional two to three hours to Hebrew.[142] This development in Greece paralleled that in the Republic of Turkey, where the project of Turkification diminished the use of the Judeo-Spanish "jargon," yet accommodated attempts to revive Hebrew, a "dead language."[143] As in Turkey, in Greece the state language dictated the educational agenda— Jewish or otherwise—and the boundaries of national belonging.

Hellenizing Jewish Communal Schools and Judaizing Greek State Schools

Even though the Greek state set some of the parameters for Jewish education in Salonica, the Jewish Community retained the right to determine much of the content of the curriculum in its schools during the 1920s and into the 1930s. The greatest challenges, however, to educational autonomy in the Jewish communal schools—ostensibly protected by the League of Nations minorities treaties—emerged in the late 1930s, during the tenure of Ioannis Metaxas as prime minister of Greece. Paradoxically, the Metaxas era enabled the most innovative attempts at partnership between the Jewish Community and the state in reforming the curricula of Jewish communal and state schools by increasing Hellenic content in the former and introducing Jewish content in the latter. In the complex realm of Jewish education and language instruction, the era of Metaxas revealed tensions while inspiring rapprochement that resulted in the creation of new textbooks, a new cohort of Greek Jewish teachers, and a new generation of Greek Jewish youth.

The developments that occurred during the Metaxas era were facilitated by significant changes in the Jewish educational leadership. Following the death in 1933 of Jacques Kohn, the inspector of the Jewish communal schools, David Florentin, the interim inspector, visited Palestine on behalf of the Zionist Federation of Greece in search of a Hebrew pedagogue and a Zionist—someone who, unlike Kohn and more like Isaac Epstein, would take a stronger stance against assimilation.[144] Selected for the position was A. Volodarsky, a Russian-born teacher who had received his master's degree in Palestine and spoke Hebrew with a Sephardic-style accent; his wife was also a teacher.[145] Shortly after his arrival, Volodarsky made two innovative propositions: to train Jewish teachers in Salonica and to produce new Hebrew textbooks.[146]

In collaboration with the new chief rabbi, Sevi Koretz, Volodarsky created a new educational program for Jewish teachers and rabbis.[147] Ironically, the first successful initiative to train Jewish teachers for the Greek future stemmed not from local Jewish leaders but from two Ashkenazic Jews imported to Salonica. The Judeo-Spanish minutes of the commission for this *klasa preparatoria de maestros i rabinos* ("preparatory class for teachers and rabbis") outlined the goals: to create a new generation of educators to "provide national and religious instruction" to Jewish youth in Salonica and Greece, to ensure that Jewish teachers and rabbis would not need to be imported in the future, and to "inspire in the hearts of the masses sentiments of love and affection for our religion and our traditions."[148]

The curriculum for the teachers- and rabbis-in-training evolved rapidly. It initially included twenty-two hours per week of instruction in Hebrew covering the Hebrew Bible, the Talmud, Hebrew literature and composition, Hebrew grammar, Jewish history, the geography of Palestine, and singing. Six hours for Greek language instruction (1934) increased to nine (1935) and then ultimately to fourteen (1936)—evidence of a greater emphasis on Hellenic aspects of the curriculum—and involved not only Greek language but also mathematics, Greek history, Greek and general geography, and natural sciences. An additional three hours focused on French language and literature.[149]

The new curriculum of the preparatory class aimed to create a new cohort of Greek Jewish teachers familiar with general European intellectual trends. In order to accomplish this goal, the Jewish Community diverted income from the Haimoucho Covo foundation (*ekdesh*) that had previously been used to fund the yeshiva Or Ahaim, which continued to serve as a religious study center for twelve rabbis and seven students, in order to provide fifteen promising Jewish students with fellowships to complete the teacher education program.[150] Koretz, Volodarsky, and a number of other local Jewish teachers—primarily graduates of the Hebrew Teachers College in Jerusalem—taught the Jewish courses; Mercado Covo taught those in French. Mr. Stefanidis, a teacher in the Jewish communal schools, contributed a set of Greek history books and taught Greek language and mathematics.[151]

Challenges emerged during the five years of study leading to the final exams in 1938: budgetary constraints, which were eventually overcome to provide students with notebooks, textbooks, tram passes, and free meals at the Matanoth Laevionim (Jewish soup kitchen); extensive negotiations to exempt students from military service; complaints from students about the low level of instruction in some subjects, particularly Talmud; debates among the teachers over how to address Jewish mysticism in the classroom (they ultimately emphasized ways to reconcile "tradition" with "science"); and concerns about "mixed results" in French.[152] Notably, complaints about lack of proficiency in the Greek language were not registered.

At the final exams, as reported in La Aksion, the students impressed their examiners and the public at large. Chief Rabbi Koretz and a certain Professor Kalogieros from the University of Salonica administered an oral exam—in Greek—in history, mathematics, philosophy, and other subjects. "Almost all" of the students, the professor reported, responded in "current and correct" Greek. The inspector for minority schools expressed satisfaction with the students' written exams. Finally, Joseph Nehama questioned them further on the Hebrew Bible, Jewish history, Greek history and geography, mathematics, and physics. Satisfied with the responses, Nehama recommended that they enroll at the university.[153] Five of the graduates instead gained employment as teachers in the Jewish communal schools; when they petitioned for a salary increase in 1939, they notably signed their names in Greek.[154] To the satisfaction of state representatives and Jewish communal leaders, the preparatory class successfully trained a new cohort of Greek Jewish teachers. The start of World War II, however, prevented the full realization of their labors, and most teachers perished in Auschwitz.

While Volodarsky helped to initiate the preparatory class, he also spearheaded the creation of new Hebrew-language textbooks for the Jewish communal elementary schools. In collaboration with local Jewish teachers and the Tora Umeleha, an organization that provided free school supplies to needy Jewish students, Volodarsky published Ba-Dereh ("On the Path") in 1934. The Judeo-Spanish preface explained the goal: to place Jewish students "on the path from the world of childhood to that of national culture and general knowledge."[155] "National culture" referred to Jewish national culture and indicated that the Jewish communal schools would now promote a Zionist agenda as part of the supplementary Jewish curriculum. The new textbooks also included lessons not in *soletreo* but rather in the Ashkenazic Hebrew script, which become the standard form of Hebrew handwriting in Palestine.[156]

After the restoration of the Greek monarchy in 1935, the Jewish communal elementary schools in Salonica came under greater scrutiny. A controversy erupted in 1936 not over allegations that the curriculum promoted a Zionist agenda, but rather over the use of a particular religious text in the classroom. During a visit to the Jewish communal schools, the new inspector of education for minority and foreign schools (the title of this new position illustrates that the state viewed non-Christians and foreigners together) opposed the use of the Passover Haggadah; only the Hebrew Bible was approved as a religious text for use in the Jewish communal schools. In response, the Ministry of Education and Religion issued order 2540 that stipulated—for the first time—that the Jewish Community must submit the Jewish studies curriculum to the Greek state for approval, that only books approved in advance by the Greek state may be used, and that only school personnel nominated and approved by the Ministry of Education and Religion may enter the Jewish communal schools.[157]

Local Judeo-Spanish newspapers, the chief rabbinate, the Communal Council, and the Commission for Jewish Instruction became furious over what they saw as a clear abrogation of their rights to "communal autonomy." The new stipulations, according to *La Aksion*, constituted a violation of Law 2456, "Concerning Jewish Communities," and thus an infringement of Jewish minority rights that contravened Greece's obligations to the League of Nations. Article 5 of Law 2456 indicated that the curriculum of the Jewish communal schools was to be "drawn up by the Communities," and that, except for courses in the Greek language, history, geography, and science, all other subjects could be taught in "whatever language each Community may wish."[158] Furthermore, the decision to prevent access to the Jewish communal schools by members of the Commission for Jewish Instruction or the Jewish Communal Council—not officially approved by the state as school personnel—constituted "a clandestine campaign" by the Ministry of Education and Religion "to wrest control of the Jewish schools away from the

Jewish Community."[159] *El Mesajero* emphasized that the issue was indeed one of jurisdiction: if the Jewish communal schools implemented the Greek state curriculum, which they did, then they should retain the right to include additional Jewish instruction. The newspaper hoped that the situation would be resolved so that "we can produce future generations of good Hellenic citizens as well as good Jews."[160]

As the chief rabbi met with the governor general of Macedonia to lobby for the annulment of the order and a delegation from the Jewish Community went to meet with representatives of the Ministry of Education and Religion in Athens to address the controversy, another set of incidents broke out in the Jewish communal schools. A Greek language teacher appointed by the state to serve in one of the Jewish communal schools decided to enforce order 2540 on his own and physically prevented Volodarsky from entering the school on the grounds that the latter did not have the authorization of the Ministry of Education and Religion. *El Mesajero* lamented: "This means, in effect, that the Jewish communal schools are no longer ours."[161] Simultaneously, at the Jewish communal school in Kalamaria, the Hebrew language books had "gone missing," an act attributed to "overzealous Greek teachers." *El Mesajero* complained that the teaching of Hebrew was "not an act of contraband" and declared that the right "to teach the Jewish language must not be stolen from us."[162]

What began as a complaint over the use of the Passover Haggadah evolved into a broader conflict between the Jewish Community and the Ministry of Education and Religion over the meaning of Jewish communal autonomy. The incidents also increased tensions between Jewish and Greek teachers. The former viewed the latter as occasionally overstepping their bounds. Yomtov Saltiel, the director of the Baron Hirsch Jewish communal school, complained about the proselytism of a Greek language teacher who "considers the students to be Christian children. Thus her students read all of the lessons in the textbook about the Christian holidays. In one of the elementary classes, she drew a crucifix on the chalkboard for the children to copy . . ."[163] Saltiel accused another Greek teacher of antisemitism for physically assaulting Jewish students: "Yesterday afternoon during recess, [the teacher] hit two students in the third grade for speaking [Judeo-]Spanish, Avram Atas with a stick to the head, and Vida Saporta he slapped."[164] A literal battle over the linguistic and religious loyalties of Jewish students erupted in the schools.

Despite tensions between Jewish and Christian teachers, the impasse between the Jewish Community and the Greek state was overcome with three
compromises: the dismissal of Volodarsky on the grounds that as a foreign
citizen of British Palestine he was not qualified to supervise the instruction
of Greek citizens, the reform of the curriculum for the Jewish communal
schools, and the creation of new textbooks in Greek and in Hebrew. The solution, in other words, was not for Hebrew or Jewish subjects to be suppressed;
on the contrary, the Jewish Community and the Greek state agreed—at least
officially—that the goal of education for Jewish youth in Greece should be to
educate them as loyal, Greek-speaking, Hellenic citizens and conscientious
Jews with knowledge of Hebrew and Judaism. They intended to codify these
dual affiliations through a new curriculum.

But in order to create a new curriculum, the Jewish Community needed
to fill the position of inspector of Jewish instruction left vacant due to the
dismissal of Volodarsky.[165] Given the new requirements that the position
be filled by a Greek citizen, the Commission for Jewish Instruction hired
Mentesh Bensanchi, the journalist, former member of Greek Parliament,
and prominent Zionist who had promoted Jewish communal education
throughout his career. Given his prominence, his experience in politics, and
his proficiency in over a half dozen languages, Bensanchi could advocate
on behalf of the Jewish Community with the Ministry of Education and
Religion and supervise the instruction of Hebrew and Greek. As a graduate of both the Talmud Tora and the Alliance, he could bridge secular and
religious instruction and promote an attachment to the Jewish Community
and to the state.[166]

As inspector of the Jewish communal schools, Bensanchi renegoti-
ated the curriculum for the Jewish communal schools with the Ministry of
Education and Religion.[167] In 1936, the proposed Jewish communal school
curriculum followed that of the Greek state schools—which paralleled "all
civilized countries"—and focused on Greek, with fewer hours on Hebrew. As
students advanced in grade level, more of the curriculum focused on studies
in Greek. *El Mesajero* indicated that the curriculum aimed to educate "good
Jews and good citizens."[168] Such rhetoric echoed the integrationist sentiment of the Alliance now more fully adopted by Jewish communal school
administrators.

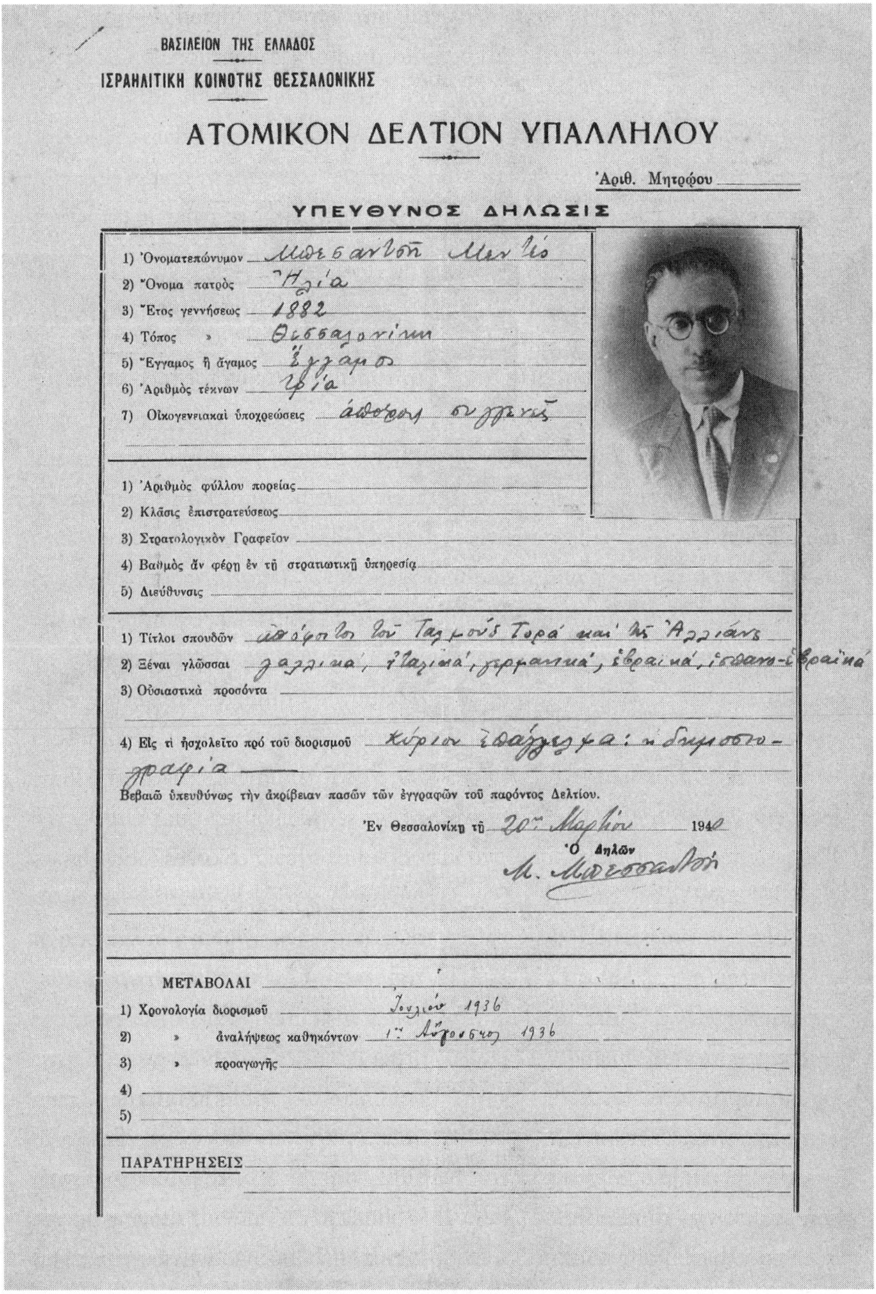

ΒΑΣΙΛΕΙΟΝ ΤΗΣ ΕΛΛΑΔΟΣ

ΙΣΡΑΗΛΙΤΙΚΗ ΚΟΙΝΟΤΗΣ ΘΕΣΣΑΛΟΝΙΚΗΣ

ΑΤΟΜΙΚΟΝ ΔΕΛΤΙΟΝ ΥΠΑΛΛΗΛΟΥ

'Αριθ. Μητρῴου _____

ΥΠΕΥΘΥΝΟΣ ΔΗΛΩΣΙΣ

1) Ὀνοματεπώνυμον _Μεντεσαντὸν Μενὶο_
2) Ὄνομα πατρός _Ἠλία_
3) Ἔτος γεννήσεως _1882_
4) Τόπος » _Θεσσαλονίκη_
5) Ἔγγαμος ἢ ἄγαμος _ἔγγαμος_
6) Ἀριθμὸς τέκνων _τρία_
7) Οἰκογενειακαὶ ὑποχρεώσεις _ἄποροι συγγενεῖς_

1) Ἀριθμὸς φύλλου πορείας _____
2) Κλάσις ἐπιστρατεύσεως _____
3) Στρατολογικὸν Γραφεῖον _____
4) Βαθμὸς ἂν φέρῃ ἐν τῇ στρατιωτικῇ ὑπηρεσίᾳ _____
5) Διεύθυνσις _____

1) Τίτλοι σπουδῶν _ἀπόφοιτος τοῦ Ταχμοῦδ Τορά καὶ τῆς Ἀλλιάνς_
2) Ξέναι γλῶσσαι _γαλλικά, ἰταλικά, γερμανικά, ἑβραικά, ισπανο-ἑβραικά_
3) Οὐσιαστικὰ προσόντα _____

4) Εἰς τί ἠσχολεῖτο πρὸ τοῦ διορισμοῦ _Κύριον ἐπάγγελμα: ἡ δημοσιο-_
γραφία

Βεβαιῶ ὑπευθύνως τὴν ἀκρίβειαν πασῶν τῶν ἐγγραφῶν τοῦ παρόντος Δελτίου.

Ἐν Θεσσαλονίκῃ τῇ _20ῃ Μαρτίου_ 194_0_

Ὁ Δηλῶν

Μ. Μεντεσαντὸν

ΜΕΤΑΒΟΛΑΙ

1) Χρονολογία διορισμοῦ _Ἰουνίου 1936_
2) » ἀναλήψεως καθηκόντων _1ᵉ Αὐγούστου 1936_
3) » προαγωγῆς _____
4) _____
5) _____

ΠΑΡΑΤΗΡΗΣΕΙΣ _____

Figure 3.4. Mentesh Bensanchi (1882–1943), Inspector of the Superior Commission of Jewish Instruction in Salonica, 1940. Jewish communal employee identification certificate. Source: Jewish Museum of Thessaloniki. Published with permission.

Grade level	1	2	3	4	5	6
Greek curriculum (hours/week)	21	22	23	24	26	26
Hebrew curriculum (hours/week)	11	10	9	8	6	6
Total hours	32	32	32	32	32	32

Figure 3.5. Proposed Hours for Greek and Hebrew language instruction in the Jewish Communal Schools, July 1936. Source: "Un projekto de programa para las eskolas djudias," *El Mesajero*, July, 10 1936.

Continued negotiations increased the number of hours for Hebrew without diminishing the hours for Greek. As Bensanchi reported in fall 1938, the nine Jewish communal elementary schools followed a unified curriculum, included more hours dedicated to Hebrew than before, and thus included more hours of weekly instruction in general. The Greek state also increased its subventions to the Jewish communal schools and permitted a half day of instruction on Sundays to accommodate the additional hours (despite the continued official imposition of the Compulsory Sunday Closing Law).[169]

The emphasis on the instruction of Hebrew continued a trend in Jewish communal schools in Salonica since the reorganization of the Talmud Tora in the late Ottoman period. By the late 1930s, the dual Jewish and Hellenic curricula corresponded to two languages alone: Hebrew and Greek. The Hebrew teachers, now required to learn Greek, attended afternoon classes beginning in 1938.[170] Of the fifty teachers examined by the Greek state for language proficiency, only thirty-three passed satisfactorily—although disappointing to state officials, still a noteworthy percentage (two-thirds) considering that Greek was not their native language.[171] Some of those teachers educated during the Ottoman period now began to perfect their signatures in Greek, including the sixty-year-old director of the Baron Hirsch school, Yomtov Saltiel.[172]

The two other languages that had vied for prominence in the Jewish communal school curriculum were thus gradually excised. Desiring to reduce so-called foreign influence in Greece, the Ministry of Education and Religion under Metaxas attempted to suppress foreign languages, including French, which was seen as a national threat due to its use in Catholic missionary schools for proselytism. The assault on French—despite complaints

Subjects	Grade 1	Grade 2	Grade 3	Grade 4	Grade 5	Grade 6
Greek language	9	9	9	9	9	9
Arithmetic	2	2	3	3	3	3
Geometry	-	-	-	-	1	1
History	-	-	1	2	2	2
Geography	3	3	2	2	2	2
Natural history	-	-	2	2	1	1
Chemistry	-	-	-	-	2	2
Singing	1	1	1	1	1	1
Calligraphy	-	2	1	1	1	1
Handicrafts	1	1	1	1	1	1
Gymnastics	2	2	2	2	2	2
Drawing	1	1	1	1	1	1
Total hours/week of classes in Greek	19	21	23	24	26	26
Total hours/week of classes in Hebrew (Judaism, Jewish history, Hebrew Bible, and Hebrew language)	12	12	12	12	10	10
Total hours/week of instruction	31	33	35	36	36	36

Figure 3.6. Curriculum of the Jewish Communal Schools, October 1938. Source: Mentesh Bensanchi, president of Superior Commission of Jewish Instruction, to Chief Rabbi Koretz, October 30, 1938, USHMM, r. 691, d. 145.

from Jewish and Orthodox Christian educators—led the Jewish communal schools to fire seven of their French teachers in 1938–1939.[173]

Increasingly marginalized and ultimately removed from the curriculum, Judeo-Spanish met a similar fate. A veteran Judeo-Spanish teacher, Alegre Samuel, was classified with the French teachers and let go in 1934. As a dedicated teacher of fifteen years, with an unemployed husband and several children to feed, Samuel even offered to teach cooking classes to keep her job. Although temporarily reinstated, she was definitively removed from the payroll in 1936.[174] Such was the fate of formal Judeo-Spanish instruction in Jewish communal schools during the era of Metaxas. Ironically, even as Jewish youth ceased learning Judeo-Spanish formally, Jewish adults continued to attend lectures at the Béné Bérith Lodge and read books and newspapers in Judeo-Spanish in order to familiarize themselves with Greek history, culture, and politics. Some Jewish adults learned to embrace Hellenism in Judeo-Spanish much like the previous generation imbibed Ottomanism in Judeo-Spanish.[175]

With the bilingual Greek and Hebrew curricula for the Jewish communal schools in place in 1938, a sense of stability prevailed even if the quality of instruction varied. Chief Rabbi Koretz indicated that relations between Greek and Jewish teachers were improving. While Greek language instruction was "perfect" in three schools, students in two others could barely speak it. Koretz requested that parents encourage their children to "speak the language of the country." Even less impressed with Hebrew instruction, Koretz reported that Greek teachers complained that the old style of teaching the Hebrew Bible by rote and through translation into Judeo-Spanish continued—a sign that, although technically no longer part of the curriculum, Judeo-Spanish retained a presence in the Jewish communal schools. He also recommended that Jewish teachers bring students to Sabbath services at the synagogues, just as Orthodox Christian teachers at state schools brought their students to church on Sunday, to increase students' engagement with their religion. Koretz lamented that, in effect, Greek education had surpassed Jewish education at Jewish communal schools. Only the most dedicated students could become proficient in Hebrew as they spoke Judeo-Spanish at home and now Greek on the streets.[176]

To strengthen the bonds between Jewish students' Jewish and Greek senses of belonging, the Jewish Community of Salonica and the Greek state partnered to establish new textbooks for Jewish communal schools and for Jewish students in Greek state schools. This final, previously unknown episode in the history of Jewish education in Salonica on the eve of World War II illuminates the prospect of fusing Jewish and Hellenic identities through education. As the controversy over the use of the Passover Haggadah in the Jewish communal schools made clear, the Ministry of Education and Religion wanted to police the books used in Jewish schools. As the complaint filed about the Greek teacher who forced her Jewish students to follow the lessons on Christianity also made clear, no suitable Greek textbooks existed that integrated Judaism. The Jewish Community of Salonica and the Ministry of Education and Religion agreed to rectify both problems.[177]

Minutes of the Communal Council from 1939 detailed plans for two new textbooks in cooperation with the Ministry of Education and Religion: one in Hebrew dealing primarily with Greek history and a second in Greek dealing with Judaism. The Hebrew textbook was to focus on "patriotic education" to enhance Jewish students' "knowledge of Greece" and the "glorious events of Hellenic history." The focus on Greece would be supplemented by passages on Jewish history and morality to inspire in the Jewish student a "love for his race and religion." The dual emphases sought to harmonize Judaism and Hellenism, Greek historical consciousness and the Hebrew language, Jewish pride in "race and religion" combined with Greek patriotism.[178] Since the Jewish Community already possessed Hebrew primers—the *Ba-Dereh* series produced in 1934—the Communal Council tabled the project and instead focused on the Greek-language textbook.[179]

The Greek textbook was deemed to be of great urgency because of the numerous Jewish students enrolled in Greek government schools for Jewish students and general Greek state elementary and secondary schools. As Joseph Nehama indicated, on the eve of World War II, 934 Jewish students attended four government schools for Jewish pupils; 1,584 attended Greek state primary schools; and 839 attended Greek state secondary schools. In short, 3,357 of 7,690 Jewish students in Salonica—over 40 percent—attended Greek state schools.[180] This figure suggests a remarkable transformation in Jewish education in the city: from the plurality of Jewish students attending Jewish communal schools in 1930, to the plurality of Jewish students enrolled in Greek state schools nearly a decade later. In effect, the Greek state had succeeded to a certain degree in co-opting the education of Jewish youth in Salonica and prying them away from the Jewish Community. Integration also brought about hardship: Saby Saltiel, the director of the Jewish Community, lamented that two "Greek boys" beat up his son, breaking his leg, in front of one of the state schools. Saltiel lost sleep worrying about his child and the state of Jewish-Orthodox Christian relations in the city.[181]

The Jewish Community sought to regain control in the domain of Jewish instruction by producing the new Greek-language textbook on Judaism. While students at government schools for Jewish students received Jewish instruction, those at the Greek state elementary and secondary schools did not. The new Greek textbook therefore targeted those Jews at general state

	Late 1920s	c. 1932	c. 1939
Jewish Communal Schools	3,365 (1928)	–	3,805
Private Jewish Schools	3,412 (1928)	–	245
Greek State Schools for Jews (est. 1929–1930)	n/a	1440	934
General Greek State Schools (elementary and secondary)	5 (1925) 46 (1927) 479 (1929)	831	2,423
Foreign Schools (secular and missionary)	c. 2,000 (1929)	–	283
Total Jewish Students	c. 9,256 (1928–1929)	–	7,690

Figure 3.7. Attendance of Jewish students at Jewish communal schools, private schools, Greek state schools, and foreign schools, 1925–1939. Sources: Minutes of Superior Commission of Jewish Instruction, 1924–1932, BZI; reports of Jewish schools, 1928, JMTh, f. 138; Figures compiled by Superior Commission of Jewish Instruction, ca. 1932, CAHJP; *Las Eskolas Komunalas*, 19; Michael Molho, *In Memoriam*, 23; Benbassa and Rodrigue, *Sephardi Jewry*, 100.

schools. The Greek state also approved a proposal for Jewish teachers to be sent not only to the government schools for Jewish students—a practice initiated in 1930—but now, in the 1939–1940 school year, for Jewish teachers to be sent to general Greek state schools to ensure that Jewish students received a Jewish education as part of the Greek state curriculum. The most respected teachers, including Michael Molho and Joseph and Simon Pessah, the sons of the chief rabbi of Volos, were assigned to six general Greek state schools that enrolled a total of 766 Jewish students.[182] The prospect of the state promoting the education of some of its citizens as both Greeks and as Jews took center stage.

The Hellenizing of Jewish students in Salonica remarkably involved the Judaizing of their curriculum at the Greek state schools. As Greece did not introduce the separation of church and state and included Orthodox Christian prayer as part of the state educational curriculum, it was deemed fair to accommodate Jewish students who flooded the state schools. The new textbook became part of a series of projects endorsed by the Jewish Community of Salonica in 1939 to translate key Jewish texts into Greek, such as *Pirke*

Avoth ("Ethics of our Fathers"), the Passover Haggadah, and a history of the Jews, all destined for use by Jewish students at Greek state schools and for Jewish youth more generally, many of whom became literate in Greek but not necessarily in Hebrew or Judeo-Spanish.[183]

Just as the Greek Ministry of Education and Religion delegated the responsibility for composing and approving passages in the textbook dealing with Orthodox Christianity to the ecclesiastical authorities, they insisted that only the rabbis could approve passages about Judaism to be included in the new Greek textbook.[184] Remarkably, all four figures linked to the project shared a similar trajectory. Due to their roots in Volos, which had been part of Greece since 1881, Simon and Joseph Pessah benefitted from a Greek-language education since their youth and served as the primary authors of the textbook. Salonican-born Eliau Barzilai, the chief rabbi of Athens, approved their work.[185] The main promoter of the new book was Samuel Saltiel, a teacher in the Jewish schools for more than twenty years. All of them had been protégés of Isaac Epstein, the head of the Talmud Tora during the final years of Ottoman rule; all attended the Hebrew Teachers College in Jerusalem; all received traditional Jewish educations infused with Ottomanism, Hebraism, and Zionism; and all were on the frontlines as they sought to transform Jewish youth into Greek citizens while strengthening their sense of Jewish religious identity and Zionist political orientation. Having been born in Greece, the Pessah brothers helped all the other teachers transform their students and themselves in a Hellenic mold: from Ottoman Jews into Hellenic Jews.

La Aksion announced the publication of the textbook on the front page in January 1940. Saltiel explained that these "special Greek books" containing "religious Jewish content for Jewish youth" resulted from a "magnanimous gesture" of the Metaxas regime. The aim of the book was to "instill in the youth a love for our beloved homeland and for Jewish religious sentiment." The book also promoted cultural interchange in order to ensure that future generations of Jews "will learn the treasures of our [Jewish] literature in the beautiful language of Homer" and to provide all Greek-speaking teachers, who form part of the Salonican elite, an unprecedented opportunity to learn about Judaism. "We should feel proud, we Jews," Saltiel asserted, "to live in a liberal country that inculcates in its children the love of national education in addition to love for their own religion." He expressed gratitude for the "favor" that the Metaxas regime did for the Jews of the city by permitting them to produce such an innovative book and by "not distinguishing between its citizens."[186]

Remarkably, such praise for the Metaxas regime recalled old-style pan-egyrics that focused on favors rather than rights and referred to the decision of the state to not distinguish between its citizens precisely when it did. But this was the idealized liberalism to which Saltiel referred, one that recognized religious differences among the citizenry by endowing both Jews and Christians with equally legitimate claims to their religion and to a sense of belonging to the Hellenic national family. The Jewish Community and the Metaxas regime thus advocated for the continued differentiation between Jews and Christians along religious lines while emphasizing their political unity. Both Jews and Christians were to be understood as Hellenic citizens. And for the first time, aspects of Jewish history and culture were to be included as part of the Greek state curriculum—a plan cut short by the war and subsequently forgotten.

Conclusion: The Jewish-Greek Future of Salonican Schools

Certain Jewish leaders, most notably Joseph Nehama, advocated for a more radical goal than preserving specifically Jewish and Christian religious instruction in public schools: the disappearance of all distinctions between Jews and Christians. Writing in 1940 in the conclusion to *Histoire des Israélites de Salonique*, Nehama ironically appealed to Christian sources, namely the New Testament, to justify this universalizing trajectory:

> For the Jew, it is a duty and a necessity to reconcile his fidelity toward his religious traditions—his honor before history—with the most complete moral assimilation with his fellow citizens of other religions. Such an enterprise is impossible and perilous among ancient and medieval people where the practices of religion envelop and penetrate all acts of political and civil life. In a secularized society, without taking into account that it constitutes an inevitable evolution, it offers neither danger nor serious difficulty. Assimilation is not identification. Moral union can be established without complete fusion. Christ said: 'There are many rooms in my father's house' [John 14:2]. At the

same time, there are many spiritual provinces in a country, and national unity is not compromised by a variety of accents and nuances. The work will be completed by the schools, which, as Edouard Herriot [a French educator and politician] said, are the temples of concord, tolerance, and national fraternity. Thanks to the schools the famous words of St. Paul, 'There are no longer Jews or Greeks' [Galatians 3:28], will become truth and reality.[187]

Taking the integrationist ideology of the Alliance to its logical endpoint, Nehama remained overly optimistic and his predictions unrealized. Greece did not follow his envisioned path toward secularization along the model of France. Despite the era of liberalism during the tenures of Venizelos and the advancement of linguistic acculturation among Salonica's Jews, the Greek state under Metaxas did not decouple national and religious identities. In this regard, the official leadership of the Jewish Community remained more in tune with the expectations of the Greek state as both embarked upon an experiment to transform Ottoman Jews into Hellenic Jews. The proposal that Jews could be Greeks or Hellenes meant that the locus of national identity and citizenship needed to shift away from Orthodox Christianity—despite it being enshrined in the constitution—and instead toward the Greek language. Such a proposal was radical itself and envisaged a capacious version of Hellenism inclusive of Jews. This version of Hellenism was a repackaged Ottomanism of the late nineteenth century according to which Jews, Muslims, and Christians could all preserve a sense of their distinctive communal identities while uniting in shared political loyalty to the state regardless of religion or language. The interwar version of Hellenism, however, added an extra dimension by insisting on the Greek language as the social glue to bind together all Hellenic citizens, regardless of religion, not only to the state but also to each other.

The endpoint of Nehama's integrationist argument posed a more grave threat to the social and religious structure of Greek society. The Jewish Community and the Greek state called for the perpetuation of Jews and Christians as discrete and recognized categories—in education as in family law—in combination with the retention of Orthodoxy as the state religion. For Nehama, however, the endpoint of the evolution of society through secularization would compel the boundaries between Jews and Christians to dissolve, religion to be relegated to the private sphere, and the introduction of the principle of separation of church and state—in short, the undermining of an organizing principle of modern Greek society. Precisely to guard against the creation of a society in which there was neither Jew nor Greek but only individual Hellenic citizens, the Jewish Community and the Greek state invested in an alternative by reinforcing communal belonging through the integration of Jewish students and Judaism into state schools. For a moment, the experiment in interwar Jewish education promised to expand the boundaries of Hellenic belonging to include Jews while nonetheless preserving the religious differences between Jewish and Christian youth in the hope of achieving harmonious relations among the country's citizens. The process, however, was cut short at a pivotal juncture due to the havoc wrought by World War II.

This chapter has illustrated the extent to which Jews in Salonica relied on Jewish educational institutions, especially those run by the Jewish Community and ultimately those under the jurisdiction of the Greek state, to help them navigate the path away from the Ottoman Empire and toward the Greek state and to reshape themselves and their children into Jews and Hellenes. Jewish communal educational administrators largely did not resist Hellenization during the interwar years but formulated a vision of Hellenism in partnership with the state that preserved their sense of identification with the Jewish Community, with Judaism, and with elements of Jewish culture, while also emphasizing allegiance to the Greek language and the Greek state. Nehama's assimilationist fantasy, which envisioned a future with neither Jew nor Greek, remained unrealized. On the eve of World War II, in contrast, the Jewish communal and state schools were on the brink of a different future in Salonica, one that would include both Jews and Greeks—and, indeed, Hellenic Jews. But this rapprochement was foiled by the war. Filled out in Greek, the Jewish communal school roll books indicate that Jewish students, ages six to twelve, continued to register for classes during the German occupation, at least until March 3, 1943, even once ghettoization commenced and until less than two weeks before deportations began to Auschwitz—the site where most of Salonica's Jewish children, the up-and-coming generation of Hellenic Jews, lost their lives.[188]

CHAPTER 4

PAVING THE WAY FOR BETTER DAYS

The Historians

Por ser un verdadero djudyo kale posedar alomenos tres livros:
un livro de tefila, una biblia, i una estorya de los djudyos.

To be a true Jew one must own at least three books:
a prayer book, a bible, and a history of the Jews.[1]

Writing in 1892 in Salonica's main Judeo-Spanish newspaper, *La Epoka*, the teacher Mercado Covo lamented that "there is no other field of study more backward today among the Jews of this country [the Ottoman Empire] than the study of Jewish history. . . . This is a void that must be filled."[2] Inspired by empire-wide celebrations in 1892 that commemorated the four hundredth anniversary not of the expulsion of Jews from Spain but of their arrival in the Ottoman realm, Covo hoped that Salonican and Ottoman Jewish in-tellectuals would heed his call, study Jewish history, and demonstrate their loyalty to the sultan. Covo further proposed the creation of a "Literary and Scientific Society" to contribute to "removing the veil of invisible history for many of our brothers of Turkey."[3] Although nothing immediately came of his proposal, beginning in 1899 a Hebraist society, *Kadima*, brought together Jewish intellectuals to explore Jewish literature and history.[4] But local Jewish newspapers observed that readers continued to view the field of history as a mere set of "curious details."[5]

The apparent absence of a popular historical awareness, let alone interest, is remarkable given later characterization of Salonica's Jews. The well-known scholar of Sephardic studies, Maír José Benardete, writing in 1953, construed Salonica as a "diminutive Jewish republic," echoing the sixteenth-century de-scription by famed Salonican rabbi, Moses Almosnino, of "our noble republic of Salonica."[6] The key ingredient that elevated Salonica to this status, in Benardete's mind, was the alleged historical awareness of the city's Jews: "There was enough learning to give these [Salonican] Jews a historical consciousness that made them aware of their existence and their relationship to the Jewish world as a whole and to the Gentile world in general. Historical awareness is the key to self-discovery."[7]

While historical awareness very well may be a key to self-discovery, Salonican Jewish elite—not to mention the broader Jewish public—developed such an attribute only gradually from the late nineteenth century until World War II. Only in the interwar years did popular interest in Jewish history blossom. As one commentator in a local Judeo-Spanish magazine, *La Nasion*, remarked in 1932: "A beautiful flourishing of history writers can be noted in our city. In almost every local Jewish publication, every day we see the growing interest in all that concerns the past of our collectivity in Salonica. This is a good sign."[8] Another Zionist magazine, *Israel*, quipped in 1932 that history writing was à la mode: "We are seeing this year a new fashion in Jewish journalism of our city: the publicizing of the history of Jewish Salonica for the readers."[9] In both of these descriptions, historical inquiry appears novel and unprecedentedly popular. Taking advantage of the new, expanded audience, Salonican Jewish intellectuals of a variety of political orientations expressed their voices as individuals and as a collective through the articulation and dissemination of historical narratives.

Jewish history migrated from the margins of Salonican Jewish attention during the 1890s to the very center of public discussion during the interwar years. In retrospect, it seemed as if that historical consciousness, that confident historical voice, had been there all along. Changing political and cultural dynamics in the city and the region, especially the upheavals of the final decades of Ottoman rule and the transition to Greek hegemony, propelled Jewish intellectuals to engage more deeply with Jewish history, to anchor themselves in their city, and to write themselves into the narratives of their country during a period in which their future prospects remained uncertain. Unlike Turkish or Greek history writers who benefitted from the support of the state in creating official national narratives, or Jewish scholars in France and Germany who gained the support of universities or rabbinical seminaries, Jewish history writers in Salonica initiated their scholarship with little institutional support.[10]

The interwar years initially afforded an opportunity for rapprochement between Jews and their Orthodox Christian neighbors through the field of historical studies. In 1929, the Greek newspaper *Nea Alithia* established a commission of local writers to compose a history of the province of Macedonia inclusive of its Jewish residents. *El Puevlo* encouraged several Jewish intellectuals to participate in this "eminently useful national project" that finally would provide an opportunity to compose a history of the Jews of Salonica.[11] But the onset of the depression, the anti-Jewish riots in 1931, and proposals to expropriate the Jewish cemetery transformed the opportunity for cooperative history writing into a tense dynamic that placed Jewish intellectuals on the defensive. In 1932, the editor of the Greek newspaper *Makedonia*, Nikos Fardis, continued to stir up anti-Jewish animosity. He published a history of Salonica in which he emphasized the key role played in the first century by the apostle Paul in bringing enlightenment (i.e., Christianity) to the city, the "Second Athens," despite, as he phrased it, the hatred, opposition, and attacks of the local, economically powerful Jews.[12] While he accepted the ancient roots of Jews in the city, Fardis cast Jewish animosity against Christians in antiquity as continuing into his own day—an impression that Jewish intellectuals sought to overturn and that rendered Jewish history a popular topic in 1932.

Confronting increasing efforts by the state to Hellenize the city, rising popular anti-Jewish sentiment, economic crisis, and the lingering effects of the fire of 1917, an energetic cohort of Salonican Jews turned to the annals of their own past to provide comfort (*afalago*), consolation (*konorte*), and inspiration to produce the necessary knowledge to overcome the present "crisis of confidence," to regain "our energy and vitality," and to bridge the divide between the Ottoman Empire and the Greek state. This historiographical enterprise, as *El Puevlo* explained in 1929, acquired the aura of a "sacred task," compared to the redaction of holy texts such as the Torah and the Talmud, written down in response to a sense of decline. For Jews in Salonica, reflection on their past eras of grandeur would help them overcome the crisis and "pave the way for better days to come."[13] In 1933, *La Aksion* celebrated Salonica as a "city of miracles and wonders," which experienced apogees and perigees in its twenty-three centuries of history and always "revived" itself, like a "phoenix rising from the ashes." The present moment, the newspaper continued, did not signify the end of that history: "More quickly than you can imagine, the good days will return . . . We make this judgment based on the past; we have faith in the star of Salonica. This star flies high . . . Salonican brothers, have courage, have confidence."[14]

The new dynamics required a complete reframing of the Salonican Jewish past from a tale of Ottoman-Jewish romance since 1492 into one of Hellenic-Jewish synergy since antiquity. Mercado Covo, Baruch Ben-Jacob, Joseph Nehama, Isaac Emmanuel, and Michael Molho each contributed to the mythologization of Salonica as a major—indeed unique—Jewish center in the world. Shaped by their ideologies and personal proclivities, they varyingly cultivated images of the city as a Jewish, Sephardic, or Macedonian (and hence Hellenic) metropolis. New historical narratives, they hoped, would endow Salonica's Jews with a new claim to the city's past and pave the way for a secure future.

Constructing a Jewish Historical Voice

The history of the Spanish Jews since their expulsion from Spain has yet to be written. Neither Graetz nor Kayserling succeeded in giving us a complete and coherent description of the life of our ancestors since their settlement in the Ottoman Empire through the present. . . . Only God knows if it will ever be possible to write it and if a historian will be found to fill this void. We are thus a branch of the tree of the people of Israel who do not have a history for a very important period of our existence. As if abandoning all desire to live, we have not judged it necessary to document our existence or leave any evidence behind. They say that we, the Jews of the Orient, are a family of mutes, a group of people without a language or literature. We add to this double negation yet a third: we do not have history . . .[15]

Included in a series of Judeo-Spanish pamphlets called "The Library of the Jewish Family" and published in Salonica in 1911 by the Alsheh Institute, Maurice Cohen's remarks illustrate the nearly complete absence of written histories of Ottoman Jews, Salonica included. It was an omission that brought shame to the empire's Jews and deprived them of their own, distinctive voice.[16] Cohen situated his endeavor, a first attempt to offer a history of Jewish women in the Ottoman realm, in the context of the already-available scholarship by Jewish scholars in Europe—such as Heinrich Graetz and Meyer Kayserling, both in Germany—who elided the Ottoman Jewish experience. Joined by other Ottoman Jewish writers like Abraham Danon, Salomon Rosanes, Moïse Franco, and Abraham Elmaleh, Salonican Jewish intellectuals initially engaged in an intra-Jewish dialogue with the prevailing German Jewish model of the *Wissenschaft des Judentums*, and with the less influential but more sympathetic French Jewish approach developed by writers linked to the Alliance Israélite Universelle. Initially internalizing their inferior position vis-à-vis French and German Jews, Salonican Jewish intellectuals ultimately harnessed aspects of both historiographic traditions, especially the sympathetic portrayal in French Jewish scholarship, to overcome their uncomplimentary characterization, to reclaim their history, and to situate Salonica at the center of their story. They used their tales to improve their image in the eyes of European Jews and to position themselves favorably within the Ottoman and subsequently Greek contexts.

To demonstrate their fitness for citizenship and full participation in European society, *Wissenschaft* scholars like Heinrich Graetz sought to recast the Jewish historical narrative in a European mold. In his renowned multi-volume work, *History of the Jews* (1853–1874), Graetz portrayed the famed Jews of medieval Spain as torchbearers of European civilization who participated fully in the surrounding society—a model Graetz thought German Jews of his own day ought to emulate. In medieval Spain, Graetz asserted, Judaism itself assumed "a European character and deviated more and more from its Oriental form."[17] But this reputation did not follow the Jews after their expulsion from Spain. Although welcomed into the Ottoman Empire, Jews living under the sultan soon declined, according to Graetz, for they "did not produce a single great genius who originated ideas to stimulate future ages, nor mark out a new thought for men of average intelligence."[18] The seventeenth-century messianic debacle of Sabbetai Sevi, who converted from Judaism to Islam, epitomized this decline for Graetz: "The glory of the Turkish Jews was extinguished like a meteor, and plunged into utter darkness."[19] Because Sevi centered his activities in Salonica, Graetz characterized the city as a "kabbalistic hotbed of old" filled with "irrational . . . madmen" tricked by false messianism, and as the site through which all of Ottoman Jewry fell into a "Jewish dark age."[20] The Jews of Salonica never reappeared in Graetz's narrative.

A passage that Graetz dedicated to sixteenth-century Salonica nonetheless became crucial for the effort by the city's Jews to valorize their history.
In describing the arrival of Jews in the Ottoman Empire after 1492, Graetz
translated into German a now well-known account in Portuguese by the
converso poet, Samuel Usque, who emphasized that Salonica became a major
Jewish center:

> The second biggest community in Turkey was Salonica (the ancient Thessa-
> lonica), which, although an unhealthy city, attracted the Sephardic emigrants.
> The main current of them went to this coastal town because this former
> Greek city offered more leisure for peaceful occupation than the noisy capital
> of Turkey.... Salonica practically became a Jewish town, in which more Jews
> dwelt than non-Jews. The poet Samuel Usque hyperbolically [*hyperbolisch*]
> called this town a "mother of Judaism" [*Mutter des Judentums*].[21]

Salonican Jewish intellectuals discovered Usque's account and held it up as
the best evidence for their city's historic grandeur. But they encountered it
as mediated not only by Graetz's translation but, more precisely, by translations from German into Judeo-Spanish and French by Rabbi Abraham
Danon from Edirne, one of the first Ottoman Jewish historians.[22] By rewriting Graetz's account, Danon and Salonican Jewish intellectuals transformed
Salonica from a "practically Jewish town" into an "unquestionably Jewish city," and from an exaggerated, hyperbolic "mother of Judaism" into a
legitimate and unquestioned "mother of Israel," an allusion to the Hebrew
ir va-em be-Israel ("city and mother in Israel") from 2 Samuel 20:19. Without
ever seeing the original Portuguese text by Usque, who had referred to the
city as *madre de Judesmo*, Salonican Jewish intellectuals naturalized their city
not as *a* "mother of Judaism" but rather as *the only* "mother of Israel" (*madre
de Israel*). The success with which Jewish intellectuals relied on Graetz's reading of Usque, massaged his text, and overturned his message by canonizing
the image of Salonica as the "mother of Israel" explains why scholars have
assumed that "Salonica: Mother of Israel" was the unquestioned motto of
Salonica's Jews for centuries.[23]

While Graetz wrote the most widely-read Jewish history in the nineteenth century, the Alliance Israélite Universelle actively transmitted
intellectual trends to Jews in the Ottoman Empire and provided another

framework for Salonican Jewish writers. Beginning in 1892–1893, Alliance schools introduced into the curriculum postbiblical Jewish history. Rather than marginalize and exclude Ottoman Jews from their narrative, as in the case of the *Wissenschaft* scholarship, French Jewish intellectuals integrated Ottoman Jews into their historical narratives to highlight the progress toward regeneration that Ottoman Jews had made thanks to the intervention of the Alliance; in so doing, they sought to validate the ideology and aims of the French Jewish establishment. Perhaps unwittingly, they also provided further proof for Salonica's Jews of their own historical merit.

Through the activities of the Alliance, French Jewish intellectuals gained firsthand knowledge of Ottoman Jews in ways that German Jewish intellectuals, such as Graetz, did not (even if French Jewish scholars' interest in Ottoman Jewry coexisted with a paternalistic gaze upon the "child-like" Oriental Jews in need of uplifting from their civilized brethren in Paris).[24] Théodore Reinach, an archaeologist and politician educated at the École des Hautes Études en Sciences Sociales and author of the most important example of French-Jewish historiography, *Histoire des Israélites* (1884), not only married into a prominent Ottoman Jewish family (Camondo) but also had visited Salonica, where he noted with pleasure the progress of Jewish education at the Alliance schools.[25]

The *Histoire* partially rehabilitated Ottoman Jewish history. Reinach noted that the sultans valued the commercial activity of the Jews, who enjoyed vast liberty under the authority of the rabbis. Unlike Graetz, who saw the seventeenth century as a period of decline that severed Ottoman Jews from their Spanish roots and their initial flourishing in the sixteenth century, Reinach hinted at continuity by still referring to the "Spanish origin" of Ottoman Jews.[26] He similarly emphasized that Salonica "was, as it still is today, a half-Jewish city where the Spanish element greatly dominated."[27] While condemning the fanaticism of Sabbetai Sevi and noting that his followers centered themselves in Salonica, Reinach viewed the movement's success as a result of the "decadence" of Jewish society in general and not as a particularly Ottoman or Salonican phenomenon.[28] Moreover, due to the *Tanzimat* and the successful intervention of the Alliance in the realm of Jewish education, Reinach emphasized that Salonican and Ottoman Jews "have begun to make serious progress"—a far cry from the continued lethargy expressed in Graetz's characterization of them.[29]

Salonica-based Jewish historians further appropriated aspects of both the German and French Jewish perspectives to compose their own narratives of their city and provide Salonica's Jews with a historical voice.

The Professor

A teacher born in Serres to parents from Salonica, Mercado Covo (1874–1940) became one of the first champions of Jewish history in the Judeo-Spanish press in Salonica and in the Ottoman Empire more broadly. He followed the examples of Abraham Danon from Edirne as well as Judah Nehama (1825–1899) from Salonica. Retrospectively nicknamed the "Turkish Mendelssohn" for introducing the Haskalah (Jewish Enlightenment) to Salonica, Nehama researched the history of Salonica's Jews, but his manuscript was lost in the fire of 1890. He did publish correspondence with eminent Jewish intellectuals across Europe, some of which dealt with history; all was in Hebrew. An admirer and eulogizer of Nehama, Covo also wrote about Jewish history but in Judeo-Spanish and encouraged Jewish allegiance to the Ottoman Empire. He referred to this endeavor as "holy work."[30] Although an adamant advocate of Ottomanism, Covo transferred his allegiance soon after Salonica became part of Greece and emerged as an ardent Jewish promoter of Hellenism. He articulated not only dominant narratives of Ottoman-Jewish romance but also narratives of Jewish-Greek symbiosis. For his role as a teacher, lecturer, and writer, he was affectionately called "the professor."

Covo was well-suited to promote the history of Salonica's Jews in both Ottoman and Greek contexts due to his schooling at Jewish, Greek, and Ottoman institutions. At a Jewish elementary school in Serres, a town about forty miles northeast of Salonica, he studied religious and general subjects including French, Hebrew, and some Turkish.[31] As he had learned Greek while helping his father in business, he then attended a Greek school but soon transferred to the new *idadi* (Ottoman imperial lycée) in Serres. Beginning in 1895, he taught at the new Alliance school in Serres before settling in his parents' hometown, Salonica, around 1905.[32] Drawn to French culture, he served as a correspondent for *L'Univers Israélite*, a Jewish magazine in Paris, and became a member of the Société des Études Juives.[33] Over the next thirty-five years, Covo became a revered teacher of French and history at the Jewish communal schools, the Alsheh and Pinto private schools, and the rabbinical colleges. Dressed in the latest European fashions, donning spectacles and a moustache (but no beard), Covo contributed to the local press, served as director of the Jewish communal library, and lectured at the Béné Bérith Lodge. He died in 1940, several months before Greece entered World War II; his wife and daughter both perished in Auschwitz.

While his formal education shaped his interest in the past, Covo traced this proclivity to family tradition. His most eminent relative on his maternal side was Rabbi Joseph Cohen (1496–1578), a Provence-born physician and author of a famous chronicle composed after the expulsion of 1492, *Emek Ha-Bakha* ("Valley of Tears"), which was translated into Judeo-Spanish in Salonica (1935), the city where Cohen's mother and sister had been buried.[34] Covo claimed that he had inherited Cohen's interest in historical recounting.[35] While *Emek Ha-Bakha* presented Jewish history as filled with persecution, Covo emphasized that a spirit of progress and coexistence shaped Jewish history in the Ottoman and Greek realms. He championed Salonica as a center for Ottoman and later Hellenic Jews—a place that represented his family's past and his own future.

Figure 4.1. Jewish teacher and writer Mercado Covo and family, early twentieth century. Source: Jewish Museum of Thessaloniki. Published with permission.

Celebrations across the Ottoman Empire in 1892 for the four hundredth anniversary of the arrival of Jews from Spain inspired the development of a popular Jewish historical consciousness for which Covo served as a driving force. In his first discussion of Jewish history, which nearly filled an issue of *La Epoka* the week before the 1892 celebration, Covo traced the expulsion of the Jews from Spain, their arrival in the Ottoman Empire, and the role of Salonica as a refuge.[36] The Ottoman Empire, he argued, was the first "open land to receive all the oppressed who desired tranquility."[37] Omitting the Sabbatean movement or any subsequent decline, Covo linked the past to the present by proclaiming that "the Jews lived and live free in Turkey."[38] Covo then turned to a discussion of Salonica, a city whose story he hoped would prove that Ottoman Jews had always blessed their enlightened empire. He repositioned Salonica as home to the "first rank" Jewish community in the Ottoman realm, "probably more important than that of Constantinople," for Salonica's "reputation had left the capital behind."[39]

In order to draw this conclusion, Covo relied on research at the Alliance in Paris. He referred to a manuscript acquired by the Alliance that had belonged to none other than Covo's purported sixteenth-century ancestor, Joseph Cohen. The manuscript included a now-famous letter apparently sent by Salonican Jews to their brethren in Provence in 1550 inviting them to come to the Ottoman Empire. The vice president of the Alliance, Isidore Loeb, first published the letter in French translation in *Revue des Études Juives* in 1888; Danon then translated it into Judeo-Spanish in his scholarly journal, *El Progreso*, in 1889; and now, in 1892, Covo presented it in Judeo-Spanish in *La Epoka* for a broader Jewish reading public. Introducing the document, *La Epoka* emphasized that the Jews in Provence had addressed themselves not to the Jews of the capital, Istanbul, but rather to the Jews of Salonica. Salonica thus became central to the image of the Ottoman Empire as a safe haven for persecuted Jews:

> It [the Ottoman Empire] is entirely open to you; settle here, our brethren, in the best of the land! . . . the poor and needy . . . will find here . . . a place where their feet can rest, and they will be able to exercise a suitable profession; they will suffer neither hunger nor thirst, they will not be afflicted by the burning fire of oppression and of exile, because the Lord has bestowed upon us

His mercy, and He has made us find favor, grace and pity in the eyes of the nations in the midst of which we are living, to such a degree that it would almost be proper to give us a new name and call us "the captives ransomed by the Lord" [Isaiah 35:10], because the Turk does not let us suffer any evil or oppression.[40]

This panegyric to the Ottoman Empire and its portrayal of the sultan's power to redeem the Jews in his land emphasized the thesis underpinning the 1892 celebrations, solidified the foundational Ottoman Jewish narrative—with Salonica at the center—and challenged the received template of Jewish history. Rather than disparaging the Ottoman Empire, Covo suggested an alternative: "Are we Jews, all across the world, not indebted to this government, which was the first to love us? . . . We must forever recognize [the Ottoman Empire] and express the most profound respect for everything bearing the name 'Ottoman.'"[41]

Covo continued to emphasize his dual sense of Jewish communal attachment and allegiance to the state. In the wake of the Young Turk Revolution in 1908, Covo embraced Jewish nationalism—cultural Zionism—while remaining a steadfast Ottomanist who supported the continued territorial integrity of the empire. He believed that, in order to conceptualize themselves as a distinct nation, Jews required not political independence but the capacity to develop their own unique voice that would transform them into "moral persons obeying their own conscience."[42] By encouraging Jewish self-awareness, he hoped to promote loyalty to the country and to strengthen "the sacred interests of my homeland [*patria*], Turkey, which I love with all my might."[43] In the local press, he also debated whether, through their embrace of "Jewish national sentiments and Ottoman patriotism," Jews in Salonica should be recognized as a model for Jews across the world: a true "citadel of Israel," "mother of Israel," or "metropolis of Judaism."[44]

Covo's endorsement of Jewish nationalism and Ottomanism ceased with the transfer of Salonica to Greek jurisdiction during the Balkan Wars. Once it became clear that Salonica would remain part of Greece, Covo sought to transform himself and his fellow Jews from Ottoman Jews into Hellenic Jews. With knowledge of Greek, he numbered among the few Jewish intellectuals in the city who could build bridges to the new state and to Orthodox

Christian neighbors. During the 1920s, he became an impassioned Hellenist while maintaining his support for Jewish nationalism. He envisioned
Hellenism to be just as capacious as Ottomanism before it—each, from his
perspective, served as an umbrella political framework that did not require
Jews to sacrifice their religion, culture, or language.

Covo wrote extensively in the French and Judeo-Spanish press on Jewish
and Greek history. His essays focused on local Jewish customs, Jewish education, Judeo-Spanish literature, Jewish culture in medieval Spain, the blood
libel, the ancient history of the land of Israel, and Greek-Jewish relations.
In a series entitled "Salonican Studies," Covo stressed that Salonica's Jews
contributed to the advancement of the city by establishing the first printing
presses in the sixteenth century and by promoting the medical sciences.[45]
He even dedicated one of his articles on Jewish printing to the library of
the University of Salonica, which he affectionately called the "alma mater
of Greece."[46] Covo also composed essays under the heading "Judeo-Greek
Studies" that highlighted cultural synergies between Greeks and Jews in antiquity: "one of the most brilliant pages in the history of civilization in the
Mediterranean basin."[47] Part of an apologetic literature composed by Jews
across Europe who sought to prove their contributions to civilization, Covo's
writing disseminated a new narrative for Salonica's Jews.[48]

Although Covo had indicated in 1892 that Jewish history began in Salonica in 1492 in order to emphasize the connection between the city's Jews
and the Ottoman Empire, he now stated in interwar Greece that Jewish
presence in the city actually dated to Hellenistic antiquity to the first century,
when the apostle Paul visited Salonica's synagogue, if not to the founding of
the city in 315 BCE. These Romaniote Jews, later absorbed by the Byzantine
Empire, formed part of the "purely Hellenic" population of Salonica in antiquity. Covo's purpose was clear: to prove to his readers, lest they should think
otherwise, that Jews belonged to Salonica just as much as Greeks, and that
they ought to continue to play a role in the city's future:

> Doubt is not permitted. The Jews have been in Salonica since the most an-
> cient times. They are as ancient as the Greeks. With the Greeks they were
> present at the dawn of the flourishing of the city and its development both
> in times of melancholy and anxiety during the invasions of the Avars, Slavs,

and Cretan corsairs; together they trembled before the Bulgarian advance and the invasion of the Lombards, Normans, Romans, and Epirotes; they suffered from threats from the Catalans, Turks, and Serbs, the revolution of the Zealots [fourteenth century], Venetian domination, and the capture of the city by the Turks. Greeks and Jews together witnessed all the triumphs and all the miseries. Following successes and failures, they now work together for the grandeur and happiness of this two-thousand-year-old city, for this pearl of the Aegean, for this ancient and ever young Thessaloniki.[49]

Covo harnessed this narrative in service of his Jewish Hellenism, which he embraced as fervently as he had his Jewish Ottomanism. He adhered to the new version of his ideology until his final days, writing on Hellenic Judaism with emphasis on Salonica and Athens as well as his native Serres.[50] He also lectured at the Béné Bérith in Judeo-Spanish to Jewish men and women over the age of forty who had not learned about Greek history and philosophy in school during the Ottoman era, in order to acquaint them with the role of Hellenic civilization in disseminating "rational and progressive humanism." He hoped that the older generations would begin to identify with the Hellenes and gain "faith in the intelligence of humankind, love for the homeland and for liberty."[51] Covo seemed to reconcile his Jewish affiliation and pride in Salonica while embracing Hellenic patriotism and remaining a steadfast Zionist as evidenced by the decision of the Jewish National Fund to honor him in 1938.[52]

The Apostle

Less concerned about shaping historical narratives to suit Ottoman or Greek frameworks, Baruch Ben-Jacob (1884–1943) aimed to educate Salonica's Jews about their own history, as Jews, in the city. Involved in the Mizrahi, the religious Zionist movement, and a respected teacher in the Jewish communal schools for forty years, Ben-Jacob was the only one of the history writers who maintained a full beard, a sign of his piety. He wrote extensively about Salonican Jewish history in Judeo-Spanish—never French, although he knew this language—yet remains the least known of the Salonican Jewish historians, likely due to his choice of language and because he ultimately perished in Auschwitz. A fundamentally Salonican Jewish history writer and

Figure 4.2. Baruch Ben-Jacob and his study of Jewish tombstone inscriptions, 1933. Page from *Israel*, the magazine of the Mizrahi youth movement. Source: Ben Zvi Institute.

popularizer who brought to the surface a strain of Jewish public engagement that he characterized as "traditionalist," "religious," and "nationalist," Ben-Jacob attracted a devoted following of readers, students, and congregants. A fellow Jewish teacher fittingly lauded him as the "apostle" of the Jewish history writers of Salonica.[53]

Ben-Jacob was a good candidate to promote Jewish national pride and the traditional observance of Judaism among Jews in Salonica. From a Jewish family of Italian origin, Ben-Jacob attended Salonica's Jewish schools, namely the Talmud Tora, where he studied under the Livorno-born rabbi Moshe Ottolenghi, and then the Beth Yosef rabbinical seminary. Through his training, he gained access to local rabbinical circles during the late Ottoman era and helped to publish the rabbinical decisions of Chief Rabbi Jacob Covo. Ben-Jacob began teaching Hebrew and Jewish history in the Jewish communal schools around 1901, served as a *hazan* at the Italia Yashan (Old Italy) synagogue and, after the fire of 1917, as a "renowned *darsan*" (preacher) in the 151 neighborhood. As a leader of the religious society Oave Tora ("Lovers of Torah," est. 1919), which promoted adherence to Jewish law and tradition, he gave sermons at the Beth Israel synagogue, which attracted 100–120 attendees each Sabbath, and 550 on the High Holidays.[54] Ben-Jacob also played a leading role in local Jewish choirs, including Naim Zemirot, which preserved the tradition of chanting Hebrew religious poetry using *makams* (Ottoman musical modes). Politically active, Ben-Jacob played a leading role in the Mizrahi, the religious-nationalist organization that placed Judaism at the core of the Jewish national ideal.[55]

Ben-Jacob's activism drew him to an array of other initiatives. When notables of the Katalan Hadash congregation reissued their *mahzor* (High Holiday prayer book) in 1927, on the four hundredth anniversary of its first publication in 1527, they commissioned Ben-Jacob to write the introduction. In 1930–1931, at the invitation of the Pro-Marrano Committee of the Spanish and Portuguese Jewish congregation in Amsterdam, Ben-Jacob travelled to Portugal to reeducate descendants of conversos in the normative practices of rabbinical Judaism. He met with acclaimed scholar and Lisbon Jewish leader, Moisés Amzalak, and with the prominent Portuguese military officer, Artur Carlos de Barros Basto, himself of converso background and the founder of the revived Jewish community in Porto.[56] Upon his return to Salonica, Ben-

Jacob participated in campaigns to document the city's Jewish cemetery, then under threat of expropriation. During the 1930s, he published more than a hundred articles in the local Judeo-Spanish press on Salonican Jewish history based on research in the cemetery and other sources that popularized the image of Salonica as a "center of scholarship and Jewish law," a city that produced or provided refuge to rabbis, kabbalists, Jewish poets, philosophers, astronomers, merchants, and doctors of world renown.[57]

It is not surprising that Ben-Jacob authored the first freestanding booklet in Judeo-Spanish on the history of the city's Jews, *Contribution to the History of the Jewish Community of Salonica*, which appeared in 1911, while Salonica remained under Ottoman rule. In this text, Ben-Jacob emphasized the exceptional status of Ottoman Jews within the annals of Jewish history. Enduring "sad and bitter" persecution nearly everywhere they went, Jews recorded their experiences and traditions, beginning with the Talmud, in order to survive across the generations. "But, fortunately," Ben-Jacob proclaimed, "this sad fate was never ours, we Ottoman Jews, who have been sheltered beneath the holy flag of Osman since our expulsion from Spain and Portugal, more than four hundred years ago." For Ben-Jacob, the notion that "massacres and persecutions are absent from Jewish history in Ottoman lands" explained, in part, why the need to record that history had not emerged.[58]

Ben-Jacob indicated that intra-Jewish tensions—not anti-Jewish persecution—spurred him to compose his booklet. As part of the Alsheh Institute's Library of the Jewish Family, the booklet targeted a local audience and sought to combat the "liberal press" and the weakening of the "national and traditional sentiments of the people."[59] Other pamphlets in the series included Maurice Cohen's *Women among the Spanish Jews of the Orient*, and Mercado Covo's *Documents on the Jewish Woman*, all of which targeted the Judeo-Spanish-reading masses.[60] A clear anxiety about the changing role of Jewish women motivated these publications.[61] But Ben-Jacob also stressed that his booklet sought to begin the work of overturning the marginalization and negative depiction of Ottoman Jews as represented in the work of great European Jewish scholars, such as Heinrich Graetz.

Ben-Jacob confronted the problem of decline in the wake of Sabbetai Sevi's conversion to Islam in the seventeenth century, an episode that, for scholars such as Graetz, embodied the decay of Ottoman Jewish society. Ben-

Jacob sought to shift the focus away from the alleged intellectual vacuity of Ottoman Jews and toward the challenging material conditions impacting Salonican Jews. The linchpin in the story was a long-forgotten "massacre" perpetrated in 1617, a reference to which he found in Jewish communal archives and in the writings of Salonican Jewish intellectual Judah Nehama.[62] In search of clues, Ben-Jacob went to the Jewish cemetery and discovered tombstone inscriptions that memorialized the victims of the tragedy.

A significant portion of Ben-Jacob's *Contribution* focused on this incident, the "Dolya massacre of 1617." He related that, on the 14th of Elul 5377, a band of brigands murdered a group of Salonican Jewish merchants returning from the annual fair in Dolya (a locale in the Former Yugoslav Republic of Macedonia). In the wake of the massacre, Salonica's rabbis signed an *askama* ("rabbinical ordinance") designating the 14th of Elul a "national fast day" for all future generations of Salonican Jews. In an unmatched act of solidarity, as Ben-Jacob presented it, all would also be required to attend annual commemoration ceremonies at the Talmud Tora. A disastrous fire in 1620, however, destroyed the Talmud Tora, and the memory of the massacre faded, in part because it became merely the first in a series of increasingly horrific calamities—fires and plagues—that wrought havoc on Salonica's Jews in the lead-up to the Sabbatean apostasy.[63] Ben-Jacob sought to demonstrate that Jews in Salonica became interested in messianism not due to lingering trauma from the expulsion from Spain in 1492, nor because of mystical practices, obscurantism, or the influence of their backward Oriental milieu, but rather as a response to anguish over specific conditions impacting their city.

In order to present the Dolya massacre within the larger framework of Jewish history, Ben-Jacob characterized it as a horrific "pogrom" and advocated for its inclusion in general Jewish histories. He wrote about it in prominent Hebrew journals in Cracow and Berlin, and in an entry on Salonica for the Hebrew-language Jewish encyclopedia *Otsar Yisrael*.[64] He also brought the episode to the attention of the acclaimed Jewish historian from Bulgaria, Salomon Rosanes, who excerpted Ben-Jacob's study in his celebrated *History of the Jews in Turkey*.[65]

But by the time Rosanes' work was published, "Turkey" (the Ottoman Empire) was no longer in control of Salonica. In fact, the transitional status of the city in 1913 was reflected in *Otsar Yisrael*'s identification of Ben-Jacob as a native of "Salonica, Europe" rather than of a specific country.[66] The redrawing of political borders, compounded by the destructive fire of 1917, provoked Ben-Jacob to reframe his historiographical endeavors by gesturing toward pre-1492 Jewish history in Salonica so as to accommodate the new dynamics of Hellenic sovereignty. He also wanted to provide a historical perspective through which to interpret the devastation of the fire and to instill confidence in the disillusioned Jewish masses. As he believed that youth would be responsible for reviving Jewish life in Salonica after 1917, Ben-Jacob, together with his brother, Aron Baruch, previously a teacher at the Alliance, published a new textbook in Judeo-Spanish, *Moral i Edukasion Djudia* ("Morale and Jewish education"), to use in a new school they established in the wake of the fire.[67] The Baruch brothers (*los ermanos Baruh*), as the Commission for Jewish Instruction referred to them, modeled their curriculum on the spirit of the Talmud Tora by focusing on Hebrew, Jewish history, and Judaism.[68] They named their school Eskola Nasionala Djudia Moderna ("The Modern Jewish National School"), which they called in Hebrew Midrash Ivrit Yavneh ("Yavneh Hebrew School"). The Baruch brothers hoped that their school would become a modern Salonican Yavneh, a center for the maintenance of Jewish national and religious sentiments following the fire, just as the original Yavneh, in Palestine, had become a Jewish stronghold after the destruction of the Temple in Jerusalem in 70 CE.

Intended for use in Jewish schools throughout the city, the Baruch brothers' new textbook concluded with a didactic chapter entitled "The History of the Jews of Salonica." Referring to the city as "The Little Jerusalem," they altered the starting point: no longer did the history of Jewish Salonica begin in 1492; it began in antiquity—"many hundreds of years ago"—when Greek-speaking Jews of the city operated their own "Greek synagogue."[69] By introducing a pre-Ottoman, Greek preamble to the history of the Jews of Salonica, the authors hoped to familiarize readers with the long-standing connections between Jews, Greek Christians, and the city itself. The Baruch brothers dedicated the rest of their historical essay—sixteen sections in total—to explicating the cyclical nature of the Jewish history of Salonica. For them, Jewish history repeated itself, and the history of Jewish Salonica, construed as paradigmatically Jewish, similarly cycled through apogees and perigees.[70] The Baruch brothers discerned three distinct cycles of the rise and fall of Jewish Salonica since 1492. The post-1917 era constituted the beginning of a fourth cycle.

For the Baruch brothers, the first period of Jewish Salonica's efflorescence transpired immediately following the arrival of the Jews from Spain in 1492. Jews in Salonica "transformed the face of the city" in terms of the economy, industry, and culture by advancing the textile industry and introducing the first printing press. The rise of "Jewish Salonica," the authors lamented, was cut short by several misfortunes. A massive fire in 1545 and a deadly epidemic in 1553 "threw the community into the darkest misery" and risked being "completely destroyed." The authors sought to demonstrate that the catastrophe of the fire of 1917 had precedent. The Jews of Salonica rebounded from their sixteenth-century misfortunes just as they could now rebound in the twentieth. After describing the fire and plague in the sixteenth century, the Baruch brothers concluded this first cycle by proclaiming: "Thus the glory was extinguished from such a brilliant community, which soon returned to life."[71]

The Baruch brothers next sketched a second cycle of the rise and fall of Jewish Salonica. Sections entitled "Sparks beneath the Ashes" and "Rays of Light" describe how Jews in Salonica reorganized their communal life under the leadership of rabbis like Samuel de Medina and Moses Almosnino. Commerce, the textile industry, and rabbinical scholarship were reborn: "All of this raised the prestige of the community and she [Salonica] approached her past glory."[72] The fortune of the Jews of Salonica, however, turned with the Dolya massacre of 1617 and the burning of the Talmud Tora in 1620.[73] But the following section, "Courage in the Face of Misfortune," enumerated how Salonican Jews aided each other: the rich donated to the poor and rebuilt the Talmud Tora. Here, as in the description of the aftermath of the fire of 1545, the twentieth-century reader was to take away a model of behavior to be emulated now in the wake of the 1917 fire.

The Baruch brothers explained the appeal of messianism in the wake of these disasters: "Until when will we suffer?! . . . is it not the hour of redemption? When will the messiah come?"[74] Within this context, the Baruch brothers explained, the purported messiah from Izmir, Sabbetai Sevi, exploited some of Salonica's Jews despite protests from several rabbis. It was important to emphasize that enlightened resistance persevered amidst the Sabbatean threat, and only several hundred Jewish families (a small minority) ultimately converted to Islam following the example of Sabbetai Sevi.

The Jews of Salonica similarly recovered from the devastation of the seventeenth century but, as the Baruch brothers suggested, it took much longer this time. They did not explicitly pinpoint a timeframe and skipped the entirety of the eighteenth century (which remains an under-researched period today). The next section, "New Era," highlights Jewish educational reform that contributed to a Jewish "awakening" in the nineteenth century. Rather than attribute the initiative to the Alliance, the authors pointed to the advances made by the Greeks and Muslims ("neighboring communities") as spurring the Jews to "catch up."[75] The authors went out of their way to emphasize the success of Jewish educational reform, which "armed" youth with "weapons for the struggle of life."[76] The Baruch brothers' livelihood and textbook depended upon, and constituted outgrowths of, these expanded educational initiatives.

During this "New Era," Salonican Jews experienced a "return" to the primary role in the city's economy. The resulting "general well-being" of the Jewish population fostered communal cohesion and the establishment of numerous philanthropic organizations, and cultural, intellectual, and sporting clubs. The synagogues became "true temples," the Talmud Tora was built anew (yet again), and the arrival of Allied troops during World War I brought additional profit.[77]

Most remarkably, the Baruch brothers did not refer to political changes, neither to the Young Turk Revolution nor the end of Ottoman rule and the incorporation of the city into Greece. The Baruch brothers told a story of Salonican Jews governing themselves autonomously. Yet, as was the case with the two previous epochs of Salonican Jewish prosperity that the brothers described, this one, too, was brought to a sudden end by fire. Describing the impact and devastation of the 1917 fire in terms mirroring those of the 1545 fire, the Baruch brothers lamented that this time, in 1917, not even the assistance sent from Europe and America could alleviate the extensive misfortune.

"The History of the Jews of Salonica" nonetheless concludes on an upbeat note. Indeed, it had to in order for the Baruch brothers' philosophy of history—their belief in the cyclical nature of Jewish history—to be legitimated. They presented a hopeful outlook, as the fourth era, one of flourishing, was an inevitable outcome of the efforts, ingenuity, and legacy of the Jews of Salonica: "The rebuilding of some synagogues and schools is being spoken about. Little by little, with time, it is certain, our great community so cruelly afflicted today, will be reborn from the ashes more brilliant than ever before!"[78] The emphatic, optimistic, and didactic message of this historical account is unmistakable. The separation that existed throughout the essay between the authors—who until then had employed the third person to discuss the Jews of Salonica—and the Jewish populace (the intended readers), now dissolved. Subject and object were conflated as the history of the Jews of Salonica was transformed into the history of "our great community." The inspiration from the past experiences of "our great community" would now teach "us" the ways to return to "our" previous heights. The pathway to the future, as Ben-Jacob and his brother saw it, was through the unique past of Jewish Salonica that again would render the city "the land of manna, milk, and honey."[79]

The Mentor

In contrast to Ben-Jacob, little remembered today, the most famous Salonican Jewish history writer, Joseph Nehama set the defining contours of the Salonican Jewish historical narrative that continue to define the field. His interest and passion for history persisted even while imprisoned in Bergen-Belsen, where he lectured about the Jews of Salonica to his fellow inmates. Friends referred to him as the "mentor" of all Salonica as well as its "minstrel," for he instilled in the city's Jews knowledge of their own poetic history. Nehama was unique among Salonican history writers, for only he was born and died in Salonica, having returned after liberation.[80] His "firm rootedness" in his native city, his "motherland" (*mère patrie*), and its Jewish population dated to the prewar years, as Nehama indicated in the 1935 preface to the first of seven volumes in his magnum opus, *Histoire des Israélites de Salonique*: "These pages powerfully evoke, in the soul of whomever would like to glance at them, a reflection of that love for the Jewish collectivity of Salonica that has sustained the author and guided him, during the long years that he has put into writing them!"[81] Given the vast influence of his writings and their accessibility in French, the single voice of Nehama, one of the city's "most illustrious sons," has often been synonymous with that of "Jewish Salonica."[82]

A relative of Judah Nehama, a rabbi and reformer in Salonica who helped bring the Alliance Israélite Universelle to the city, Joseph Nehama followed family tradition and played a leading role in Jewish communal life for more than thirty years. A life-long struggle with kyphosis compelled him to use a walking stick but never hindered his success as a teacher, writer, business-man, or communal leader. As a graduate of the Alliance school himself, he participated in the Association des Anciens Élèves de l'Alliance Israélite Universelle and the Hebraist society, Kadima, one of the city's first Jewish groups to cultivate an interest in history. After studying in Paris at the École Normale Israélite Orientale, the Collège de France, and the Sorbonne, Ne-hama returned to Salonica and served as the director of the local Alliance beginning in 1910; he was also a member of the Consultative Council of the Jewish Community that advised the Communal Council. Before the fire of 1917, he had lived in the city center; afterwards, he moved to Queen Olga Street, beyond the White Tower, to a well-to-do district inhabited by Or-thodox Christians and Jews alike. As the founder of the Banque Union in Salonica (est. 1926), Nehama invited an Orthodox Christian business leader to serve on the board—a sign of his desire for cross-communal cooperation.[83] Nehama utilized some of the fortune he earned as a banker for his research, at times commissioning other local scholars, such as Michael Molho, to undertake research on his behalf.[84]

Promoting the ideology of the Alliance, Nehama vociferously opposed Zionism and advocated for Jewish integration in both the Ottoman and Hel-lenic contexts. Involved in Freemasonry and a member of the Grand Lodge de Orient, Nehama supported the Young Turks, promoted Ottomanism, and dabbled in socialism.[85] First and foremost, he was Salonicanist. When ques-tioned about his position on Zionism in 1919, Nehama quipped: "What is this Palestine you're telling us about now? This [Salonica] is Palestine."[86] During the interwar years, he converted his staunch Ottomanism into Hellenism without forfeiting his Salonicanism. In 1928, he helped found the Associa-tion of Jewish Assimilationists, which "sought to create and develop among Salonican Jews feelings utterly identical to those of their fellow-citizens irre-spective of religious persuasion, without however distancing themselves from the Jewish faith, the Jewish tradition and the spirit of Jewish solidarity."[87] Although only a segment of the Jewish bourgeoisie joined this association,

Nehama advanced its ideology in his historical writings, which conveyed the secularizing, integrationist politics of the Alliance.

Nehama undertook two early historical projects that set the tenor for his later work. His first study, fittingly published in the *Revue des Écoles de l'Alliance Israélite* in 1902, addressed the polemical topic of Sabbetai Sevi. While all Jewish historians in Salonica confronted the so-called problem of Sabbetai Sevi, only Nehama celebrated it. Nehama emphasized what he saw as the progressive and civilizing forces of the Sabbatean movement that resulted in the conversion of several hundred Jews to Islam, who became known as the Dönme. Despite the influences of the Kabbalah—"the Pandora's box of Judaism"[88]—he stressed that Sabbateanism also initiated a powerful, reforming "fight against the rabbis."[89] The unique position of the Dönme in Salonica—rejected both by Muslims and by Jews—advantageously rendered them "free thinkers," whose "enlightened youth" studied in Europe and formed an "advanced and liberal class."[90] Nehama provocatively concluded that, while the Dönme were becoming "extinct," their "faculty for assimilation," which stemmed from their "Jewish ancestors," would permit them to rise in society and prepare them for "action." The Dönme, Nehama submitted, "will rank among the avant-garde of the army of civilization that will propagate the ideas of justice and progress in Turkey."[91]

Nehama appeared to predict the Young Turk Revolution launched in Salonica in 1908 and attributed it to Dönme influence. At the heart of his essay, therefore, lay a paradox. By demonstrating the progressive potential of the Sabbatean movement, Nehama could clear the record of Salonican Jewish history from its purportedly most shameful historical stain. By attributing Jewish origins to the capacity of the Dönme to bring progressive ideas to the Ottoman Empire, Nehama ironically presented an argument later adopted by antisemites who denounced the Young Turk Revolution as a Dönme-Jewish-Freemason conspiracy.[92] Strikingly, this Salonican Jewish Freemason with connections to Paris had hoped that the Dönme would bring "justice and progress" to the Ottoman realm.[93]

The question of descent also intrigued Nehama in connection to the Spanish ancestry of Salonica's Jews. He numbered among a handful of Salonican Jews—purportedly "Spaniards without a homeland"—who corresponded with Spanish senator Angel Pulido, whose "philosephardic" campaign sought to reconnect the dispersed Sephardic Jews with Spain out of cultural and economic interest. Pulido became aware of lectures that Nehama gave about the relationship between Spanish Jews and Spain.[94] Nehama also contributed an article to *El Liberal de Madrid* on the same topic.[95] In a letter to Pulido, "D[on] José Nehama"—the rendering of Joseph as José and the addition of the Spanish honorific are already telling—described an ambitious textbook on the history of the Jews that he was preparing in 1903. Inspired by Pulido's campaigns, Nehama hoped to write in "clean and clear" Judeo-Spanish free from Turkish, Greek, or Italian words; it is unclear if the book was ever published.[96] In a manual for composing business and family correspondence in Judeo-Spanish that he did publish in 1906, Nehama also advised his readers to write in "clear" prose, free of French and of Hebrew.[97]

Through contact with Pulido, Nehama introduced terms such as "Sephardic" and "Spanish" into his vocabulary. Although absent from his earlier article on Sabbateanism, the notion that Jews in Salonica retained indelible links to Spain greatly shaped how Nehama developed his subsequent historical narratives. In 1914, in Paris, on the eve of World War I and just after Salonica had come under Greek control, Nehama published a book about his native city, titled *La Ville Convoitée* (The Coveted City). Written in lively French under the pseudonym P. Risal (standing for Paris-Salonique), the book targeted a foreign audience and was reissued more than a half dozen times. The book presents an idealized vision of this coveted, cosmopolitan "metropolis of the Balkans," this "Macedonian metropolis," a "modern Babel of races, languages, beliefs, customs, ideas, and aspirations."[98] A bold history, *La Ville Convoitée* enshrined an image of Salonica as a fundamentally Jewish—and Sephardic—city.

While Nehama hoped to present an overview of Salonica's history spanning twenty-five centuries, he emphasized that the city's "hybrid spirit" rendered it, since the fifteenth century, "Latin in thought, Jewish in religion."[99] In other words, Salonica was doubly Jewish for, as he suggested, the Latin aspect of the city was also Jewish—Sephardic. Salonica therefore ought to be understood as an "exception" in the Balkans, Nehama argued, for "it is a parcel of medieval Judaic Iberia" that "the Hispanicized Jews" had "conquered peacefully" and transformed into their "adopted homeland."[100] The Jews made Salonica "simultaneously Jewish and Spanish," as if it were "a lost canton of

Judea and a makeshift district of Castile."[101] While other peoples had ruled or invaded Salonica, "today it [Salonica] is Jewish and Spanish: it is Sephardic. It is, in our days, that which Toledo was just until modern times."[102]

In the remainder of *La Ville Convoitée*, Nehama surveyed the various periods of the city's history and the dominant populations: the Macedonians, Romans, Christians, Slavs, Bulgarians, Normans, Venetians, Turks, Jews, and Greeks. But Jews remained the focus in numerous sections. The section on the Christian period began with a discussion of the Jews;[103] even the rise of Greek merchants in the eighteenth century was possible, so Nehama argued, because Jews paved the way for the city to "return" to its role as the regional entrepôt.[104] Nehama emphasized how Salonica "became a veritable Jewish city in the Balkan region," an "autonomous state," a "model of perfection" for all Jewish communities in the Orient and, indeed, *La Mère en Israël*.[105]

While Nehama paid attention to the other populations in this cosmopolitan city, he prioritized his discussion of Jews. In one of the final chapters, "The Current Situation," Nehama focused on Jews for eight paragraphs; Greeks for two; and the Dönme, Turks, Bulgarians, and Europeans for one each. He dedicated only one line each to Serbs, Armenians, Romanians, and Gypsies. "The Jews are everywhere here," Nehama observed, "and the city is Jewish in language, appearance, and religion." The Jews, he continued, "are the incontestable masters of commerce, banking, education, the Bar."[106]

Nehama accentuated the importance of Spanish and French cultures for Jews in Salonica in order to demonstrate their status as Latin and European rather than Eastern and backward. Nehama galvanized the myth that Jews spoke "very pure" Castilian, "the language of Cervantes," which non-Jews spoke as if it were a local Esperanto.[107] He sought to show that Jews spoke an unadulterated European language but ignored the extensive influence of languages like Turkish, Greek, and Hebrew on local Judezmo. Emphasizing the impact of Alliance schools, Nehama referred to the "purely French education" of Salonica's Jews, who "think in the language of Racine." Alluding to his anti-Zionism, Nehama indicated that, since Salonica's Jews looked to Paris rather than Palestine, the city had the aura of "a province of France."[108] This, too, was an exaggeration, for it presented a minority of the French-oriented middle and upper classes, to which Nehama belonged, as representative of the entire Jewish population.

For Nehama, the Spanish and French cultural attributes of the Jews rendered the city Latin in mentality and held the key to the Salonica's future. "Tomorrow," Nehama hoped, "Salonica may become the City of Light of the Balkans." This would be possible, he asserted, due to its "Latin affinities"—made possible by Jewish presence—that rendered Salonica a suitable locale for a university.[109] He thus concluded his book by arguing that the best solution for the city's future would be internationalization.[110] Although he recognized the reality that "fate has decided otherwise"—the Greeks had already captured the city—Nehama referred to the unpredictability of the city's history and concluded that nothing was "definitive."[111] He hoped that, whatever the fate of Salonica, it would continue to be a prosperous port and a city where Jews would continue to play a prominent role. Some commentators, however, later accused Nehama of lacking objectivity and overstating his pride in the Sephardic character of Salonica's Jews, which *Israël*, a newspaper in Cairo, construed as an expression of chauvinism that undermined the unity of the Jewish people.[112]

Although interrupted by World War I, the fire of 1917, and the series of difficulties confronting the city's Jewish residents during the interwar years, Nehama continued to assemble source materials for a master narrative of Salonica's Jews. He hired Michael Molho to study inscriptions in the Jewish cemetery; consulted numerous rabbis—Haim Habib, Pinhas Barzilai, Isaac Brudo, and Shaul Amariglio—who combed through four hundred rabbinical responsa with him; and synthesized historical essays published in the local press over the past decade by Molho, Baruch Ben-Jacob, Mercado Covo, and Isaac Emmanuel. He also acknowledged that each prepared the groundwork for his ultimate "history of the community" and helped bring to fruition plans formulated four decades earlier to compile a comprehensive history of the Jews of Salonica.[113] Nehama also relied on the Hebrew writings of a previous generation of Salonican rabbis, namely Judah Nehama and David Pipano, and utilized studies by Ottoman and Turkish Jewish historians Abraham Danon, Salomon Rosanes, and Abraham Galante. To their work, he added the writings of the major scholars of Jewish history, Heinrich Graetz, Théodore Reinach, Cecil Roth, and Simon Dubnov, whose methodology of highlighting not only religious but also social and economic developments in Jewish history Nehama adopted. Seeking to integrate his history into the

Greek framework, he relied on "decisive research" on Greek antiquity and Byzantine history, which he read in French.[114]

With his seven-volume *Histoire des Israélites de Salonique* (while all written by 1940, only four volumes had been published by then), Nehama produced a "monument" to the history of the Jews of Salonica that sought to reroot them in the context of interwar Greece and situate them favorably in the eyes of their Orthodox Christian neighbors and firmly within the narratives of what Nehama called "the Macedonian Metropolis" and of Hellenic history. He also wanted his scholarship to resonate with Salonican Jews, no matter where they resided, and to remind them of their native community and its rich history:

> Our ambition has been to prevent a rich past of events and ideas, from which it is possible to extract useful information, from falling into oblivion. We have thought, in particular, of the innumerable swarms of Salonican Jews who, over the last fifteen years [sic], have established themselves in various points on the globe, in America, in France, in Palestine and elsewhere, and who, away from their ancestral hive, risk losing all specific memory of it.
>
> To these distant compatriots and to their children born under other skies, to Salonicans remaining faithful to their corner of land [*coin de terre*], to those who have a curiosity in Jewish matters, we offer this tableau, covering twenty centuries of social, economic, religious, and intellectual life of the Judaism of the Macedonian Metropolis, which is the most important and enduring branch of the great Sephardic family.[115]

In the mid-1930s, after twenty years under Greek rule and with increased Jewish emigration, Nehama aimed to memorialize the Jewish grandeur of the city. Although he did not anticipate a renaissance of Jewish culture in Salonica and instead advocated for Jews to embrace Hellenism, readers nonetheless found in his work inspiration to foment the revival of Jewish Salonica. The Judeo-Spanish press summarized each volume so that those who could not read French nonetheless could familiarize themselves with "a general idea of this great work." Those who knew only a little French were encouraged to read all the volumes in order to understand the "brilliant origins" of the Jews in the city.[116] *El Mesajero* indicated that Nehama's work was "indispensible to the community," for it presented "useful lessons" about how the community dealt with past ills and how "men of valor" always stepped forward to return the community to its proper course.[117] The implication was that Nehama's *Histoire* ought to serve as a guidebook, a kind of Salonican Bible in which Salonican sages of old—Moses Almosnino, Joseph Taitachek, Samuel de Medina—were cast as the new archetypes: indeed, through their model leadership, the pathway to the future could be found in the past.

Although not religiously inclined, Nehama recognized the sacred task of writing the history of Jewish Salonica. He referred to his work as a "pourana," the Sanskrit term for the sacred poems that contain the theological corpus of Hinduism.[118] Into this *pourana*, Nehama folded his earlier analysis from *La Ville Convoitée* and his interpretation of the Sabbatean movement from thirty years earlier. But the differing political tenor and the less assertive, less populous Jewish population demanded an altogether different framing of that history. No longer could Salonica be conceived of as a Jewish city par excellence or an exclusively Sephardic one. Rather, in coming to terms with the reality of Greek hegemony, Nehama rerendered his native city not as the Spanish and Jewish metropolis but rather as the Macedonian Metropolis. It was a Macedonian metropolis—a fundamentally Greek site—where Jews had played a central role over the course of two thousand years and where they ought to continue to do so.

At the start of the first volume of *Histoire des Israélites de Salonique*, Nehama emphasized the long-standing relationship between Jews and the capital of Macedonia. He argued that Jews arrived in Macedonia as merchants with the Phoenicians prior to the establishment of Thessaloniki. With the founding of the city, Jews gained rights as "regular citizens" and contributed to the flourishing of the port. Speaking Greek fluently, Jews numbered among the "finest interpreters of Greek philosophy."[119] The Jewish population increased during the Roman era due to the influx of Jews from elsewhere in the Mediterranean basin and, significantly, due to the conversion of Greek pagans, who were "won over by the clarity and logic of the Jewish religion."[120] Judeo-Spanish newspapers highlighted this point, reinforcing Nehama's assertion that, at that time, Greek pagan converts to Judaism outnumbered born-Jews and the two "elements" mixed together strengthening the "race"; only with Roman persecutions did this mixing cease.[121] The obvious points readers were to take away from these passages were that Jews ought not to be considered a separate "race" from Greeks, and that some of the present-day Jews in Salonica may have descended from the ancient Hellenes.

Byzantine history also played an important role for Nehama in providing the historical and philosophical frame for Hellenic Judaism.[122] Rather than present "the Jews" in opposition to the dominant category of "the Greeks," Nehama argued they could be conceived as complementary to each other. For Nehama, the Byzantine Empire preserved the knowledge of classical antiquity during an era of barbarism in western Europe.[123] Such an enlightened perspective promoted cordial relations between Jews and Greeks. The principles of Greek Orthodoxy proved tolerant and permitted the development of a Jewish messianic movement in the eleventh and twelfth centuries that echoed the miracles of St. Demetrius, Salonica's patron saint.[124] The fall of Constantinople represented a calamity in the eyes of Nehama, but it also unwittingly provided the spark for the birth of modern Europe as Byzantine Greeks, spreading throughout Europe after 1453, brought with them classical knowledge that had been lost in the West. Offering a pro-Greek reading of history, Nehama argued that the fall of Constantinople and the creation of a Europe-wide Hellenic diaspora contributed to the Renaissance. He lectured on this theme at the Béné Bérith Lodge in 1937, instilling in his Jewish audience elements of the Greek nationalist narrative.[125]

In addition to focusing on the linkages between Jews and Greeks in antiquity and Byzantium, Nehama argued that the two populations "never missed an opportunity to demonstrate their solidarity" even during the Ottoman period. Although often characterized through religious animosities and economic competition, Greek-Jewish relations in Ottoman Salonica emerged in Nehama's telling as cordial and mutually supportive. He described how, in the nineteenth century, Greeks and Jews helped to fund each other's educational enterprises and the metropolitan bishop and chief rabbi were "friends." Nehama further highlighted how Jews came to the defense of the Greeks during a controversy in 1880, when the Romanian consul published a report that no Greeks lived in Salonica. In response, the Jewish Communal Council condemned the consul's egregious claim and announced in the press that twenty thousand Greeks dwelt in Salonica, and boasted a large clergy and six communal schools.[126]

Cooperative dynamics such as these set part of the tone for Nehama's depiction of Salonica once the city came under Greek rule. Nehama lamented that the Jews of Salonica lost much of their cachet, especially after 1923, when they no longer constituted the plurality of the city's population. But he also celebrated what he perceived to be the opening up of Hellenic society which, he argued, no longer relegated Jews to the margins as Ottoman society had but rather cultivated complete "symbiosis." Rapprochement between Jews and Greeks, he believed, would be forthcoming in ways not possible with Muslims, whose society he perceived as too closed. Due to the purported intellectual and historical affinities among Jews and Greeks—the first promoting faith in God and the latter a sense of art, culture, and science—Nehama believed that the Salonican Jew would cease to be "an exclusive citizen of his little communal republic" and instead become a true citizen of Greece, of Europe, and of the world.[127]

For Nehama, Athens and Jerusalem constituted the dual pillars of universal modern civilization, which were entwined in Salonica more than anywhere else. Nehama's version of the historical precedents of antiquity and Byzantium, the late Ottoman era, and to a certain extent the dynamics of post-1912 Salonica, evoked productive, complementary dynamics between Jews and Greeks that could serve as a model for the present. Concluding the final volume of his *Histoire*, written in 1940 (but published posthumously), Nehama drew upon an image of two thousand years of symbiosis between Jews and Greeks in Salonica, the Macedonian Metropolis, and hoped that the universalist words of the apostle Paul (Galatians 3:28) would provide the model for the future: "there is neither Jew nor Greek . . . " for, he implied, they are all one in Mother Salonica.[128] The subordination of the Jewish Metropolis to the Macedonian Metropolis was complete.

The new frame of Greek hegemony in Salonica during the 1930s thus contributed to the consolidation of the emergent category of "Hellenic Judaism" that not only competed with but at times displaced the established notions of Salonican or Sephardic Judaism. Channeling once again his integrationist ideology, Nehama sought to harmonize the image of Salonica as the Jewish Metropolis with that of the city as an essentially Macedonian Metropolis, part and parcel of the Greek nationalist narrative. But much of this perspective remained unpublished until after the war. The first four volumes nonetheless drew the attention of the German Foreign Office, whose representative sent copies to the Reich Institute for the History of the New Germany in Munich in 1940 and praised Nehama's work as a "valuable addition to our library" even though the available volumes did not bring the narrative up to "our times."[129]

Nehama's purported integrationist ideology continued to sit in tension with his personal decisions in life-or-death circumstances: despite his embrace of Hellenism, on the eve of World War II, he traded Greek citizenship for Spanish citizenship by appealing to his Sephardic ancestry—a move that ultimately saved him and his family from certain death at Auschwitz. Instead, along with several hundred other Jews from Salonica, primarily well-to-do merchants who also had acquired Spanish citizenship, he spent the war in Bergen-Belsen—and survived. Realizing that his faith in the state to protect its citizens and the ability or desire of Greece to accept its Jews may have been misplaced, Nehama became more sympathetic to the cause of Zionism; the final volume of his *Histoire*, which had celebrated Jewish-Greek symbiosis, remained unpublished until after his death.[130]

A Faithful Son

The year after Nehama's death, Isaac Emmanuel (1896–1972) died in Cincinnati, a world apart from his native Salonica. Stanley Chyet, director of the American Jewish Archives, eulogized him:

> He was Don Quixote. Not the Don Quixote who tilted with windmills, or not only that Don Quixote. He was the Don Quixote who brooded over the passing of an ancient and honorable inheritance. . . . For him scholarship, scholarly research, was no mere diversion, no game of cerebration. It was a visceral force, an act of *hazkarat neshamot*, a weapon against decay. It was a weapon against the decay of a cherished past, against the decay of all the ancestral values and usages he had learned to honor as a youngster in Salonika. It was a weapon against threats to his own pride and his own identity. He would not submit. He would never submit . . .[131]

According to Chyet, Emmanuel conceived of his scholarship more in his soul than in his mind, for the sake of conscience rather than science. Maír José Benardete, in contrast, viewed Emmanuel's writing style as "dry" and "unornamented," "documented and to the point," and imbued with the "positivistic school of historical scholarship."[132] As the only Salonican Jewish historian to earn a PhD and to be trained in *Wissenschaft des Judentums*, Emmanuel deployed his scholarship as a weapon against what he perceived to be the unraveling of Salonican Jewish culture during the interwar years and against insults to his sense of self. Despite the comparison to Quixote—an allusion to Emmanuel's Sephardic and ostensibly Spanish descent—Emmanuel saw himself as a Jewish scholar who sought to demonstrate to Jews across the world the significance of Salonica as a Jewish city.

Although not descended from long line of rabbis, Emmanuel nonetheless benefitted from family connections and from his activities with the Mizrahi, the Jewish religious-nationalist organization in the city. Isaac's father, Samuel Emmanuel (1866–1943), numbered among the communal rabbis; his mother, who died in childbirth, was connected to the prominent Brudo rabbinical family.[133] Living in the Jewish working-class Vardar district, however, the Em-

Figure 4.3. Isaac Emmanuel student identification card, University of Berlin, 1927. Source: Archive of Isaac S. Emmanuel, published with permission of Dr. Gary S. Schiff.

manuel family was of modest means and appealed to the Jewish Community for financial assistance.[134] Growing up in Vardar, Isaac Emmanuel frequented the Evora synagogue where he befriended Abraham Recanati, the founder of the Mizrahi. In addition to joining the Mizrahi, Emmanuel and his younger half-brother, Haim, launched a Zionist youth group, Shivat Sion, in 1923, and helped Recanati promote the two-thousand member Shomre Shabat, "the league for the defense and safeguarding of the Sabbath," which protested the Compulsory Sunday Closing Law in 1924.[135] Emmanuel attended the Or Ahaim seminary, where he studied under Chief Rabbi Bension Uziel and served as an officiant at the Sisilia Yashan synagogue.[136] Given his promise as an up-and-coming rabbi, the Jewish Communal Council sent Emmanuel to the Jewish Theological Seminary in Breslau and the University of Berlin to continue his studies. The hope was that he would return with academic credentials in hand to serve his native community, perhaps even as chief rabbi.

Despite his best efforts, Emmanuel never returned to serve Salonica. After living abroad for thirteen years and upon the completion of his dissertation at Lausanne, Emmanuel made his final attempt to secure a position in Salonica. He applied to become the inspector of the Commission for Jewish Instruction in 1936. Despite the endorsements he received from the well-known journalist Sam Lévy, who characterized Emmanuel as "one of the most cultivated Salonicans," and the Union Universelle des Communautés Sepharadites, with offices in Paris and London, Emmanuel failed to secure the post.[137] Instead, later that same year, he published his dissertation as *Histoire des Israélites de Salonique*, in Paris (notably sharing the same title as Nehama's magnum opus).[138] It followed Emmanuel's shorter but well documented *Histoire de l'industrie des tissus des Israélites de Salonique*, which appeared in 1935 and which great Jewish historians such as Cecil Roth and Salo Baron later cited.

Only after he left Salonica did Emmanuel become interested in the history of his community. In the preface to his own *Histoire des Israélites de Salonique*, Emmanuel recalled that, upon arriving in Breslau in 1923, he was "touched" that Jewish scholars he met had attached great significance to the past of their communities. He decided that he, too, could make a scholarly contribution by presenting the history of his own community, Salonica—*la ville mère en Israël*. He admitted that to the work of "science" he would add a "sense of familial affection."[139] The family connection deeply resonated with Emmanuel, who never ceased to mourn his own mother, who died giving birth to him and to whose memory he dedicated his first book about the sages buried in Salonica's Jewish cemetery.[140] Jewish Salonica became a kind of surrogate mother for Emmanuel, who dedicated his time and energy to promoting his mother city and her history.

This familial affection also invested his scholarship with passion and urgency and inspired him to dedicate his *Histoire des Israélites de Salonique* to the Communal Council in Salonica, which had sent him abroad and inaugurated his interest in history.[141] Emmanuel hoped that endowing the Jews of Salonica with a legitimate scholarly history would bring them both honor and consolation, as measures imposed by the Greek state appeared to be unraveling their long-standing communal, religious, and national autonomy. Emmanuel concluded his preface with a wish: "I hope that these pages will be useful to Jewish history and serve to uplift the soul of the Jews of Salonica, who in recent years, have bared the burden of so many troubles. As in the past, they will continue to be proud of their community, more than two thousand years old."[142]

Seeking to uplift the souls of his Salonican Jewish brothers and inspire in them a sense of pride in the accomplishments of their ancestors, Emmanuel fittingly concluded his *Histoire* in 1640, prior to the Sabbatean debacle. Despite plagues, fires, and other calamities (e.g., the Dolya massacre), the status of the Jewish community, according to Emmanuel, remained "brilliant" until 1640; Jewish schools, commerce, industry, and rabbinic scholarship "still flourished." "We have desired," Emmanuel explained, "to relate the relatively fortunate history of Jewish Salonica."[143] Emmanuel sought to etch into the minds of his readers an image of the grandeur of *la ville mère en Israël*, frozen in time and thus rendered timeless. His target audience included Jews and non-Jews at home and abroad—hence its publication in the universal language of the era, French. While Emmanuel had written a second volume as part of his dissertation at Lausanne covering the history of Jewish Salonica from 1640 to the twentieth century, he did not publish it at that time and thus, for the moment, avoided making public his views on the questions of Sabbateanism and decline so entrenched in the established historical paradigms.

As a Salonican son abroad, Emmanuel conducted research in libraries and archives across Europe—in Berlin, Paris, London, and Oxford—to collect the necessary documentation to construct his image of Jewish Salonica. An original work of scholarship, Emmanuel's three-hundred-page treatise included 1,175 meticulous footnotes citing previously unknown sources, especially rabbinical literature, that offered proof of Salonica's status as *la ville mère en Israël*. Serving as an ambassador of his city, he conceptualized himself as part of a long-standing tradition: since the sixteenth century, he reported, "the Salonican Jew . . . upon leaving for another city, was proud of his community like the Roman in the epoch of Augustus was proud to belong to the Empire."[144] Emmanuel's pride in the metropole inspired him to organize the "colony" of "faithful Salonicans" in Lausanne to send donations back home.[145]

Emmanuel also relied on his pride to maintain a sense of self-respect and sangfroid while abroad. Upon arrival at the Jewish Theological Seminary in Breslau in 1923, the director granted Emmanuel special exemptions due to his "Oriental" background and his lack of European training; unlike the other students, he did not have a baccalaureate.[146] He was permitted to attend Talmud class but could not participate; although he knew Judeo-Spanish, Hebrew, French, and some Turkish and Greek, he did not yet know German.[147] While the Jewish Community of Salonica gave Emmanuel a stipend for tuition and living expenses, it was not enough. He begged the seminary director to intervene to increase his allowance in order to alleviate his "suffering." The lack of funds, he worried, reinforced the stereotype of the impoverished "Oriental."[148] In the face of these dilemmas, Emmanuel presented himself as a proud "Spanish Jew of Salonica" rather than as an enfeebled Oriental.[149] In a report to Jewish communal leaders back in Salonica, the Breslau seminary director soon praised Emmanuel's knowledge and scholarship, as well as the extent to which classmates came to respect him.[150] Symbolizing a kind of Sephardic-Ashkenazic rapprochement, Emmanuel married Chanah Frenkel in 1930 (although their marriage ended in divorce).

Regaining his confidence, Emmanuel began publishing articles on the history of Jewish Salonica in the Judeo-Spanish press back home. His first (1925) focused on prominent Salonican Jewish families.[151] He soon wrote for *El Djidio*, the annual magazine of the Mizrahi in Salonica.[152] During holidays, Emmanuel returned to Salonica, where he undertook research in

the Jewish cemetery which became the subject of his first scholarly publication—in German no less—in the prestigious journal of the *Wissenschaft des
Judentums*.[153] A colleague, Rabbi Isaac Jerusalmi, later characterized the theme
of Emmanuel's life and work with an allusion to Genesis: "I am seeking my
brethren" (37:16). "Dead or alive," Jerusalmi recalled, Emmanuel sought fellow
"Sepharadim, portrayed on tombstones or in archival documents." It was a
"continual adventure of the heart and the spirit into their glorious history."[154]

The initial searches for the past of his brethren paved the way for Emmanuel's *Histoire des Israélites de Salonique*. Although tracing social, economic,
and literary aspects of the history of Salonica's Jews from 140 BCE until
1640 CE, the book was also a history of the city itself—as *El Mesajero* remarked, a history of "great interest for the [Jewish] community of Salonica
and similarly for the history of the Macedonian capital."[155] His tale, therefore, began not with the Jews themselves but with the foundation of the
city of Thessaloniki as the Macedonian capital. Emmanuel then traced the
beginnings of the Jewish presence with Romaniote Jews who, fleeing persecution in Alexandria, settled in the city in 140 BCE. He also referenced the
apostle Paul's letters to the Thessalonians—which the German New Testament expert, Gustav Adolf Deissman, authenticated for Emmanuel—and to
second- and third-century inscriptions in the cemetery as further proof of
Jewish presence in the Roman era.[156] While emphasizing Jewish activity in
Byzantine Salonica, Emmanuel highlighted uninterrupted Jewish presence
in the city and in Macedonia beginning in antiquity and continuing through
the Middle Ages. He sought to render the Jews of Salonica visible, as a distinct community, within the framework of Hellenic history.

The bulk of the volume focused on the period from 1492 to 1640, during which Salonican Jews (*Israélites Saloniciens*), having transplanted the
grandeur of medieval Jewish Iberia to their new city, created their own
"Judeo-Salonicien Civilization," an autonomous social, cultural, and political
entity that formed part of the Macedonian Metropolis.[157] Emmanuel may
have been the first to use the phrase "Jerusalem of the Balkans" to describe
his native city:

> [I]t was to Salonica that all of the great Jewish [rabbinical] families of [medi-
> eval] Spain migrated . . . In effect, the Jews possessed in Salonica that which

all the other [Jewish] communities of the Diaspora lacked, Jewish liberties. They operated a rabbinical police and a Jewish prison, being a state within a state. The [Jewish] Sabbath was that of the city. The small congregations or *kehiloth*, which deployed much zeal to maintain the traditions imported from their countries of origin, gave to each Jewish event the imprint and character of a Jerusalem of the Balkans. Commerce, industry, customs, the port, leasing fees and taxes were also in Jewish hands. . . .

[. . . Salonica] is where the poor [Jews] from Germany, Hungary and all the countries of the Mediterranean found refuge. It is for all of these reasons that it [Salonica] was called "Mother City in Israel."[158]

This was the idealized image of Salonica as a major—indeed, unique—Jewish center in the world. Salonican-born Zionist Isaac R. Molho similarly referred to Salonica as the "Jerusalem of the Balkans" in Cairo's *Actualités* (1942), and the moniker gained greater currency following the war.[159] While the Spanish origins of the great sages who settled in the city retained pride of place for Emmanuel, he projected an image of Salonica not as a Sephardic city but as a Jewish center of unequaled grandeur. After World War II, Emmanuel concretized this Jerusalmic image of his native city in a massive memorial book, aptly titled *Zikhron Saloniki: Yerushalayim del Balkan*, which appeared posthumously in 1972. As he explained to his editor, Abraham Recanati, Emmanuel wrote in Hebrew so that "Ashkenazi rabbis and scholars will know what Salonica really was."[160] The Jewish framework retained primacy for Emmanuel's Jerusalem of the Balkans. While he had also written important studies on the Jews of Curaçao, where he had served as rabbi during World War II, he asked in his will to be remembered as "Haham Ishac Shemuel Emmanuel," historian of the Jews of Salonica.[161]

The Historian of the Future

Although he was the last of the main Salonican Jewish historians to begin researching and writing, Michael Molho (1890–1964) became one of the most influential and best remembered. His first work, an eighty-five-page Judeo-Spanish book, *Contribution to the History of Salonica*, published in 1932 in the depths of the depression, stood out for emphasizing the Iberian character of the Jews of Salonica, which he called the "Citadel of Sephardism."[162]

He saw his study as the first to treat the history of the Jews of Salonica in a serious manner since an article by Abraham Danon that had appeared in *Revue des Études Juives* in 1900.[163] More importantly, Molho's *Contribution* became the first work of scholarship in Judeo-Spanish by a Salonican Jew to draw attention in intellectual circles abroad; its appearance contributed to the renaissance of the field of Sephardic studies in Salonica and beyond. Less than a decade later, however, due to changing political dynamics, Molho notably subdued his Sephardic pride in favor of a new Hellenic framework for the history of Salonica's Jews.

A scion of a prominent rabbinical dynasty, Molho intended to pursue a rabbinical career. His father, Rabbi Salomon Molho (1850–1918), served in the honored position as head of the Hevra Kadisha, the burial society.[164] The younger Molho studied at the Talmud Tora, the Beth Yosef rabbinical seminary, and the Gattegno School. He began teaching Hebrew and Jewish history at Beth Yosef and later at Or Ahaim, the other yeshiva.[165] Following his father's death after the fire of 1917, however, Molho abandoned his rabbinical career in favor of a textile business to support his family. He also began writing for *El Puevlo* and became the secretary of the Zionist Federation of Greece.[166]

A decade-long hiatus from the Jewish communal schools created a barrier for Molho when he sought to return to his position as a teacher in the late 1920s. In 1929, he applied for a position in Kavalla, a port town northeast of Salonica, as director of the Jewish communal school. Despite his family status, educational credentials, and references—which included Mentesh Bensanchi, the member of parliament; Joseph Nehama, the director of the Alliance; Leon Recanati, the president of the Béné Bérith Lodge; and the Zionist Federation of Greece—the position fell through due to lack of funds.[167] Later in 1929, Molho applied to the Jewish communal schools of Salonica but initially could not secure that position either.[168] It was proposed that he work at a new Greek state school that recently added courses to accommodate Jewish students, but Molho refused. Changing dynamics among Jewish teachers in 1930—Baruch Ben-Jacob's visit to Portugal to aid conversos there and Isaac Hassid's appointment to the Beth Din—finally permitted Molho to a secure a position in the communal schools and to delve into historical studies.[169]

As a teacher of Hebrew and Jewish history at the Jewish communal schools and a journalist, Molho promoted the history of the Jews of Salonica as part of the Iberian Jewish story. He had indicated in his applications that he could teach Hebrew and French, knew Turkish, had some knowledge of Greek—which improved every day—and was fluent in "Castilian (the pure Spanish language)."[170] Yet Molho confessed to his cousin, Henry Besso, a Salonican intellectual in New York, that, while he could read Castilian in Latin script, he could not write it because he did not know the orthography.[171] Besso encouraged Molho to learn the archaic spelling of Castilian so that he could transcribe Judeo-Spanish into Latin script in a way that showed the antiquity of the language, as if it were a living museum of medieval Spanish. Doing so would show how the grandeur of medieval Iberian Jews was transferred intact to Salonica's Jews and preserved over the centuries.[172]

Within this context, Molho authored his first substantive study in Judeo-Spanish on the history of the Jews of Salonica and emphasized the city's status as the historic "Citadel of Sephardism." Rather than seek rapprochement with the Greek state and integrate the Jews of Salonica into Greek national history, Molho conceived of his narrative as a key feature of the Sephardic Jewish experience. The dissolution of the Ottoman foundation of earlier historical accounts of the Jews of Salonica and increased Christian-Jewish tensions in the city, especially following the Campbell attack in 1931, prompted Molho to cleave to his distinctive Sephardic, Jewish identity. Although entitling his book *Contribution to the History of Salonica*, Molho's contribution eschewed the presence of Orthodox Christians and Muslims and focused exclusively on Jews. For Molho, Jews acted as the protagonists in Salonica's history, which he narrated in present tense: "Our community, which constitutes the essential and progressive element in the city, experiences a period of glory and fortune."[173]

Molho's *Contribution* contained three parts: a historical narrative, a section on folklore, and epigraphs culled from the Jewish cemetery. He began the story with the era of Alexander the Great and the initial so-called Hellenizing Jews who resided in the city. He continued his tale through the Byzantine era and described the twelfth-century visit of Benjamin Tudela, who encountered a significant Jewish population in the city. He also noted that Ashkenazic Jews fleeing the crusades "found shelter within the walls of

Salonica," and that the first Iberian Jews, escaping anti-Jewish persecution, apparently fled to Salonica in 1391.[174]

Even though Molho referred to antiquity and the medieval era, he saw these periods as preamble to the main story, which began in 1492 when "*we arrived in Salonica*," namely the bulk of ancestors of the present Jewish population. He encouraged his readers to think of themselves as the heirs of the grandeur of medieval *Sefarad*. By using "we," the first person plural, Molho sought to dissolve the boundary between author and reader, and render his account as one written unabashedly by a Salonican Jew for Salonican Jews.[175] He explained that doctors, rabbis, and philosophers of "universal fame" arrived in Salonica and constituted the "flower of the Sephardic intellectuals," versed in religious and secular studies.[176] Molho presented the initial wave of Iberian arrivals as the "aristocratic class" of the Jews who "conserved their refined tastes" and spoke an "elegant language."[177]

Molho emphasized that the continued potency of the Iberian connections maintained by Jews in Salonica protected them against the obscurantism of the Orient. Secular studies—"universal science"—equaled if not surpassed religious study as the first generations in Salonica "transplanted" their "Latin culture" to the Orient. Molho contributed to the mythologizing of Jewish Salonica by attributing to the sixteenth-century poet Samuel Usque the designation of the city as "The Mother in Israel." According to Molho, Jews imbued this "Citadel of Sephardism" with a "Spanish character": they allegedly spoke the "pure" language of Cervantes as evidenced, so Molho argued, in the writings of Moses Almosnino.[178] Despite the interruption caused by Sabbateanism, the continual arrival of conversos from Portugal into the eighteenth century "did not permit the intellectual level of their coreligionists to decline totally."[179] The conversos, Molho asserted, as university-educated polyglots, nobles, and knights, brought with them "a certain intellectual vivacity," retained contact with "Latin civilization," and endowed "a certain brilliance to our community."[180] For Molho, the emphasis on the Sephardic, Iberian, Latin, and European character of Salonican Jews demonstrated their continued vivacity in the face of their benighted, Oriental environment.

Molho had a vested interest in presenting the Portuguese conversos as key figures in buttressing the grandeur of Jewish Salonica. As an officiant at the Lisbon Hadash and Portugal congregations, Molho presented himself as a descendant of famous Portuguese conversos.[181] He emphasized that one of his ancestors—Rabbi Joseph Molho, the father of the Molho dynasty of Salonica[182]—numbered among those rabbis who excommunicated Sabbetai Sevi by countering mysticism with European rationalism. Molho concluded the final section of his book—containing transcriptions of epitaphs of famous Salonican Jews—with his own father.[183] Molho presented the chain of Salonican grandeur as being transmitted from fifteenth-century Iberia to sixteenth-century Salonica and down to the present age as embodied in his family and his father—and, by extension, in Molho himself.[184]

Although his ancestors deserved attention in their own right, Molho incorporated them into his story of Salonican flourishing as part of a strategy to access the inner circles of the Jewish communal structure from which he had been absent—the first in a long line of Molhos who had *not* served in any high rabbinical position in Salonica. His desire to ensure continuity also led him to guide the administration of the Jewish Community in determining the congregational affiliations of its members once the fire of 1917 had destroyed the synagogue buildings. Molho wanted Jewish families during the interwar years to recall and reclaim their ancestral linkages with synagogues that also permitted them to claim roots in Europe, whether Spain, Portugal, Italy or elsewhere, since most of the city's synagogues bore the name of the place from which their founders came.[185]

Due to its dynamic, vivacious portrait of Salonican Jewry over the centuries, Molho's *Contribution* received an enthusiastic welcome in the local and international press. *El Puevlo* indicated that Molho popularized the history of the Jews of Salonica while maintaining a high level of scholarship that satisfied "our most well-versed rabbis."[186] *La Nasion* lauded Molho as the "historian of the future" but lamented that the book sold only four hundred copies by early 1932—nonetheless a significant number for that time.[187] *La Nasion* also encouraged Molho to publish in Hebrew so that Jews far and wide would recognize "the glory of all of Salonican Judaism"—and accord Molho well-deserved fame.[188]

Following this advice, Molho published four booklets in Hebrew under the title *Be-veth Ha-almin shel Yehudei Saloniki* ("In the Cemetery of the Jews of Salonica"), which presented a selection of 150 of the 4,000 tombstone inscriptions that Molho ultimately recorded from the Jewish cemetery of Salonica.[189] In the French preface, Mercado Covo celebrated Molho's research as forming part of a broader intellectual movement to revive Jewish culture in the city. Covo boasted that readers would discover "the first specimens of the monument that the author proposes to erect to the glory of the Jewish community of Salonica," "a metropolis of Judaism in the Orient." Molho emerged as "the first among us" to bring the treasures of the necropolis to life, and to garner the admiration of scholars and "compatriots."[190] Covo saw Molho's work as a base upon which future scholars would build.

Molho's *Contribution* became the first work of scholarship in Judeo-Spanish to be reviewed in the popular London Jewish newspaper, *The Jewish Chronicle*: "Most research on the history of the Jews of Salonika has come hitherto from outside sources." The review continued by indicating that Molho, "a local scholar," sought "to remedy this state of affairs." Presented as "very solid" and "containing much important information," Molho's *Contribution* received a favorable reception in *The Jewish Chronicle*, which added a few words about the importance of the tombstone inscriptions contained in his *Be-veth Ha-almin*.[191]

Across the Atlantic, Henry Besso penned a laudatory review in the *Jewish Quarterly Review*, the oldest English-language journal of Jewish scholarship.[192] The *JQR* provided a forum for Besso to promote the work of his relative and cotownsman and to introduce the readership to original research undertaken by Salonican Jews about their own community. Like Covo, Besso also recognized that Molho's work constituted only a beginning. The writing of a full, integrated history of the "Spanish Jews" of Salonica "will require the bending of efforts on the part of many learned persons in generations to come."[193]

Both Besso and Molho saw the publication of *Contribution* as a turning point and hoped it would inspire the "rebirth" (*renasimiento*) of Sephardic culture in Salonica and beyond. Besso elaborated in a letter to Molho: "I was extremely happy to learn . . . that you seek to revive [*hacer renacer*] the Judeo-Spanish culture that flourished during the Middle Ages in Spain and until the eighteenth century in Holland, France and Turkey. I was interested, moreover, to learn that the youth of Salonica is awakening from the lethargy that had veiled them in ignorance for many years."[194] Molho hoped to contribute significantly to the process, as he wrote to Besso: "I am a very passionate researcher and I consecrate much time and money to historical work." He hoped that his research would one day make "a lot of noise in the scholarly world."[195]

Notably, Besso reconceptualized Judeo-Spanish culture as extending beyond the borders of the former Ottoman realm and including other Jewish communities of Iberian origin, namely Amsterdam and Bordeaux.[196] The new rhetoric about the unity of Judeo-Spanish and Sephardic culture developed simultaneously in intellectual circles in Sarajevo and Vienna.[197] While Besso envisioned a renewed Sephardic culture across the continent, Molho continued to focus on the circumscribed geography of the former Ottoman world. Molho planned trips "to the different localities of the Balkan countries to collect books, to conduct historical research in the cemeteries, archives, libraries, to collect folklore such as *romansas*, traditions, habits, customs, proverbs, archaic expressions, etc."[198]

Molho published the results of his research in Salonica and abroad. He wrote about Sephardic wedding customs in Judeo-Spanish for *La Aksion* and in French for *La Volonté* (1934); Besso subsequently translated these pieces for publication in magazines in English and Castilian in the Americas.[199] The Spanish connection also led Molho to publish on Judeo-Spanish liturgical poetry in *Bulletin Hispanique* (1940), one of the most important academic journals in the field.[200] Molho also salvaged from the German occupation his full-length French manuscript, subsequently published in Castilian in Madrid in 1950 (and in English in 2006), as *Traditions and Customs of the Sephardic Jews of Salonica.*

As he developed his work within the framework of Sephardic history through the 1930s, Molho remained focused on elevating the status of Salonican Jewry and relied on the support of patrons to satisfy this goal. The merchant and writer Judah Haim Perahia, in nearby Xanthi, commissioned a family history. With the publication in French of a history of the Perahia family (1938), Molho promoted the grandeur of Salonican Jews through the case of one family, inclusive of rabbis, doctors, and philanthropists who, over the course of four centuries, "enhanced the prestige of the Jewish Community of our city."[201] Molho saw in the Perahia family a key counterexample to the assumption that prominent Sephardic families in the Orient eventually withered and declined. While they faced the same challenges as all of the other residents of the "pious Thessalonican cité," the Perahias always succeeded in reestablishing their economic and intellectual position in society.[202]

Another commissioned project provided Molho with an opportunity to expand the framework of his research to consider the Jews of the region of Macedonia as an integrated unit. With the support of Jews from Kastoria living in New York, Molho wrote a history in Judeo-Spanish of the Jews of Kastoria.[203] Published in 1939, the book formed part of a broader effort to document the smaller Jewish populations near Salonica. Mercado Covo also contributed to this trend by publishing studies on Jews in his hometown, Serres. Together, the studies promoted a historical framework for Macedonian Jews that resonated with the broader discussions in Greek national discourse about the central place of Macedonia within Greek history.[204]

The broadening scope prepared Molho for an unexpected and novel historical project on the eve of World War II: a Jewish history to be published in Greek. In the summer of 1939, the Jewish Community of Salonica embarked on a new program to promote Greek education at Jewish communal schools, and to teach Jewish students enrolled in Greek state schools—and the general Greek public—about Judaism by publishing new textbooks in Greek. The Communal Council also decided to publish an unprecedented book dealing with Jewish history and to do so in Greek. To oversee a competition for the best monograph, the council formed a committee comprised of the well-known intellectuals Joseph Nehama and Mercado Covo; Mentesh Bensanchi, then the inspector of Jewish communal schools; Daniel Saïas, a Hebrew teacher; and Abram Levy, a member of the Communal Council. Chief Rabbi Koretz presided over the committee.[205]

The local Judeo-Spanish press announced the competition in the autumn of 1939. It was the first time that the Jewish Community agreed to support historical writing financially. All previous efforts emerged out of individual initiative, through the support of patrons, or through societies such as Kadima. While preference would be given to the best three-hundred-page manuscript submitted in Greek, submissions would also be accepted in other languages, but the award would be reduced from eight thousand to five thousand drachmes to accommodate translation costs.[206] The intended audience for the book—Greek-speaking Jews and Orthodox Christians alike—was clear, as was the desire to rewrite Jews into the official course of Hellenic civilization—and to do so just as war began to engulf Europe.

In the cover letter that accompanied his submission, Molho outlined the goals of his manuscript. He applauded the Communal Council for the initiative, which he viewed as an important "sign of the interest of our leaders in the rapprochement of our element with the Greek public, and for the enlightenment . . . of our youth . . . and of Greek public opinion regarding our past and the beliefs of [the people of] Israel." He aimed to provide a broad account of Jewish history across eras and countries but with particular attention to the relations between Judaism and Hellenism as well as Byzantine Jews and the Jewish community of Salonica. Reflecting on his research into Jewish history, Molho observed that, since scholars in other countries tailored their theses to suit the context, he tried to do the same for the case of Greece. Molho thus concluded on an optimistic note:

> If a cry of pain or a suffering calls out, from one moment to the next, from
> the valley of tears—which is the history of Judaism—a hallelujah is also sung
> in this valley, a hallelujah of indelible faith in human justice, a hallelujah
> in favor of knowledge and the light of intelligence that guide the people
> of Israel and all of civilized humanity across the painful path of historical
> evolution.[207]

The timing of the competition was remarkable: Molho submitted his manuscript on September 25, 1940, a year into the war, just before the Jewish New Year, and a month prior to Italy's invasion of Greece. Yet at that moment, neither Greece nor its Jewish population was directly affected by the war; rather than Jews being expelled from public spaces or from schools as in other parts of Europe, the new initiatives to transform Greek-Jewish education in Salonica suggested the possibility of a cordial future between Jews and Christians in the city and the country. These dynamics motivated Molho to proclaim "hallelujah" from the "valley" of Greece, a country that, for the moment, appeared to have avoided another sad chapter in Jewish history.

Molho conceded that rapprochement between Jews and Christians was by no means complete, as evidenced by his own inability to compose his manuscript in Greek. Instead, he wrote it in "clear" and "pure" Judeo-Spanish in Latin script with his best attempt at Castilian-style orthography.

As a translator, he proposed Isaac Kabelli, one of the few Jewish writers in Salonica who published in "erudite and elegant" Greek and was thus, according to Molho, "the Jew in Greece most qualified" for the translation work. Kabelli gained recognition for working to bring together Jews and Christians under the framework of Hellenism. He spoke about Greek-Jewish partnership on the local radio and published an essay on the Jews of Salonica as well as a booklet, *Jewish Civilization*, which, in Greek, charted the development of Jewish culture, morality, religion, literature, art, and music; the local press praised its emphasis on the "brotherly relations" between Jewish and Hellenic civilizations.[208] He later played a contested role during the German occupation.

While Molho won the competition, the outbreak of the war with Italy cut short the publication project; it was never completed, and Molho never received his prize money. Unfortunately, his complete manuscript was lost during the war, but Molho salvaged a partial, handwritten draft of two hundred pages that offers additional insight into how he framed his historical narrative on the eve of the war. Molho began his preface by emphasizing the complementarity of Hellenism and Judaism:

> Two peoples, having their roots in the highest antiquity, subsist still today in our days, vivacious and strong, young and vigorous, despite their four millennia of existence. These two peoples are the Jews and the Greeks. Both worked together actively for the formation of human civilization; the first gave the world its morality, its monotheistic conceptions, the idealized and sublime belief in religious sentiment that resides in the human heart; the other ignited the sparks of the sciences and art that today still enlighten human intelligence, and deepen reason nurtured by truth and beauty. It is in the bosom of the vast empire, first founded by Alexander the Great, and later by the Romans, that Jewish knowledge and Hellenic reason met, fused, informed each other, and, due to political power, imposed themselves on humanity by constituting the soul and the spirit of civilized men in our day.[209]

In this opening paragraph, Molho outlined the intellectual and ideological framework for his work by drawing Judaism and Hellenism together as the two pillars of modern civilization forged for the first time during the reign of Alexander the Great. He confirmed Greek nationalist claims to continuity between Alexander and the modern Greeks. The prospect of a bright future in a Salonica modeled on the ancient past, where the threads of Hellenism and Judaism converged, inspired Molho to proclaim "hallelujah." But it was a call cut short—in fact, obliterated—by the war. From an emphasis on the Sephardic aspects of Salonica's Jews, Molho now shifted to the Hellenic framework. He solidified this national framework in the wake of the war with a memorial volume he dedicated not to the Jews of Salonica but all of Greece: *In Memoriam: Hommage aux victims Juives des Nazis en Grèce*.

Conclusion: History as the Faith of Fallen Jews?

Adopting the language of some of the Salonican writers cited here, present-day scholars have assumed that both Jews and non-Jews described Salonica since the sixteenth century as the "Jerusalem of the Balkans."[210] There is only one problem with this claim: the term "the Balkans," as a geographic signifier, is a nineteenth-century neologism. According to Balkan specialist Maria Todorova, the term "the Balkans" entered common usage only during the twentieth century with the eponymous Balkan Wars (1912–1913).[211] The Salonican Jewish intellectuals discussed in this chapter thus invented the designation, the "Jerusalem of the Balkans." They appealed to it as well as other monikers—"Jewish Salonica," "Citadel of Judaism," "Sephardic Metropolis," "The Hebrew City in the Diaspora," *Shabbatopolis*, "Our noble Republic," and "Mother of Israel"—that they rediscovered, augmented, or popularized in order to promote the historic grandeur of the Jews in the city, to stake a claim on their city, to integrate themselves into the Ottoman political framework, and subsequently to rewrite themselves into the narratives of modern Greece. The fact that scholars today attribute sixteenth-century origins to the expression "the Jerusalem of the Balkans"—a cipher for the grandeur of Salonica as a Jewish city—indicates the extent to which the twentieth-century architects of this discourse successfully propagated their message.

Those who developed these historical narratives relied on modern innovations—Jewish communal schooling, expanded associational activity, the popular vernacular press, modern historical scholarship, and increased political activity—to reconceptualize Salonica as a fundamentally Jewish site and symbol. But in order to do so, they also depended upon a knowledge base at the heart of the traditional Salonican rabbinical world. Most of the sources necessary to "erect" (*fraguar*, in Judeo-Spanish) this history were in Hebrew, whether rabbinical decrees, communal statutes, eulogies, or tombstone inscriptions. It is, therefore, no surprise that the main figures writing the history of the Jews of Salonica—except for Joseph Nehama—received rabbinic training or were associated with the rabbinical seminaries in Salonica. Aside from Nehama and Mercado Covo, the other figures served as Hebrew teachers in the Jewish communal schools.

The scholar of Jewish history Yosef Hayim Yerushalmi famously observed that the study of history became "the faith of fallen Jews." He argued that, in the modern era of nationalism and secularization, the historian, who produced a past for his people and served as an intermediary between Jews and their traditions, encroached upon and sometimes displaced the role previously occupied by the rabbi.[212] But the process developed differently for Jewish intellectuals in Salonica, as three of the five main Salonican Jewish history writers (Ben-Jacob, Emmanuel, and Molho) received rabbinical training, served in religious roles as either rabbis or *hazanim*, and remained faithful to Jewish religious observance. As much as history became part of the faith of fallen Jews, as in the case of Nehama, it also became sacralized and integrated into the belief and practice of faithful Jews. Covo, who stood somewhere between Nehama and the others in terms of religious observance, illustrates that Jewish intellectuals in Salonica who engaged in historical research often stayed close to traditional Jewish practice.

Jewish history in Salonica also became the purview of Jewish nationalists, although the boundaries between the different political groups remained fluid. Nehama remained exceptional in the entire enterprise, for not only did he engage least with traditional Jewish practices, but he also emphasized assimilation and opposed Jewish nationalism. But Nehama relied on Molho and vice versa. As respected intellectuals, they transcended their political views and gained favor among a wide swath of the Jewish population. While the progressive organization Béné Bérith sponsored talks by Nehama and Covo (and one by Emmanuel), Ben-Jacob, Molho, and Emmanuel primarily operated in the realms of the Jewish schools, Zionist parties and publications, and synagogues. Covo more successfully operated in a variety of contexts—secular and religious, Zionist and assimilationist, Ottomanist and Hellenist—with

impressive dexterity. Despite their varying personalities and political proclivities, what united these intellectuals was their belief that writing the history of
Salonica's Jews would help them secure their position in the city.

These Salonican Jewish intellectuals focused their historiographical enterprise on the production of a narrative of their mother city—a sacred task
they dedicated to the Jewish family of Salonica. They did not compose universal Jewish histories as did colleagues elsewhere in Europe, nor did they
follow the paths of their Jewish colleagues elsewhere in the former Ottoman
Empire who wrote national or regional histories of the Jews in Turkey or in
the Orient.[213] Salonican Jews stood apart by focusing their energies primarily on composing local histories that sought to promote and legitimize the
status of Salonica within universal Jewish history and within the Ottoman
and subsequently Hellenic frameworks.

Observers believed that the historians' efforts during the interwar years
bore fruit and made a significant impact. As part of the history fad in 1931–
1932, journalist Sam Lévy re-published the memoirs of his father, the first
Judeo-Spanish journalist in the city, Saadi a-Levi, in Judeo-Spanish (*La
Aksion*) and French (*Le Progrès*).[214] The memoirs drew the attention of the
authorities and the mayor, Charisios Vamvakas, named a street in Saadi's
honor significantly, and perhaps unexpectedly, during a tense moment in
Jewish-Christians relations after the riots of 1931.[215] In the conclusion to his
pamphlet, *Les Juifs de Salonique* (1933), Lévy argued that the writings of figures like Michael Molho and Mercado Covo provoked a "veritable movement
of spiritual renaissance" among the Jews of Salonica. Lévy intimated that
the crisis of confidence experienced by the city's Jews was being overcome
by the very act of writing history. Lévy wondered whether Salonica could
approximate its former glory as "The Citadel of Israel" by recording and disseminating that very history.[216] Jewish communal leaders certainly hoped so.
They capitalized on the increasing excitement about history in the 1930s by
highlighting the arrival of the Jews to Salonica in 1492—not their expulsion
from Spain nor their entrance into the Ottoman Empire, in general—at the
center of the Jewish communal school history curriculum, which ran from
biblical times to the Balfour Declaration. Moreover, the chief rabbi encouraged teachers to inculcate in students a deep "emotional" attachment to their
history in order to definitively "influence the new generation."[217]

In the belief that Jerusalem again would stand at the center of the Jewish world, the founders of the Jewish Studies Institute of the Hebrew University of Jerusalem in 1925 appealed to the passage from Isaiah (2:3)—"For from Zion shall go forth Torah"—in support of their initiative.[218] Yet Covo proclaimed just a few years later in 1928: "For from *Salonica* shall go forth Torah."[219] He boldly positioned Salonica and Jerusalem, and the scholarly pursuits of Jewish intellectuals in both cities, on a par. The dynamic visions of Salonica that Covo, Ben-Jacob, Nehama, Emmanuel, and Molho ultimately bequeathed to us—the Jerusalem of the Balkans, the Citadel of Sephardism, the Macedonian Metropolis, and others—constitute the crowning achievements in the historiography of Salonican Jews. I. S. Révah, a scholar of Salonican background, declared in 1938 that the immense scholarship on Salonican Jews by Nehama and Emmanuel would be "without a doubt, impossible to surpass in the future."[220] This successful historiographical outpouring, which transformed an empty field in the 1890s into an unsurpassable one on the eve of World War II, demonstrates that, even if Salonican Jews experienced an unprecedented crisis in confidence during the interwar years, they also produced their most enduring scholarship about the past, which they hoped would lead them to a better future.

CHAPTER 5

STONES THAT SPEAK

The Cemetery

Solo ni al bedahey.

Alone, not even in the cemetery.

—Judeo-Spanish expression[1]

In his memorial to the "true metropolis of Israel," teacher and historian Michael Molho recorded the tragic scene of the final destruction of Salonica's vast Jewish cemetery:

> On December 6, 1942, at ten o'clock in the morning, a meeting is held at the cemetery, near the University buildings. . . . At the request of [Chief Rabbi] Koretz, we point out a great number of tombs with historical importance. Merten [the Nazi Military Administrative Director] listens to the arguments of the Jews and those of the proponents of the final expropriation presented by the secretary of the [Greek] government and decides on the spot: [only] the part closest to the University will be expropriated. . . . At the moment that Merten gets in his car, the representatives of the state authorities, anticipating the indulgence and full-fledged German approval for any increased, harsh anti-Jewish measures, ignore the decision just made in front of them by the German representative, and give the orders for everything to be demolished. . . . Five hundred workers are hired by the municipality to hastily execute the destructive and impious work. . . . The vast necropolis, strewn with heaps of stone and rubble, soon resembles a city violently bombed, or destroyed by a volcanic eruption.[2]

Stretching across 86 acres and housing an estimated 350,000 densely packed graves, the Jewish cemetery in Salonica had been the largest Jewish burial ground in all of Europe (the next largest, in Warsaw, housed 150,000 graves covering 74 acres).[3] Amidst the debris of the graves that dated to 1493—and in some cases to the Roman era—Molho transcribed the most important inscriptions, etched in stone and now reduced to shards by the municipal workers' pickaxes. Even after Merten initiated the ghettoization of the Jews on February 6, 1943, Molho continued his research amidst the cemetery ruins.[4] The following month, on March 15, deportations to Auschwitz began. The destruction of the Jewish necropolis thus preceded the liquidation of the Jewish metropolis.

Today, the extensive campus of Aristotle University of Salonica—the largest university in the Balkans—sits atop the former Jewish burial ground. A modest memorial, erected on the campus in 2014 after decades of silence, for the first time acknowledges the previous use of the site and commemorates "the old Jewish cemetery located for centuries on these grounds until its destruction in 1942 by the Nazi occupation forces and their collaborators." The monument continues, referring to the Jewish graves that stretched across the land "until 1943 when the forces of evil crushed all human substance; but people were not enough. They wanted to eradicate the memory too. And as they were sending the living to their death, they were shattering the tombs of the dead and scattering their bones. Those buried here died for a second time." While acknowledging the role that collaborators played in the destruction of the burial ground, the monument remarkably attributes initiative and responsibility to the Nazis, who are characterized as wishing to eradicate the memory of Jewish presence in the city by razing the cemetery. Despite the availability of accounts such as Molho's (first published in 1953), which implicates the Greek government and the municipality as the authors of the act, the new monument joins a long-standing trend of attributing primary—if not exclusive—responsibility for the demolition of the cemetery to the German occupation forces and thereby exculpating the local authorities.[5]

The initiative to remove the Jewish cemetery of Salonica, however, stemmed not from the Nazi occupation forces but rather from certain members of the Orthodox Christian population, government officials, and university representatives. Germans did not destroy most of the Jewish burial grounds in occupied Europe. Those in Berlin, Munich, Hamburg, and Breslau, as well as Paris, Amsterdam, Budapest, Vienna, Prague, Warsaw, and

Lodz survived the war largely intact. In Cracow, however, the German occupation forces razed two adjacent Jewish cemeteries and transformed the
terrain into the Plaszow concentration camp depicted in Steven Spielberg's
film, *Schindler's List.*[6] The decisive role played by the local population in the
fate of the Jewish burial ground in Salonica has been described as "a unique
phenomenon in modern European history, unique within the history and
memory of the destruction of the European Jews."[7] But the destruction of
a Jewish cemetery to make way for a university was not unique to Salonica
within the annals of modern Greek history; a similar process transpired in
Izmir while the city was under Greek control in the wake of World War I.

As significantly, the story of the ultimate destruction of the Jewish cemetery of Salonica began well before the arrival of the Germans. While the
Jewish cemetery sustained damage during the late Ottoman era, the prospect
of its complete expropriation emerged only after Salonica came under Greek
rule (1912). Following the massive fire of 1917, the city expanded beyond its
medieval walls, and the Jewish cemetery, previously on the eastern outskirts
of the city, soon became the new center of what was supposed to become
modern Greek Thessaloniki. Prime Minister Venizelos requested that the
French and British architects invited to redesign the city conceive of it as a
"blank slate"—in effect, ignoring the centuries-long physical imprint made
on the city by Jews and Muslims.[8] The new city plans envisioned the removal
of all cemeteries from within the city limits and posed the first major existential threat to the Jewish burial ground. Despite plans for its transfer, the
Orthodox Christian cemetery, Evangelistria, located across the street from
the Jewish cemetery, was never touched and remains in place today.[9]

Not resigned to the removal of their burial ground, official and unofficial representatives of the Jewish Community of Salonica successfully
safeguarded their cemetery from 1917 through the late 1930s—an effort
that demonstrated their continued power to shape local political dynamics. Some Jewish journalists, teachers, and communal leaders argued that
the Jewish cemetery should be preserved due to the inviolability of Jewish
burial grounds according to Jewish law, which dictated that Jewish graves
must not be disinterred. Jewish practice sat in stark contrast with Orthodox
Christian custom, which typically involved the exhumation of the remains
of the deceased after a period of three years and the reuse of the plots for

new burials.[10] Recognizing the divergent rituals among Jews and Orthodox Christians, other Jewish activists argued that the principle of religious tolerance—which required respect for Jewish customs—should not be violated and certainly not in the name of urban planning. Others argued that the tombstones "spoke" (*piedras ke avlan*), that the inscriptions narrated the integral role played by Jews—as Salonicans—in Jewish history and therefore should be preserved as Jewish historical artifacts. Still others argued that the burial ground ought to be considered an archaeological landmark of relevance to the entire city if not all of Greece, for it included graves of individuals who contributed to the city and endured hardship together with their Christian neighbors. If the Jewish monuments were preserved in the urban landscape, Salonica's Jews hoped to continue to play an integral role in the city's economic, political, and cultural life and bridge the divide between the Ottoman Empire the Greek nation-state.

The House of Life

The significance of the Jewish cemetery stemmed from its role not only as a space of the dead but also as a space of the living. The Hebrew term euphemistically applied to the Jewish burial ground, *Beth Ahaim* ("House of Life") or, in popular Judeo-Spanish, *Bedahey*, evokes the place of the cemetery as a connecting point between past and present, living and dead. Historically located to the east of the medieval city walls, the *Beth Ahaim* in Salonica stretched over a surface of more than four hundred thousand square meters. To the south, it bordered the Dönme cemetery and one of several Muslim burial grounds, which the municipality destroyed in the 1920s following the exchange of populations and the departure of their owners. The Dönme cemetery became the PAOK (Pan-Thessalonikian Athletic Club of Constantinopolitans) soccer field, whereas that of the Muslims became the International Fair Ground (est. 1926); another Muslim cemetery at the other end of the city, near Vardar, was also removed.

The erasure of the Muslim and Dönme cemeteries, along with the demolition of dozens of minarets, formed part of the state-sponsored process of Hellenizing the urban space by removing markers of the former "Turkish occupiers" in the city. Tombstones from these cemeteries were used for construction in the city; some with Arabic inscriptions can still be seen in the yard of the Rotunda (a Roman monument). In 1931, however, the Greek newspaper, *Makedonia*, lamented the disappearance of these picturesque Muslim burial grounds, for they once contained tombs of historical significance and had attracted European tourists to the city. A Judeo-Spanish newspaper wondered whether its Greek counterpart would agree that the Jewish cemetery also counted as a "historical monument."[11]

As the largest Jewish cemetery in Europe—thirty-five times larger than the famous Jewish cemetery in Prague—the *Beth Ahaim* served as a mirror of and nexus to the living world. Like the metropolis, the necropolis was divided into sectors, such as Allatini, Bitran, and *Sinyor* Jacques, often arranged by family or synagogue affiliation and according to class. Built from marble brought from nearby towns like Drama and Verria, the Aegean island of Tinos, or Italy, the gravestones usually sat parallel to the ground, more modern ones raised on brick foundations, and packed tightly: proximity to deceased rabbis or kabbalists believed to be close to God was considered advantageous. Modeling themselves on their Muslim neighbors, Jews in Salonica as throughout the Ottoman Empire participated in the tradition of *ziyara*, the pilgrimage to visit the tombs of loved ones on the anniversaries of their deaths, and the tombs of sages—such as the famed sixteenth-century Talmudic scholar, Samuel de Medina—in anticipation of the Jewish New Year and Passover. A class of lower-ranking rabbis, called *honadjis* ("callers"), made their living by guiding visitors to specified tombs and reciting memorial prayers. Bad dreams, illness, the impending birth of a child, business problems, or upcoming travels would provoke visits to the burial ground to implore divine protection. Among popular classes, the Jewish cemetery also served as the shrine for mystical practices—for Jews, Christians, and Muslims alike. Soil from the tomb of a loved one or sage constituted a central ingredient in folk remedies and kabbalistic recipes.[12]

To the chagrin of Jewish leaders, the *Beth Ahaim* also served as a grazing pasture for farm animals; a hangout for transients and squatters, prostitutes and teenage lovers; a battlefield for Jewish and Christian children engaged in rock fights; the site of several suicides; and a center for the hashish trade. In the interwar years, spectators at the adjacent PAOK and Iraklis (Hercules) sports fields dislodged tombstones to erect stadium-style seating in order to better view the games. Newspapers chastised the hired guards for attending to their bean garden rather than preventing trespassing. A British traveler lamented the "conspicuous absence of dignity about the Jewish cemetery; we find no reposefulness, no soothing influence, and the entire surroundings bespeak temporariness rather than permanency."[13]

Controversy over the Jewish cemetery dated back centuries. In the sixteenth century, Christians and Jews quarreled over a burial plot they each claimed, and the Christians ultimately purchased the right to use that particular terrain. Ottoman court records from 1709 reveal another conflict that erupted over the expansion of the Jewish cemetery to the displeasure of the Orthodox Christian and Muslim populations. Later in the eighteenth century, the Jewish cemetery became the site of a makeshift hospital during an outbreak of the plague. Amidst the Greek War of Independence in the 1820s, the Ottoman administration appropriated Jewish tombstones to fortify the city walls against rebels at Kassandra.[14] The Jewish burial ground nonetheless continued to expand in order to accommodate the needs of the Jewish population through the acquisition of adjacent terrain in 1873, 1893, 1911, and 1916—although the *tapus* ("title deeds") for some of these plots were lost over the years.[15]

More serious anxieties regarding the status of the Jewish cemetery developed during the late nineteenth-century project of urban transformation. The Ottoman modernization agenda included the building of a new port and a train station, and the establishment of companies for potable water, gas, and other amenities.[16] As hygiene became a major preoccupation, the municipality began to dump the "filth of the city" on the Jewish cemetery, located just outside the city limits.[17] "Our ancient *Beth Ahaim*," *La Epoka* exclaimed in 1889, "is at the point of being lost . . . since a large part is already covered in trash or other things that the [municipal] wagons throw out."[18] To protect the site, a Jewish philanthropic society, Hesed ve-Emeth, began erecting a wall around the cemetery in the 1890s. The organization promoted the upkeep of the burial ground: "So that we will not be the shame of the nations" and because "the respect for the dead is an absolute duty."[19]

But the duty to respect the dead came into conflict with public interest. In the wake of the massive fire in 1890, the municipality began to expand the city eastward and appropriated a section of the Jewish cemetery to construct the new Hamidiye Boulevard (now Ethnikis Aminis Street) and to erect the building of the Ottoman lycée (*idadi*).[20] *La Epoka* lamented the repurposing of terrain from the Jewish cemetery but also welcomed the creation of one of "the greatest preparatory schools in Turkey."[21] Michael Molho later speculated that the construction of the road and the *idadi* destroyed the oldest Jewish graves, dating from the Roman and Byzantine eras, as well as those of famous sixteenth-century rabbis, such as Moses Almosnino.[22] After Salonica came under Greek control, the building of the *idadi* became the philosophy building of the University of Salonica (1926), which overlooked the Jewish cemetery and hoped to expand further.

Figure 5.1. The University of Salonica overlooking the Jewish cemetery, interwar years. A view of the philosophy school. Source: Jewish Museum of Thessaloniki. Published with permission.

Prophets of Misfortune

Following the fire of 1917, the new city plan by Ernst Hébrard for the first time envisioned the complete removal of the Jewish cemetery from Salonica's urban fabric. In response to this existential threat, the Hesed ve-Emeth society hurried to complete the walls in the hope that the Town Planning Office would redraw the urban plan to accommodate the Jewish cemetery as a permanent feature of the city's topography.[23] Jewish communal leaders realized, however, that drawing more attention to their burial ground might only further "whet the appetite of the authorities."[24] They nonetheless successfully foiled attempts to expropriate the Jewish cemetery in 1919, partly due to a petition sent by journalist Sam Lévy directly to Prime Minister Venizelos, and again in 1925 and 1927.[25] By 1929, however, Hebrew teacher and journalist Samuel Saltiel preferred "not to predict the worst" nor serve as a "prophet of misfortune" but lamented that the existence of the Jewish cemetery could no longer be assured.[26] He feared that the Town Planning Office would dispose of the tombstones—"like trash."[27]

The arrival of Orthodox Christians from Asia Minor with the exchange of populations in 1923 exacerbated the already acute housing crisis in Salonica stemming from the fire of 1917. In 1929, in order to create new housing developments for refugees, the Ministries of Agriculture and Social Welfare and the governor general of Macedonia proposed expropriating sections of the Jewish cemetery on the grounds that the terrain "has been abandoned for hundreds of years," meaning that no new burials had taken place in those areas for some time.[28] City engineers began measuring nearby streets and hopped from tomb to tomb in order to survey the premises; new houses were being built on the adjacent land every day.[29]

The University of Salonica, established in 1926 as the main institution of higher education in Northern Greece, posed an additional threat to the existence of the Jewish cemetery in 1929. Seeking to expand the campus, the university demanded that the Jewish Community cede 6,500 square meters of the terrain of the Jewish cemetery.[30] Even though the university initially requested just a segment of the Jewish burial ground, the Town Planning Office explained to the governor general of Macedonia that the plans for the new university buildings involved "almost the whole area of the [Jewish] cemeteries" and insisted that no other "suitable" location for the

campus expansion could be found in the city.[31] The university's request ironically transpired simultaneously with the creation of a new chair of Hebrew
language and literature that ostensibly aimed to promote rapprochement between Jews and Christians. The rector of the university publically praised the
new position for providing an opportunity to "work toward reciprocal appreciation among Greeks and Jews . . . for the greatest benefit to the shared
homeland."[32] But he privately pressured Jewish leaders to capitulate to his
demand to cede part of the Jewish cemetery for the sake of higher education
and the "shared homeland."

Orthodox Christians living nearby also began to resent the inconve-
nience posed by the presence of the Jewish burial ground. Those in search
of shortcuts to the city center took pickaxes to the walls of the cemetery to
burrow their own passageways when they found the cemetery gates locked
and, in one instance, destroyed sixty to seventy tombstones along their path.
At least one tombstone, from 1863, was appropriated as building material
for a nearby military hospital. Over 150 more tombstones were destroyed in
another episode. Some Jewish newspapers sought to excuse these acts of van-
dalism as "child's play," whereas others viewed them as part of a "regular and
systematic" plan instigated by "evil-doing antisemites."[33]

In response to threats to the cemetery beginning in 1929, Jewish journalists, the chief rabbinate, the Communal Council, the new Commission
for the Defense of the Jewish Cemetery, and other Jewish activists appealed
varyingly to historical, archaeological, religious, moral, and legal arguments—
all charged with an emotional undercurrent—to defend their burial ground.
In an open letter to the Communal Council in *El Puevlo*, journalist and
teacher Samuel Saltiel initially prioritized a historical argument: "Our *Beth
Ahaim* contains truly precious monuments," the "best sources" with which to
write the history of the Jews of Salonica.[34] Because these "priceless tombs"
represented the only physical evidence of the centuries-long Jewish presence
in Salonica to survive the fire of 1917, Saltiel argued that the authorities must
be convinced of the significance of the Jewish burial ground to the city as a
whole.[35] He recommended that the Rabbinical Council take up the issue, for
it constituted a "spiritual question" of the greatest "moral" significance.[36]

Responding to Saltiel's call, the Rabbinical Council demanded that the
Communal Council take immediate action to halt the expropriations.[37] The

rabbinate elaborated on the spiritual and moral aspects of the issue and argued that, according to the "Jewish religion," the burial ground may not be touched and no graves may be moved, not even from a desecrated tomb to a new one. Rabbi Haim Habib justified this position with reference to the Jerusalem Talmud (Mo'ed Qatan 3) and the Jewish code of law, *Shulhan Arukh* (Yoreh De'ah 363). The rabbinate argued that due respect for the cemetery was so strong that "we consider the cemetery as a temple."[38] The Judeo-Spanish press soon echoed the chief rabbinate: "Cemeteries are not only historical monuments, but they also have a holy character."[39]

In responding to the public outcry, the Communal Council searched for precedents and sought information about how other Jewish communities dealt with proposed cemetery expropriations. The Salonican-born rabbi, Isaac Emmanuel, responded that, in Breslau, where he had been a student, Jewish leaders successfully halted the expropriation of their cemetery on the grounds that it constituted a "historical monument of the city." Emmanuel recommended that the Communal Council advocate that the Jewish cemetery of Salonica gain comparable status, especially considering that its tombs were more ancient. (Breslau's dated only to 1750.)[40] But the Communal Council recalled an earlier proposal by journalist Sam Lévy that the Jewish burial ground in Salonica be recognized as a "historical monument," in response to which the royalist Greek newspaper, *Taxydromos*, retorted that the Jewish cemetery "does not have any value" and recommended that the municipality transfer it outside of the city.[41] More promisingly, Jewish leaders in Bordeaux, Bayonne, Algiers, Prague, Vienna, and Berlin replied that they had successfully (or at least partially, in the case of Prague) prevented their burial grounds from being expropriated by evoking the principle of religious toleration.[42] The Greek Ministry of Foreign Affairs conducted a parallel investigation into the fate of cemeteries that produced mixed results. According to various Greek embassies, Jewish cemeteries had been preserved despite urban redesign initiatives in Istanbul, Adrianople, Alexandria, Bucharest, and Paris—in some instances out of respect for Jewish tradition—whereas they had been moved in Varna and Burgas, in Bulgaria, and removed in Izmir.[43]

The case of Izmir offers an intriguing parallel to Salonica. The Ottoman governor commandeered part of Izmir's Bahri Baba Jewish cemetery (est. 1565) to house Muslim refugees of the Russo-Ottoman War (1877–1878).

During World War I, in 1914, the Ottoman governor appropriated terrain from the Jewish burial ground in the name of urban development in order to build a school. While Jewish leaders protested—and asked Haim Nahum, the chief rabbi of the empire, to intervene on their behalf—they ultimately did not succeed, as the government was in the process of transferring all of the city's burial grounds, including the Muslim one, without distinction. The Beth Din begrudgingly developed procedures to transfer the remains.

During the Greek occupation of Izmir (1919–1922), the Greek administration completed the demolition of the Jewish cemetery to make way for the anticipated campus of the Ionian University. Jewish tombstones were used as construction material. Protests to the French and British consuls failed. A Salonican Jewish deputy in the Greek Parliament, David Alhanati, also tried to intervene with the Greek authorities to halt the perpetration of this "anti-Jewish act," which offended him as a "Hellene."[44] He did not succeed either. Instead, rabbis in Izmir arranged for the transfer of the remains of the dead on June 28, 1921, which was declared a day of mourning for local Jews, who closed their shops to grieve. Due to the expulsion of the Greeks from Asia Minor in 1922, however, the Ionian University never opened. At first a teachers college and a maternity ward, and now an ethnography museum and a vast park, occupied the site of the former Jewish burial ground.[45] As the University of Salonica took the place of the unrealized Ionian University as Greece's second institution of higher learning, the uncanny resemblance in the coveted status of these two Jewish burial grounds cannot be missed.

Aware of the precedent of Izmir's Jewish cemetery, the Communal Council in Salonica sent an official protest memorandum, jointly signed with the chief rabbinate, to Prime Minister Venizelos in December 1929. Appealing to the legal status of the Jews in Greece as a religious minority recognized by the state and protected by the League of Nations, the council emphasized the religious nature of the question of the cemetery: "Regardless of the historical value of our cemetery, what is most important is the position of cemeteries in general in the Hebrew religion, which accords them unique significance."[46] The council referred to precedents in Vienna, Bordeaux, and Bayonne, where proposals for the expropriation of Jewish cemeteries in the middle of cities for "public benefit" were abandoned out of respect for Jewish religious principles.[47] The council concluded that the proposal must have

emerged without knowledge of the inviolability of Jewish cemeteries according to Jewish law. Having been informed of Jewish tradition—which, unlike
that of Orthodox Christians, forbids the disinterment of the dead—the government would reconsider, or so the council hoped.[48]

The Communal Council also established a special Commission for the
Defense of the Jewish Cemetery, which sent delegations to the governor general of Macedonia, the university rector, and government ministries in Athens
to annul the expropriation initiatives.[49] As these efforts met with mixed results, the commission sought to document the most important tombstone
inscriptions—before it was too late—in order to compose "the history of the
community" and to publicize the "glorious" past of Salonica's Jews.[50] But the
commission discovered that numerous tombstones were strewn about, and
sheep and a horse—both belonging to one of the guards—posed obstacles.
The head of the commission, Isaac Alsheh, a communal notable and school
director, proposed an alternative strategy: to invite a "professor of valor" to
Salonica to study the tombstones, verify their historical merit, and present a
new case to the government.[51]

Officially on a mission throughout Europe in 1930 in search of suitable
candidates for a new chief rabbi of Salonica, Alsheh also investigated the
status of Jewish cemeteries in Belgrade, Vienna, Berlin, Prague, Geneva, and
Paris. His trip culminated in London in a meeting with the eminent Jewish
activist and diplomat, Lucien Wolf, the secretary of the Joint Foreign Committee of the Board of Deputies of British Jews.[52] Wolf had already been
involved in the affairs of Salonican Jews by advocating on their behalf during
the Balkan Wars and at the Paris Peace Conference, and by submitting an
official complaint to the League of Nations claiming that the Sunday closing
law (1924) violated the Greek Minorities Treaty.

Taking up the cause of the Jewish cemetery of Salonica, Wolf wrote to
Demetrios Kaklamanos, the Greek ambassador in London, requesting that
the proposed expropriation be reconsidered. While he referred to the "deeply
rooted religious susceptibilities" of Salonican Jews in connection to their
burial ground, Wolf also emphasized a historical argument: "This cemetery
is regarded with special reverence far beyond the limits of Hellenic Jewry, as
a historical monument, inasmuch as it shelters the remains of many of the
illustrious rabbis and martyrs who in the fifteenth century found a generous

asylum on the hospitable shores of the Aegean."[53] Kaklamanos responded that, although the "historical and sentimental reasons" had been taken into account, a burial ground could not continue to exist in the city center, for it was deemed "incompatible with modern exigencies of public welfare." He promised that "every measure would be taken in order that monuments and inscriptions of historic interest as well as the religious feelings of the Jewish community of Salonica would be safeguarded."[54] Wolf characterized this reply as "extremely amiable" yet "decidedly unsatisfactory"—it offered no "definitive prospect" of modifying the proposed expropriation.[55]

In conversation with Wolf and accompanied by Sam Lévy, Alsheh proposed the creation of an international Jewish Committee of Historical Studies, composed of scholars from the United States, England, France, and Germany. The committee would come to Salonica to document the Jewish cemetery and, at the very least, "would gain time" and postpone the proposed expropriation. Wolf endorsed the idea "without reservation."[56] By the end of the meeting, the discussion no longer focused on the creation of a "historical" committee, but rather on an "archaeological school." In the context of interwar Greece, the shift from a historical to an archaeological lens, it was believed, would resonate with the ascendance of archaeology as a tool of Greek nationalism.[57]

Despite interest on the part of the Jewish Historical Society of England and the Alliance Israélite Universelle, the archaeological school never materialized, due in part to Wolf's death (1930). New petitions sent to the Board of Deputies of British Jews from the Mizrahi, the Jewish religious-nationalist party in Salonica, conceded that the expropriation of the Jewish cemetery was a fait accompli and argued that international attention should be focused on overturning the Sunday closing law, which had become more stringently enforced.[58] Left to their own devices and spurred by mounting crises, Salonican Jewish intellectuals took the task of documenting their cemetery into their own hands.

Tombstones that Speak

Jewish teachers and journalists in Salonica initiated a campaign to document the Jewish cemetery and its most important tombstones in order to demonstrate the key role Jews played in the city's history and to justify the preservation of the burial ground as a site of archaeological and historical significance. As Baruch Ben-Jacob proclaimed, the cemetery was filled with "stones that speak."[59] In the face of claims circulating in the Greek press that Jews were Christ-killers, foreign Spaniards, cosmopolitan Francophiles, Turkish sympathizers, Bulgarian irredentists, communist insurgents, and otherwise anti-Greek, disloyal, and had no place in the city or the country, the funerary inscriptions, so Ben-Jacob argued, documented the long-standing contributions of Jews to the development of Salonica, Macedonia, and all of Greece. According to this logic, the Jewish cemetery must remain, not only for the sake of the Jews but also as a record of the city and the region. But tensions emerged as some preferred to emphasize the significance of the cemetery to Jewish history alone and published their findings exclusively in Judeo-Spanish or Hebrew. Even those who sought to demonstrate the greater importance of the cemetery to the city or to Greece reached a primarily Jewish audience, as they rarely published in Greek (although occasionally in French). The local Jewish press nonetheless insisted that the Jewish dead should remain buried just as the Jewish living should continue to exercise vital roles in the life of the city.

By reference to the tombstone inscriptions and the historical tales imbedded therein, the campaigners, writing initially in the Judeo-Spanish press, sought to remind their readers of "our beautiful traditions and customs," "the spirit of our forefathers," and "the beautiful history of our important community, which has more than one glorious page to register." The writing of history offered "comfort and consolation" and the knowledge to inspire Jews to regain "our energy and vitality."[60] As the only local repository of Jewish history in the city that survived the fire of 1917, the cemetery became a unique historical source: "In reproducing the inscriptions of the tombstones, tomorrow it will be seen, as in a clear mirror, the glorious life of the Jews of Salonica throughout the centuries."[61] In an editorial entitled "What the tombs say" (*Loke Dizen las Tombas*), Joseph Nehama emphasized that the significance of the inscriptions lay in the stories they told of "our families," generations of Jews who had called Salonica home.[62]

The tombstone inscriptions offered stories of famous figures who made the city their home and provided evidence of the status of Salonica as a center of Jewish culture since the fifteenth century—if not earlier. While inscribed with names and dates of death, the tombstones often included Jewish symbols and iconography representative of the deceased's profession. Some sixteenth-century inscriptions highlighted great figures of Jewish Spain who contributed to the "glory of Sephardi Judaism in Salonica": "This inscription is in honor of the eminent / sage, the doctor R[abbi] Salomon / son of Don Samuel son of his eminence the prince Don Shemtov / Habib, a native of / the city of Castresana / in the kingdom of Castile / and he died on the 17th of Elul 5264 [1504]." While the majority of the tombstone inscriptions, including Habib's, were in Hebrew, those in Judeo-Spanish first appeared in 1709. They were joined by those in Portuguese on the gravestones of former conversos who were buried as Jews; those in Italian of Livornese Jewish merchant families; and those in French, preferred by the upwardly mobile from the nineteenth century on. A handful appeared in Yiddish. Several also included the languages of the state, whether Ottoman Turkish—for example, Jacques Nissim Pasha (d. 1903), a physician for the Ottoman military—or Greek—for example, David Matalon (d. 1931), an active Zionist and member of Greek Parliament. In short, the inscriptions revealed the diverse cultural orientations of Salonica's Jews.

Unlike most cemeteries in northern and eastern Europe, the one in Salonica, like those in Istanbul and parts of Italy, often included Hebrew inscriptions in flowery verse that endowed them with literary significance.[63] Some included detailed biographies, although few were as elaborate as this one:

He who lies [here] in refuge
was the chief poet who composed several
poems for the visit of the sultan and his entourage [1859] and songs
to be sung for Purim
and many Jewish hymns in praise of the Almighty,
pleasant melodies for Israel. To every gathering, for the sake of heaven,
with all of his strength and with his feet, he would run like a deer.
This man is Saadi a-Levi.
This tombstone was erected here
in honor of a man full of wisdom.
From him [came] counsel and insight.

He was girded with justice and faith.

Behold it is he "the great and blessed" Saadi a-Levi Ashkenazi, "may his soul
   rest in paradise."

He was the first Jew in this city who brought to light newspapers.

In 1875 he published a newspaper in the Sephardic language
   La Epoka.

In 1895 he published in the French language
   Journal de Salonique.

He "departed for his eternal home" on the 8th day of Tevet 5663 [1903].

This inscription offered evidence of Jewish contributions to "this city" as a
whole. When Michael Molho published the inscription in Judeo-Spanish
translation in 1931, he massaged his version to suit his goals: he referred to
Saadi as the first person, rather than the first Jew, to publish newspapers in
Salonica; and he referred to Salonica not as "this city" but as "our city."[64]

The campaigns to record and disseminate the historical tales spoken by
tombstones such as these involved "epigraphists" compiling inscriptions and
composing historical "chapters" for local newspapers from 1929 to 1932.[65]
Popular essays about the history of Salonica appeared as front-page stories in *El Puevlo* and *La Aksion* with headlines such as "The History of
Salonica," "Salonican Studies," "The History of Jewish Salonica," "The History of Our Community," and "Our Popular University" that sought to
disseminate the knowledge produced by reference to the tombstones and
supplementary sources. Judeo-Spanish newspapers motivated the discovery
of inscriptions of historical merit by publishing the picture of the discov-
erer on the front page. Newspapers soon complained about the increase in
amateur involvement: owning "a magnifying glass does not suffice to make
you a historian."[66]

The more serious epigraphists formed teams, inclusive of "callers"
(*honadjis*) familiar with the layout of the burial ground and equipped to lead
the way to historic tombs. Isaac Emmanuel, then living in Lausanne, led one
of the teams and paid Isaac Samuel Brudo, a cemetery guard, to serve as his
research assistant and transcribe relevant tombstone inscriptions. In his letters to Emmanuel, Brudo explained that the great pilgrimages, or *ziyaras*, at
the times of the Jewish holidays plus bad weather turned the cemetery into

a big mud bath and delayed the work. Brudo indicated that two other teams also busied themselves in the cemetery: those of Baruch Ben-Jacob and Michael Molho. Brudo described Ben-Jacob as a "charlatan" and indicated that he "butchered" his transcriptions of inscriptions.[67] In contrast, Brudo indicated that Molho recruited a formidable team. Funded by Joseph Nehama, Molho brought along several *honadjis* and Rabbi Isaac Emanuel Brudo (a member of the Beth Din). By 1932, Molho had commissioned photographs of forty of the most important tombstones. The cemetery guard thus warned Emmanuel that Molho posed the most serious competition, especially once he gained additional support from the Alliance in Paris, due to the intervention of Nehama.[68] Molho, Emmanuel, and to a lesser extent Ben-Jacob, Mercado Covo, and Rabbi Shaul Amariglio, ultimately published collections of hundreds of the most significant inscriptions they had discovered under titles such as *The Great Jews of Salonica across the Generations.*[69]

Competition between the various teams intensified and provoked a major controversy from 1933 to 1934 over accusations that certain individuals involved in the campaigns had intentionally disfigured tombstone inscriptions by covering them up with cement or chiseling out names and dates so that their rivals would not find them. As many as two hundred tombstones may have been damaged in this way, including those of famed sixteenth-century sages such as David ben Nahmias and relatives of the Hebrew poet Gedalia Ibn Yahya. The chief rabbinate opened an investigation and temporarily banned researchers from entering the burial ground. This "*Beth Ahaim* affair" revealed the desperation with which the researchers wrote, the intrigues of fame and fortune, and the fragility of the situation of the city's Jews in the depths of economic depression.[70]

The convergence of scandal and intense public interest in tombstone inscriptions and historical essays in the local press led the cemetery guard to pun that a "historical epidemic" (*epedemia estoryana*) had overtaken the city's Jews. But to the common reader unaware of the intrigue, newspapers revealed tombstone inscriptions of Salonica's "great men" and their achievements in order to show that faith in tradition and ingenuity had enabled the city's Jews to overcome catastrophes in the past—whether fire, plague, or economic crisis—and that they could do so again. By issuing a decree suppressing debts, for example, eighteenth-century rabbis emerged as economic theorists who brought the city's Jews out of a depression worse than the current one of the 1930s. The tombstone inscriptions of these rabbis were brought to light, contextualized, and touted as reminders of their salutary deeds.[71]

Researchers and publications focused particular attention on the activities of Jewish physicians in Salonica. Michael Molho's articles on the subject and Baruch Ben-Jacob's booklet, *The Community of Doctors* (1932), emphasized that Jewish doctors across the generations cared not only for Jews but also for all communities in the city, including Orthodox Christians.[72] The most frequently evoked of these physicians, Amatus Lusitanus (1511–1568), a famed Portuguese-born converso, made important discoveries about the circulation of blood. Settling in Salonica, where he embraced the open practice of Judaism, Lusitanus helped rescue the city's residents—Jews, Christians, and Muslims alike—from an outbreak of the plague. His ecumenical heroism and attachment to his adoptive land was enshrined on his tombstone in Latin, which the press creatively paraphrased in Judeo-Spanish: "Amatus Lusitanus, who created life for kings and princes, rich and poor, came to die far from his country and sleeps in the soil of Macedonia."[73] The reference to the "soil of Macedonia" served the interests of the campaigners seeking to demonstrate the connection of the Jews of Salonica to the larger Macedonian Metropolis, to illustrate their contributions to the city, and to show that the cemetery ought to be considered a historical monument of value for all of Salonica's residents.

The campaigns in the press, combined with political lobbying, succeeded in postponing all attempts to expropriate the Jewish cemetery, in the short term. In 1930, prominent Jews and Orthodox Christians banded together to form a new association, the League of Peace, and visited the police chief, the mayor, and the governor general of Macedonia to protest desecrations in the Jewish cemetery and to advocate for the terrain's security.[74] The Commission for the Defense of the Jewish cemetery reinforced the protective walls—"the holiest of holy work"—and together with the police chief erected a police station, manned by three gendarmes, on the grounds of the Jewish cemetery in 1932: true evidence, the press reported, of the spirit of Orthodox Christian-Jewish fraternity.[75] The Commission also mobilized to prevent various government agencies from expropriating Jewish graveyards in towns across the country, including Drama, Kavalla, Larissa, and Halkida. Finally, in 1933,

Prime Minister Venizelos, municipal officials, the governor general, the metropolitan, and the rector of the university all promised that they would "not consider expropriation [of the cemetery] for many years to come."[76] It appeared as if the Jewish cemetery had been saved and would remain part of the urban topography of Greek Thessaloniki.

From the House of Life to the House of Intellect

With the fall of Venizelos (1933) and the rise of Metaxas (1936), the "delicate question"—as both the Judeo-Spanish and Greek newspapers called it—of the Jewish cemetery reemerged in an unprecedented fashion. The resurgent debate underscored the limits of Orthodox Christian-Jewish rapprochement and the extent to which Jews—and their burial ground—could be considered "Greek." Despite the apparent goodwill of Metaxas, often remembered for having alleviated much of the anti-Jewish pressure that characterized the tenures of Venizelos as prime minister, it was during Metaxas' regime that the long-standing plans to expropriate the Jewish cemetery, debated and delayed for twenty years, finally began to be implemented. The battle over the burial ground ultimately polarized Orthodox Christian-Jewish relations and revealed fractures among the city's Jews.

The Salonica-based Orthodox Christian instigators of the successful expropriation of the Jewish cemetery dismissed or minimized not only the religious but also the archaeological and historical appeals in support of the preservation of the *Beth Ahaim*. Some who promoted expropriation justified their stance by reference to urban planning, hygiene, or property law. But the most influential of these "partisans of expropriation" justified their goal in the name of "the progress of Hellenic civilization," which, they strategically argued, required not only the expansion of the university over the cemetery terrain but also the elimination of the Jewish cemetery as a major marker—like the Dönme and Muslim cemeteries before—of non-Hellenic civilization in the center of what was supposed to be the Second City of Greece.

That the university could have expanded in other directions and spared the Jewish cemetery—the alternatives were well-known at the time yet not pursued—demonstrates that the proponents of expropriation believed they had proved that the progress of Hellenic civilization *required* the replacement of the "House of the Living"—the Jewish *Beth Ahaim*, embodied by the cemetery—with the "House of the Intellect"—the Greek *pnevmatikí estía*, represented by the Hellenic university. Such a transformative project revealed not only Orthodox Christian-Jewish tensions but also the struggle between Salonica and Athens for power and influence in the consolidating Greek state.

The competition between Athens—and especially its port at Piraeus— and Salonica began with the incorporation of Salonica into the Greek state in 1912. Piraeus represented the commercial interests of Athens and Old Greece, and Salonica, the major port of entry to Macedonia and New Greece. The central government sought to give Piraeus the advantage in order to transform Athens from a provincial village into an economically vibrant city connected to a thriving port and worthy of the designation as capital of modern Greece. Salonica's port suffered after 1912 because it was cut off from markets in the Balkans that had previously provided much of the city's wealth. The effort in Salonica to Hellenize the port—a process that resulted in the dismissal of many Jewish stevedores—found a parallel in the national arena with the simultaneous effort to solidify the dominant position of the capital and its port. By 1932, headlines in the press lamented: "Piraeus ruins Salonica."[77]

As part of these inter-city struggles, the Jewish cemetery of Salonica became a bargaining chip under Metaxas. The catalyst was the implementation by Athens of new measures restricting imports to Salonica in 1935–1936. Hoping to assure the continued vitality of the city's economy, the Chamber of Commerce of Salonica objected to the new restrictions. In debates at the Chamber of Commerce, certain participants argued for a quid pro quo. If the central government in Athens continued to impose economic restrictions on Salonica, it must support the expansion of the University of Salonica, the "only intellectual sanctuary of higher [education] in Northern Greece," which, like the city's port, continued to "suffocate" from the "boa constrictor of national abandonment."[78]

The Judeo-Spanish press reported on every move in favor of the new initiative to expropriate the Jewish cemetery. *El Mesajero* feared that the general governor of Macedonia was organizing the Chamber of Commerce, the municipality, and the university in a "serious movement" in favor of expropriation.[79] The paper noted that the students of the university also mobilized, especially the Panfitiki Enonis ("Student Union"), anxious to find space for a new student center. Significantly, the Student Union's leadership had passed out manifestos that had encouraged the Campbell attacks in 1931.[80] Soon, Orthodox Christian representatives of neighborhoods near the Jewish cemetery, including Saranda Ekklisies, Pavlou Mela, Aghion Pandon, and Megalo Revma, petitioned the mayor and the chief rabbi arguing that, in addition to the needs of the university, in the interest of their own health they were "not prepared to tolerate" the continued existence of the Jewish cemetery inside the city. The City Health Department had already requested that burials be at least two meters away from the cemetery walls because the odor offended nearby residents.[81] "We will do what it takes," the neighborhood representatives proclaimed.[82] The municipality also began construction of a road bisecting the cemetery and of a canal.[83] *El Mesajero* "feared that the difficulties to be faced this time will be great."[84] Among the immediate responses, Chief Rabbi Koretz requested that the municipality plant trees in the cemetery to improve its "desolate" appearance while the Communal Council asked the Town Planning Office for permission to establish new Jewish burial plots outside the city center.[85]

In contrast to the Judeo-Spanish press, which reported on the "question of the cemetery," Greek newspapers focused on the "question of the university." *Makedonia*, which had instigated the Campbell riots in 1931, led the campaign. The editors complained that the "suffocating" of the university was due not only to the restrictions imposed by Athens but also to the literal lack of space. Chemistry and physics students were forced to conduct their lab experiments in the dark, unhygienic basements of the university building: "The students draw the springs of knowledge like the first Christians executed the duty of worshipping their religion. In the catacombs." Responsible for this despicable situation in the "university sanctuary," wrote philosophy professor Avrotelis Eleftheropoulos—again emphasizing religious metaphors—were none other than the Jews, who continued to prevent the university from expanding by refusing to relinquish the space of the Jewish necropolis.[86] A native of Istanbul, educated in Leipzig, and previously a professor in Zurich, Eleftheropoulos joined the faculty in Salonica in 1929 and ultimately served as rector of the university in 1937–1938. As a prominent intellectual, he galvanized support for the cemetery's expropriation.

Seeking to "enlighten" Chief Rabbi Koretz in 1936, Eleftheropolous argued that Jews in Salonica obstructed the expansion of the university and hindered the "elevation of humanity" by exploiting Greek politics. "You insist that those tombs remain in their place," he decried, "you insist and you succeed, having as an aid the political hardships of miserable Greece, whose deprivations you know perfectly and exploit." Eleftheropoulos presented the Jews of Salonica as unique in Europe: nowhere else, he assured his readers, would Jews get away with defending their cemetery for "supposedly religious reasons." He

Figure 5.2. The Greek newspaper *Makedonia*, reporting on the university and the Jewish cemetery, April 1, 1936. Headline: "An important matter for the city. The space of the Jewish monuments will be given as quickly as possible to the city and the university." Source: Union of Journalists of Thessaloniki.

reminded Koretz of "the persecutions you [i.e., 'the Jews'] endure in Germany [i.e., under Hitler's regime]" and assured him that elsewhere in Europe, Jews would not be permitted to "drown the evolution of the city and university" for the sake of their alleged beliefs. He referred to the prohibition against Jewish ritual slaughter in Poland and lamented that if Greece were more *advanced*, if the mayor of Salonica were not "a slave" to Jewish votes, the Jews would be compelled to forgo their "religious dogmas" and cede their burial ground for the "common good." Finally, the professor recommended that the chief rabbi transfer the Jewish cemetery outside the city limits at his "own initiative" so that he would not have to be "blackmailed by a law" compelling him to do so in the future. Eleftheropoulos argued that, by taking the initiative, the Jewish Community would demonstrate its desire to contribute to the "development of our country for the common good and particularly [that] of the university and in that way contribute to real brotherhood between the two elements of Thessaloniki, the Jews and the Greeks (Christians)."[87]

The absence of Jewish students at the University of Salonica in 1936 reinforced the perception that they did not support Jewish-Orthodox Christian solidarity or the advancement of Hellenic civilization. While repudiating Eleftheropoulos' "insolence" and "disrespect" of Chief Rabbi Koretz, *El Mesajero* lamented the absence of Jews among the 1,500 students at the university. Since its founding in 1926, only ten Jews had graduated from the faculty of law, while two Jews from nearby Verria graduated from the faculty of agronomy. No Jews had enrolled in the previous three years. The temporary suspension of the Béné Bérith scholarship program and the lack of Greek language proficiency among Jewish graduates of the Lycée Français numbered among the explanations offered.[88] Perhaps continued resentment over the role of the Student Union in the Campbell riot and the disdainful attitude of ostensibly well-respected faculty such as Eleftheropoulos contributed to a climate that young Jews preferred to avoid.

Despite the absence of Jewish students at the university, the rector made overtures toward the Jewish Community in 1936 to fill the vacant chair of Hebrew philology. Previously held by Lazarus Belleli, the chair was offered by the Ministry of Public Education to Chief Rabbi Koretz.[89] While an ostensible gesture toward firming up Orthodox Christian-Jewish "fraternity," the proposal to appoint the chief rabbi as a professor served as a kind of preemptive compensation—a bribe—for the removal of the Jewish cemetery to benefit the university. Proposing another quid pro quo, the minister of public instruction offered to permit more hours of French language instruction in the Jewish communal school curriculum if the cemetery were ceded.[90]

The university, the municipality, the Greek press, the governor general of Macedonia, and residents of various Orthodox Christian neighborhoods had campaigned over the course of two decades to acquire parts of the Jewish burial ground for planned parks, roads, neighborhoods, and the university. The introduction of a new player, the Chamber of Commerce, enhanced the efficacy of the expropriation initiatives. The Judeo-Spanish press identified G. Loulis—a staunch Venizelist, the head of the Union of Industrialists, and the manager of a major flour mill (notably founded by a Jewish family, Allatini)—as the "theoretician . . . without a doubt" of the new expropriation campaign.[91]

Loulis furtively raised the "question of the university" during a discussion of "miscellaneous" topics at a July 2, 1936, meeting of the Chamber of Commerce.[92] The extant minutes reveal in handwritten Greek that, by framing the question of the university as a national issue, Loulis garnered support from almost all the attendees. According to the Judeo-Spanish press, however, several Orthodox Christian notables—namely, Athanasios Rozis, the director of the Salonica branch of the National Bank of Greece, and Alexandros Krallis, a merchant of Vlach origin who later became the president of the Chamber of Commerce during the German occupation—discretely argued against the expropriation of the Jewish cemetery on the grounds that the university could open new buildings elsewhere in the city.[93] But their views remained in the minority. Building upon Eleftheropoulos' earlier scare tactics, Loulis warned that chemical explosions would occur in the basement science labs, destroy the university, and kill a generation of up-and-coming Greek scientists. Such sensational rhetoric formed part of a larger argument that Northern Greece had an "absolute necessity" (*apolyti anagki*) to increase the flourishing of the university, Salonica's "House of the Intellect" (*pnevmatiki estia*). Loulis argued that if millions of drachmae of new laboratory equipment, which sat in warehouses due to lack of space on campus, were to be used, then the University of Salonica would become a prestigious research institution on a par with those in Europe.

The solution, Loulis announced, was easy: expand the university to make way for new science labs. Loulis indicated that the university shared its boundaries not only with the Jewish cemetery, but also with the two sports fields of Iraklis and PAOK, as well as with an orphanage. Without addressing the last institution, Loulis stressed the prime significance of exercise and sport for the development of the youth. While he hoped that Iraklis would consider ceding its stadium and relocate elsewhere in the city, he argued that the most convenient terrain for the expansion of the university was the Jewish cemetery. Loulis contended that, if the Jews, led by the chief rabbi—a man of "uncommon understanding"—would "recognize the ... educational necessity" at hand and "eliminate [their] superstitions and prejudices" that permitted them, *without reason*, to object to the transfer of their cemetery, the success of the university would be guaranteed. The issue came down to whether Jewish prohibition against disinterment constituted legitimate religious practice to be tolerated and protected, or whether it was a superstition to be ignored.

Loulis insisted that he should not be accused of being antisemitic or of lacking respect for the dead. Appealing to the history of the city and to the heritage of many of the members of the Chamber of Commerce who were born in Turkey and arrived in Salonica in the 1920s, Loulis proclaimed: "You should know that Thessaloniki is built over graves and that in Asia Minor and Thrace we have abandoned graves upon graves of loved ones and brothers. But I believe that respect for graves should not limit progress. Nobody could ever think that it would be possible for graves to be an obstacle to progress and to the improvement of life."[94] In one fell swoop, Loulis dismissed the efforts of Jewish leaders over the previous decade to demonstrate the historical and archaeological significance of their cemetery. The only remaining obstacle was the alleged religious sentiment of the Jewish population. Framing his claim in terms of universal progress, Loulis reiterated that the solution to the problem lay in convincing the Jews to "erase their prejudices." He urged the members of the Chamber of Commerce to help the university complete its mission and called for a vote to this effect.

The initial responses among the members of the Chamber of Commerce were mixed. Albert Ginio, a Jewish member of parliament and the treasurer of the Chamber of Commerce, objected. He argued that this "delicate" matter of a religious nature fell beyond the "competence" of the Chamber and, moreover, involved a conflict between the university and Iraklis, not the Jewish Community. He agreed to do whatever was necessary to promote the expansion of the campus—just not over the Jewish cemetery. Isaac Simantov Sciaky, a Jewish merchant, observed that the University of Athens did not house all of its faculties on the same campus but had several annexes throughout the city. Precisely such planning explained why, when a fire did break out in the Athens chemistry department, no other departments of the university were affected. His suggestion to create new university buildings in other sectors of Salonica fell on deaf ears. In contrast, Haim Benroubi, a moderate and a member of the General Assembly of the Jewish Community, damningly conceded that "progressive" Jews like himself might agree with Loulis: the so-called psychological objections of the Jewish masses to the transfer of the cemetery amounted to mere "superstitions" and "prejudices." Loulis insisted that his proposal be voted on, but the meeting was adjourned due to the "aggression being built up during the discussion."[95]

Such aggression transferred to the pages of the local newspapers reporting on the meeting. While the royalist *Taxydromos* provided a reasoned summary of the debate at the Chamber of Commerce, *Makedonia* referred to Loulis' perspective alone by emphasizing that the existence of a graveyard "does not stop the living from building cities and institutions of civilization."[96] *Makedonia* published a front-page article by Loulis, who now claimed that the presence of the science labs in the basement was "criminal."[97] Loulis also alleged—falsely so—that the Jewish cemetery was "no longer in use," had been "free for many years," and was waiting to be taken: "not even a remote family memory could be offended today." Loulis then noted that, according to Efstratios Pelekidis, an archaeology professor at the university, the allegedly Jewish cemetery in question had been a Christian burial ground, as evidenced by certain tombstone inscriptions in Latin, and therefore did not belong to the Jews at all. He concluded that the Jewish cemetery must be removed in accordance with the principles of "liberalism" so that the "Greek spirit," embodied in the University of Salonica, may elevate the "level of civilization in the Balkans."[98]

Invited by the Greek paper *To Fos* to rebut Loulis' arguments, Chief Rabbi Koretz reiterated the religious and historical character of the Jewish burial ground; the unquestionable desire of the Jewish Community to promote the

university; the possibility of establishing additional university buildings elsewhere in the city, as in Athens and in Europe; and the precedents in France,
Germany, Poland, and Czechoslovakia where Jewish cemeteries in the heart
of the city were preserved. He also countered the claims of the archaeologist Pelekidis by invoking the earlier research in the Jewish cemetery: the
tombs to which Pelekidis referred belonged not to Christians but to conversos—such as Amatus Lusitanus—who returned to Judaism in Salonica and
were buried as Jews.[99] Despite Koretz's pleading, the rector of the university
decided to bring his case to the central government in Athens. The Jewish
Community begged its lawyer in the capital to intervene and "neutralize" the
rector's effort.[100]

The local Judeo-Spanish press realized that the question of the Jewish
cemetery had become "serious, very serious this time."[101] Jewish newspapers
abroad, such as one in Cairo, also worried: "Will the ancient necropolis of
more than five centuries that synthesizes all the glory of Sephardi Judaism
be demolished?"[102] Since Sam Lévy, writing from France, recognized that
this time "we will not win," he proposed that the Jewish Community transfer
the Jewish cemetery to a new terrain outside of the city center. This would
be the only way, he argued, to ensure both the perpetuation, in any capacity, of the burial ground—"the scared patrimony that proves the existence of
oriental Sephardism"—and the integration of this "'living' page of the history of the Macedonian metropolis" into the urban fabric of Greece. But by
ignoring the inviolability of the religious prohibitions against disinterment
and reburial, Lévy met the wrath of the chief rabbinate, which condemned
his callous proposal for giving fodder to those who wished to destroy the
cemetery.[103]

The Courage to Unbury the Dead

The campaign in the Greek press for the expansion of the university over
the terrain of the Jewish burial ground gave rise to a decisive meeting at the
Chamber of Commerce, this time under the auspicies of the governor general of Macedonia in late July 1936. The meeting revealed that the views of
Loulis were triumphing, and Jewish leaders believed that the only way they
could preserve the cemetery was to take their case to Athens. Loulis similarly
believed that the central government would look favorably on his endeavor.

This decisive meeting at the Chamber of Commerce, which guided the fate of the university, the Jewish cemetery, the urban arrangement of Salonica as a whole, and the tenor of Orthodox Christian-Jewish relations, strikingly took place on the Jewish holiday of Tisha Be-av (the ninth day of the Hebrew month of Av), which commemorates the destructions of the Temples in Jerusalem.

The symbolic and practical impact of this apparent coincidence must not be underestimated. Due to the observance of Tisha Be-av, a day of solemn mourning on the Jewish calendar, Chief Rabbi Koretz and the president of the Community, Eliaou Benosiglio, spent the day at synagogue mourning, praying, and fasting. Downtown on Tsimiski Street, those at the Chamber of Commerce fashioned themselves into Talmudic exegetes qualified to interpret the "true" meaning of Jewish law. Albert Ginio, a Jewish parliamentary deputy who attended the meeting despite the holiday, unsucessfully sought to table the debate on the grounds that the only person authorized to judge the precepts of the Talmud was the chief rabbi, who was absent.[104]

The rector of the university, following the lead of Loulis and Eleftheropoulos, rejected Ginio's suggestion by declaring that there was "only one possible solution" to the question of the expansion of the university—the Jewish cemetery: "But the Jews refuse to cede to us the terrain we need by posing historical and religious arguments. . . . They make reference to the Talmud. Certainly the religion must be respected, but we cannot sacrifice the future for the past and stop the progress of life because of the dead. I believe that their religious precepts are not violated if we disinter the bones . . ."[105] *La Aksion* feared that Koretz would not have fared well even if he had been present, as Loulis wanted to "win at any cost." He would have learned Hebrew, the paper surmised, to debate with Jewish texts in hand whether the religion permits the disinterring of bones.[106] *Makedonia* emphatically announced the winner of the debate: Loulis, "with solid arguments, destroys the pretentions of the Jews."[107]

In addition to Ginio, the only other Jewish representative at the Chamber of Commerce, the journalist and Zionist Baruch Shiby, tried in vain to convince the audience to abandon the plan for expropriation by invoking numerous precedents of cemeteries that remained in city centers, such as those in Tunis, Vienna, Vitoria (Spain), Cologne, Prague, and Altona.[108] *Taxydromos* did not even mention Shiby's final attempt to sway the audience, while *Makedonia* focused on the "fanaticism" and "unjustifiable religiosity" of the Jews without mentioning the other possibilities available to expand the university—in another part of the city or on top of the football fields of Iraklis and PAOK.[109] In a similar vein, Eleftheropoulos wrote another editorial in *Makedonia* focused exclusively on overturning the historical and religious arguments mounted by the Jews, concluding that if the transfer of the cemetery "constitutes a sin, the Greeks will take the responsibility upon themselves and be accountable before God."[110]

The Judeo-Spanish newspapers condemned the vituperative attacks against the Jews and lamented the collapse of the project of Hellenic Judaism and of Orthodox Christian-Jewish rapprochement. "Do we constitute the lowest rung of society?" mourned *La Aksion* in a front-page story.[111] The newspaper had hoped that the tides would change and reproduced a photograph of the laying of the first brick of the police station in the Jewish cemetery from 1932, a symbol of Orthodox Christian-Jewish cooperation, however fragile, that the editors hoped would endure. But they also worried that Christians would never understand Jewish religious tradition (the prohibition against disinterment) just as Jews could not understand Christian traditions.[112]

Jewish leaders convened a special assembly to assure a united front in the face of the expropriation initiative. In the lengthy Judeo-Spanish-language minutes of this meeting, however, competing perspectives among divergent Jewish factions emerged. Koretz noted that the division was very "dangerous" to the interests of the Jewish Community as a whole. The first delegation, composed of seven communal "notables," namely, upper-class, more-assimilated Jewish bankers, industrialists, and a journalist, urged the communal leadership to consider concession. "We must defend our cemeteries," asserted the spokesman for the notables, banker Moïse Morpurgo, "but not to the point of proving our intransigence which itself may provoke anti-Jewish troubles."[113] That the most Hellenized Jews feared a physical backlash if they did not concede demonstrated the fragility of the Orthodox Christian-Jewish dynamic and definitively called into question the alleged Jewish-Greek synthesis the elite had sought to cultivate during the previous decade. The common assumption that the era of Metaxas proved to be a period of calm must be reconsidered as Jewish elite remained anxious for they feared the repetition of the Campbell pogrom.

The Jewish elite in Salonica thus saw themselves, like Jews across Europe, as embattled and on the denfensive. Communal Council member Peppo Benosiglio feared the university rector's threats, the distribution of manifestos by students (similar to the campaign that preceded the Campbell riots), and the governor general's declarations, which were "not tranquil." "The general atmosphere in the world is against us," Benosiglio cried in reference to growing antisemitism in Germany and elsewhere in Europe, "and the proverbial liberalism of the Greeks has been influenced."[114] He and his colleague Abram Levy, also a member of the Communal Council, agreed that "in principle" all Jews were against the cession of the cemetery but argued that only out of fear of "anti-Jewish troubles" should 10 percent of the cemetery be sacrificed to save the other 90 percent, and to protect the Jewish population.[115] Others referred to promises made by government and university spokesmen that if fifteen thousand square meters of the Jewish cemetery were ceded, the university would *under no circumstances* request more for one hundred years. A member of the Béné Bérith Lodge, Moïse Benveniste, similarly agreed that concession should be made not out of fear of violent retaliations but out of fear that the government would reduce or cancel its subventions to Jewish philanthropic and educational instititions. Those in favor of concession invoked the Talmudic dictum *Dina de-malkhuta dina* ("the law of the land is the law") in support of their position, but Rabbi Haim Habib rejected the proposal, explaining that this Talmudic imperative applies only if state law does not conflict with Jewish law—not the case in this instance.[116]

While communal notables presented their wishes to the Communal Council in a discrete manner, two other factions publically and loudly expressed their opposition to expropriation. A delegation from the Federation of Jewish Corporations, which represented a cross-section of Jewish merchants, artisans, professionals, and shop owners, published a resolution in the Judeo-Spanish press: "Make no concessions!" The members of this Federation implored communal leaders to do whatever necessary to defend the Jewish cemetery, a site of "primordial significance"—even if that required defending it with their "own existence."[117] Echoing the demands of the Federation of Jewish Corporations, the Mizrahi published the position of the religious Jews. "The Jewish population of our city," the Mizrahi declared, "oppose the expropriation only and exclusively for religious reasons; we categorically defend our holy law against the unburying of our dead and the transfer of their remains." Although appealing explicitly to religious reasons, the Mizrahi quickly added the historical significance of the cemetery, in which rest "venerable, wise, famed rabbis and illustrious personalities of the Jewish community of Salonica." In addition to the religious and historical appeals, the Mizrahi threatened the Jewish notables by "inviting" them to "stop their damaging efforts so that the curse of history does not weigh upon your shoulders and those of your children."[118] In a less hostile manner, Chief Rabbi Koretz agreed: "If we have the right to demand respect for our cemeteries from the non-Jews, we have an even stronger reason to demand this respect from our progressive Jews."[119]

The perspectives expressed by the progressive Jewish notables and by the Federation of Jewish Corporations and the Mizrahi demonstrate that the threat of expropriation divided not only Jews and Orthodox Christians but also Jews themselves. Koretz had convened the special assembly precisely to address the intra-Jewish division and to restore a unified front in the battle to save the Jewish cemetery. Some wanted to continue to fight for the expansion of the university over the Iraklis field. Koretz proposed establishing a Society of Friends of the University that would collect donations from Greeks in the diaspora, namely the United States and Egypt, in order to raise the requisite million drachmae to purchase the Iraklis field. But others indicated that the university would not accept such a project because it was deemed too difficult to disassemble the Iraklis stadium; it was against state policy for the university to accept private funds; and that bringing private money into the question would make the university lose its "moral effect."[120] The local Greek press never raised the issue.

At the conclusion of the debate, representatives of the Jewish Community resolved not to cede the Jewish cemetery and to urge the Jewish public to present a unified front against the expropriation initiatives. The Jewish notable Morpurgo, who had previously advocated for acquiesence, instead promised the cooperation of the notables in the name of Jewish unity. The assembled leaders decided to dispatch representatives to Athens where they hoped Metaxas and King George II would exhibit the purportedly classical spirit of Greek liberalism lacking among local government representatives and thwart the efforts of the "partisans of expropriation"—if only by preserving the burial ground as an archaeological park closed to future burials. While all present agreed that Athens could proclaim a decree compelling the Jewish Community to relinquish the land of its cemetery, Koretz concluded with confidence that "even if the decree passes, the authorities will not have the courage to unbury the dead."[121] He was wrong.

Metaxas had already intimated that he would resolve the question in favor of the university. He assured the rector and Loulis full cooperation in promoting Hellenic civilization in Greek Macedonia as embodied in its university, the "House of the Intellect." He also sympathized with petitions submitted by organizations of scientists, merchants and industrialists, professionals and artisans, and army reservists—virtually every significant association in Salonica composed of Orthodox Christians—to the president of the government and the Ministries of Education and Religion, Agriculture, National Economy, Finance, and Welfare. In the name of "the collective will of the Macedonians [*koini Makedonon thelisis*]," they demanded the immediate removal of the Jewish cemetery for the installation of the "indispensible laboratories" functioning at present in dangerous conditions in the basement of the university so that the "mission of the Institution of Higher Education of Macedonia" may be realized.[122] The petition also demanded that the central government intervene in this case in order to compensate for the decreased income from Macedonian imports resulting from the new restrictions at the port of Salonica. Athens's boa constrictor hold on Salonica was released for a moment to accommodate the "will of the [Orthodox Christian] Macedonians" and the progress of Hellenic civilization. The general (Orthodox Christian) Macedonian will was harnessed to overturn the particularist (Jewish) Salonican will.

The cession of the *Beth Ahaim* transpired piecemeal. Obligatory Law 890, decreed in Athens in September 1937, comprised three articles regarding the "disposition of the land used in the city of Thessaloniki as a Jewish cemetery." The first article required that burials cease in one year, at which time the municipality was to plant trees and maintain a park without harming the tombs that lay therein. The second article transferred the rights of exploitation and usufruct of 12,300 square meters of the northern part of the Jewish cemetery to the University of Salonica. This plot of land was exempted from the requirements to plant trees and not touch the tombstones. The third article required that the city plan of Salonica be altered to accommodate the new arrangement as decreed by the law.[123] Joseph Nehama, writing to the Alliance headquarters in Paris, expressed relief that only a section of the cemetery—not the whole terrain—was affected.[124] In a certain sense, the approach advocated by the Jewish notables won out insofar as a section of the Jewish cemetery was ceded with the hope that the remainder would stay intact. The only difference was that the Jewish Community did not volunteer the land but was compelled to surrender it.

The removal and reburial of the tombstones and remains from the part of the *Beth Ahaim* ceded to the university provoked deep mourning. From February to March 1938, the Jewish Community arranged for the removal of 562 tombstones and 1,000 remains, including those of several sixteenth- and seventeenth-century sages, such as the kabbalist Samuel Gaon.[125] Twelve rabbis supervised the excavations in shifts, reciting psalms and praying for the repose of the souls of those whose tombs were affected and whose remains were reburied, ten per grave, in another part of the cemetery. A Jewish communal functionary spent twelve days, from eight o'clock in the morning until six o'clock in the evening, overseeing the process, taking breaks only to nibble on *halva* and bread.[126] The excavations provided an opportunity for Molho and Ben-Jacob—who took off two weeks from teaching at the Jewish communal schools and discovered 150 new inscriptions—to demonstrate their archaeological acumen as they debated, along with Mercado Covo and Isaac Emmanuel, the significance of unexpected finds lurking underground, such as a cave, a human skeleton 2.1 meters long, and the 300-year-old remains of a famous Jewish mystic whose teeth "miraculously" remained intact.[127]

Describing the somber ceremony for the reinterring of the uprooted remains with fifty Jewish notables in attendance, Judeo-Spanish newspapers sympathetically portrayed the rabbis who, uncertain of how to proceed in such an unprecedented situation, treated the burial as if it were for those who had just died and chanted special dirges as if for a chief rabbi. They begged forgiveness for violating holy law, proclaimed a day of "national mourning for the Jewish people," and recited a special *kaddish* (memorial prayer) reserved for Tisha Be-av, the annual commemoration of the destruction of the Holy Temples in Jerusalem.[128] In a sense, the Holy Temple of Jewish Salonica, symbolized by the cemetery, was being destroyed.

The extent to which the vision of Hellenic Judaism failed to insert the Jews of Salonica into the narrative of their city, province, and country became

clear with the removal of a part of the Jewish cemetery. Certain Jewish intellectuals, journalists, and politicians had advocated that the Jewish cemetery
ought to be preserved as a historical monument, a marker of the generations
of Jews who contributed to the progress of the city of Salonica, if not the
country of Greece, and were laid to rest in the soil of Macedonia. Ironically,
the expropriation of the cemetery was ultimately justified on the opposite
grounds: that the progress of Salonica, of Macedonia, and of Hellenic civilization *required* the destruction of the Jewish cemetery. The discourse of Hellenic
Judaism constituted a sad, solemn Jewish monologue. The destruction of the
Jewish cemetery had commenced. The belief of certain Jewish communal
leaders that giving 10 percent would save the remaining 90 proved naïve.

Nearly every article of Law 890 was violated at least once within two
years. In February 1939, the university demanded and received, this time out
of the Jewish Community's "good will" and without any law being passed,
another segment of the *Beth Ahaim* for the erection of the new Student
Union.[129] The Jewish Community, shocked by the new, illegal demand, nonetheless justified the "donation" in the requisite laudatory terms: "to make
clear"—because it apparently still was not—"the interest of our city's Jewish
society in favor of the development of the university, a lighthouse of education and Greek civilization in Northern Greece."[130] The same year, Law 890
was violated yet again: numerous tombstones were broken by municipal and
university builders during construction and without agreed-upon rabbinic
supervision.[131] And again: approximately twenty graves were desecrated or
broken during the municipality's effort to plant trees in the remaining terrain of the Jewish cemetery. The National Youth Movement (the Greek Boy
Scouts) planted the trees and perpetrated the desecrations in the process.[132]
And Law 890 was violated yet again as the Jewish Community continued to
bury its dead in the Jewish cemetery even during the German occupation,
which commenced in April 1941.

Conclusion: Who Listened?

Although the final and complete destruction of the Jewish cemetery began
in December 1942, during the Nazi occupation, the process had begun in
1936 under the reign of Metaxas, and the initial proposal emerged with the
Hébrard Plan after the fire of 1917. The success with which Jewish representa-

tives postponed all plans of expropriation for two decades signifies the extent to which they made their voices heard and achieved their goals. The defense of the dead—on religious, historical, and archaeological grounds—enabled Jews to reassert their own religious, cultural, economic, and political aspirations and begin to adapt to the new context of the Greek state. Jewish leaders in Salonica sought to render their cemetery and their history legible, literally by reinscribing it into the sphere of print culture, transcribing it from the ephemeral physical realm to the enduring textual domain. In so doing, they disseminated images of Salonica as the Jewish Metropolis or, by modifying Greek nationalist rhetoric, the Macedonian Metropolis in which Jews played a key role for two millennia in this capital of Hellenic Judaism. Only due to the campaigns to document the Jewish cemetery undertaken during the interwar years has any information about the historically significant tombstones of Salonica's *Beth Ahaim* been bequeathed to posterity.

One of the lawyers of the Community, Yomtov Yacoel, who had served on the Commission for the Defense of the Jewish Cemetery, recorded the final destruction of the Jewish cemetery. He explained that the governor general of Macedonia advocated for the German command to compel the Jewish

Figure 5.3. The destruction of the Jewish cemetery of Salonica, January 1943. Source: Institut Der NSDAP zur Erforschung Der Judenfrage, RG-222, YIVO Institute for Jewish Research. Published with permission.

Community to relinquish claims to the burial ground. The opportunity came when the Nazis conscripted Jewish men for forced labor outside of Salonica in July 1942. When Jewish notables began to rally to raise a ransom to redeem the laborers, the local Greek authorities requested that the Jews give over their cemetery as part of the deal. According to Yacoel, the German forces agreed to do so even though they were not particularly interested in the fate of Jewish cemeteries in order to "satisfy the sentiments of the Christian population":

> The hurried manner, and the excessive zeal shown by the Greek authorities make it obvious that it wasn't only out of motives aimed at the city's beautification that they were moved to dismantle the Jewish monuments so quickly. Christian delegations visited the German military commander to thank him on behalf of the Greek population of the city for the final settlement of this matter. Therefore it was in order to satisfy an old demand of the Christian public opinion that the Germans got involved in this non-military but clearly political matter, and that the local Greek authorities proceeded to this hurried and destructive action . . . only a few hundreds of families, acting privately, took care to transport the bones of their beloved relatives to the new cemeteries. Thus came to a close in the most sad and unseemly manner, by its massive destruction and looting, the story of the ancient Jewish cemetery, a precursor to the imminent total destruction of the whole Jewish community of Salonica, the most populous center of Judaism in the East.[133]

Betrayed while in hiding, as he penned these very lines, Yacoel was deported to his death at Auschwitz in 1944.

Writing to Joseph Nehama in December 1942, shortly after the final destruction of the Jewish cemetery commenced, Michael Molho lamented that the extensive efforts to preserve the burial ground had been in vain. Molho confessed his wish that the Jewish Community had surrendered the burial ground earlier, under more favorable circumstances, in order to gain time to transfer the graves outside of the city and save those tombstones of historical and artistic significance, to benefit from financial compensation for the land, and to negotiate to use a piece of the terrain to erect a new neighborhood for impoverished Jews.[134] Instead, Molho hastened to transfer the remains of several dozen well-known rabbis to the new Jewish burial ground in the suburb of Stavroupolis, where they were deposited in a single grave.[135]

Figure 5.4. A swimming pool constructed with Jewish tombstones. Source: Jewish Museum of Thessaloniki. Published with permission.

Back in the city center, the "rape" of the cemetery escalated, marble flooded the market, and its price plummeted. Jewish tombstones were stacked up in masons' yards and, with the permission of the director of antiquities of Macedonia and overseen by the metropolitan bishop and the municipality, used to pave roads, line latrines, and extend the sea walls; to construct pathways, patios, and walls in private and public spaces throughout the city, in suburbs such as Panorama and Ampelokipi, and more than sixty kilometers away in beach towns in Halkidiki, where they decorated playgrounds, bars, and restaurants in hotels; to build a swimming pool—with the Hebrew-letter inscriptions visible; to repair the St. Demetrius Church and other buildings

damaged during the war; and to fashion the courtyard of the National Theater of Northern Greece, the cafeteria of the Yacht Club of Thessaloniki, and
the very campus of the university, including the new medical school facility,
whose students appropriated Jewish tombstones for use as dissection tables
and skulls, which they gave so-called Jewish nicknames, to place atop their
office desks. Other looters targeted graves with tombstone inscriptions in
French or Italian—indicators of wealth—to extract gold fillings from the
skulls and to search for alleged buried treasure. Hebrew-letter tombstones
remain visible today, more than seventy years later, on the university campus
as throughout the city and in several church courtyards.[136] "And what of our
dead?" one survivor cried, "[t]he bones of generations of Jews, who came to
Greece seeking refuge in a tolerant country, were thrown into the sea."[137]

The tombstones in Salonica's *Beth Ahaim* indeed spoke. But, ultimately,
few listened.

JEWISH SALONICA

Reality, Myth, Memory

El muerto no save nada,
todo es para el ojo del bivo.

The dead know nothing;
Everything is in the eye of the living.

—Judeo-Spanish expression

Like Jewish populations throughout Europe, the almost total annihilation of Salonica's Jews during the Holocaust was an unprecedented catastrophe—an irrevocable rupture in the centuries-long and demographically significant Jewish presence in the city. Of the roughly fifty thousand Jews in Salonica on the eve of World War II, almost all perished during the Holocaust, mostly in Auschwitz-Birkenau. Less than two thousand could be counted in 1945. Michael Molho reported that, of the thirty-two synagogues whose locations he could identify that year, only one remained intact due to its use as a storage facility for the Red Cross. He indicated that local Orthodox Christians had stripped many of the others to their foundations—if not destroyed them completely—and pillaged furniture, religious objects, chandeliers, doors, and window frames in order to "beautify" their homes or nearby churches. Pilfered Jewish tombstones lay strewn about the city and the cemetery continued to be looted and utilized as a quarry despite protests from Jewish survivors, the local police, the American Jewish Committee, and the British military. Stationed in Salonica by the British War Office, the historian Cecil Roth recoiled at the sight of a Torah scroll cut into pieces to serve as soles for shoes.[1] Jewish Salonica was in ruins.

Ironically, perhaps more than ever before, the few survivors who returned from the camps or from fighting with the partisans, or who came out of hiding across the country, depended on the official Jewish Community for their "rehabilitation." As a first step, they reestablished the Communal Council on December 9, 1944, five weeks after the Germans fled (October 30). Structural continuities persisted from before the war, although on a much smaller scale. The Jewish Community registered as official members all the Jews in the city. Appointed as chief rabbi, Molho reconvened the Beth Din to perform and regulate marriage, divorce, and conversion to Judaism. Additional institutions reemerged under the auspices of Law 2456 of 1920, "Concerning Jewish Communities." This law had recast the older Ottoman privileges in the language of minority rights and had designated the Jewish Community as a "corporate person under the law." Remarkably, the 1920 law, with certain modifications, continues today.

The destruction wrought by the Holocaust also, ironically, solidified the pre-war images of Salonica as a grand Jewish metropolis through the processes of mourning and nostalgia.[2] Salonica's Jews became ever more enshrined in collective Sephardic memory even as they were increasingly excised from local consciousness and marginalized within the broader framework of Jewish history. The afterlife of the Jewish Salonica mythos became the prerogative of Salonican survivors as well as Sephardic Jews abroad. Writing in post-war Salonica, Joseph Nehama articulated his vision of Jewish Salonica in *In Memoriam*:

> At the moment when the Teutonic hordes [the Nazis] swept across the Macedonian lands, the ancient Thermaic metropolis [Salonica] still housed a small Jewish city, enriched by more than fifty thousand souls, endowed with its own internal communal government, language, press, synagogues, schools, clubs, libraries, printers, superb philanthropies of mutual aid and of solidarity, its currents of ideas and opinions, its sui generis life, with its own traditions and customs, its craftsmen, industrialists, merchants, [and] intellectual class. Born with the city itself, many centuries before the Christian era, it had survived, for two thousand years, as a confessional group, yet vivacious and always present. At the dawn of modern times, and for a half millennium, it had nourished the social and economic life of the city and remained the essential

element, until the war of 1914–1919, and one of the most important and most
prosperous elements until the enemy invasion.[3]

Continuing his perspective from before the war, Nehama notably insisted not
that Salonica as a whole was Jewish but that a kind of autonomous Jewish
city resided within this Macedonian Metropolis. In keeping with his liberalism and eschewing nationalism, he also designated Jews as a confessional
or religious group rather than a national one. Despite the nuance, Nehama
reinforced an image of the sui generis, self-sustaining Jewish collectivity in
Salonica, one linked to the city since its foundation in antiquity—with roots
deeper than those of Christians—and of the continuing contributions and
centrality of Jews to the life of the city until World War II.

In the United States, France, and Israel, Salonican and Sephardic Jews
envisioned Salonica both as the most exceptional Jewish center in the East
and as the most representative one. The Salonican tragedy became *the* Sephardic tragedy. The last Judeo-Spanish newspaper in the world written in
Hebrew characters, *La Vara* of New York, proclaimed in 1944 that the deportations from Salonica inaugurated a "national tragedy" that destroyed
"the Zion of the Balkans."[4] A similar sentiment characterized the reception in the Judeo-Spanish press in New York of the first notable post-war
memoir, Leon Sciaky's *Farewell to Salonica* (1946), which constituted a final
farewell to Salonica—a city destroyed, a Jewish community obliterated during the Nazi occupation, yet one that Sciaky had fled thirty years before.
The enthusiastic reviews of the book in *La Vara* enshrined Salonica as a
quintessential Sephardic homeland and a crucial site of memory. Maír José
Benardete, a Dardenelles-born, American Sephardic studies scholar, proclaimed: "*Farewell to Salonica* is a book not only for Salonicans. It is for all
Sephardim. More or less, the lives of us all were how Sciaky presents it.
The customs, traditions, people, language, problems, pains and pleasures that
Sciaky recalls were the same for us all."[5] Salonica, the local and exceptional,
came to be globalized and universalized, understood as the homeland for all
Sephardim and as nothing less than a Jerusalem in its own right. Another
review of *Farewell to Salonica* in *La Vara*, by a Sephardic Jew from Bucharest,
made the universality of Salonica explicit: Salonica—and no greater region
or country—constituted "the third homeland [*patria*] of the Sephardic

Jews," following Israel and Spain.[6] This conception of Salonica gained traction due in part to the irrevocable transformation of Jewish Salonica from reality to memory.

Salonicans in Paris also elevated the status of Salonica, seeking to emphasize its unique character within the framework of Jewish history and its relevance to world history. In his magazine, *Cahiers Sephardis*, Sam Lévy reinforced the image of Salonica as "the Citadel of Israel" and "the Citadel of Sephardism": the "most compact, the most flourishing, and, during certain epochs, the most celebrated [Jewish community] in the world." Salonica, the "martyred city," was the only location in the world, Lévy declared, where the name "Jew" never gained currency as a pejorative term. "We have the firm wish," Lévy optimistically asserted, "to see Salonican Sephardism, a new phoenix, be reborn from the ashes." One day, he hoped, Salonica would again flourish as in the Roman era or the sixteenth and seventeenth centuries, or at the very least, leave its imprint in "the heart of Judaism" and serve as an example in the quest of humanity "to attain universal harmony."[7]

Salonican Jewish leaders in Israel focused on registering their mother community in collective Jewish memory. The crowning achievement in the effort to memorialize and immortalize Salonica was embodied in the two-volume *Zikhron Saloniki* ("A memorial to Salonica"), edited by David Recanati in Tel Aviv; Isaac Emmanuel composed the bulk of the first volume. This publication solidified the narrative of Salonican Jewish grandeur and reconfirmed the dedication of the "sons of Salonica" to their "mother city" that had developed in the decades before the war. The text of *Zikhron Saloniki* was published in Hebrew—with a Jewish and specifically Israeli audience in mind—albeit with short summaries in Latin-lettered Judeo-Spanish. The one-page preface, in the traditional Rashi script, divulged, *entre mozotros*, to Salonican and Sephardic Jews, the book's purpose: to erect a "monument" to the "glorious community of Salonica," to the "Jerusalem of the Balkans, the Citadel of Sephardic Judaism." The preface continued: "We consider it our sacred duty as sons of this marvelous Judaism [of Salonica], unique in its genre, to take upon ourselves the burdensome task of erecting an eternal monument" to the Jewish community of Salonica, once characterized by its "complete autonomy," in order to "elevate Jewish Salonica [*Saloniko la djudia*]—which exists no longer—to the high level it deserves in the consciousness of all those across the globe who are interested in the past of the Jewish people."[8] Other Salonicans in Israel echoed this rhetoric by mourning *la difunta Saloniko la djudia* ("the deceased Jewish Salonica"), the "pearl of the Aegean."[9]

The efforts after the war to stake a claim on Salonica as an exalted Jewish space represented a postscript to the expansive writing campaigns and political and cultural activities undertaken by Salonican Jews in the five decades prior to the Holocaust. During this period, Salonican Jewish intellectuals and leaders desired collective self-affirmation, as Salonicans and as Jews. They sought to transform their ideal vision of the inextricable link between themselves and their city into a reality while grappling with a multiplicity of evolving political and cultural frameworks, especially Ottomanism and later Hellenism, Zionism, integrationism, and socialism, as well as Sephardism.

Through self-valorization, Salonican Jewish elites departed from the established, self-effacing practices of an earlier era. Scholars have argued that late nineteenth-century Ottoman Jews could imagine becoming modern only by overcoming their Oriental origins through westernization. One scholar summarized this perspective by arguing that editors of Judeo-Spanish newspapers in Salonica and Istanbul "talked about their own community with deliberate self-deprecation. . . . The contrast between 'us' (Ottoman Jews) and 'them' (European Jews), always present in the Ladino press, made it clear to the readers that there was only one way to perfection: to become like *them*, both in appearance and essence—that is, to westernize."[10]

The story told in this book about Salonica's Jews from the final decades of Ottoman rule until World War II demonstrates that while the earlier generation's zeal for westernization continued in some circles, others developed a new program of self-affirmation. Westernization and its accompanying self-evisceration now came to be viewed as but one pathway to modernity. Jewish elites of a variety of political affiliations co-opted methods from the West—institutional reform, modern schooling, popular print culture, historical scholarship—and recast them in ways that resonated with local mentalities, practices, and priorities. They demonstrated that, rather than becoming *them*—the other, the Westerner—Salonican Jews could also become self-conscious, modern, European, and citizens of their state by embracing their history and their distinctive identity. They sought to attain a sense of individual and collective dignity by holding a mirror up to their past, whether the golden age of Sephardic Jews after 1492 or the flourishing era of Greek-speaking Jews in Hellenistic antiquity, both of which, they argued, endowed them with legitimate claims to modernity and to Europe—and to their city. They actively remade themselves in their historic images, as heirs to the legacy of the Jerusalem of the Balkans, a designation they devised precisely to achieve this end. The embrace of the often-derogatory toponym "the Balkans," in the expression "Jerusalem of the Balkans," indicates that Jews in Salonica ultimately championed their status as Balkan, within Europe, yet embedded in the interstices of East and West.

By invoking images of Salonica's past as a model for the present and future, Salonican Jews created blueprints for themselves according to which they hoped to reconfigure their sense of belonging to a discrete entity, which Isaac Emmanuel designated the "Judeo-Salonican civilization."[11] The case of Salonica's Jews illuminates a range of strategies harnessed by Jews to cope with the collapse of empire and to re-anchor themselves in the contested spaces of the modern nation-state. By serving as the interpreters of their past and believing in the capacity to shape their destiny, Salonica's Jewish elites embodied—and simultaneously challenged and expanded—the very meanings of "modern," "Jewish," and indeed, "European." Localizing their sense of citizenship and rooting it in their city, they actively shaped the contours of imperial and national belonging, engaged with the discourses of Ottomanism and subsequently Hellenism, and sought to articulate visions of these political frameworks that would be capacious enough to include them.

The ostensible transition, however, from multicultural empire to homogeneous nation-state was neither a linear process nor part of a natural succession. With the collapse of multiethnic, multireligious, and multilinguistic empires during the early twentieth century, nation-states aspired to organize themselves along ethnically, religiously, and linguistically homogenous lines. The ensuing disentanglement of populations in the wake of imperial disintegration contributed to the formation of new nation-states through a process famously referred to as the "unmixing of peoples." But peoples were not only disentangled and unmixed but also re-entangled, re-mixed—indeed, refashioned. In the case of post-Ottoman Greece, as in other Ottoman successor states, imperial-style dynamics did not disappear. Religion remained the primary category defining national belonging. Religious affiliation had dictated the terms of the exchange of populations between Greece and Turkey that resulted in the influx of Orthodox Christians into places like Salonica, which became a meeting point for Greek-speaking Orthodox Christians and Turkish-speaking Orthodox Christian refugees who were supposed to fuse together to form the Greek nation. The Greek state recognized non-Orthodox Christians, namely Muslims and Jews, as distinct communities with certain powers of self-government—a legacy of the Ottoman *millet* structures—but suppressed the linguistic and cultural diversity among Orthodox Christians (e.g., Slavic-speakers). Although Greece has been identified as the "most homogeneous national state of the Balkans," the state's strategy of governance continued to differentiate "minorities" while concealing the diversity within the "majority," and permitted ongoing negotiations with the country's citizens over the nature of national belonging.[12]

Conceiving of themselves as modern actors capable of shaping their own destinies, Salonica's Jewish leaders did not believe that the nation-state was an established, fixed, prepackaged entity invented in the West that would be transplanted to their world in the Balkans; rather, they believed in their ability to influence the precise form that this new polity would take and actively participated in shaping its parameters. They sought to restitch the multicultural tapestry of the Ottoman world in a manner that would resonate with the development of Greek state ideology in order to guarantee their continued presence in Salonica and the country. Some scholars have claimed that a proclivity to resist homogeneity or to perpetuate their status as a discrete community meant that Salonican Jews did not understand the nature of nationalism. But a more nuanced reading would indicate instead that they proposed a different vision of what the new nation-state could become, one animated by aspirations for civic inclusion capable of accommodating a certain degree of religious, linguistic, and cultural diversity. They did not unequivocally resist Hellenization but sought to define Hellenism as a shared, overarching, supracommunal civic framework—for Zionists, a supranational one, and for the supporters of the Alliance, a suprareligious one. They wanted to be part of Greece without relinquishing their Jewishness, although they disagreed precisely on how it ought to be preserved or adapted and how they ought to engage with the state.

In the late Ottoman era, Jewish elite in Salonica insisted on their status as "Ottomans" by virtue of their citizenship—rarely as "Turks," a term more often used as an ethnic designation. So, too, in interwar years, they recast this tiered sense of belonging by accentuating their status as "Hellenes," which they distinguished from and viewed as more inclusive than the term "Greeks." The civic category of "Hellenes," the Judeo-Spanish press emphasized, was not synonymous with the ethnic identifier "Greeks," although there was sometimes slippage between the two. By using the term "Hellenes," they evoked and underscored Enlightenment conceptions of ancient Greece animated by democracy and liberalism in contrast to notions of Greekness rooted in Byzantine and Ottoman emphases on Orthodox Christianity. Judeo-Spanish newspapers developed a taxonomy according to which "Jews" and "Greeks," or "Jews" and "(Orthodox) Christians," ostensibly had equal claim to their status as "Hellenes."

They deployed this aspirational conception of political belonging—based on civic rather than religious or ethnic criteria—in defense of themselves and of other maligned populations in the country. In the wake of the 1920 elections, Greek nationalists, led by the newspaper *Makedonia*, falsely blamed Jews and Muslims for the defeat of Venizelos and charged that these two so-called foreign populations had revealed their true antipathy against Greece. Characteristic of the posture that Jewish intellectuals adopted to combat these kinds of accusations, *La Verdad* argued that *Makedonia* was actually the one guilty of expressing "anti-Hellenic" sentiments by dividing "Hellenic citizens" into Greeks, Jews, and Muslims in order to scapegoat the latter two. *La Verdad* turned the tables and contended that the supporters of *Makedonia* emerged as "anti-Hellenic Greeks" who, by separating the country's citizens into disparate "national elements," violated the country's constitution and perpetrated the "greatest crime against the homeland." The "Hellenic people," *La Verdad* insisted, included all of the country's citizens—Greeks, Jews, and Muslims alike.[13]

Salonican Jewish leaders insisted on an inclusive definition of Hellenism but wavered between defining its constituent populations as ethnic groups (e.g., Jews, Greeks, and Turks) or religious groups (e.g., Jews, Christians, and Muslims). As the interwar years progressed, Judeo-Spanish newspapers increasingly referred to the latter set of categories in line with the stipulations of Greek law and the Minorities Treaties endorsed by the League of Nations, which characterized Greece's Jews and Muslims as religious minorities. Even after the formation of the Hellenic Republic (1924), the state insisted on recognizing only religious differences—vestiges of the categories of governance employed by the Ottoman state. Judeo-Spanish newspapers followed suit and formally and cordially referred to their non-Jewish fellow citizens as "Christians" as often as "Greeks." After the Campbell attacks in 1931, a new Judeo-Spanish newspaper, *Derito*, which promoted Jewish integration, described its mission as "work[ing] for the continued maintenance of good relations between the Christian and Jewish elements."[14]

A Jewish version of Hellenism emerged as an idealized, suprareligious, supranational ideology, inclusive of Jews. Jewish elites appealed to this broader conception of Hellenism to defend the right of different groups to express differing viewpoints even as Greece moved toward dictatorship. In the wake of a controversy over the 1936 elections, for example, the Judeo-Spanish newspaper *La Aksion* argued that the city's Jews aimed to maintain "close and cordial relations with our fellow Christian citizens, both natives and refugees." The newspaper emphatically argued for a capacious definition of Hellenism: "For us, as we have said and we say again today with much greater force, all of the citizens of this country—natives, refugees, and Jews—are Hellenes, children of a common homeland, and as such have the full right to express themselves."[15]

Salonican Jews—Zionists, Moderates, and Socialists—wanted to be citizens of Greece without relinquishing their Jewishness, although they disagreed over how it ought to be preserved or adapted. "How to measure these sentiments?" *El Puevlo* asked in 1928. "What percentage will one be a Hellene and what percentage a Jew?" The newspaper concluded that "questions of the heart," such as this one, cannot be measured.[16] Yet different Jewish groups privileged Hellenic and Jewish affiliations differently—"Jewish Hellenes" or "Hellenic Jews"—but always acknowledged both aspects. Zionists insisted on the preservation of Jewish communal self-governance whereas Moderates advocated that Jews prioritize their status as individual citizens of the state. In 1936, the Judeo-Spanish daily *El Mesajero* preferred a more integrationist formulation by referring to its readers as "Jewish Hellenes" (*elenos djidios*).[17] In contrast, also in 1936, the founder of the country's Socialist movement,

Abraham Benaroya, influenced by the principles of national federalism
that had shaped the city's Socialist Workers' Federation, preferred the category "Hellenic Jews" but endorsed integration no less: "Before everything,
do all that the country asks of us, embrace its undertakings, its ideals, its
aspirations—Hellenize ourselves! This does not impede us from remaining
Hellenic Jews [*djidios elenos*]. That each class of Jews fraternizes with its class,
that each political party has a number of Jews among its partisans—there is
nothing more natural or necessary."[18] Benaroya insisted that a balance could
be found between Hellenization and the retention of a Jewish identity, that
a hybrid Hellenic Jew, divided according to class affiliation like all the other
citizens of the country, remained not only a possibility but also a reality.
Some Salonican Jews were convinced that they belonged—or at least could
belong—in Thessaloniki and in Greece, more generally, by "Hellenizing their
souls" even if they did not yet speak Greek fluently.[19]

Depending on their class, political affiliation, and cultural orientation,
Jews in Salonica reshaped their sense of self and attempted to unite several seemingly contradictory allegiances. They promoted multiple affiliations
that challenged certain assumptions about the nation-state by incorporating
imperial sensibilities that emphasized communal identity as well as trans-
national influences that linked them to institutions and movements beyond
the boundaries of the state: the Alliance Israélite Universelle in Paris, Zionism connected to Palestine and Zionist organizations throughout Europe,
and a renewed Sephardist movement that fostered links with Spain and
with other Sephardic populations across the continent. Jewish socialists also
looked across national borders and cultivated links with the Communist
International.[20]

In Salonica itself, different cultural and political threads of identification
coexisted among the city's Jews. The best evidence for these multiple affinities was a new Hebrew prayer book, *Sidur Sha'are Tefila*, published in 1941,
amidst World War II, by the *Tora Umelaha* society under the auspices of two
Hebrew teachers in the Jewish communal schools, Zionists Eliau Estroumsa
and Daniel Saïas, both born during the Ottoman era and the latter educated
in Palestine. The timing is remarkable: Greece was already at war with Italy
on the Albanian front. Estroumsa's son was serving in the Greek military at
that time and, indeed, the book was dedicated, in Judeo-Spanish (in Rashi

typeface), to a Salonican Jewish solider, Shabetai (Henri) Raphael Andjel, who had fallen in battle defending his "beloved homeland, Greece" (*kerida patria la Grecha*).

The editors of this prayer book therefore believed that they—and their constituency, more generally—could be religiously Jewish, Zionists, and Hellenic patriots and that they could convey these affinities in Judeo-Spanish (and hence be culturally Jewish and specifically Sephardic) without provoking an existential crisis or the unmitigated ire of their non-Jewish neighbors or the Greek state. They made only one change to the liturgy to accommodate their Hellenic patriotism.[21] Most importantly, the publication of this new prayer book in mid-February 1941 meant that Salonican Jews still, at such a late date, envisioned a future for themselves *as Jews* in Salonica and in Greece. The Germans occupied the city less than two months later, and only then did a future Salonica without Jews become thinkable.

Perhaps Salonica's Jews faced resentment from some of their neighbors not necessarily because they refused to become Greek, but rather because they were successfully becoming Greek while remaining Jews and members of the Jewish Community—a dual status preserved from the Ottoman era by agreement between the Greek state and Jewish communal elite. Salonica's Jews could anticipate this trajectory coming out of an Ottoman context, but segments of the Orthodox Christian population launched perhaps the greatest resistance, pushing against the prospect of the expansion of Hellenic national identity to accept Jews as equal citizens and members of the national family. If, along the liberal model of France, civic criteria such as political loyalty and proficiency in the state language—rather than religion or "blood"—constituted the pillars of national belonging, then Jews could become—or were becoming—just as Greek as Orthodox Christians, including those whose lives were uprooted from their ancestral homes in Asia Minor solely due to their religion and forced to come to the place now designated as their real homeland: Greece. The prospect of equality between those who suffered on account of their Orthodox Christianity and those who did not made it seem as if the sacrifices made by the refugees were in vain. When an anti-Venizelist politician described the Jews of Salonica as "more Greek" than the Orthodox Christian refugees from Asia Minor, many of whom did not arrive speaking Greek, could he have been painting a reasonable portrait of the situation?[22] Did he pinpoint an underlying anxiety?

Until World War II, the social distance between Jews and Orthodox Christians generally remained due in part to choice but also to law. With civil marriage (and thus intermarriage, except via conversion) nonexistent—in continuity with Ottoman practice—and the governance of civil status for Jews delegated to the exclusive authority of the Beth Din, the prospect of bringing Jews and Orthodox Christians together via marriage and forming a new, integrated national family remained extremely limited. Educational institutions became one of the domains in which the populations interacted, but only gradually. Jewish youth attended primarily Jewish communal schools or private schools until the mid-1920s but increasingly integrated into Greek state schools thereafter. The persistent distance between the two populations nonetheless became clear during the German occupation of Salonica. When the vast majority of Jews were deported, few Orthodox Christians intervened, and the two populations continued to imagine themselves as constituting distinct communities with divergent fates.

The most noteworthy exception to this dynamic tellingly arose not in Salonica but in Athens. In a letter of protest against the deportations of Salonican Jews in March 1943, Archbishop Damaskinos implored the citizens of Greece to help their fellow persecuted citizens. Notably, Damaskinos indicated that Jewish men had earned their citizenship and proven their patriotism—apparently this point was not self-evident to his audience—by sacrificing themselves on the front lines as soldiers in the Greek army. He also noted that he had no interest in defending Jews across the world, but only "our fellow citizens, who are Jews." He appealed to the New Testament, specifically to the passage in Paul's epistle to the Galatians (3:28) that Jewish intellectuals such as Joseph Nehama had evoked earlier in seeking to achieve rapprochement between the two populations. Damaskinos proclaimed: "Our holy religion does not recognize differences—superior or inferior—based on race and religion; it teaches that there is 'neither Greek nor Jew.'" He continued by proclaiming: "We are all children of the same father."[23] But it appears that, perhaps by virtue of their different "mothers," Jews and Orthodox Christians in Salonica—although not necessarily the whole of Greece—remained apart, tethered to their Ottoman-era affiliations during a most grievous period of suffering.[24] No Orthodox Christian leaders in Salonica endorsed Damaskinos's appeal, which neither stopped nor delayed the deportations.

Despite the overwhelming silence of their Orthodox Christian neighbors and fellow citizens during deportations to Auschwitz-Birkenau, young Salonican Jewish men did not abdicate the sense of connection and belonging to their Greek homeland that they had cultivated during the interwar years. While some scholars have suggested that Jews from Salonica came to define themselves and be identified by others as "Greeks" only outside of Greece—in Auschwitz, for example—the reality was that this kind of self-identification was not new and instead was transported, especially among the younger generations, from Salonica to the camps.[25] Imprisoned at Auschwitz, a number of Salonican Jews forced to work in the *Sonderkommando*, the squad of Jewish prisoners charged with the horrific task of transferring corpses from the gas chambers to the crematoria, recalled singing patriotic Greek songs, such as *"Tin Elliniki simea"*: "The Greek flag, God how I love it, my mother, I will never abandon my native land to foreigners, I would rather die."[26] Tales circulated that in the wake of the *Sonderkommando* uprising in October 1944, Salonican and other Greek Jews dramatically intoned the Greek national anthem prior to being executed for their role in the revolt.[27] The surviving fragment of recollections penned in Greek in late 1944 by Salonican Marcel Nadjary regarding his experiences in the *Sonderkommando* similarly revealed the author's sense of Greek patriotism and his love for his "Beloved Fatherland, 'Hellas,'" especially his concluding words: "I die content because I know that at this moment . . . our Greece is liberated. I will not live, but let survive . . . my last words will be: Long Live Greece."[28] Although imprisoned in Auschwitz because they were Jews, these Salonican men faced death as Jews and as Hellenes.

The extent to which Salonica's Jews came to view themselves as Hellenes was, by the time of the war, not matched by those Orthodox Christian neighbors who remained reticent—if not hostile—to the prospect of accepting Jews as authentic members of the Greek national family. Although some scholars consider Salonican Jews as Greece's most unwanted compatriots who suffered from unrelenting decline in the lead up to World War II, we must also recognize that they engaged actively with the state and civil society, achieved some victories, and forged some compromises within the new framework of Hellenism. To the rhetoric of "decline" (*deskadensya*)—remembered today—must therefore be added the rhetoric of "rebirth" (*renasensya*), long occluded from the historical narrative but very much present in the interwar sources. Both came hand in hand, the first a diagnosis and the latter a prognosis. Both tropes permeated the Jewish press during the interwar years and presented a paradox. Salonica's Jews reached the height of their cultural productivity during the tenure of Venizelos (1928–1932), perhaps when the situation was the most tense around the time of the Campbell riot in 1931. During this period Jewish intellectuals and activists published the greatest number of Judeo-Spanish newspapers in the history of the city and wrote the greatest number of articles dealing with Jewish history and inscriptions from the Jewish cemetery. Jewish notables and communal leaders simultaneously achieved a victory—albeit a pyrrhic one—by postponing the plans to expropriate the Jewish cemetery. Only under Metaxas did the expropriation of the Jewish cemetery and intensive interference in the Jewish school curriculum begin, and these constituted severe blows to the morale and confidence of Jewish leaders. But it by no means signified the beginning of the end of Jewish Salonica or the dissolution of Jewish identification and communal affiliation, even if the number of Jews in the city had decreased. Notably, even when Jewish commentators expressed anxieties about the diminishing status or numbers of the city's Jews, they did so by reference to a Hellenic framework, warning, for example, in 1935, that "the ship of Hellenic Judaism risks sinking" and, in 1936, that "Hellenic Judaism is in agony."[29] They made these calls precisely because they were not resigned to their fate.

Other contributors to the Judeo-Spanish press responded to those who saw the period since the transfer of Salonica to Greek control as one of decline by urging them to "stop crying." A close review of the past fifty years, one writer argued in 1938, would reveal that Salonica's Jews found themselves in a better position in the 1930s than during the late Ottoman era. Those who clung to nostalgia for imagined "good old days" full of "manna, milk and honey" misplaced their energies.[30] While motivated by a particular ideological perspective, the author nonetheless made a salient point by encouraging Greece's Jews to look forward in time rather than only backward: crisis and creativity, decline and rejuvenation, came together. The minutes of the Communal Council from 1938, for example, reveal plans for the offices of the Jewish Community to be transferred from their location beyond the White Tower, where they had been since the fire of 1917, *back* to the city center—to again stake a claim in the heart of Salonica.[31] The outbreak of World War II delayed the plan.

Amid the processes of transition from Ottoman to Greek jurisdiction over Salonica after 1912, the city's Jews grappled with numerous attempts to adapt to the new environment, which should call into the question the ineluctable trajectory of the homogenizing nation-state. The multiple ways that Salonica's Jewish leaders envisioned the relationship between themselves and their city, their neighbors, their province, and their country remind us that at particular conjunctures, in particular places, and among particular people socio-political configurations could be imagined in different terms, with different futures and dreams. The fact that many of these visions ultimately did not materialize—whether the plans for autonomy or internationalization during the Balkan Wars or the complete rebuilding of Jewish institutional life in the city center after the fire of 1917—does not mean Salonica's Jews should be dismissed as passive victims or as disconnected from the realities of their world.

While suffering from demographic diminution, economic weakening, and political fragmentation, Salonica's Jewish leaders, despite internal disagreement, ultimately convinced the state to recognize the Jewish Community as a legal entity across the Ottoman-Greek divide. The Community expanded the number and reach of its institutions upon which the Jewish masses relied, from the religious courts to neighborhoods and schools, as it if were its own municipality or state. After increasing debate, Jewish leaders crowned the community with chief rabbis who served as strong representatives and encouraged the Jewish public to engage with the state ideology. After a decade-long interruption after World War I, Jewish lay leaders believed their newest selection for chief rabbi would advance their status as a worldwide Sephardic center, achieve rapprochement with Ashkenazic Jewry, and embrace the new environment of Hellenism. As the most important institutions operated by the Jewish Community, the Jewish communal schools educated new generations of Jewish youth as Jews and as citizens and, during the interwar years, did so both increasingly in conflict but also in partnership with the state. The schools served as the laboratories where the children of the last generation of Ottoman Jews would become the first generation of modern Hellenic Jews in Salonica—proficient in Greek and loyal to the country.

A cohort of Jewish intellectuals also composed histories of their city—Jewish histories of Salonica—as a way to secure their position first in the Ottoman context and subsequently in Greece, all the while emphasizing their sense of belonging to the city, whether since 1492 or antiquity. They developed master narratives that highlighted a romance between Jews and the Ottoman state since 1492, in which Salonica played a key role as the demographic and cultural center of Ottoman Jews. The story of Salonica could be harnessed to illustrate the purportedly special relationship between Jews and the Ottoman state. In the interwar years, Jewish intellectuals in Salonica completely reframed their historical narratives, now emphasizing the historic symbiosis of Hellenism and Judaism since antiquity and the synergies between the heirs of Plato and Moses, of Deucalion and Adam.[32] Salonica, too, emerged at the center of the story as the meeting point of the traditions of Athens and Jerusalem, the two founts of European civilization. Salonica was situated at the heart of each endeavor as the symbol of the pinnacle of Ottoman Judaism and subsequently Hellenic Judaism.

The successful, two-decade-long postponement of the attempt by the Greek state to expropriate the Jewish cemetery and the prospect of the cemetery's recognition as a site of Hellenic patrimony or its protection on the grounds of religious tolerance, liberalism, and minority rights demonstrate that official and unofficial representatives of the Jewish collectivity deployed creative methods as they sought to navigate the transition from the Ottoman Empire to modern Greece. More dramatically than in other instances, the ultimate initiation of the expropriation of the cemetery prior to World War II revealed the limits of the power of the city's Jews to exert their collective will and the overall fragility of the campaigns for rapprochement.

Elusive aspirations and lost dreams nonetheless ought to be granted serious and full consideration, for they reflected a dynamic Jewish collective imbued with agency as they confronted the socio-political reconfigurations of the late nineteenth and early twentieth centuries. They invested their efforts with what they described as sacred significance—the sacred missions of the Jewish Community, of the chief rabbi, of the Jewish communal schools, of the history writers, of the defenders of the Jewish cemetery—a sign that those issues most pressing and most important remained cast in the language of sanctity. Moreover, the self-fashioned status of Salonican Jews as Salonican, Jewish, Sephardic, Ottoman and subsequently Hellenic, Oriental, or European, and traditional or modern resulted in the creation of multiple ideas and realities of Jewish Salonica and of Salonica in general, versions of the city that interfaced, coexisted, and competed with other notions of what that city had been or should become. But the city—idea and locale— remained one thing throughout: home.

These visions of the city remained inextricably linked to contested, localized conceptions of citizenship: by formulating their visions for civic participation from their own perspective and location in the city, Salonican Jewish leaders sought to express their status as citizens. The case of Jewish Salonica invites broader reflection on the formulation of hybrid identities, the relationship between empire and nation-state, and the ideal of a plural society that still remains elusive today. The quest for a framework to accommodate individual and collective rights and to determine the place of minorities in society constitutes a central, unresolved dilemma of modernity.

﹁

While the physical presence and the material traces of Jewish Salonica have largely disappeared, the reverberations of the constitutive discourses may still be heard. This was the great success and legacy of the making of the mythic Jewish Salonica. When one visits Salonica today, he or she will find echoes of this historical agency still at work amidst the city's ghosts. In an era of economic crisis, rising xenophobia, and resurgent antisemitism, some of the city's leaders look to the past for inspiration. In recent years, the mayor has delved into discussions that previously remained within the purview of Jewish activists alone: "Thessaloniki is looking back and accepting its identity. We cannot look into the future without knowing the past. Not for nothing was it called the Jerusalem of the Balkans, and it could be that again."[33] At a Holocaust commemoration in Salonica—one of the first public ones in the city—the minister of Macedonia and Thrace acknowledged Salonica as the city not only of Aristotle but also of Salomon Alkabetz, the famed sixteenth-century rabbi and kabbalist.[34] As the city continues to reckon with its past, visitors to the Jewish Museum of Salonica (est. 2003), run by the Jewish Community, can discover traces of the city's Jewish past as guests of the "Mother of Israel" and the "Metropolis of Sepharadism." Upon entering the museum, one's introduction is none other than a remarkable arrangement of fragmentary tombstones salvaged from the wreckage of the vast Jewish necropolis. Fittingly, the physical remnants of the city's *Beth Ahaim*, the "House of Life," introduce the visitor to Jewish Salonica—reality, myth, and memory.

ARCHIVAL ABBREVIATIONS

ABDBJ   Archive of the Board of Deputies of British Jews, London Metropolitan
         Library

AIU   Alliance Israélite Universelle, Paris
         Fond Grèce

AUSC   Archives of the Union of Sephardic Congregations, American Sephardi
         Federation, New York

BZI   Ben Zvi Institute, Jerusalem
         Amariyo collection
         Dapim Saloniki

CAHJP   Central Archives for the History of the Jewish People, Jerusalem
         Gr/Sa refers to the Greece/Saloniki collection

FMBTN   Fondo Molho de la Biblioteca Tomás Navarro,
         Consejo Superior de Investigaciones Científicas, Madrid
         Papers of Michael Molho

HBA   Henry Besso Archive, American Sephardi Federation, New York

IEA   Isaac Emmanuel Archive, in the possession of Gary Schiff,
         Chestertown, MD

JMTh   Jewish Museum of Thessaloniki
         All references are to Jewish community archives unless otherwise noted

NARA   National Archive and Records Administration, Washington, DC

USHMM   United States Holocaust Memorial Museum in Washington, DC
            Unless otherwise indicated, references are to RG-11.001M.51, records of
            the Jewish Community of Thessaloniki, fond 1428, microfilmed from the
            Russian State Military Archive in Moscow

            GMFA refers to the archives of the Greek Ministry of Foreign Affairs,
            RG-45.001M

            RG-44.003M refers to the New Archives of the History of Jews in
            Greece, 1940–1951

YIVO   YIVO Institute for Jewish Research, New York
            RG-207 refers to the Records of the Jewish Community of Salonika

NOTES

Introduction

1. P. Risal, *La Ville Convoitée: Salonique* (Paris, 1914); Aron Astruc Gueron, *Salonique et son avenir* (Sofia, 1913), iii.

2. "A Zionist's proposal to make Salonica an international city," as translated in Julia Phillips Cohen and Sarah Abrevaya Stein, eds., *Sephardi Lives: A Documentary History* (Stanford, 2014), 145–149. See also N. M. Gelber, "An Attempt to Internationalize Salonika," *Jewish Social Studies* 17 (1955): 105–120. Rena Molho, "The Jewish Community of Thessaloniki and Its Incorporation into the Greek State, 1912–1919," *Middle Eastern Studies* 24, no. 4 (1988): 391–403; K. Skordyles, "Réactions juives à l'annexion de Salonique par la Grèce (1912–1913)," in *The Jewish Communities of South-Eastern Europe from the 15th Century to the End of World War II*, ed. I. Hassiotis (Thessaloniki, 1997), 501–516; Mark Levene, "'Ni grec, ni bulgare, ni turc'—Salonika Jewry and the Balkan Wars, 1912–1913," *Simon Dubnow Institute Yearbook* 2 (2003): 65–97; Carole Fink, *Defending the Rights of Others: The Great Powers, the Jews, and International Minority Protection, 1878–1938* (Cambridge, England, 2004), 57–60; K. E. Fleming, *Greece—A Jewish History* (Princeton, 2008), 68–69; Matilde Morcillo Rosillo, "La comunidad sefardí de Salónica después de las guerras balcánicas (1912–1913)" *Sefarad* 57, no. 2 (1997): 307–331; Paris Papamichos Chronakis, "De-Judaizing a Class, Hellenizing a City: Jewish Merchants and the Future of Salonica in Greek Public Discourse," *Jewish History* 28, no. 3–4 (2014): 373–403.

3. Joseph B. Schechtman, *The Life and Times of Vladimir Jabotinsky: Rebel and Statesman* (New York, 1956–1961), 1:157; Shabtai Teveth, *Ben-Gurion: The Burning Ground, 1886–1948* (Boston, 1987), 78; Victor Bérard, *La Turquie et l'hellénisme contemporain* (Paris, 1897), 320–321; Lucy Garnett, "A New Jerusalem," *The Catholic World* 69, no. 425 (August

1900): 612–622; G. F. Abbott, *A Tale of a Tour in Macedonia* (London, 1903), 18–30; H. N. Brailsford, *Macedonia: Its Races and their Future* (London, 1906), 83.

4. *Jewish Chronicle*, May 16, 1913; Richard E. Hibbard, "The Emergence of Salonika as a Problem in Modern Diplomacy," *The Historian* 6, no. 1 (September 1943): 53–75.

5. Yura Konstantinova, "The Race for Salonica," *Études Balkaniques* 49, no. 2 (2013): 44–67. See also Lucien Frary, "Russian Interests in Nineteenth-Century Thessaloniki," *Mediterranean Historical Review* 23, no. 1 (June 2008): 15–33.

6. *New York Times*, November 10 and December 29, 1912.

7. *El Tiempo*, November 11, 1912.

8. Quoted in "A Muslim-Jewish-Vlach Committee for Internationalizing Salonica," in Cohen and Stein, eds., *Sephardi Lives*, 150–153.

9. Paris Papamichos Chronakis, "The Jewish, Greek, Muslim and Donme merchants of Salonica, 1882–1919: Class and ethnic transformations in the course of Hellenization," (PhD Dissertation, University of Crete, 2011) (Greek).

10. Devin E. Naar, "From the 'Jerusalem of the Balkans' to the 'Goldene Medina': Jewish Immigration from Salonika to the United States," *American Jewish History* 93, no. 4 (December 2007): 435–473.

11. John A. Mazis, "The Idea of an Eastern Federation: An Alternative to the Destruction of the Ottoman Empire," in *Russian-Ottoman Borderlands: The Eastern Question Reconsidered*, ed. L. J. Frary and M. Kozelsky (Madison, 2014), 251–279.

12. Matilde Morcillo Rosillo, "Aproximación al pensamiento del sefardita salonicense Alberto Samuel Asseo (1912)," *Revista de la Facultad de Humanidades de Jaén* 1, no. 2 (1992): 81–92.

13. Sam Lévy, "Le Salut des Balcans," [c. 1919], AIU, Grèce II C 53.12, b. 13. Lévy identified Danzig and the Free State of Fiume (Rijeka, in present-day Croatia) as models for Salonica. On the fate of the port, see Shai Srougo, "The Geopolitical Status of the Port of the City of Thessaloniki during an Age of Change: 1869–1929," in *Greece in the Balkans: Memory, Conflict and Exchange*, ed. O. Anastasakis et al. (London, 2009), 92–109.

14. Kevin Featherstone, et al., *The Last Ottomans: The Muslim Minority in Greece, 1940–1949* (New York, 2011), 27–29.

15. *Avanti*, December 9, 1912 and November 3, 1918.

16. Aron Rodrigue, *Jews and Muslims: Images of Sephardi and Eastern Jewries in Modern Times* (Seattle, 2003), 236–238.

17. *El Liberal*, November 15, 1912, 1; *El Avenir*, December 1, 1912; Minna Rozen, *The Last Ottoman Century and Beyond: The Jews in Turkey and the Balkans, 1808–1945* (Tel Aviv, 2005) 1:170.

18. See weekly reports in *Jewish Chronicle*, March–April 1913.

19. Reşat Kasaba, *A Moveable Empire: Ottoman Nomads, Migrants, and Refugees* (Seattle, 2009).

20. Karen Barkey and George Gavrilis, "The Ottoman Millet System: Non-Territorial Autonomy and its Contemporary Legacy," *Ethnopolitics* 15, no. 1 (2016): 24–42. For an exploration of Greece and Turkey as post-Ottoman states, see Christine Philliou, "The Ottoman Empire between Successors: Thinking from 1821–1922," in *Religion, Ethnicity and Contested Nationhood in the Former Ottoman Space*, ed. J. Nielsen (Boston, 2012), 29–44.

21. *Avanti*, April 4, 1913, 1.

22. Joseph Uziel, *ha-Migal ha-Lavan: Reshamim, zikhronot ve-sipurim me-haye 'ir 'ivrit ba-golah* (Tel Aviv, 1929).

23. Maír José Benardete, *Hispanic Culture and Character of the Sephardic Jews* (New York, 1953), 17.

24. See extensive correspondence regarding the production and distribution of *matza*, 1922–1937, YIVO, RG-207, f. 88–96.

25. *El Mesajero*, April 16, 1936.

26. Rogers Brubaker, "Aftermaths of Empire and the Unmixing of Peoples," in *After Empire: Multiethnic Societies and Nation-Building: The Soviet and the Russian, Ottoman, and Habsburg Empires*, ed. K. Barkey and M. von Hagen (Boulder, 1997), 155–180; Renée Hirschon, "'Unmixing Peoples' in the Aegean Region," in *Crossing the Aegean: An Appraisal of the 1923 Compulsory Population Exchange between Greece and Turkey*, ed. R. Hirschon (New York, 2003), 3–12; Ryan Gingeras, *Sorrowful Shores: Violence, Ethnicity, and the End of the Ottoman Empire, 1912–1923* (New York, 2011); Nicholas Doumanis, *Before the Nation: Muslim-Christian Coexistence and its Destruction in Late-Ottoman Anatolia* (Oxford, 2013).

27. Bernard Wasserstein, *On the Eve: The Jews of Europe Before the Second World War* (New York, 2012), 100.

28. K. E. Fleming, "'Salonica's Jews': A Metropolitan History," *Jewish History* 28, no. 3–4 (2014): 449–455, esp. 454–455, illustrates how the Septuagint, the Greek translation of the Hebrew Bible from the second century BCE, rendered *ir va-em be-Israel* as *polin kai metropolin en Israel*—a metropolis, literally a "mother city." Mark Mazower, *Salonica, City of Ghosts: Christians, Muslims, and Jews, 1430–1950* (London, 2004), 83; Nikos Gabriel Pentzikis, *Mother Thessaloniki*, trans. L. Marshall (Athens, 1998); Yorgos Ioannou, *Refugee Capital: Thessaloniki Chronicles*, trans. F. Reed (Athens, 1997).

29. Andrew Apostolou, "Mother of Israel, Orphan of History: Writing on Jewish Salonika," *Israel Affairs* 13, no. 1 (January 2007): 193–204.

30. Henriette-Rika Benveniste, "The Coming Out of Jewish History in Greece," *Usages Publics du Passé* (February 2011) (http://anciensiteusagespublicsdupasse.ehess .fr/index.php?id=130); Fleming, *Greece*, 11. Among the publications that appeared in connection to the 1997 celebrations was I. K. Hassiotes, ed., *Queen of the Worthy: Thessaloniki, History and Culture* (Thessaloniki, 1997), which includes Albert Nar, "Social Organisation and Activity of the Jewish Community of Thessaloniki," 191–210. See the

website for the Group for the Study of the History of the Jews of Greece (http:// www
.histjews.blogspot.com). See also Rena Molho, "État de Recherche," in *Salonica and
Istanbul: Social, Political and Cultural Aspects of Jewish Life* (Istanbul, 2005), 73–84; Rena
Molho, "Problems of Incorporating the Holocaust into the Greek Collective Memory: The Case of Thessaloniki," *Journal of Turkish Studies* 40 (December 2013): 301–314;
Odette Varon-Vassard, "L'intérêt pour les Juifs de Grèce," *Historein* 1 (1999): 157–162;
Rika Benveniste, "Gia tēn Istoria tōn Evraiōn tēs Elladas" [On the History of the Jews
of Greece], in *Istoriografia tēs neoterēs kai sygchronēs Elladas, 1833–2002* [Historiography
of Modern and Contemporary Greece], ed. P. Kitromilides and T. Sklavenitēs (Athens,
2004), 2:315–328. The historiographical essays in a recent issue of *Jewish History* 28, no.
3–4 (2014), on the Jews of Salonica, are of great significance: Tony Molho, "Introduction," 249–259; Efi Avdela, "Toward a Greek History of the Jews of Salonica," 405–410;
Maurice Aymard, "Salonica's Jews in the Mediterranean: Two Historiographical Perspectives (1945–2010)," 411–429; Edhem Eldem, "Salonica and its Jewish History in
Turkish Historiography," 431–438; Aron Rodrigue, "Salonica in Jewish Historiography,"
439–447; Fleming, "'Salonica's Jews.'"

31. Mazower, *Salonica, City of Ghosts*, 10.

32. Risal, *La Ville Convoitée*; Gueron, *Salonique*, 6.

33. Mazower, *Salonica, City of Ghosts*, 299–300.

34. George Th. Mavrogordatos, *Stillborn Republic: Social Coalitions and Party
Strategies in Greece, 1922–1936* (Berkeley, 1983), 257; Giorgos Margaritis, *Anepithymētoi
Sympatriōtes: Stoicheia gia tēn Katastrophē tōn Meionotētōn tēs Elladas: Evraioi, Tsamēdes*
[Unwanted Compatriots: Elements for the Destruction of the Minorities of Greece:
Jews and Chams] (Athens, 2005); Aristotle A. Kallis, "The Jewish Community of Sa-
lonica Under Siege: The Antisemitic Violence of the Summer of 1931," *Holocaust and
Genocide Studies* 20, no. 1 (Spring 2006): 34–56.

35. For further analysis of the relationship between the interwar and war years, see
Hagen Fleischer, "Greek Jewry and Nazi Germany: The Holocaust and Its Anteced-
ents," in *Les Juifs en Grèce: Questions d'Histoire dans la Longue Durée*, ed. R. Molho and
R. Benveniste (Athens, 1995), 185–208; Andrew Apostolou, "'The Exception of Salonika':
Bystanders and Collaborators in Northern Greece," *Holocaust and Genocide Studies* 14,
no. 2 (Fall 2000): 165–196; Steven Bowman, *The Agony of Greek Jews* (Stanford, 2009);
René Levine Melammed, *An Ode to Jewish Salonika: The Ladino Verses of Bouena Sarfatty*
(Bloomington, 2013); Rena Molho, "The Close Ties between Nationalism and Antisem-
itism: The Hellenization of Salonika, 1917-1948," in *Jahrbuch für Antisemitismusforschung*
24 (2015): 217–228.

36. Michael Molho, *In Memoriam: Hommage aux Victimes Juives des Nazis en Grèce*
(Salonica, 1948), 16.

37. Fleming, *Greece*, 91; see the critique by Andrew Apostolou, "When Did Greek
Jews Become Greek?" *Yad Vashem Studies* 38, no. 2 (2010): 205–219.

38. While offering a seemingly convenient explanation, this interpretation requires further evaluation given that the few thousand Romaniote Jews who had been living in Ioannina for generations spoke Greek exclusively but nonetheless suffered the high mortality rate of 90 percent as a result of the Nazi deportations. For Ioannina Jews, being assimilated did not improve their fate. Rae Dalven, *The Jews of Ioannina* (Philadelphia, 1990); George Th. Mavrogordatos, "The Holocaust in Greece: A Vindication of Assimilation?" *Études Balkaniques* 48, no. 4 (2012): 5–17.

39. Mark Mazower, *The Balkans: A Short History* (New York, 2000), 39. On the persistence of religious allegiances, see Frederick Anscombe, *State, Faith, and Nation in the Ottoman and Post-Ottoman Lands* (New York, 2014).

40. My framework is informed by scholarship in modern Greek studies on the development of Greek nationalism and the place of minority populations. Salient perspectives include: Peter Mackridge and Eleni Yannakakis, eds., *Ourselves and Others: The Development of a Greek Macedonian Cultural Identity Since 1912* (Oxford, 1997); Richard Clogg, ed., *Minorities in Greece: Aspects of a Plural Society* (London, 2002); Anna Triandafyllidou and Anna Paraskevopoulou, "When Is the Greek Nation? The Role of Enemies and Minorities," *Geopolitics* 7, no. 2 (Autumn 2002): 75–98; Efi Gazi, "Constructing the National Majority and Ethnic/Religious Minorities in Greece," in *Statehood Beyond Ethnicity: Minor States in Northern and Eastern Europe, 1600–2000*, ed. L. Eriksonas and L. Müller (Brussels, 2005), 303–317; Philip Carabot, "Aspects of the Hellenization of Greek Macedonia, ca. 1912–ca. 1959," *Kampos: Cambridge Papers in Modern Greek* 13 (2005): 21–61; Philip Carabott, "State, Society and the Religious 'Other' in Nineteenth-Century Greece," *Kampos: Cambridge Papers in Modern Greek* 18 (2011): 1–33.

41. On the development of Greek nationalism, see, inter alia, Paschalis Kitromilides, "'Imagined Communities' and the Origins of the National Question in the Balkans," in *Modern Greece: Nationalism and Nationality*, ed. M. Blinkhorn and T. Veremis (Athens, 1990); Stathis Gougouris, *Dream Nation: Enlightenment, Colonization and the Institution of Modern Greece* (Palo Alto, 1996); Victor Roudometof, "From *Rum Millet* to Greek Nation: Enlightenment, Secularization, and National Identity in Ottoman Balkan Society, 1453–1821," *Journal of Modern Greek Studies* 16 (1998): 11–48; Effi Gazi, "Revisiting Religion and Nationalism in Nineteenth-Century Greece," in *The Making of Modern Greece: Nationalism, Romanticism & the Uses of the Past (1797–1896)*, ed. R. Beaton and D. Ricks (Burlington, 2009), 95–106.

42. Patricia Kennedy Grimsted, "Twice Plundered or 'Twice Saved'? Identifying Russia's 'Trophy' Archives and the Loot of the Reichssicherheitshauptamt," *Holocaust and Genocide Studies* 15, no. 2 (Fall 2001): 191–244; Minna Rozen, "The Archives of the Salonika Community as a Key to the Economic Life of the Jews of Salonika between the Two World Wars; Desiderata, Possibilities, and Constraints," in *Professional Occupations, Production Business, Social Life of Thessaloniki, 18th–20th centuries*, ed. A. Dagas and H. Antoniadis Bibicou (Thessaloniki, 1998), 121–126; Maria Vassilikou, "The Archive

of the Jewish Community of Salonika," *Bulletin of Judaeo-Greek Studies* 21 (1997–1998): 35–37.

43. Report by the grand rabbinate on the Office of Civil Status of the Jewish Community of Salonica, c. 1934, USHMM, r. 691, d. 145.

44. Moshe David Gaon, *Ha-'Itonut be-Ladino: bibliyografyah: shelosh me'ot 'itonim* [A bibliography of the Judeo-Spanish (Ladino) press] (Jerusalem, 1965), 133–134.

45. For *La Epoka*, see Olga Borovaya, *Modern Ladino Culture: Press, Belles Lettres and Theater in the Late Ottoman Empire* (Bloomington, 2011), 54. I compiled the figures for 1927 from Manolis Kandylakis, *Efimeridografia tis Thessalonikis: Simvoli stin Istoria tou Tipou* (Thessaloniki, 2005), 3:490–546.

46. Hans Kohn, "Letters from Abroad, Saloniki: New Régime in Greece," *The Menorah Journal* 16, no. 5 (May 1929): 442–445.

47. H. G. Dwight, "Saloniki," *National Geographic* 30 (September 1916): 203–232. On Judeo-Spanish reading practices, see Matthias Lehmann, *Ladino Rabbinic Literature and Ottoman Sephardic Culture* (Bloomington, 2005).

48. *Pro-Israël*, September 19, 1923.

49. *La Renasensia Djudia*, March 11, 1932.

50. *El Puevlo*, July 19 and 27, 1932; *La Aksion*, June 4, 1939; David Bunis, "Judezmo Glossaries and Dictionaries by Native Speakers and the Language Ideologies behind them," in *Lexicologia y lexicografía judeoespañolas*, ed. W. Busse and M. Studemund-Halévy (Berne, 2011), 339–431, esp. 420–421.

51. Business card of Sotirios Papadimas, YIVO, RG-207, f. 100.

52. Yosef Hayim Yerushalmi, "Exile and Expulsion in Jewish History," in *Crisis and Creativity in the Sephardic World, 1391–1648*, ed. B. Gampel (New York, 1997), 3–23; Yosef Hayim Yerushalmi, "Servants of the Kings and not Servants of Servants: Some Aspects of the Political History of the Jews," in *The Faith of Fallen Jews: Yosef Hayim Yerushalmi and the Writing of Jewish History*, ed. D. Myers and A. Kaye (Waltham, 2014), 245–276.

53. *Sidur Sha'are Tefila* (Thessaloniki, 1941), 270–271. Barry Schwartz, "*Hanoten Teshua*: The Origin of the Traditional Jewish Prayer for the Government," *Hebrew Union College Annual* 57 (1986): 113–120; Edwin Seroussi, "*Ha-noten teshu'a la-mlakhim*: Identity and Nationality in 19th-century Synagogue Music in Europe," *Mit Pauke und Reigen* (Hannover, 2002), 51–59.

54. *La Verdad*, January 10, 1921.

55. *La Esperansa*, November 28, 1919.

56. Isaac Jerusalmi, ed., *Kanun Name de Penas*, Auxiliary Materials for the Study of the Semitic Languages 8 (Cincinnati, 1975), 9ff. (Articles 49, 50, 55). The sentiment captured by the distinction between *turko* and *turkino* echoes in modern Turkish with the terms *Türk* (ethnic Turk) and *Türkiyeli* (citizen of Turkey). Ioannis Grigoriadis, "Türk or Türkiyeli? The Reform of Turkey's Minority Legislation and the Rediscovery of Ottomanism," *Middle Eastern Studies* 43, no. 3 (May 2007): 432–438.

57. Aron Rodrigue and Sarah Stein, eds., *A Jewish Voice from Ottoman Salonica: The Ladino Memoir of Sa'adi Besalel a-Levi*, trans. I. Jerusalmi (Stanford, 2012), 142–147; Elena Romero, *Entre dos (o más) fuegos: Fuentes poéticas para la historia de los sefardíes de los Balcanes* (Madrid, 2008), 283–286.

58. On these tensions, see Kemal Karpat, "*Millets* and Nationality: The Roots of In-congruity of Nation and State in the Post-Ottoman Era," in *Christians and Jews in the Ottoman Empire*, ed. B. Braude and B. Lewis (New York, 1982) 1:149–169; Aron Rodrigue, "From *Millet* to Minority: Turkish Jewry," in *Paths of Emancipation: Jews, States, and Citizenship*, ed. P. Birnbaum and I. Katznelson (Princeton, 1995), 238–261; Benjamin Braude, "The Strange History of the Millet System," in *The Great Ottoman-Turkish Civilisation*, ed. K. Cicek (Ankara, 2000), 2:409–418; Dimitrios Stamatopoulos, "From *Millets* to Mi-norities in the 19th-Century Ottoman Empire: An Ambiguous Modernization," in *Citizenship in Historical Perspective*, ed. S. G. Ellis, G. Hálfadanarson, and A. K. Isaacs (Pisa, 2006), 253–273; Karen Barkey, *Empire of Difference: The Ottomans in Comparative Perspective* (Cambridge, England, 2008); Aron Rodrigue, "Reflections on *Millets* and Minorities: Ottoman Legacies," in *Turkey Between Nationalism and Globalization*, ed. R. Kastoryano (New York, 2013), 36–46; Benjamin C. Fortna, "The Ottoman Empire and after: From a State of 'Nations' to 'Nation-States,'" in *State-Nationalisms in the Ottoman Empire, Greece and Turkey: Orthodox and Muslims, 1830–1945*, ed. B. Fortna (Hoboken, 2012), 1–11.

59. Karen Barkey, "Thinking about the Consequences of Empire," in *After Empire: Multiethnic Societies and Nation-Building: The Soviet and the Russian, Ottoman, and Habsburg Empires*, ed. K. Barkey and M. von Hagen (Boulder, 1997), 99–114; M. Şükrü Hanioğlu, *A Brief History of the Late Ottoman Empire* (Princeton, 2008); Michelle Cam-pos, *Ottoman Brothers: Muslims, Christians, and Jews in Early Twentieth-Century Palestine* (Stanford, 2010); Julia Phillips Cohen, *Becoming Ottomans: Sephardi Jews and Imperial Citizenship in the Modern Era* (New York, 2014); Bedross Der Matossian, *Shattered Dreams of Revolution: From Liberty to Violence in the Late Ottoman Empire* (Stanford, 2014).

60. Cohen, *Becoming Ottomans*; Selim Deringil, *The Well-Protected Domains: Ideol-ogy and the Legitimation of Power in the Ottoman Empire, 1876–1909* (New York, 1998).

61. Romero, *Entre dos (o más) fuegos*, 397–413, 496–497.

62. See Esther Benbassa, "Zionism in the Ottoman Empire at the End of the 19th and the Beginning of the 20th Century," *Studies in Zionism* 11, no. 2 (1990): 127–140; Ilber Ortayli, "Ottomanism and Zionism During the Second Constitutional Period, 1908–1915," in *The Jews of the Ottoman Empire*, ed. A. Levy (Princeton, 1994), 527–536; Rena Molho, "The Zionist Movement in Thessaloniki, 1899–1919," in *The Jewish Com-munities of Southeastern Europe*, ed. I. K. Hassiotis (Thessaloniki, 1997), 327–355; Rozen, *Last Ottoman Century*; Ioannes Skourtes, "The Zionists and their Jewish Opponents in Thessaloniki between the Two Worlds Wars," in *The Jewish Communities of South-Eastern Europe from the 15th Century to the End of World War II*, ed. I. Hassiotis (Thes-saloniki, 1997), 517–525.

63. Aron Rodrigue, *French Jews, Turkish Jews: The Alliance Israélite Universelle and the Politics of Jewish Schooling in Turkey, 1860–1925* (Bloomington, 1990), 136.

64. Şükrü Ilicak, "Jewish Socialism in Ottoman Salonica," *Southeast European and Black Sea Studies* 2 (September 2002): 115–146; Paul Dumont, "A Jewish, Socialist and Ottoman Organization: The Worker's Federation of Thessaloniki," in *Socialism and Nationalism in the Ottoman Empire, 1876–1923*, ed. M. Tuncay and E. J. Zürcher (London, 1994), 49–76; Efi Avdela, "Class, Ethnicity and Gender in Post-Ottoman Thessaloniki," in *Borderlines: Genders and Identities in Peace and War (1880–1930)*, ed. B. Melman (New York, 1998), 421–438; Donald Quataert, "The Workers of Salonica, 1850–1912," in *Workers and the Working Class in the Ottoman Empire and the Turkish Republic*, ed. D. Quataert and E. J. Zürcher (New York, 1995), 59–74; Gila Hadar, "La renovasion de Judeo-espaniol en Salonika: edukar las masas socialistas en muestra lengua maternal," in *Lexicología y lexicografía judeoespañolas*, ed. W. Busse and M. Studemund-Halévy (Berne, 2011), 143–158.

65. Esther Benbassa and Aron Rodrigue, *Sephardi Jewry: A History of the Judeo-Spanish Community, 14th–20th Centuries* (Berkeley, 2000), 116.

66. Yosef Uziel, *El Sionismo. Su Orijen i Su Eskopo* (Salonica, 1909), 1.

67. Ibid., 11–20.

68. Maria Vassilikou, "Politics of the Jewish Community of Salonika in the Inter-War Years: Party Ideologies and Party Competition" (PhD Dissertation, University of London, 2000); Maria Vassilikou, "Post-Cosmopolitan Salonika—Jewish Politics in the Interwar Period," *Simon Dubnow Institute Yearbook* 2 (2003): 99–118; Bernard Pierron, *Juifs et Chrétiens de la Grèce Moderne: Histoire des relations intercommunautaires de 1821 à 1945 (Paris, 1996)*, 158–164; Paula Daccarett, "Shabbat, Noël, and Jewish Temporal Modernity: A Comparative View from Salonica," *Jewish Social Studies* 19, no. 2 (Winter 2013): 109–150.

69. "Raporto sovre los incidentes dela keila en Castoria," April 7, 1934, USHMM, r. 752, d. 109; *Jewish Telegraphic Agency*, May 14, 1934.

70. Richard Clogg, *A Concise History of Greece* (Cambridge, England, 2002), 47. See Kitromilides, "'Imagined Communities,'" 23–66; Anastasia Stouraiti and Alexander Kazamias, "The Imaginary Topographies of the *Megali Idea*: National Territory as Utopia," in *Spatial Conceptions of the Nation: Modernizing Geographies in Greece and Turkey*, ed. N. Diamandouros, T. Dragonas and C. Keyder (London, 2010), 11–34.

71. Clogg, *Minorities in Greece*, xvii.

72. Ioannis Grigoriadis, *Instilling Religion in Greek and Turkish Nationalism: Sacred Synthesis* (New York, 2013), 30–33.

73. Efi Gazi, "'Fatherland, Religion, Family': Exploring the History of a Slogan in Greece (1880–1930)," paper presented at the Modern Greek Studies Association, New York University (October 2011).

74. Gazi, "Revisiting religion," 95.

75. *El Liberal*, November 29, 1913.

76. Michael Molho, "La Nouvelle Communauté Juive d'Athènes," in *Joshua Starr Memorial Volume* (New York, 1953), 231–239; Yitzchak Kerem, "The Multicultural Background of Greek Jewry: Factors in their Diversity and Integration in Modern Greece," *Mesogeios* 20–21 (2003): 57–79.

77. Richard Clogg, "The Greek *Millet* in the Ottoman Empire," in *Christians and Jews in the Ottoman Empire*, ed. B. Braude (London, 2014), 109–132, esp. 115.

78. *El Puevlo*, December 6 and 7, 1932.

79. Jewish Community of Salonica to the president of the Greek government and ministers of Interior, Justice, and Foreign Affairs, February 21 and 24, 1928, JMTh, f. 95.

80. Mathew Arnold, "Hebraism and Hellenism," in *Culture and Anarchy: An Essay in Political and Social Criticism* (London, 1869), 142–166; Louis Feldman, "Hebraism and Hellenism Reconsidered," *Judaism* 43, no. 2 (Spring 1994): 115–126; Nicholas de Lange, "Hebraism and Hellenism: The Case of Byzantine Jewry," *Poetics Today* 19, no. 1 (Spring 1998): 129–145.

81. Yaacov Shavit, *Athens in Jerusalem: Classical Antiquity and Hellenism in the Making of the Modern Secular Jew* (London, 1997); Miriam Leonard, *Socrates and the Jews: Hellenism and Hebraism from Moses Mendelssohn to Sigmund Freud* (Chicago, 2012).

82. Dimitris Livanios, "The Quest for Hellenism: Religion, Nationalism and Collective Identities in Greece (1453–1913)," *The Historical Review* 3 (2006): 33–70; Antonis Liakos, "Hellenism and the Making of Modern Greece: Time, Language, Space," in *Hellenisms: Culture, Identity, and Ethnicity from Antiquity to Modernity*, ed. K. Zacharia (Burlington, 2008), 201–236.

83. Konstantinos Tsitselikis, "Aspects of Legal Communitarianism in Greece: Between *Millet* and Citizenship," *Oñati Socio-Legal Series* 2, no. 7 (2012): 106–118; Dimitris Katsikas, "*Millet* Legacies in a National Environment: Political Elites and Muslim Communities in Greece (1830s-1923)," in *State-Nationalisms in the Ottoman Empire, Greece and Turkey: Orthodox and Muslims, 1830–1945*, ed. B. Fortna (Hoboken, 2012), 47–72; Dimitris Katsikas, "*Millets* in Nation-States: The Case of Greek and Bulgarian Muslims, 1912–1923" *Nationalities Papers* 37, no. 2 (March 2009): 177–201.

84. Krishan Kumar, "Nation-States as Empires, Empires as Nation-States: Two Principles, One Practice," *Theory and Society* 39 (2010): 119–143 observes that, although often considered antithetical forms of state formation, empires and nation-states may share practices of governance.

85. *La Verdad*, December 1, 1920.

86. David Sorkin, "Religious Minorities and Citizenship in the Long Nineteenth Century: Some Contexts of Jewish Emancipation," in *Politics of Religious Freedom*, ed. W. Fallers Sullivan, et al. (Chicago, 2015), 115–126.

87. Thomas Mawson, *The Life and Work of an English Landscape Artist* (New York, 1927), 273. On the fire and its consequences, see, inter alia: Alexandra Yerolympos, *Urban Transformations in the Balkans (1820–1920): Aspects of Balkan Town Planning and the Re-*

making of Thessaloniki (Thessaloniki, 1996); Rena Molho, "Jewish Working-Class Neigh-borhoods Established in Salonika Following the 1890 and 1917 Fires," in *Last Ottoman Century*, ed. M. Rozen, 2:173–194; Vilma Hastaoglou-Martinidis, "The Jewish Commu-nity of Salonica after the Fire of 1917: An Unpublished Memoir and Other Documents from the Papers of Henry Morgenthau Sr," in *The Jewish Communities of Southeastern Europe from the Fifteenth Century to the End of World War II*, ed. I. K. Hassiotis (Salonica, 1997), 147–174.

88. *El Puevlo*, September 30, 1917.

89. *El Puevlo*, December 31, 1917; January 3 and 13, 1918.

90. Interclub Israélite, Salonica, to the Joint Foreign Committee of the Jew-ish Board of Deputies and the Anglo-Jewish Association, London, August 14, 1924, ABDBJ, acc. 3121/E3/158/2 and Lucien Wolf, "Minorities in Greece: Letters Addressed to the Secretary General of the League of Nations and the High Commissioner for Refugees, Relative to the Guarantee of the Greek Minorities Treaty of August 10, 1920," London, August 29, 1924, ABDBJ, acc. 3121/G2/16.

91. Shomre Shabat to the Communal Council, Av 5, 5685, CAHJP, Gr/Sa 74; Beth Din cases, 1938–1939 (v. 22, pp. 88a and 93a), YIVO, RG-207, f. 15; *La Aksion*, February 10, 1938.

92. *El Puevlo*, November 25, 1931.

93. Venizelos outlined his offer in *Archives Israélites* in 1929 as described in Bracha Rivlin, "History of the Jews of Greece," in *Pinkas HaKehillot. Encyclopedia of Jewish Communities from their Foundation till after the Holocaust—Greece*, ed. B. Rivlin (Jerusa-lem, 1998), 18 (Hebrew).

94. "The Influence of the French Revolution" in *The Movement for Greek Inde-pendence, 1770–1821: A Collection of Documents*, ed. Richard Clogg (Macmillan, 1976), 149–176; Paschalis Kitromilidis, "An Enlightenment Perspective on Balkan Cultural Pluralism: The Republican Vision of Rhigas Velestinlis," *History of Political Thought* 24, no. 3 (Autumn 2003): 465–479; Maria Lopez Villalba, "Balkanizing the French Revolu-tion: Rhigas's *New Political Constitution*," in *Greece and the Balkans: Identities, Percep-tions and Cultural Encounters since the Enlightenment*, ed. D. Tziovas (Burlington, 2003), 141–154; Gougouris, *Dream Nation*, 74–75.

95. *La Aksion*, January 5, 1936.

96. *La Esperansa*, April 4, 1916.

97. *El Puevlo*, October 1, 1928.

98. *Ester Matalon: Romanso inedito sovre la vida a Saloniko en los anyos de la gera mondiala* (Salonica, 1935), 2.

Chapter 1

1. *El Puevlo*, April 10, 1921.

2. M. Bensanchi, "La mision de la komunita. Todo loke es djidio deve interesarla," *El Makabeo* (5691): 15–21.

3. *Avanti*, May 2, 1913.

4. See Johann Gottlieb Fichte, "A State within a State (1793)," in *The Jew in the Modern World: A Documentary History*, ed., P. Mendes Flohr and J. Reinharz (New York, 1995), 308–310.

5. Quoted in David Biale, Introduction to *Cultures of the Jews: A New History* (New York, 2002), 3:725. Scholars like Biale have begun to reinterpret the now-extensive literature on the question of Jewish emancipation through the lens of cultural studies. See also P. Birnbaum and I. Katznelson, eds., *Paths of Emancipation: Jews, States, and Citizenship* (Princeton, 1995).

6. Rena Molho, "The Zionist Movement in Thessaloniki, 1899–1919," in *The Jewish Communities of Southeastern Europe: From the Fifteenth Century to the End of World War II*, ed. I. K. Hassiotis (Thessaloniki, 1997), 327–350, esp. 348.

7. Anastasia Karakasidou, *Fields of Wheat, Hills of Blood: Passages to Nationhood in Greek Macedonia, 1870–1990* (Chicago, 1998), viii.

8. Daout Levy, "Rapporto sovre la Communidad Djudia de Thessaloniki a partir del anio 1870 asta el 1940 sea por ouna perioda de circa 60/70 anios," June 1942, JMTh, f. 20.

9. Yaron Ben-Naeh, *Jews in the Realm of the Sultans: Ottoman Jewish Society in the Seventeenth Century* (Tübingen, 2008), 166; Avigdor Levy, "Introduction," in *The Jews of the Ottoman Empire*, ed. A. Levy (Princeton, 1994), 68.

10. Eyal Ginio, "Coping with Decline: The Political Responses of the Jewish Community to the Eighteenth Century Crisis in Salonica," in *Political Initiatives 'From the Bottom Up' in the Ottoman Empire*, ed. A. Anastasopoulos (Rethymno, 2012), 69–90.

11. Ben-Naeh, *Jews in the Realm of the Sultans*, 211–214; Aron Rodrigue and Sarah Stein, eds., *A Jewish Voice from Ottoman Salonica: The Ladino Memoir of Sa'adi Besalel a-Levi* (Stanford, 2012), 41–42, 134.

12. Aron Rodrigue, "From *Millet* to Minority: Turkish Jewry," in *Paths of Emancipation: Jews, States, and Citizenship*, ed. P. Birnbaum and I. Katznelson (Princeton, 1995), 238–261.

13. For a recent, comprehensive overview, see the contributions in Eyal Ginio, ed., *Greece: Jewish Communities in the East in the Nineteenth and Twentieth Centuries* (Jerusalem, 2014) (Hebrew).

14. *El Liberal*, December 1, 1913; Levy, "Rapporto sovre la Communidad Djudia"; J. Almaleh, "Statistica sovre la population sephardite djudia de Thessaloniki," May, 27, 1941, JMTh, f. 16, p. 4.

15. Orly Meron, "Budgeting in Judeo-Spanish: Jewish Administration in the Age of Crisis, Salonica, 1928–1934," *Ladinar* 7–8 (2014): 179–200, esp. 199.

16. *El Mesajero*, August 29, 1940.

17. Circular from the president of the Communal Council, June 24, 1918, BZI, Dapim Saloniki/41; *La Aksion*, November 11, 1930; *La Volunté*, May 28, 1934.

18. Selections drawn from register listing 3,165 voters stamped by "Komision Elektoral" of the Jewish Community, 1933–1934, USHMM, r. 687, d. 21.

19. See the series "La Komunita Israelita de Saloniko," *El Liberal*, December 4, 8, 9, 10, and 22, 1913.

20. Emanuel Isaac Brudo to the Communal Council, Nisan 5, 5680, USHMM, r. 751, d. 107.

21. See the reports in YIVO, RG-207, f. 87.

22. Meron, "Budgeting in Judeo-Spanish"; "Subventiones a los journalés," 1936, CAHJP, Gr/Sa 305.

23. Declarations of communal employees, 1934–1940, JMTh, ff. 26–29; documents pertaining to Association de Fonctionarios de la Administration Centrala de la Comunita Djudia de Salonicco, 1932–1937, JMTh, ff. 47–49; reports on communal institutions, 1939, YIVO, RG-207, f. 87; lists of *shohatim, moalim, hazanim*, judges of the Beth Din, members of the Rabbinical Council, etc., and their salaries, 1936, USHMM, r. 727, d. 293.

24. *La Epoka*, January 6, 1911.

25. M. Bensanchi, "En la komunita djudia: el estado aktual," *El* Makabeo (5678): 9–16, esp. 15. See also "'We Are a National Minority': A Greek Jewish Manifesto Issued After the Paris Peace Conference," in *Sephardi Lives: A Documentary History*, ed. J. P. Cohen and S. A. Stein (Stanford, 2014), 238–240.

26. *Avanti*, April 7, May 2 and 5, 1913.

27. S. Protonotarios, director, Thessaloniki Press Bureau, to the minister of foreign affairs, May 17, 1920, as translated in *Documents on the History of Greek Jewry: Records from the Historical Archives of the Ministry of Foreign Affairs*, ed. P. Constantopoulou and T. Veremis (Athens, 1999), 101–102.

28. Molho, "Zionist Movement," 347.

29. J. Cazes to the governor general of Thessaloniki, March 17, 1919, as translated in *Documents on the History of Greek Jewry*, 92.

30. Quoted in Carole Fink, *Defending the Rights of Others: The Great Powers, the Jews, and International Minority Protection, 1878–1938* (Cambridge, England, 2004), 61.

31. K. E. Fleming, *Greece—A Jewish History* (Princeton, 2008), 67.

32. Bernard Pierron, *Juifs et Chrétiens: Histoire des relations intercommunautaires de 1821 à 1945* (Paris, 1996), 128.

33. Stefanos Katsikas, "*Millet* legacies in a national environment: Political Elites and Muslim Communities in Greece, 1830s–1923," in *State-Nationalisms in the Ottoman Empire, Greece and Turkey: Orthodox and Muslims (1830–1945)*, ed. B. Fortna et al. (New York, 2012), 52–74, esp. 70, n. 86; Law 2456 Concerning Jewish Communities, as translated in *Documents on the History of Greek Jewry*, 110.

34. Stefanos Katsikas, "Hostage Minority: The Muslims of Greece (1923–41)," in *State-Nationalisms in the Ottoman Empire, Greece and Turkey: Orthodox and Muslims (1830–1945)*, ed. B. Fortna et al. (New York, 2012), 153–175.

35. Evangelos Hekimoglou, *O Nikolaos Manos kai o Mesopolemos sti Thessaloniki* (Thessaloniki, 2010), 130.

36. Philip Carabot, "The Politics of Integration and Assimilation vis-à-vis the Slavo-Macedonian Minority in Inter-war Greece," in *Ourselves and Others: The Development of a Greek Macedonian Cultural Identity since 1912*, ed. P. Mackridge and E. Yannakakis (Oxford, 1997), 59–78, quote 66; Karakasidou, *Fields of Wheat.*

37. "A Muslim Journalist Calls upon Turkey's Jews to Forgo Minority Rights (1925)," "Dance Halls and Decadence in Istanbul: The Turkish Press Airs Concerns About Non-Muslims (1926)," and "A Turkish Jew's 'Ten Commandments' for Turkification (1928)," in *Sephardi Lives,* ed. Stein and Cohen, 169–174, 252–253.

38. Rifat Bali, *The Silent Minority in Turkey: Turkish Jews* (Istanbul, 2013).

39. Victor Meyer, Athens, to the Jewish Community of Salonica, July 29, 1935, CAHJP, Gr/Sa 202.

40. Michael Molho, "Dos obras maestras en Ladino de Moises Almosnino," in *Estudios y ensayos sobre tópicos judíos* (Buenos Aires, 1958), 95–102.

41. *El Liberal,* November 30, 1913.

42. Elias Messinas, *The Synagogues of Salonika and Veroia* (Athens, 1997).

43. "Defter nefus resansiman primo echo del 1300," CAHJP, Gr/Sa 358; "Defter nufus yabandji i bakli mekyan muvakat," JMTh, f. 1; Devin Naar, *With Their Own Words: Glimpses of Jewish Life in Thessaloniki Before the Holocaust* (Thessaloniki, 2006), 12–14.

44. Mark Cohen, *The Last Century of a Sephardic Community: The Jews of Monastir* (New York, 2003), 130, 138.

45. As tabulated from "Rejistro de nasensias" of the Jewish Community of Salonica, 1932–1939, USHMM, r. 728, d. 10.

46. Asher Moisis, *Greek-Jewish Patrimony* (North Charleston, 2012).

47. *El Puevlo,* May 2, 1921.

48. David M. Bunis, *Voices from Jewish Salonika* (Jerusalem, 1999), 62–63; Sarah Bunin Benor, "Lexical Othering in Judezmo: How Ottoman Sephardim Refer to Non-Jews," in *Languages and Literatures of Sephardic and Oriental Jews,* ed. D. M. Bunis (Jerusalem, 2009), 65–85, esp. 82.

49. *El Puevlo,* February 19 and December 12, 1932; Gila Hadar, "Prostitución: espacio, comunidad y nacionalidad en Salónica a fines del período otomano y después de él," in *Gender and Identity,* ed. T. Alexander et al. (Beer-Sheva, 2009), 141–154.

50. Minna Rozen, "Strangers in a Strange Land: The Extraterritorial Status of Jews in Italy and the Ottoman Empire in the Sixteenth to Eighteenth Centuries," in *Ottoman and Turkish Jewry,* ed. A. Rodrigue (Bloomington, 1992), 123–166; Eyal Ginio, "Perceiving French Presence in the Levant: French Subjects in the Sicil of 18th Century Ottoman Salonica," *South-East Studies* 65–66 (2006–2007): 137–164; Eyal Ginio, "Jews and European Subjects in Eighteenth-Century Salonica: The Ottoman Perspective," *Jewish History* 28, no. 3–4 (2014): 289–312.

51. David Bunis, "Writing more or less 'Jewishly' in Judezmo and Yiddish," *Journal of Jewish Languages* 1 (2013): 9–75, esp. 70.

52. Minna Rozen, *The Last Ottoman Century and Beyond: The Jews in Turkey and the Balkans, 1808–1945* (Tel Aviv, 2005), 1:168.

53. Matilde Morcillo Rosillo, "La communidad sefardita de Salónica: cuestíon del reconocimiento de la nacionalidad española. Desde el final de las gueras balcánicas hasta la segunda gerra mondial," *Sefárdica* 17 (2008): 47–56. The fate of five hundred Jews who had benefitted from Greek protection while Salonica remained part of the Ottoman Empire is unclear. *La Epoka*, December 27, 1907, quoted in Olga Borovaya, "Ladino Periodical Transcriptions," (http://stanford.edu/dept/jewishstudies/programs/sephardi/borovaya_texts_files/periodicals/Ladino_Periodicals.Transcription.pdf).

54. P. Risal, *La Ville Convoitée: Salonique* (Paris, 1914), 255.

55. "Rejistro de nasensias."

56. Irith Dublon-Knebel, ed., *German Foreign Office Documents on the Holocaust in Greece (1937–1944)* (Tel Aviv, 2007), 298–319.

57. Minna Rozen, *Facing the Sea: The Jews of Salonika in the Ottoman Era 1430–1912* (Afula, 2011), 29–30.

58. İpek Yosmaoğlu, *Blood Ties: Religion, Violence and the Politics of Nationhood in Ottoman Macedonia, 1878–1908* (Ithaca, 2014).

59. *El Liberal*, November 30, 1913.

60. *El Sinistrado*, September 12, 1917.

61. "Regolamento por los servizios del Grand-Rabbinato y particolarmente por el delivramiento de assertationes y certificatos," February 13, 1934, JMTh, f. 16.

62. Meron, "Budgeting in Judeo-Spanish."

63. *La Verdad*, January 2 and 4, 1921.

64. *La Aksion*, January 30, 1930.

65. *La Aksion*, June 3, 1934.

66. *El Mesajero*, January 26 and 27, 1938.

67. *La Aksion*, February 2, 1938.

68. Yomtov Yacoel, "The Memoir of Yomtov Yacoel (1943)," in *The Holocaust in Salonika*, ed. S. Bowman (New York, 2002), 7.

69. Theofano Papazissi, "Family Law of Greek Jews: Transition from Jewish Law to the Greek Civil Code," *Justice: The International Association of Jewish Lawyers and Jurists* (Spring 1999): 22–29.

70. Joseph Nehama, *Histoire des Israélites de Salonique* (Paris/Salonique, 1935–1978), 7:793–794.

71. Karen Barkey, "Aspects of Legal Pluralism in the Ottoman Empire," in *Legal Pluralism and Empires, 1500–1850*, ed. R. Ross and L. Benton (New York, 2013), 83–107.

72. Nehama, *Histoire*, 6:121–126; Michael Molho, *Kontribusion ala istoria de Saloniko* (Salonica, 1931), 17–18.

73. Rodrigue and Stein, eds., *Jewish Voice from Ottoman Salonica*, 94–95.

74. *La Epoka*, June 29 and July 20, 1888.

75. *La Nasion*, October 29, 1909.

76. Clipping of "La ley sovre las komunidades," USHMM, r. 691, d. 145.

77. Minutes of Beth Din, November 7, 1938, USHMM, r. 694, d. 185.

78. List of twenty-two *hazanim*, 1936, USHMM, r. 727, d. 293.

79. Beth Din cases, 1938–1939 (v. 22, p. 24a) and 1938–1940 (v. 23, p. 87b), YIVO, RG-207, ff. 15–16.

80. See registrations of "Seksion de las taksas: raporto del kapo presiado" and "Detalyo de presiado," 1940, USHMM, r. 726, f. 289.

81. Renée Levine Melammed, *Ode to Salonika: The Ladino Verses of Bouena Sarfatty* (Bloomington, 2013), 62–63.

82. *La Epoka*, March 30, 1900.

83. *El Puevlo*, June 6, 1932; Susana Weich-Shahak, *Ventanas Altas de Saloniki: Sephardic Songs, Coplas and Ballads from Thessaloniki* (Haifa, 2013), 36.

84. *El Puevlo*, March 17, 1933.

85. Koretz to the Communal Council, May 27 and June 16, 1938, and reply, July 7, 1938, JMTh, f. 59.

86. *El Puevlo*, March 14, 1932.

87. *El Puevlo*, January 9, 1933.

88. *Jewish Telegraphic Agency*, January 16, 1934.

89. In contrast, 8 percent of marriages in Zagreb from 1928 to 1932 involving a Jewish spouse were intermarriages. And as much as 20 percent of the Jewish population converted to Christianity. Rozen, *Last Ottoman Century*, 1:188, 312.

90. Haim Habib, "La instruksion djudia de muestras ijas," *Israel* (5691): 1.

91. *El Djaketon*, Nisan 30, 5682, 1; Kostas Tomanas, *The Coffee-Houses of Old Thessaloniki* (Skopelos, 1997), 30.

92. Matt Goldish, *Jewish Questions: Responsa on Sephardic Life in the Early Modern Period* (Princeton, 2008), 99–101.

93. Rifat Bali, *A Scapegoat for all Seasons: The Dönmes or Crypto-Jews of Turkey* (Istanbul, 2008); Marc Baer, *The Dönme: Jewish Converts, Muslim Revolutionaries, and Secular Turks* (Stanford, 2010); Rozen, *Facing the Sea*, 27–28.

94. Selim Deringil, *Conversion and Apostasy in the Late Ottoman Empire* (New York, 2012); Leah Bornstein-Makovetsky, "Jewish Converts to Islam and Christianity in the Ottoman Empire in the Nineteenth Century," in *Last Ottoman Century*, ed. Rozen, 2:83–127; Isaac Levy, *Chants Judéo-Espagnols* (London, 1959), 15; Eyal Ginio, "Childhood, Mental Capacity, Conversion to Islam in the Ottoman Empire," *Byzantine and Modern Greek Studies* 25 (2001): 90–119.

95. *La Epoka*, April 3, 1890.

96. Bülent Özdemir, "Political Use of Conversion in the Nineteenth Century

Ottoman Context: Some Cases from Salonica," *Journal of the Study of Religious Identities* 7 (2004): 155–169.

97. Michael Molho to Joseph Nehama, November 20, 1942, FMBTN, 44.2.

98. Beth Din cases, 1920–1931 (v. 12, p. 152, entry 372) and 1932–1934 (v. 17, p. 98, entry 12), YIVO, RG-207, f. 12–13.

99. *El Puevlo*, June 15, 1932.

100. Rabbi Haim Habib and Rafael Menashe to Chief Rabbi Koretz, November 9, 1938, USHMM, r. 691, d. 145.

101. *El Mesajero*, September 10, 1937; *La Aksion*, February 1, 1940, 1. See also: *El Puevlo*, May 10, 1928; *El Mesajero*, December 19, 1935 and June 14, 1938; *La Aksion*, July 25, 1939.

102. *El Mesajero*, May 20, 1938.

103. *El Puevlo*, September 16, 1924.

104. As quoted in *La Aksion*, July 7, 1935.

105. As quoted in *El Mesajero*, January 11, 1938.

106. Declaration signed by Diamante Abolafia, September 20, 1938, USHMM, r. 689, d. 138.

107. Rafael Menashe to the Office of Civil Status of the Jewish Community of Salonica, July 3, 1939, USHMM, r. 689, d. 138. A similar case transpired in Istanbul in 1910: Rozen, *Last Ottoman Century*, 1:103.

108. Rabbi Isaac Brudo to Alberto Rousso, Sivan 19, 5694, USHMM, r. 689, d. 138.

109. Zvi Zohar, *Conversion (Giyyur) in Our Times: A Study in the Halakhic Responsa of Rabbi Uzziel* (Jerusalem, 2012), 35–53 (Hebrew).

110. *El Mesajero*, June 17, 1936; *La Aksion*, June 21, 1936.

111. Beth Din cases, 1938–1939 (v. 22, pp. 88b, 92a, 93a, and 96b), YIVO RG-207, f. 15.

112. Beth Din cases, 1938–1940 (v. 23, p. 91a), YIVO RG-207, f. 16.

113. Melammed, *Ode to Salonika*, 176–177.

114. Alberto Nahmias to Chief Rabbi Koretz, September 20, 1938, USHMM, r. 691, d. 145.

115. *El Puevlo*, July 19, 1932 and June 12, 14, 15, and 20, 1933.

116. *La Aksion*, June 3, 1934; Minna Rozen, "Jews and Greek Remember Their Past: The Political Career of Tzevi Koretz (1933–1943)," *Jewish Social Studies* 12, no. 1 (Fall 2005): 111–166.

117. *La Aksion*, June 21, 1936.

118. *La Aksion*, January 12, 1938.

119. *La Aksion*, January 14 and March 9 and 11, 1938.

120. *La Aksion*, August 22, 1938.

121. *La Aksion*, July 27, 1937; November 23, 1938; February 9 and 10, 1939; *L'Indépendent*, February 16, 1941.

122. Dublon-Knebel, ed., *German Foreign Office Documents*, 74–75.

123. Quoted in David Saffan, "The Fall of Jewish Salonika, 1900–1944," unpublished paper, State University of New York at Old Westbury (1974), 44.

124. Melammed, *Ode to Salonika*, 170–171.

125. *El Puevlo*, February 15, 1932; *El Mesajero*, February 17, 1936.

126. S. Revah, *La Socheta Podrida: Shenas dela vida reala de Saloniko* (Salonica, 1930–1931).

127. Meropi Anastassiadou, *Salonique, 1830–1912: Une ville ottomane à l'âge des Réformes* (New York, 1997); Basil Gounaris, "Salonica," *Review: Fernand Braudel Center* 16 (Fall 1993): 499–518; Vassilis Colonas, "The Contribution of the Jewish Community to the Modernization of Salonika at the End of the Nineteenth Century," in *Last Ottoman Century*, ed. Rozen, 2:165–172.

128. *El Puevlo*, January 22, 1931; Rena Molho, "Jewish Working-Class Neighborhoods Established in Salonika Following the 1890 and 1917 Fires," in *Last Ottoman Century*, ed. Rozen, 2:173–194.

129. Gila Hadar, "Régie Vardar: A Jewish 'Garden City' in Thessaloniki (1917–1943)," lecture at the Seventh International Conference on Urban History: European City in Comparative Perspective, Athens (October 27–30, 2004).

130. Robert Campbell to the Jewish Community of Salonica, November 6, 1932, CAHJP, Gr/Sa 73.

131. Hadar, "Prostitución"; Gila Hadar, "Space and Time in Salonika on the Eve of World War II and the Expulsion and Extermination of Salonika Jewry (1939–1943)," *Yalkut Moreshet* 4 (2006): 42–80.

132. *El Puevlo*, March 18, 1918.

133. Yaacov Handeli, *A Greek Jew from Salonica Remembers* (New York, 1993), 44.

134. Evangelos Hekimoglou, "Jewish Pauperism in Salonika, 1940–1941," in *Last Ottoman Century*, 2:195–205.

135. *El Puevlo*, August 12, 1931.

136. Molho, "Jewish Working-Class Neighborhoods."

137. J[oseph] N[ehama], "Ce qu'était la communauté juive de Salonique à la veille de la catastrophe," in *In Memoriam: Hommage aux Victimes Juives des Nazis en Grèce*, ed. M. Molho (Salonica, 1988 [first edition 1948]), 34.

138. *Statutos dela Socheta de Damas Devora del Kuartier Israelita 151* (Salonica, 1920).

139. *El Puevlo*, March 8, 1921.

140. "Socheta de Damas 'Devora,'" *El Djidio* (5686): 57.

141. *El Puevlo*, July 29, 1931.

142. "Prochesos verbales de la Komision de Instruksion," September 4, 1933, BZI, A1719, v. 5, p. 144.

143. Female residents of the 151 neighborhood to Chief Rabbi Koretz, November 2, 1937, USHMM, r. 692, d. 145.

144. Nina Moshe, Feminist Society for the Rights of Women, Regie, to the Jewish Community of Salonica, June 1, 1936, JMTh, f. 147.

145. David Matalon to the Communal Council, December 10, 1926, CAHJP, Gr/Sa 195.

146. See over one hundred requests for housing, 1927–1928, YIVO, RG-207, ff. 98–100.

147. "Estatutos de la Union de Moradores del Kuartier Hirsch," February 2, 1924, YIVO, RG-207, f. 102.

148. Residents of the Hirsch quarter to the Communal Council, February 5, 1932, YIVO, RG-207, f. 102.

149. In the 1934 elections for the General Assembly of the Jewish Community of Salonica, the Foburgistas received 677 of the 7,083 votes cast, enough to win five of the fifty seats; *La Volunté*, May 28, 1934.

150. Ben Shem, "Los kuartieres populares en perikolo," *El Makabeo* (5682): 22–24.

151. Gabriel Levi, "Manifesto del primo kongreso dela federasion a todos los moradores de los foburgos populares," September 22, 1924, CAHJP, Gr/Sa 74.

152. *La Aksion*, January 9, 1938, 1.

153. Levi, "Manifesto del primo kongreso."

154. Association de moradores del foburgo 151 to Komision de Kuartier 151, November 12, 1926, CAHJP, Gr/Sa 218.

155. Mayor of Salonica to the Jewish Community, August 19, 1925, YIVO, RG-207, f. 84.

156. *La Aksion*, March 2 and 26 and May 30, 1938.

157. Teneke Maale Commission to the Communal Council, February 24, 1939, JMTh, f. 59.

158. Minutes of the Administrative Council of the Jewish Community of Salonica, June 11 and July 2 and 9, 1939, USHMM, r. 691, d. 145.

159. Minutes of the Administrative Council of the Jewish Community of Salonica, July 26, 1939, USHMM, r. 691, d. 145; see also "Programme de la inauguration de la polycatikia fraguada en el quartier Aghia Paraskevy," USHMM, r. 691, d. 145.

160. Translated in Shmuel Refael, "Spain, Greece, or Jerusalem? The Yearning for the Motherland in the Poetry of Greek Jews," in *Homelands and Diasporas: Greeks, Jews and Their Migrations*, ed. M. Rozen (London, 2008), 211–223, esp. 220.

161. Derek Penslar, *Jews and the Military: A History* (Princeton, 2013).

162. Moisis, *Greek-Jewish Patrimony*, 165–176.

163. *La Epoka*, November 25, 1892.

164. Quoted in Aron Rodrigue, *Jews and Muslims: Images of Sephardi and Eastern Jewries in Modern Times* (Seattle, 2003), 237.

165. Mercado Covo, *Los djidios komo soldados a traverso los siekolos* (Salonica, 1911).

166. *El Liberal*, December 12, 1912 and January 20, 1913; Eyal Ginio, "*El Dovér el Mas Sànto*: The Mobilization of the Ottoman Jewish Population during the Balkan

Wars (1912–13)," in *Conflicting Loyalties in the Balkans: The Great Powers, the Ottoman Empire and Nation-Building*, ed. H. Grandits et al. (London, 2011), 157–181.

167. *El Liberal*, October 4, 1915.

168. Entries for Djako Naar and Yosef Salem, December 23 and 24, 1923, CAHJP, Gr/Sa 280.

169. *La Aksion*, May 18, 1937.

170. Statutes of the Jewish Community of Salonica, JMTh, f. 11, art. 108.

171. Yom Tov Saltiel to the Superior Commission of Communal Schools, Tammuz 6, 5682, YIVO, RG-207, f. 135.

172. "Komunikado del gran rabinato," Adar 25, 5675, BZI, Dapim Saloniki/39.

173. *El Puevlo*, June 16, 1933; Nessim Mattatias, president of the Jewish Community of Athens, to the chief rabbi of Salonica, August 23, 1932, USHMM, r. 690, d. 144; Yosef David Florentin to the Communal Council, April 5, 1940, CAHJP, Gr/Sa 165.

174. Letter from Mordehai Yosef Menashe, Moshe Eliaou Koen, Vitalis S. Bendjouïa, and Izhak David to the Rabbinical Council, Adar and Nisan 5681, USHMM, r. 751, d. 107; Commission of Italia Yashan synagogue to the chief rabbinate, c. 1930, JMTh, f. 129; Haim Habib to the Communal Council, Shevet 16, 5692, JMTh, f. 56.

175. *El Puevlo*, September 6, 1932.

176. CAHJP, Gr/Sa 11, 234, 326; Jewish Community to the Minister of Military, June 25, 1933, JMTh, f. 100.

177. Penslar, *Jews and the Military*, 123.

178. *El Puevlo*, October 13, 1932.

179. *Jewish Telegraphic Agency*, June 1, 1938.

180. *El Mesajero*, April 19, 1938.

181. Deklarasion responsavle, Benyamin Presiado, March 9, 1941, USHMM, r. 688, d. 64.

182. Fleming, *Greece*, 106.

183. *La Aksion*, April 20, 1938.

184. Joseph Matarasso, Kefalonia, to the chief rabbi of Salonica, August 20, 1932, USHMM, r. 690, d. 144.

185. I. Florentin et al. to the chief rabbi of Salonica, April 6, 1932, USHMM, r. 690, d. 144.

186. Minutes of the Administrative Council of the Jewish Community of Salonica, September 3, 1939, USHMM, r. 691, d. 145.

187. David Naar to the Jewish Community of Salonica, June 26, 1935, and Union of Veterans and Soldiers of Macedonia to the Jewish Community of Salonica, December 7, 1936, CAHJP, Gr/Sa 119.

188. Flor Nar to the president of the Jewish Community of Salonica, Adar 12, 5700, CAHJP, Gr/Sa 165.

189. Yomtov Saltiel to Samuel Aelion, February 15, 1938, YIVO, RG-207, f. 135.

190. Committee of the Association of Revisionist Zionists to the Communal Council, November 1, 1926, CAHJP, Gr/Sa 74.

191. Juda Saporta to the Communal Council, November 9, 1939, CAHJP, Gr/Sa 165.

192. *El Puevlo*, April 26, 1932; Shabetai David Beraha to the Jewish Community of Salonica, April 9, 1935, CAHJP, Gr/Sa 363.

193. Registration for Izhak Shemuel Nefusi and family in the census of the Jewish Community of Salonica, YIVO, RG-207, f. 1, p. 368 (entry 536); *El Puevlo*, April 9, 1930.

194. Matanoth Laevionim and Adassa, both to the Communal Council, May 14, 1939, YIVO, RG-207, f. 87.

Chapter 2

1. Beki Bardavid and Fani Aelion Ender, *Trezoro Sefaradi: Folklor de la Famiya Djudiya* (Istanbul, 2006), 34.

2. *Jewish Chronicle*, November 18, 1932. On the question of the chief rabbi, see Minna Rozen, "Jews and Greeks Remember Their Past: The Political Career of Tzevi Koretz (1933–1943)," *Jewish Social Studies* 12, no. 1 (Fall 2005): 111–166; Steven Bowman, "Salonikan Memories," in *The Holocaust in Salonika: Eyewitness Accounts* (New York, 2002), 7; Georgios Tousimes, "Ē Elleipsē Archiravvinou stēn Evraikē Koinotēta tēs Thessalonikēs kata to Mesopolemo kai oi Synepeies tēs," ["The Absence of a chief rabbi in the Jewish community of Thessaloniki during the interwar years and its consequences"] *History* 2 (September 1990): 109–120; Maria Vassilikou, "Politics of the Jewish Community of Salonika in the Inter-War Years: Party Ideologies and Party Competition" (PhD Dissertation, University of London, 2000), 91–92, 220–221; Alberto Nar, '*Keimenē epi aktēs Thalassēs . . .*': *Meletes kai arthra gia tēn Evraikē Koinotēta tēs Thessalonikēs* [Studies and articles on the Jewish community of Salonica] (Thessaloniki, 1997), 144–151.

3. M. Allatini, *A Sketch of the State of Primary Education Among the Jews of the East and Especially among the Jews of Salonica*, trans. J. Picciotto (London, 1875), 17.

4. *La Epoka*, May 3 and 24, 1907.

5. Joseph Nehama, *Histoire des Israélites de Salonique* (Paris/Salonique, 1935–1978), 7:637.

6. Ibid., 6:96–107, 7:779; Rena Molho, *"La Jerusalem des Balkans": Salonique, 1856–1919* (Thessaloniki, 2000), 38–40; Daout Levy, "Rapporto sovre la Communidad Djudia de Thessaloniki," JMTh, f. 20.

7. Eyal Ginio, "Coping with Decline: The Political Responses of the Jewish Community to the Eighteenth-Century Crisis in Salonica," in *Political Initiatives 'From the Bottom Up' in the Ottoman Empire*, ed. A. Anastasopoulos (Rethymno, 2012), 69–90.

8. *Hahamhane Nizamnamesi, Estatuto organiko dela komunidad Israelita* (Constantinople, 1913).

9. Avigdor Levy, "*Millet* Politics: The Appointment of a Chief Rabbi in 1835," in *The Jews of the Ottoman Empire* (Princeton, 1994), 425–438; Avigdor Levy, "Introduction," in

The Jews of the Ottoman Empire, ed. A. Levy (Princeton, 1994), 105–108; Minna Rozen, *The Last Ottoman Century and Beyond: The Jews in Turkey and the Balkans, 1808–1945* (Tel Aviv, 2005), 1:77–130; Esther Benbassa, *Haim Nahum: A Sephardic Chief Rabbi in Politics, 1892–1923* (Tuscaloosa, 1995).

10. Canan Seyfeli, "Osmali Devlet Salnamelerinde Hahambasilik (1847–1918)," *Milel ve Nihal* 7, no. 1 (2010): 95–136.

11. Isaac Emmanuel, "Toldot Yehudei Saloniki," in *Zikhron Saloniki: Gedulata ve-hurbana shel Yerushalayim de-Balkan*, ed. D. Recanati (Tel Aviv, 1972–1985), 1:148.

12. *La Epoka*, September 2, 1887, December 30, 1887, and January 6, 1888.

13. *La Epoka*, September 2, 1887.

14. *La Epoka*, January 13 and 20, 1888.

15. *La Epoka*, November 4, 1887.

16. *La Epoka*, April 12, 1907.

17. *La Epoka*, November 18 and 25, 1887. On the curses, see Emmanuel, "Toldot Yehudei Saloniki," 1:149; Aron Rodrigue and Sarah Stein, eds., *A Jewish Voice from Ottoman Salonica: The Ladino Memoir of Sa'adi Besalel a-Levi* (Stanford, 2012), 10–11.

18. *La Epoka*, January 13, 1888.

19. Nehama, *Histoire*, 7:650.

20. Emmanuel, "Toldot Yehudei Saloniki," 1:174–175; Nehama, *Histoire*, 7:639–640, 736–737.

21. Paula Daccarett, "Jewish Social Services in Late Ottoman Salonica (1850–1912)" (PhD Dissertation, Brandeis University, 2008).

22. *La Epoka*, April 12, 1907.

23. Ibid.; *El Tiempo*, April 15 and 18, 1907.

24. Nehama, *Histoire*, 7:697; Emmanuel, "Toldot Yehudei Saloniki," 1:161–193.

25. *El Tiempo*, May 30, 1907.

26. *La Epoka*, May 3, 1907; *El Tiempo*, May 7, 1907.

27. *El Tiempo*, April 26, 1907.

28. *El Tiempo*, May 3, 1907.

29. *El Tiempo*, May 7, 1907; *La Epoka*, May 17, 1907.

30. *El Tiempo*, May 14 and 23, 1907; *La Epoka*, May 17 and October 18, 1907.

31. *La Epoka*, May 24, 1907; *El Tiempo*, May 17, 1907.

32. On this controversy, see Bedross Der Matossian, "The Young Turk Revolution: Its Impact on Religious Politics in Jerusalem (1908–1912)," *Jerusalem Quarterly* 40 (Winter 2009–2010): 18–33.

33. David Ashkenazi, "Mi Yerushalaiam le-Saloniki ve-Hazara: ha-Minhiguto shel ha-Rav Ya'akov Me'ir, Haham Bashi be-Yerushalaiam ve-Rav Rashi be-Saloniki" (PhD Dissertation, Bar Ilan University, 2008).

34. *El Avenir*, quoted in *El Tiempo*, May 30, 1907.

35. *La Epoka*, April 10, 1911.

36. *La Epoka*, May 11, 1907.

37. *El Tiempo*, June 21 and 25, 1907.

38. *El Tiempo*, October 11 and 25, 1907.

39. *El Tiempo*, November 1, 1907.

40. *El Tiempo*, December 13 and 20, 1907.

41. Ibid.; *El Tiempo*, January 17, 21, and 24, 1908; *La Epoka*, January 24, 1908.

42. *La Epoka*, January 21, 1908.

43. La Epoka, Adar 2, 1908; *El Tiempo*, February 4 and 7, 1908.

44. La Epoka, Adar 2, 1908; *El Tiempo*, February 4, 1908.

45. *El Tiempo*, January 10, 1908.

46. *Jewish Chronicle*, September 4, 1908.

47. *La Epoka*, August 8, 1908.

48. Benbassa, *Haim Nahum*; Yaron Harel, "'Save the Museum': Rabbi Chaim Soloveitchik and the question of the Chief Rabbinate in the Ottoman Empire," *Journal of Jewish Studies* 66, no. 2 (Autumn 2015): 360–386.

49. *La Bos*, January 11, 1909.

50. Ibid.

51. As evidenced by the correspondence from Salonica as preserved in the archive of the *haham bashi* of Istanbul located at CAHJP. Stationery printed during the tenure of Meir's predecessor, Jacob Covo, as *haham bashi* did not include reference to "City and Mother in Israel."

52. *El Puevlo*, June 1 and September 3, 1919.

53. *La Aksion*, November 25, 1935.

54. *La Liberasion de Saloniko: La Aliansa balkanika kontra la Turkia. La entrade de la armada grega. Los deportos entre gregos i djidios* (Salonica, 1931).

55. *El Mesajero*, June 8, 1939.

56. Mark Mazower, *Salonica, City of Ghosts: Christians, Muslims, and Jews, 1430–1950* (London, 2004), 309–311.

57. See the headlines in *El Liberal*, September–November, 1920; *La Vara* (Salonica), November 17, 1922.

58. Sam Hassid, "Further on the 1920 Elections," *Newsletter of the Jewish Museum of Athens* 4 (Autumn–Winter 1996): 5–7; Dimosthenis Dodos, *Oi Evraioi tis Thessalonikis stis Ekloges tou Ellinikou Kratous, 1915–1936* [The Jews of Thessaloniki in the Greek State Elections, 1915–1936] (Athens, 2005).

59. *El Puevlo*, September 29, 1919.

60. *El Puevlo*, November 2 and 3, 1919.

61. *El Puevlo*, December 12, 1919.

62. *El Puevlo*, August 26 and 27, 1919.

63. *El Puevlo*, November 1, 1919.

64. *El Liberal*, March 25, 1920.

65. Catalogue, August 25, 1920, JMTh, f. 127; *El Puevlo*, December 15, 1924.

66. *El Puevlo*, December 12, 1919.

67. "Prochesos verbales dela komision superiora de instruksion Talmud Tora," November 6, 1917, CAHJP, Gr/Sa 8, p. 9.

68. *El Puevlo*, July 7, 1919 and October 30, 1919.

69. *El Puevlo*, November 6, 1922.

70. *El Puevlo*, December 10, 1919.

71. The newspaper recommended Jacob Maze, a rabbi in Moscow; *El Liberal*, May 26, 1919.

72. *El Puevlo*, December 10, 1919.

73. *El Puevlo*, June 23, 1923.

74. *El Puevlo*, December 10, 1919.

75. *El Puevlo*, July 9, 1923.

76. Victor Schonfeld, a Hungarian-born, University of Vienna-educated rabbi in London, was eliminated before the vote; *El Puevlo*, October 6, December 3, and December 5, 1920.

77. *El Liberal* first referred to Uziel as Meir's appointed successor on January 30, 1919.

78. *El Puevlo*, December 5, 1920.

79. *El Chaketon*, Tevet 6, 5681.

80. *El Puevlo*, January 13, 1921.

81. *El Puevlo*, January 16, 1921.

82. *El Puevlo*, March 6, 1921.

83. *La Verdad*, February 28, 1921.

84. Marc Angel, *Loving Truth & Peace: The Grand Religious Worldview of Rabbi Benzion Uziel* (New Jersey, 1999), 81–82.

85. Chabetaï Don-Yihye, *Bension Meir Hay Ouziel: Vie et Oeuvre d'un Gran Rabbin d'Israel* (Jerusalem, 1974), 34–41; Yitzchak Kerem, "Harav Uziel ka-rav rashi shel Saloniki ve-kesherav im ha-kehila lahar mihen," in *Rabbi Uzziel and His Peer: Studies in the Religious Thought of Oriental Rabbis in 20th Century Israel* , ed. Z. Zohar (Jerusalem, 2009), 166–189.

86. *La Verdad*, March 28, 1921.

87. Bension Uziel, "Un apelo del gran rabino por el shabat," Tevet 19, 5682, CAHJP, Gr/Sa 74; *El Puevlo*, January 20, 1922.

88. "Prochesos verbales dela komision superiora de instruksion Talmud Tora," January 21, 1921 (p. 112) and Tammuz 29, 5682 (p. 189), CAHJP, Gr/Sa 8; Bension Uziel to the Communal Council and General Assembly, March 16, 1923, CAHJP, Gr/Sa 74; *La Aksion*, July 12, 1939.

89. Asher Simha, Agudat Hahamim, to the Communal Council, Av 4, 5683, CAHJP, Gr/Sa 74.

90. Bension Uziel to the Communal Council, with attached letter from the Jewish Community of Yafo and Tel Aviv, Nisan 23, 5683, CAHJP, Gr/Sa 74.

91. *El Puevlo*, March 18, 1923.

92. *El Puevlo*, May 3, 10, and 14, 1923.

93. *El Puevlo*, June 5, 8, and 20, 1923.

94. *El Puevlo*, May 13 and 24, 1923.

95. *El Puevlo*, May 18, 1923; *Jewish Chronicle*, May 4, 1923.

96. *El Puevlo*, July 17, 1923.

97. *Jewish Chronicle*, September 7, 1923.

98. *El Puevlo*, July 8, 1923.

99. *El Puevlo*, March 4, 1925; resignation letter from Emanuel Isaac Brudo to Communal Council, Sivan 26, 5684, CAHJP, Gr/Sa 74; *El Puevlo*, December 22, 1925; *El Djidio* (Tishre, 5687): 13–14.

100. *El Puevlo*, September 1, 1926.

101. Ehrenpreis, Stockholm, to Alberto [Pipano], September 14, 1925, BZI, Osef Amarilio, f. 180, doc. 4; *El Puevlo*, October 15, 1925.

102. *El Puevlo*, October 18 and December 23, 1925.

103. *El Puevlo*, October 15 and November 2, 1925.

104. *El Puevlo*, January 24, 1926.

105. Ehrenpreis, Stockholm, to Alberto [Pipano], September 14, 1925, and Ehrenrpeis to Jewish Community of Salonica, October 23 1925, BZI, Osef Amarilio, f. 180.

106. *El Puevlo*, December 18, 1925.

107. *El Puevlo*, December 30, 1925.

108. *El Puevlo*, December 27, 1925; Nouveau Club Sioniste to the Communal Council, Tevet 8, 5686; Bensanchi, Fédération Sioniste de Grèce, to the Communal Council, December 25, 1925, CAHJP, Gr/Sa 74.

109. *El Puevlo*, March 26, 1926.

110. *El Puevlo*, January 24, 1926.

111. Ehrenpreis to the Communal Council of Salonica, January 20, 1926, BZI, Osef Amarilio, f. 180.

112. *El Puevlo*, February 16, 1926.

113. *El Puevlo*, February 23, 1926.

114. *La Renasensia Djudia*, January 28, 1927.

115. *El Puevlo*, January 24, 1927.

116. Saül Mézan, *Les Juifs Espagnols en Bulgarie* (Sofia, 1925), 21.

117. *El Puevlo*, March 29, 1926; September 26 and 29, 1930.

118. *El Puevlo*, March 9, 1926.

119. *El Puevlo*, February 28, 1926 and September 29, 1930.

120. Mézan, *Les Juifs Espagnols en Bulgarie*, 150. Notably, the chief rabbi of Emanuel Isaac had been the Salonican rabbi, David Pipano (1920–1924).

121. *El Puevlo*, March 9, 1926.

122. *El Puevlo*, March 29, 1926.

123. Marcus Ehrenpreis, *Ben Mizrah le-Ma'arav* (Tel Aviv, 1953), 171–172.

124. N. M. Gelber, "An Attempt to Internationalize Salonika," *Jewish Social Studies* 17 (1955): 105–120.

125. Tousimes, "Ēlleipsē," 109–120.

126. *El Puevlo*, August 20 and 31, 1926.

127. *El Puevlo*, July 21, 1927. Haim A. Toledano, "Harbi Haim Habib zts"l," *Zikhron Saloniki: Gedulata ve-hurbana shel Yerushalayim de-Balkan*, ed. D. Recanati (Tel Aviv, 1972–1985), 2:462–463 (Hebrew); I. Matarasso, "Harbi Haim Habib," *Chronika* 70 (September 1984): 68–69 (Greek); David Benveniste, "R[abbi] Haim Habib the Last Rabbi of Salonica," in *Leket: Collected Essays on the Heritage of Oriental Jewry* (Jerusalem, 1990), 63–67 (Hebrew).

128. Marcus Ehrenpreis, *The Soul of the East: Experiences and Reflections* (New York, 1928), 46–47.

129. Quoted in Vassilikou, "Politics," 247.

130. *El Puevlo*, June 23, 1927.

131. See Aelion's contract with the Jewish Community of Salonica, December 11, 1928; Aelion to the Communal Council, August 30, 1932; Vitalis Stroumza, Rhodes, to the Jewish Community of Salonica, October 23, 1933; and "Rapporto," October 17, 1934, CAHJP, Gr/Sa 243.

132. Yitzchak Moshe Emanuel, *Eretz Israel Kor ha-Chetuch* (Holon, 1988), 240–256.

133. Isaac S. Emmanuel, "Zikhronot yeledot ve-bahorot," in *Avraham Ha-Ivri: Kovets mukdash lamanhig vehalohem Avraham S. Rekanati* (Tel Aviv, 1958), 16–18.

134. Emmanuel to Recanati, February 20, 1967, IEA.

135. *El Puevlo*, March 9, 1925.

136. Isaac S. Emmanuel, "Kuestiones Komunalas. Nuestros seminarios," *El Djidio* (5688): 33–34.

137. Ibid., 34.

138. *L'Indépendant*, September 12 and 17, 1926.

139. Press Office of Thessaloniki to the GMFA, Athens, September 14, 1926, USHMM, GMFA, r. 1.

140. Emmanuel, Lausanne, to the Communal Council, February 3, 1928, CAHJP, Gr/Sa 333.

141. Emmanuel, Lausanne, to the Communal Council, April 29, 1927 and February 3 and 26, 1928, CAHJP, Gr/Sa 333.

142. Emmanuel, Breslau, to the Communal Council, October 23, 1927, CAHJP, Gr/Sa 333; *El Puevlo*, May 8, 1929.

143. *La Verdad*, June 28, 1929; *El Puevlo*, July 1, 1929; *Le Progrès*, July 2, 1929.

144. Emmanuel to Abraham Recanati, March 13, 1967 and Emmanuel to his attorney, Dr. Lerner, November 1, 1971, IEA.

145. Emmanuel, Lausanne, to David de Sola Pool, New York, November 5, 1928, AUSC.

146. De Sola Pool to Buena Blok, April 8, 1929, AUSC.

147. Buena Blok, London, to de Sola Pool, August 18, 1929, AUSC.

148. *El Puevlo*, June 26, 1929.

149. *El Puevlo*, November 7, 1929.

150. *El Puevlo*, December 26, 1929.

151. *El Puevlo*, July 14, 1930.

152. Press Office, Salonica, to GMFA, Athens, July 2, 1930; Ministry of Education and Religion to GMFA, August 13, 1930, USHMM, GMFA, r. 1.

153. Izak Yakov Alsheh, "Raporto sovre la mision de gran rabino," August 31, 1930, YIVO, RG-207, f. 18.

154. David Florentin first mentioned Herzog as a candidate in *El Puevlo*, October 18, 1923; Bracha Rivlin, ed., *Pinkas HaKehillot: Encyclopedia of Jewish Communities from their Foundation till after the Holocaust—Greece* (Jerusalem, 1998), 245; Steven Bowman, *The Agony of Greek Jews* (Stanford, 2009), 295 n. 5.

155. Alsheh, "Raporto sovre la mision de gran rabino."

156. Ibid.

157. The Communal Council, Salonica, to Herzog, Dublin, June 22, June 26, and November 17, 1931; Herzog to the Communal Council, October 15, 1931; the Communal Council, Salonica, to Dr. J. M. Hertz, London, October 12, 1931, CAHJP, Gr/Sa 70.

158. *El Puevlo*, September 26 and 29, 1930.

159. *El Puevlo*, October 9, 1930.

160. Herzog to the Jewish Community of Salonica, September 8, 1932, CAHJP, Gr/Sa 70.

161. *El Puevlo*, December 13, 1932.

162. *El Puevlo*, November 15, 1932.

163. *El Puevlo*, July 27, 1932.

164. A. S. Yahuda, London, to the Jewish Community of Salonica, June 6, 1932, CAHJP, Gr/Sa 70.

165. *El Puevlo*, November 8, 1932.

166. Koretz, Berlin, to the president of the Jewish Community, Salonica, n. d. [1932], CAHJP, Gr/Sa 70.

167. Transcript of interview by Joseph Ben with Gita Koretz, July 22, 1976, Yad Vashem Archive, Jerusalem, f. 3527/304.

168. *El Puevlo*, January 20, 1933.

169. *El Puevlo*, December 18, 1932.

170. *El Puevlo*, December 28, 1932.

171. *El Puevlo*, December 13, 1932.

172. *El Puevlo*, December 18, 1932.

173. *El Puevlo*, December 21, 1932.

174. *El Puevlo*, December 15, 1932 and February 15, 1933.

175. *El Puevlo*, February 14, 1933.

176. *El Puevlo*, February 19, 1933.

177. *El Puevlo*, February 26, 1933.

178. *El Puevlo*, March 1 and 2, 1933.

179. *El Puevlo*, March 13, 1933.

180. *El Puevlo*, May 22, 1933.

181. Macedonia General Direction to GMFA, February 14, 1933 and March 10, 1933; GMFA to Macedonia General Direction, May 3, 1933, USHMM, GMFA, r. 2.

182. Greek Embassy, Berlin, to GMFA, Athens, March 11, 1933, USHMM, GMFA, r. 2.

183. *El Puevlo*, March 30, 1933.

184. Simcha Zaiden, "Harav Dr. Tzvi Koretz," in *Kehilat Rzeszow: Sefer Zikaron* (Tel Aviv, 1967), 1:275.

185. "Lista del personnel ordinario de la Communita," June 29, 1934, JMTh, f. 47.

186. Rozen, "Jews and Greeks Remember Their Past."

187. René Levine Melammed, *An Ode to Jewish Salonika: The Ladino Verses of Bouena Sarfatty* (Bloomington, 2013), 232–233.

188. JMTh, ff. 30–31.

189. Communal Council, Processo-verbal no. 51, August 6, 1939, USHMM, r. 691, d. 145.

190. Report on Konstantinopel, Sofia, and Saloniki by M. Ussishkin, Bucarest, to Bernard Kahn, Paris, January 1938, American Joint Reconstruction Foundation, YIVO, RG-335.2, b. 19, f. 185A.

191. "Gastes por embiar lulavim, etrogim, i adas de diversas sivdades de Polonia," September 24, 1940, CAHJP, Gr/Sa 290.

192. *La Aksion*, June 28, 1936.

193. "Le ténor Albert Rousso," *Le Judaisme Sepharadi* 4, no. 25 (1935): 14.

194. *La Aksion*, June 28, 1936.

195. Ibid.

196. See Fourth of August Regime celebratory materials, 1938–1939, JMTh, f. 99.

197. As reported in *La Aksion*, June 28, 1936.

198. *El Mesajero*, June 15, 1936.

199. Andrew Apostolou, "Strategies of Evasion: Avoiding the Issue of Collaboration and Indifference during the Holocaust in Greece," in *Collaboration with the Nazis: Public Discourse after the Holocaust*, ed. R. Stauber (London, 2010), 138–165, esp. 144.

200. Melammed, *Ode to Jewish Salonika*, 234–235.

201. Interview with Salvatore and Lili Katan, August 18, 1981, Voice/Vision Holocaust Survivor Oral History Archive, University of Michigan-Dearborn (http://holocaust.umd.umich.edu/).

202. Rozen, "Jews and Greeks Remember Their Past"; also see Apostolou, "Strategies of evasion."

203. Rabbinical Association of Switzerland, St. Gallen, to Minister of Greek Delegation, Bern, March 3, 1945, USHMM, RG45.003, f. 18.

204. *Homenaje a Don Michael Molho ofrecido por un núcleo de amigos y simpatizantes* (Buenos Aires, 1961), 11, 28–31.

205. Emmanuel, "Toldot Yehudei Saloniki," 1:261–264.

206. Central Board of the Jewish Communities of Greece, Athens, to Emmanuel, Panama City, March 22, 1949, and reply, April 25, 1949, IEA.

207. Emmanuel, "Toldot Yehudei Saloniki," 1:227–229.

208. Recanati, Tel Aviv, to Emmanuel, Nisan 13, 5724, IEA.

209. Emmanuel, "Toldot Yehudei Saloniki," 1:227–229.

210. *La Aksion*, June 21, 1938.

211. *Jewish Telegraphic Agency*, November 14, 1941.

212. *Palestine Post*, January 11, 1940.

213. He referred to Josiau Pardo; Emmanuel, Curaçao, to de Sola Pool, New York, June 28, 1936, AUSC.

214. *El Mesajero*, April 6, 1941.

215. *La Epoka*, June 14, 1907.

Chapter 3

1. Mathila Koén Sarano, *Kurso de Djudeo-Espanyol (Ladino) para Adelantados* (The Negev, 1999), 68.

2. *Rekontos morales seguidos de una chika instruksion relidjioza. Livro de lektura a uzo de las eskolas del Oriente* (Salonica, 1880), 6.

3. Ipek Yosmaoğlu, *Blood Ties: Religion, Violence and the Politics of Nationhood in Ottoman Macedonia, 1878–1908* (Ithaca, 2014).

4. Selçuk Akşin Somel, *The Modernization of Public Education in the Ottoman Empire, 1839–1908: Islamization, Autocracy, and Discipline* (Boston, 2001); Benjamin Fortna, *Imperial Classroom: Islam, the State, and Education in the Late Ottoman Empire* (Oxford, 2002); Emine Evered, *Empire and Education Under the Ottomans: Politics, Reform and Resistance from the Tanzimat to the Young Turks* (New York, 2013).

5. Evie Zambetta, "Religion and National Identity in Greek Education," *Intercultural Education* 11, no. 2 (2000): 145–155.

6. Peter Mackridge, *Language and National Identity in Greece, 1766–1976* (New York, 2009).

7. The Direction of the Thessaloniki Press Bureau to the General Governance of Thessaloniki, December 16, 1926, as translated in *Documents on the History of the Greek Jews: Records from the Historical Archives of the Ministry of Foreign Affairs*, ed. P. Constantopoulou and T. Veremis (Athens 1999), 122.

8. Eyal Ginio, "'Learning the Beautiful Language of Homer': Judeo-Spanish Speaking Jews and the Greek Language and Culture between the Wars," *Jewish History* 16 (2002): 235–262.

9. *Statutos del Orfelinato de Ijas Mair Aboav fondado el 11 Iyar 5683* (Salonica, 1926). From five girls in 1924, the orphanage cared for forty-five in 1939, ages six to sixteen. While the orphanage initially taught the girls in house, by the late 1930s they were sent to public school and then to a factory to learn to sew. Saltiel Koen, Aboav Orphanage, to the Communal Council, May 12, 1939, YIVO, RG-207, f. 87.

10. *La Aksion*, July 15, 1938.

11. Yitzchak Kerem, "The Talmud Tora of Salonika: a Multi-faceted Changing Institution from 16th Century Traditionalism until Modern Political Zionism," in *The Heritage of the Jews of Spain*, ed. A. Doron (Tel Aviv, 1994), 159–168; Rena Molho, "Education in the Jewish Community of Thessaloniki in the Beginning of the Twentieth Century," *Balkan Studies* 34, no. 2 (1993): 259–269.

12. Aron Rodrigue and Sarah Stein, eds., *A Jewish Voice from Ottoman Salonica: The Ladino Memoir of Sa'adi Besalel a-Levi* (Stanford, 2012), 35–37; Fortna, *Imperial Classroom*, 15.

13. Cengiz Sisman, "Failed Proselytizers or Modernizers? Protestant Missionaries Among the Jews and Sabbateans/Dönmes in the Nineteenth Century Ottoman Empire," *Middle East Studies* 51, no. 6 (2015): 932–949; Hans-Lukas Kieser, *Nearest East: American Millennialism and the Mission to the Middle East* (Philadelphia, 2010).

14. *Autobiography of William G. Schauffler, for forty-nine years a missionary in the Orient* (New York, 1887).

15. Rodrigue and Stein, eds., *Jewish Voice from Ottoman Salonica*, 38.

16. "Mission to the Jews," in *Report on the American Board of Commissioners for Foreign Missions* (Boston, 1850), 98.

17. Rachel Wolfe, "From Protestant Missionaries to Jewish Educators: Children's Textbooks in Judeo-Spanish," *Neue Romania* 40 (2011): 135–151.

18. As recalled by teacher Gracia Salem to the Communal Council, November 30, 1937, YIVO, RG-207, f. 125.

19. "Sultan Abdul Majid's Islahat Fermani Decree Reaffirms the Privileges and Immunities of Non-Muslim Communities in the Ottoman Empire, February 18, 1856," in *Sources in the History of the Modern Middle East*, ed. Akram Khater (Boston, 2004), 14–18.

20. Evered, *Empire and Education*.

21. Julia Phillips Cohen, *Becoming Ottomans: Sephardi Jews and Imperial Citizenship in the Modern Era* (New York, 2014).

22. Evangelia Balta and Mehmet Ölmez, *Between Religion and Language: Turkish-Speaking Christians, Jews and Greek-Speaking Muslims and Catholics in the Ottoman Empire* (Istanbul, 2011); Johann Straus, "Who Read What in the Ottoman Empire (19th–20th Centuries)?" *Middle Eastern Literatures* 6, no. 4 (January 2003): 39–76.

23. "The Ottoman Chief Rabbi Urges His Coreligionists to Learn Turkish (1840)," in *Sephardi Lives: A Documentary History,* ed. J. P. Cohen and S. A. Stein (Stanford, 2014), 185.

24. Sarah Abrevaya Stein, *Making Jews Modern: The Yiddish and Ladino Press in the Russian and Ottoman Empire* (Bloomington, 2004).

25. *La Epoka,* December 6, 1895.

26. *La Epoka,* March 2, 1900.

27. *El Avenir,* March 14, 1900.

28. Isaac Yeoshua, *Nosiones Sumarias de la Estorya del Imperio Otomano: Lisyones i Refleksiones: Kompozado partikularmente para los elevos de las eskolas djudias* (Salonica, 1902).

29. Attempts to introduce more Turkish into Greek Christian schools met resistance on the grounds that it violated privileges and immunities guaranteed to them by the 1856 reform decree. Vangelis Kechriotis, "The Modernization of the Empire and the Community 'Privileges': Greek Orthodox Responses to the Young Turk Policies," in *The State and the Sublatern: Modernization: Society and State in Turkey and Iran,* ed. T. Atabaki (New York, 2007), 53–70.

30. Moise Allatini, *A Sketch of the State of Primary Education Among the Jews of the East and Especially among the Jews of Salonica,* trans. J. Picciotto (London, 1875).

31. Aron Rodrigue, *French Jews, Turkish Jews: The Alliance Israélite Universelle and the Politics of Jewish Schooling in Turkey, 1860–1925* (Bloomington, 1990); Molho, "Education," 259–269.

32. Moize Alatini, *Las Instituciones Izraelitas en Saloniko* (Salonica, 1880–1881).

33. Cercle des Intimes, *Opinion i dezeo sovre la ovra de membrasion aparejada en onor del Doktor Moize Alatini* (Salonica, 5643).

34. *El Liberal,* December 25, 1913; January 2 and 6, 1914.

35. *La Epoka,* September 27, 1895.

36. Sarah Abrevaya Stein, "The Permeable Boundaries of Ottoman Jewry," in *Boundaries and Belonging: States and Societies in the Struggle to Shape Identities and Local Practices,* ed. J. S. Migdal (London, 2004), 49–70.

37. Esther Benbassa, "Questioning Historical Narratives—The Case of Balkan Sephardi Jewry," *Jahrbuch des Simon-Dubnow-Instituts* 2 (2003): 15–22.

38. Rodrigue, *French Jews, Turkish Jews,* 87.

39. *El Avenir,* October 21, 1900.

40. The others were Daniel Saporta, Abraham Burla, Isaac Faraggi, and Leon Salem. *El Mesajero,* May 11, 1938.

41. "Ambivalent Recollections of a Jewish Border in an Ottoman Imperial High School [1880s]," in *Sephardi Lives,* ed. Cohen and Stein, 74–75.

42. *El Liberal,* February 26, 1913.

43. "Liste de adherents," *Association des anciens élèves de l'Alliance israélite universelle—*

Salonique: bulletin annuel 14 (1910): 80–85; "Liste de adherentes," *Association des anciennes élèves de l'Alliance israélite universelle—Salonique: bulletin annuel* 1 (1909–1910): 12–13.

44. Abraham Recanati, *Ke es el Sionismo Mizrahi? Konferensia organizada por la sudjeta Mizrahi i echa por el Se. Avraam Shemuel Rekanati en el Midrash Karaso el 4 Shevat 5680* (Salonica, 5680), 27–28.

45. *El Avenir*, December 19, 1900; "Prof. Rabbino Maggiore Mosè Ottolenghi," *Il Corriere Israelitico* 39, no. 8 (1900): 185–186.

46. Joseph Nehama, Salonica, to the Alliance, Paris, January 9, 1903, AIU, r. 14.

47. *La Epoka*, June 18, 1891.

48. *La Epoka*, March 8, 1893.

49. *La Epoka*, April 7, 1905.

50. Paula Daccarett, "Jewish Social Services in Late Ottoman Salonica (1850–1912)" (PhD Dissertation, Brandeis University, 2008), 56–57.

51. Ibid., 68.

52. *La Epoka*, April 4, 1890.

53. *La Epoka*, October 2, 1895.

54. *El Avenir*, April 11, 1900.

55. *El Avenir*, August 29, 1900.

56. *La Epoka*, August 31, 1900.

57. *El Avenir*, September 5, 1900; *La Epoka*, September 7, 1900.

58. Michael Molho, *Traditions and Customs of the Sephardic Jews of Salonica*, trans. A. Zara and ed. R. Bedford (New York, 2006), 114–115; Elias Messinas, *The Synagogues of Salonika and Veroia* (Athens, 1997), 76–79.

59. *El Avenir*, December 14, 1904; Daccarett, "Jewish Social Services."

60. Daccarett, "Jewish Social Services."

61. *El Avenir*, March 20, 1904.

62. Daniel Saïas, "Yitzhak Epstein," *Israel* 4 (5692): 7–8.

63. *La Epoka*, January 1, 1906.

64. *El Liberal*, December 23, 1913; *Avanti*, October 31, 1913.

65. *El Liberal*, September 25, 1912.

66. *El Liberal*, January 15, 1914; Cheskel Zwi Klötzel, *In Saloniki: Schriften des Ausschusses für jüdische Kulturarbeit* (Berlin, 1920), 49, 70–83; Eli Bar-Chen, with comment by Aron Rodrigue, "Two Communities with a Sense of Mission: The Alliance Israélite Universelle and the Hilfsverein der deutschen Juden," in *Jewish Emancipation Reconsidered*, ed. M. Brenner et al. (London, 2003), 111–128.

67. Moshe Attias gained recognition for his work on Judeo-Spanish folklore, David Benvenisti became a well-known geographer and educator, and Baruch Uziel became a prominent lawyer and recruited Salonican stevedores for the port of Haifa. *La Aksion*, June 25, 1939.

68. These teachers included Daniel Saïas, Eliau Stroumsa, Samuel I. Saltiel, Eliau

Barzilai (who became the chief rabbi of Athens), and Joseph and Simon Pessah (the sons of the chief rabbi of Volos).

69. "Law 2456 Concerning Jewish Communities," in *Documents on the History of the Greek Jews*, ed. Constantopoulou and Veremis, 103–110.

70. *El Liberal*, November 1, 1912.

71. "Prochesos verbales dela komision superiora de instruksion," October 10, 1918, CAHJP, Gr/Sa 8, p. 47. This notebook contains the minutes of the Superior Commission for Jewish Instruction from 1917 until 1921. The Ben Zvi Institute in Jerusalem holds the subsequent minutes from 1922 to 1934, cited below, in the Amariglio Collection, 1719: v. 1, 1922–1927; v. 2, 1927–1928; v. 3, 1929–1930; v. 4, 1931–1932; v. 5, 1932–1934.

72. "Prochesos verbales dela komision superiora de instruksion Talmud Tora," October 10 and 26, 1918, and February 5, March 11, April 7 and 30, 1919, CAHJP, Gr/Sa 8, pp. 47, 50, 59, 62–63, 65–68.

73. Protest of residents of the Regie Quarter to the Communal Council, November 18, 1922, CAHJP, Gr/Sa 74.

74. Based on a survey of 497 birth certificates registered, 1934–1935, 1938–1939, 1939–1940, YIVO, RG-207, ff. 8–10.

75. "Prochesos verbales dela komision superiora de instruksion," February 15/28 and 22, 1922; March 3/16, 1922; April 26, 1922, CAHJP, Gr/Sa 8, pp. 162, 167, 168, and 176.

76. "Prochesos verbales dela komision superiora de instruksion," November 11, 1924 and February 2, 1925, BZI 1719, 1:54, 69–70.

77. Yom Tov Saltiel to the Superior Commission of Communal Schools, August 27, 1923, YIVO, RG-207, f. 135.

78. To the Communal Council, June 1, 1924, CAHJP, Gr/Sa 74.

79. Asher Simha, Commission for the rebuilding of Talmud Tora, to the Communal Council, January 5, 1925, CAHJP, Gr/Sa 74.

80. See the extensive correspondence and architectural plans regarding this school, CAHJP, Gr/Sa 186–188.

81. *El Puevlo*, January 1, 1932.

82. Statistics compiled from reports to the Superior Commission for Jewish Instruction, December 1928, JMTh, f. 138.

83. Esther Benbassa and Aron Rodrigue, *Sephardi Jewry: A History of the Judeo-Spanish Community, 14th–20th Centuries* (Berkeley, 2000), 100.

84. "Prochesos verbales dela komision superiora de instruksion Talmud Tora," August 23, 1922, CAHJP, Gr/Sa 8, p. 195.

85. Yom Tov Saltiel to the Superior Commission of Communal Schools, August 27, 1923, YIVO, RG-207, f. 135.

86. "Prochesos verbales dela komision superiora de instruksion," April 17, 1928, BZI 1719, 2:64; December 9, 1930, BZI 1719, 3:195; December 31, 1931, BZI 1719, 4:40;, January 8, 1932, BZI 1719, 4:42; November 7, 1933, BZI 1719, 5:150.

87. *El Puevlo*, March 16, 1931.

88. Stefanos Katsikas, "Hostage Minority: The Muslims of Greece (1923–41), in *State-Nationalisms in the Ottoman Empire, Greece and Turkey: Orthodox and Muslims (1830–1945)*, ed. B. Fortna et al. (New York, 2012), 160.

89. The director of the Thessaloniki Press Bureau to the Ministry of Foreign Affairs, September 26, 1926, as translated in *Documents on the History of the Greek Jews*, ed. Constantopoulou and Veremis, 113.

90. "Nécrologie: Jacques Kohen," *Hamenora: Organe périodique des Béné Bérith du District d'Orient* (January-February-March 1933): 30–33; Michael Molho, *Matsevot bet ha'almin shel yehudei Saloniki* (Tel Aviv, 1974), 630.

91. "Oeuvre d'éducation sociale: Fondation Béné Bérith," March 15, 1925, AIU, Grèce IIC 54.2; cf. Béné Bérith to the Communal Council, July 6, 1925, CAHJP, Gr/Sa 343.

92. Béné Bérith to the Communal Council, September 8, 1924, CAHJP, Gr/Sa 343.

93. Sidney O'Donague to the Secretary of State, "The Anti-Semitic Movement in Saloniki," December 19, 1923, NARA, RG84, v. 113, doc. 840.1/3217.

94. *El Puevlo*, December 21 and 23, 1923.

95. *Evraïkon Vēma tēs Ellados*, April 8, 1925, 1.

96. Mackridge, *Language and National Identity*, 299–300.

97. "A Greek Orthodox Writer Promotes Rapprochement Between Jews and Christians in Greece (1925)," in *Sephardi Lives*, ed. Cohen and Stein, 240–242.

98. Eleni Kourmantzi-Panayotakou, "Josef Eliya and Sabbetai Kabili: Ideological Problems in Ioannina's Pre-war Jewish Community," in *The Jewish Communities of Southeastern Europe from the Fifteenth Century to the End of World War II*, ed. I. K. Hassiotis (Salonica, 1997), 262–280.

99. Rae Dalven, *Poems by Joseph Eliyia* (New York, 1944); "Lodge de Salonique," *Hamenora* (April–May–June 1934): 75–76; *La Aksion*, January 10, 1939.

100. "Prochesos verbales dela komision superiora de instruksion," August 5 and 19, 1924, BZI 1719, 1:46–48.

101. Béné Bérith to the Jewish Communal Council, November 9, 1925, CAHJP, Gr/Sa 343.

102. "Prochesos verbales dela komision superiora de instruksion," October 9, 1921, BZI 1719, 1:144.

103. "Prochesos verbales dela komision superiora de instruksion," January 2, 1921 and September 20, 1921, BZI 1719, 1:127–128, 143.

104. "Prochesos verbales dela komision superiora de instruksion," February 15, 1921, BZI 1719, 1:116.

105. Kohn to Jewish communal schools, October 30, 1930, JMTh, f. 147.

106. *La Nasion*, October 29, 1909.

107. *El Puevlo*, July 29, 1926.

108. "Prochesos verbales dela komision superiora de instruksion," July 15, 1930 and August 19, 1930 BZI 1719, 3:171–172, 175–176.

109. *La Nasion*, September 29, 1909; *El Liberal*, May 7, 1912.

110. *El Puevlo*, May 18, 1930; "Estabelisimientos eskolarios Alsheh," July 1932, BZI, dapim S/46.

111. Menahem Sion, Ottowa, to Samuel Josafat, Salonica, February 6, 2002, JMTh, Families documents/Sion.

112. *El Puevlo*, July 9, 1926.

113. *La Aksion*, June 21, 1938.

114. *Las Eskolas Komunalas de Saloniko—Loke eyos son loke eyos deven ser. Konferensia echa por s. J. Kon, inspektor de las eskolas komunales. En la lodja Bene Berith, el Shabat 5 Marso 1927* (Salonica, 1927), 19.

115. "A Jewish Secondary School or a Greek-Jewish Secondary School?," in *Documents on the History of the Greek Jews*, ed. Constantopoulou and Veremis, 119; Ginio, "'Learning the beautiful language of Homer.'"

116. *Las Eskolas Komunalas de Saloniko*, 18.

117. Ibid., 20.

118. *El Puevlo*, July 19, 1931.

119. "Prochesos verbales dela komision superiora de instruksion," April 7, 1927, BZI 1719, 2:4.

120. *El Puevlo*, May 18, 1928.

121. *La Aksion*, June 27, 1939.

122. *El Puevlo*, January 24, 1928.

123. Katsikas, "Hostage Minority," 160–161.

124. "Prochesos verbales dela komision superiora de instruksion," October 16, 1930, BZI 1719, 3:185.

125. Benbassa and Rodrigue, *Sephardi Jewry*, 100.

126. "Prochesos verbales dela komision superiora de instruksion," November 3, 1931, BZI 1719, 4:23.

127. "Prochesos verbales dela komision superiora de instruksion," January 21, 1932, BZI 1719, 4:46–47.

128. Statistics of Jewish students attending Greek schools, [early 1930s], CAHJP, Gr/Sa 273.

129. Béné Bérith to the Jewish Community of Salonica, May 15, 1939, YIVO, RG-207, f. 87; "Loge de Salonique," *Hamenora* (April–May–June 1931): 102–109 and (January–February–March 1934): 12–22.

130. "Prochesos verbales dela komision superiora de instruksion," October 23, 1930 BZI 1719, 3:186–187; February 19, 1931 BZI 1719, 4:5.

131. "Prochesos verbales dela komision superiora de instruksion," November 4, 1930, BZI 1719, 3:189.

132. "Prochesos verbales dela komision superiora de instruksion," December 16, 1930, BZI 1719, 3:197; and February 9, 1932, BZI 1719, 4:52; Bensanchi, Athens, to the Communal Council, Salonica, May 8, 1931, CAHJP, Gr/Sa 339.

133. The position was originally supposed to be in Jewish history but was changed, likely due to the perception that history would be too politicized; *Jewish Telegraphic Agency*, November 10, 1927 and January 4, 1929.

134. See Charalampou Papastathē, "Lazaros Velelēs ōs kathēgētēs panepistēmíou Thessalonikēs," *Chronika* 61 (September 1983): 6–8; Vasileios Phoukas, "Oi istorikes spoudes stē Philosophikē Scholē Thessalonikēs kata tēn periodo tou Mesopolemou," in *30th Panellēniko Istoriko Synedrio 29–31 Maiou 2009. Praktika* (Thessaloniki, 2009), 337–358, esp. 350; Vasileios Phoukas, "Ē Philosophikē Scholē tou Panepistēmiou Thessalonikēs" (PhD Dissertation, University of Thessaloniki, 2009), 93–100, 193–195; Bernard Pierron, *Juifs et Chrétiens de la Grèce Moderne: Histoire des relations intercommunautaires de 1821 à 1945* (Paris, 1996), 152.

135. *Makedonia*, November 1, 1927.

136. *El Puevlo*, February 14, 1929.

137. Ibid.

138. *El Puevlo*, April 11, 1929.

139. See Joshua Seth Goode, *Impurity of Blood: Defining Race in Spain, 1870–1930* (Baton Rouge, 2009), 182–206.

140. Dēmētrēs Philippēs, *Prophasismos, ekphasismos, pseudophasismos, Ellada, Italia kai Ispania ston mesopolemo* (Thessaloniki, 2010), 199–201.

141. Secretary of the Société Chivat-Sion to the Superior Commission for Jewish Instruction, Elul 13, 5686, YIVO, RG-207, f. 149.

142. "Prochesos verbales dela komision superiora de instruksion," September 18 and October 30, 1928, BZI 1719, 2:81 and 89.

143. *Jewish Telegraphic Agency*, December 12, 1924.

144. "Prochesos verbales dela komision superiora de instruksion," February 10 and May 2, 1933, BZI 1719, 5:115 and 125; *La Renasensia Djudia*, May 5, 1933.

145. "Prochesos verbales dela komision superiora de instruksion," July 4 and 25, August 30, and September 28, 1933, BZI 1719, 5:132–133, 135–136, 142, and 148–149.

146. "Prochesos verbales dela komision superiora de instruksion," November 13, 1933, BZI 1719, 5:150.

147. "Prochesos verbales dela komision superiora de instruksion," December 5, 1933, BZI 1719, 5:156–157.

148. "Prochesos verbales de la klasa preparatoria de maestros i rabinos," June 29, 1934, USHMM, r. 694, d. 181, p. 2.

149. "Prochesos verbales de la klasa preparatoria de maestros i rabinos,", November 19, 1934, USHMM, r. 694, d. 181, p. 19; and November 17, 1935, USHMM r. 690, d. 144, p. 371.

150. "Prochesos verbales de la klasa preparatoria de maestros i rabinos," September 9, 1934, USHMM, r. 694, d. 181, p. 10; Haim Habib to Koretz, November 1, 1938, USHMM, r. 691, d. 145.

151. "Prochesos verbales de la klasa preparatoria de maestros i rabinos," November 19, 1934, USHMM, r. 694, d. 181, p. 19.

152. For the debates over classroom instruction, see "Prochesos verbales de la klasa preparatoria de maestros i rabinos," October 14 and December 20, 1934, and February 21, 1935, USHMM, r. 694, d. 181, pp. 13, 26, and 29. For the other issues, see Jacques Alkalai to the Communal Council, March 15, 1936, USHMM, r. 694, d. 181; Isaac Haim Carasso to commission for the class of rabbis and teachers, December 16, 1936, USHMM, r. 694, d. 181; students in the class of rabbis and teachers to Chief Rabbi Koretz, January 1, 1937, USHMM, r. 694, d. 181; La Aksion, July 1 and December 11, 1937; Mercado Covo to Chief Rabbi Koretz, May 6, 1938, USHMM, r. 691, d. 145.

153. La Aksion, July 4, 1938.

154. Notably, the students signed their initial petition for employment as teachers at the Jewish communal schools in Ashkenazic Hebrew cursive, a sign of the literary imprint that figures such as Volodarsky and Koretz had in shaping their educational trajectory. Students in the class of rabbis and teachers to the Commission of Superior Education, July 27, 1938 and Alumni of the class of rabbis and teachers to the Communal Council, October 22, 1939, USHMM, r. 688, d. 111.   ·

155. "Nota sovre la edision," *Ba-Dereh: Sefer Kria Le-shanat ha-limudim ha-sheniya* (Salonica, 5694).

156. Controversy erupted when not all of the Jewish children could get a hold of the new books and were sent home from school. *La Aksion*, November 29, 1934.

157. *El Mesajero*, April 1, 1936.

158. "Law 2456 Concerning Jewish Communities," in *Documents on the History of the Greek Jews*, ed. Constantopoulou and Veremis, 104.

159. *El Mesajero*, April 1, 1936.

160. *El Mesajero*, April 2, 1936.

161. *El Mesajero*, April 21, 1936.

162. Ibid.

163. Yomtov Saltiel to Superior Commission for Jewish Instruction, July 1, 1937, YIVO RG-207, f. 135; Mentesh Bensanchi to the Communal Council, December 14, 1936, JMTh, f. 147.

164. Yomtov Saltiel to Mentesh Bensanchi, inspector of Jewish communal schools, February 24, 1939, YIVO, RG-207, f. 135.

165. *Jewish Telegraphic Agency*, April 5, 1936.

166. Superior Commission for Jewish Instruction to the Communal Council, June 24, 1936, CAHJP, Gr/Sa 200; Employee declaration, March 20, 1940, JMTh, f. 40.

167. *Jewish Telegraphic Agency*, November 20, 1936.

168. *El Mesajero*, July 10, 1936.

169. *Jewish Telegraphic Agency*, March 17, 1937; Yomtov Saltiel to the Commission for Jewish Instruction, July 6, 1938, YIVO, RG-207, f. 135.

170. *La Aksion*, May 5, 1938.

171. Katerina Lagos, "Hellenism and Minority Education: The Promotion of Literacy and Cultural Assimilation," paper presented at the Modern Greek Studies Association, New York University (2011).

172. Yomtov Saltiel to the Commission for Jewish Instruction, February 22, 1940, YIVO, RG-207, f. 135.

173. "Notas por los anios de servicio por el Personnel de fransès alongiado del servicio al 1938/39," USHMM, r. 691, d. 145.

174. Alegre Samuel to the Commission for Jewish Instruction, July 24, 1934; November 5, 1934; February 8, 1935; July 14, 1935; September 8, 1936; November 8, 1937, YIVO, RG-207, f. 136.

175. Ginio, "'Learning the Beautiful Language of Homer.'"

176. Seduta del 25 Agosto 1938 de la Commission de la Instruction. Koretz requested again the following year that Jewish teachers bring their students to synagogue; minutes of the Administrative Council of the Jewish Community of Salonica, August 30, 1939, USHMM, r. 691, d. 145.

177. Minutes of the Administrative Council of the Jewish Community of Salonica, May 4, 1939, USHMM, r. 691, d. 145.

178. Minutes of the Administrative Council of the Jewish Community of Salonica, June 7, 1939, USHMM, r. 691, d. 145.

179. Minutes of the Administrative Council of the Jewish Community of Salonica, June 7, 1939, USHMM, r. 691, d. 145.

180. To this number, he added fifty Jewish students who had attended the University of Salonica; J[oseph] N[ehama], "Ce qu'était la communauté juive de Salonique a la veille de la catastrophe," in *In Memoriam: Hommage aux Victimes Juives des Nazis en Grèce*, ed. M. Molho (Salonica, 1988 [first edition 1948]), 23.

181. Saby Saltiel, Salonica, to Joseph and Isaac Saltiel, New York, February 14, 1938, HBA, b. 36, f. 24.

182. Minutes of the Administrative Council of the Jewish Community of Salonica, August 27, 1939, USHMM, r. 691, d. 145, pp. 4–6.

183. *La Aksion*, April 6, 1939, 2. On the proposal to translate *Pirke Avoth* into modern Greek, see minutes of the Administrative Council of the Jewish Community of Salonica, July 30, 1939, USHMM, r. 691, d. 145.

184. Minutes of the Administrative Council of the Jewish Community of Salonica, June 25, 1939, USHMM, r. 691, d. 145.

185. Minutes of the Administrative Council of the Jewish Community of Salonica, September 3, 1939, USHMM, r. 691, d. 145.

186. *La Aksion,* January 25, 1940.

187. Nehama, *Histoire des Israélites de Salonique,* 7:806–807.

188. Mathitologio, 3° Israilitikon Sxoleion, 1939–1943, JMTh, f. 1–RE.

Chapter 4

Portions of this chapter are adapted with kind permission from Springer Science+Business Media from Devin E. Naar, "Fashioning the 'Mother of Israel': The Ottoman Jewish Historical Narrative and the Image of Jewish Salonica," *Jewish History* 28, no. 3–4 (2014): 337–372.

1. *El Eko Judaiko,* October 25, 1902, adapted from the transcription by Olga Borovaya, "Ladino Periodical Transcriptions" (http://stanford.edu/dept/jewishstudies/programs/sephardi/borovaya_texts_files/periodicals/Ladino_Periodicals.Transcription.pdf).

2. *La Epoka,* May 20, 1892.

3. *La Epoka,* May 31, 1892.

4. Baruch Ben-Jacob recalled those active in Kadima: Isaac R. Molho, Jacob Eliau Cohen, Moise Aron Cohen, Moise I. Cohen, Rabbi Isaac Brudo, Rabenu Jacob de Botton, and Joseph Nehama; *El Puevlo,* October 14, 1932.

5. *La Epoka,* November 23, 1900.

6. Moysen Almosnino, *Extremos y Grandezas de Constantinopla,* trans. I. Cansino (Madrid, 1638), 1.

7. Maír José Benardete, *Hispanic Culture and Character of the Sephardic Jews* (New York, 1953), 17.

8. Mérodach, "La istoria de los djidios de Saloniko. Kale konchentrar los esforsos," *La Nasion* 1, no. 3 (January 1932): 7.

9. S. I. Livros, "Kontribusion ala istoria de Saloniko," *Israel* 4, no. 3 (February 1932): 5.

10. On the development of official Greek and Ottoman Turkish national narratives, see Stathis Gougouris, *Dream Nation: Enlightenment, Colonization, and the Institution of Modern Greece* (Palo Alto, 1996); Paschalis M. Kitromilides, "On the Intellectual Content of Greek Nationalism: Paparrigopoulos, Byzantium, and the Great Idea," in *Byzantium and the Modern Greek Identity,* ed. D. Ricks and P. Magdalino (Brookfield, 1998), 25–33; Ioannis Kouboulis, "European Historiographical Influences upon the Young Konstantinos Paparrigopoulos," in *The Making of Modern Greece: Nationalism, Romanticism, and the Uses of the Past (1797–1896),* ed. R. Beaton and D. Ricks (Brookfield, 2009), 52–63; M. Şükrü Hanioğlu, *A Brief History of the Late Ottoman Empire* (Princeton, 2008), 98; Selim Deringil, *The Well-Protected Domains: Ideology and the Legitimation of Power in the Ottoman Empire, 1876–1909* (New York, 1998); Serif Mardin, *The Genesis of Young Ottoman Thought: A Study in the Modernization of Turkish Political Ideas* (Syracuse, 2000), 133–168; Christoph K. Neumann, "Whom Did Ahmed Cevdet Represent?" in *Late Ottoman Society: The Intellectual Legacy,* ed. E. Özdalga (London, 2005), 117–134; Ebru Boyar, *Ottomans, Turks, and the Balkans: Empire Lost, Relations Altered* (London, 2007), 9–28.

NOTES TO CHAPTER 4

11. As discussed in *El Puevlo*, May 29, 1929.

12. Nikos Fardis, *Thessaloniki* (Thessaloniki, 1932).

13. *El Puevlo*, June 30, 1929.

14. *La Aksion*, October 8, 1933.

15. "A Blind Spot of Wissenschaft des Judentums Scholars: 'Spanish Jews in the Orient' (1911)" as translated in *Sephardi Lives: A Documentary History*, ed. J. P. Cohen and S. A. Stein (Stanford, 2014), 395–397.

16. See Julia Phillips Cohen and Sarah Abrevaya Stein, "Sephardic Scholarly Worlds: Toward a Novel Geography of Modern Jewish History," *Jewish Quarterly Review* 100 (2010): 349–384. None of the major works on Jewish historiography mention Jews in the Ottoman Empire or its successor states: Michael A. Meyer, *Ideas of Jewish History* (New York, 1974); Shmuel Feiner, *Haskalah and History: The Emergence of a Modern Jewish Historical Consciousness* (Oxford, 2002); Michael Brenner, *Prophets of the Past: Interpreters of Jewish History* (Princeton, 2010). See also Yitzchak Kerem, "The Development and Current State of Research on Ottoman Jewry," *Archivum Ottomanicum* 19 (2001): 79–85.

17. Heinrich Graetz, *Geschichte der Juden* (Leipzig, 1853–1874), 5:269, trans. B. Löwy, *History of the Jews* (Philadelphia, 1891–1898), 3:187–188. See also Ismar Schorsch, *From Text to Context: The Turn to History in Modern Judaism* (Hanover, 1994), 71–92; Sarah Abrevaya Stein, "Sephardic and Middle Eastern Jewries since 1492: The Sephardic Mystique/The Sephardic Mistake," in *The Oxford Handbook of Jewish Studies*, ed. M. Goodman (Oxford, 2002), 327–362; Daniel Schroeter, "From Sephardi to Oriental: The 'Decline' Theory of Jewish Civilization in the Middle East and North Africa," in *The Jewish Contribution to Civilization: Reassessing an Idea*, ed. J. Cohen and R. I. Cohen (Oxford, 2008), 125–150; John M. Efron, *German Jewry and the Allure of the Sephardic* (Princeton, 2016).

18. Graetz, *Geschichte der Juden*, 9:399–401, trans. Löwy, *History of the Jews*, 4:611–12.

19. Graetz, *Geschichte der Juden*, 9:409, trans. Löwy, *History of the Jews*, 4:630.

20. Graetz, *Geschichte der Juden*, 9:390; 10:213, 222, 227, trans. Löwy, *History of the Jews*, 4:617; 5:126–127, 135, 140.

21. Graetz, *Geschichte der Juden*, 9:40–42.

22. Dina Danon, "Abraham Danon: La vie d'un maskil ottoman, 1857–1925," in *Itinéraires sépharades: Complexité et diversité des identités*, ed. E. Benbassa (Paris, 2010), 181–192.

23. Anthony Molho, "The Jewish Community of Salonika: The End of a Long History," *Diaspora* 1 (1991): 109.

24. Aron Rodrigue, *French Jews, Turkish Jews: The Alliance Israélite Universelle and the Politics of Jewish Schooling in Turkey, 1860–1925* (Bloomington, 1990), 76.

25. Aron Rodrigue, "Léon Halévy and Modern French Jewish Historiography," in *Jewish History and Jewish Memory*, ed. E. Carlebach, J. M. Efron, and D. N. Myers

(Hanover, 1998), 413–427; Aron Rodrigue, "Totems, Taboos, and Jews: Salomon Reinach and the Politics of Scholarship in Fin-de-Siècle France," *Jewish Social Studies* 10 (2004): 1–19.

26. Théodore Reinach, *Histoire des Israélites: Depuis l'époque de leur dispersion jusqu'à nos jours* (Paris, 1884), 373.

27. Ibid., 232.

28. Ibid., 272.

29. Ibid., 372–376.

30. *La Epoka*, July 15, 1892.

31. Merkado Yosef Kovo, "Suvenires de chikes i de manseves: Mi entrada al lyseo imperial (Fragmentos)," *El Maccabeo* (5681): 57–65. Covo's writings on his native town were published posthumously as *Aperçu historique sur la communauté israélite de Serrès* (Tel Aviv, 1962).

32. D[avid] R[ecanati], "Merkado Yosef Kovo," in *Zikhron Saloniki: Gedulata ve-hurbana shel Yerushalayim de-Balkan*, ed. D. Recanati (Tel Aviv, 1972–1985), 2:460–461; Merkado J. Kovo, *Los djidios komo soldados a traverso los siekolos* (Salonica, 1911). For a summary of this booklet, see Eyal Ginio, "*El Dovér el Mas Sànto*: The Mobilization of the Ottoman Jewish Population during the Balkan Wars (1912–13)," in *Conflicting Loyalties in the Balkans: The Great Powers, the Ottoman Empire and Nation-Building*, ed. H. Grandits et al. (London, 2011), 165–166.

33. M. Covo, "Lettre de Turquie," *Univers Israélite* 56 (1901): 663–664; "Procès-verbaux des séances du conseil—Séance du 20 novembre 1900," *Revue des Études Juives* 44 (1902): 27–28.

34. Clipping of Judeo-Spanish newspaper article by Baruch Ben-Jacob on *Emek Ha-Bakha* [1930s], Marcel Yoel Papers, JMTh.

35. Kovo, "Suvenires de chikes," 58. See Joseph Hacohen, "The Vale of Tears," as translated in *The Expulsion 1492 Chronicles: An Anthology of Medieval Chronicles Relating to the Expulsion of the Jews from Spain and Portugal*, ed. D. Raphael (North Hollywood, 1992), 105–111; Yosef Hayim Yerushalmi, *Zakhor: Jewish History and Jewish Memory* (Seattle, 1989), 60–62.

36. *La Epoka*, April 11, 1892.

37. Ibid. In subsequent articles he recounted the travails of the conversos who had crossed the Atlantic to settle in Peru, Mexico, and Brazil, where they suffered at the hands of the Inquisition and survived only a few generations; *La Epoka*, April 29 and May 20, 1892.

38. *La Epoka*, April 11, 1892.

39. Ibid.

40. Ibid.; "The Provencal Jews in Salonica to the Jews in Provence," in *Letters of Jews through the Ages*, ed. Franz Kobler (New York, 1978), 2:344–347.

41. *La Epoka*, April 11, 1892.

42. *La Epoka*, December 25, 1910.

43. *La Epoka*, December 22, 1910.

44. *La Epoka*, January 1 and 6, 1911.

45. M. J. Covo, "Les Synagogues de Tolède," *Almanach National* (Salonica, 1915), 94–96; M. J. Covo, "Contribution à l'histoire des institutions scolaires de la Communauté israélite de Salonique," *Almanach National* (Salonica, 1916); 97–103; M. J. Covo, "Des origins de l'accusation du meurte ritual," *El Makabeo* (5682): 51–54; M. J. Covo, "Études Saloniciennes: Un médicin juif du Pape à Salonique au XVIe siècle," *El Makabeo* (5688): 19–22; *El Puevlo*, September 30, 1931; *La Aksion*, March 22, 1932; M. J. Covo, "Purim a traverso los siekolos," *Israel* (5692): 4–6; Merkado Yosef Kovo, "Literatura relidjioza djudeo-espanyola: Meam Loez," *Israel* (5693): 11–13; *La Volunté*, May 19, 1935; *El Mesajero*, April 15, 1938; *La Aksion*, November 23, 1938.

46. See the copy held in the library of the Aristotle University of Salonica, catalog no. 9540.

47. M. J. Covo, "Études Judéo-greques. Rapports entre Athéniens et Hiérosolymites d'après la Midrasch Ekha," *El Makabeo* (5690): 1–6.

48. M. J. Covo, *Kolpo de ojo sovre la antiguedad grega (istoria, literatura, sensia, filozofia, arte* (Salonica, 1937).

49. M. J. Covo, "Premiers Établissements Juifs à Salonique," *El Makabeo* (5691): 11–19.

50. M. J. Covo, "Istoria dela komunidad djudia de Sheres de los tiempos antiguos asta nuestros dias," *Aksion Prensa*, May 1938.

51. Covo, *Kolpo de ojo sovre la antiguedad grega*, 4–5.

52. *La Aksion*, February 17, 1938.

53. *El Puevlo*, November 28, 1932.

54. Yitzchak Kerem, "The Fate of Greek Sephardic Cultural Personalities in the Holocaust," *Jewish Studies at the Turn of the Twentieth Century: Proceedings of the 6th EAJS Congress* (Leiden, 1999), 1:523–529.

55. Joseph Nehama, "Baruch Ben-Jacob, z"l," in *Zikhron Saloniki: Gedulata vehurbana shel Yerushalayim de-Balkan*, ed. David Recanati (Tel Aviv, 1972–1985), 2:464–465.

56. Baruch Ben-Jacob to the Superior Commission for Jewish Instruction, October 10, 1930 and May 31, 1931, CAHJP, Gr/Sa 296; "Visita Pastoral," *Ha-Lapid: Órgão de Comunidade Israelita de Porto* 5, no. 31 (November–December 1930): 1; *El Puevlo*, January 4, 5, and 6, 1931.

57. *El Puevlo*, October 9, 1931.

58. Baruch Ben-Jacob, *Kontribusion ala Istoria de la Komunidad Djudia de Saloniko* (Salonica, 1911).

59. According Ben-Jacob's recollections in *El Puevlo*, October 14, 1932.

60. Elena Romero, *La Creación Literaria en Lengua Sefardí* (Madrid, 1992), 206.

61. Beatriz León, "Dos conferencias sobre el papel de la mujer," in *"Sala de Pasa-*

tiempo": Textos judeoespañoles de Salónica impresos entre 1896 y 1916, ed. B. Schmid, Arba 14: Acta Romanica Basiliensia (Basel, 2003), 124–164.

62. *El Puevlo*, October 14, 1932

63. Ben-Jacob, *Kontribusion*, 6–11; 18–22.

64. Recalled in *El Puevlo*, October 14, 1932; Baruch Ben-Jacob, "Saloniko," in *Ozar Yisrael: An Encyclopedia of all Matters concerning Jews and Judaism, in Hebrew*, ed. J. D. Eisenstein (New York, 1913), 10:125–130 (Hebrew).

65. Salomon Rosanes, *Divrei Yame Israel be-Togarma* (Husiatin, 1914), 3:331–334.

66. *Ozar Yisrael*, ed. Eisenstein, 10:iii.

67. With the assistance of the French government, which helped procure the location, and financial support from the Talmud Tora committee, the Baruch brothers opened their new school; Ben-Jacob and Baruch to the Talmud Tora Agadol, Av 12, 5679, CAHJP, Gr/Sa 296.

68. E.g., "Prochesos verbales dela komision superiora de instruksion Talmud Tora," August 14 and 21, 1919, CAHJP, Gr/Sa 8, pp. 75, 79. Baruch Ben-Jacob and Aron Baruch to the administrative commission of the Talmud Tora Agadol, Av 12, 5679, CAHJP, Gr/Sa 296.

69. [Baruch] Ben-Jacob and Aron Baruch, *Moral i Edukasion Djudia: Livro de lektura redijido espesialmente a la intesion [sic] de las eskolas djudias i de las famiyas* (Salonica, c. 1922), 85.

70. Jay R. Berkovitz, "Does Jewish History Repeat Itself? Paradigm, Myth, and Tradition," in *The Solomon Goldman Lectures Vol. VII*, ed. D. P. Bell (Chicago, 1999), 131–153.

71. Ben-Jacob and Baruch , *Moral i Edukasion Djudia*, 85–88.

72. Ibid., 89.

73. Ibid., 90.

74. Ibid., 90.

75. Ibid., 92.

76. Ibid., 93.

77. Ibid., 93.

78. Ibid., 94.

79. *El Puevlo*, November 18, 1932.

80. Iacob M. Hassán, "In memoriam: Joseph Nehama (1881–1971)," *Sefarad* 31, no. 2 (1971): 470–474; Maurice Benusiglio, "Hors texte: Joseph Nehama (1881–1971)," in *Salonique: Raconte-nous tes histoires*, ed. J. Aelion (Tarascan, 1998), 209–216.

81. Joseph Nehama, *Histoire des Israélites de Salonique* (Paris/Salonique, 1935–1978), 1:6.

82. Adolfo Arditti, "Jos. Nehama," *Voz Sefaradi* 1, no. 8 (1967): 23.

83. Orly Meron, *Jewish Entrepreneurship in Salonica, 1912–1940: An Ethnic Economy in Transition* (Portland, 2012), 3–4.

84. Michael Molho, Salonica, to Henry Besso, New York, August 10, 1935, HBA, b. 32, f. 4.

85. See Paul Dumont, "Freemasonry in Turkey: A By-product of Western Penetration," *European Review* 13, no. 3 (2005): 481–493.

86. Quoted in Rena Molho, "The Zionist Movement in Thessaloniki, 1899–1919," in *The Jewish Communities of Southeastern Europe*, ed. I. K. Hassiotis (Thessaloniki, 1997), 349.

87. Quoted in Mark Mazower, *Salonica, City of Ghosts: Christians, Muslims, and Jews, 1430–1950* (London, 2004), 407.

88. Joseph Nehama, "Sabbetaï Cevi et les Sabbatéens de Salonique," *Revue des Écoles de l'Alliance Israélite* 5 (April–June 1902): 289–323; esp. 291. He drew on Abraham Danon, "Une secte Judéo-Musulmane en Turquie," *Revue des Études Juives* 33 (1897): 264–281.

89. Nehama, "Sabbetaï Cevi," 303.

90. Ibid., 322.

91. Ibid., 323.

92. Elie Kedourie, "Young Turks, Freemasons and Jews," *Middle Eastern Studies* 71, no. 1 (1971): 89–104; Mim Kemâl Öke, "Young Turks, Freemasons, Jews and the Question of Zionism in the Ottoman Empire (1908–1913)," *Studies in Zionism* 7, no. 2 (1986): 199–218.

93. He later published his perspectives in Judeo-Spanish; Joseph Nehama, *Shabetai Sevi i los Maminim* (Salonica, 1932). Finally, Nehama also folded these interpretations into his magnum opus, *Histoire des Israélites de Salonique*.

94. Ángel Pulido, *Españoles sin Patria y la Raza Sefardí* (Madrid, 1905), 447.

95. Ibid., 118.

96. Ibid., 447–448.

97. Paloma Díaz-Mas and Teresa Madrid Álvarez-Piñar, *Cartas sefardíes de Salónica* (Barcelona, 2014), 15.

98. P. Risal, *La Ville Convoitée: Salonique* (Paris, 1914), 165.

99. Ibid., 5.

100. Ibid., 5, 96.

101. Ibid., 6.

102. Ibid., 6.

103. Ibid., 22.

104. Ibid., 100.

105. Ibid., 97.

106. Ibid., 165–166.

107. Ibid., 166.

108. Ibid., 165, 167.

109. Ibid., 8.

110. Ibid., 171–174.

111. Ibid., 175.

112. *Israël*, August 12, 1936.

113. Nehama, *Histoire*, 2:5–8.

114. Ibid.

115. Ibid., 1:5–6.

116. *La Aksion*, October 27, 1935 and November 3, 1935.

117. *El Mesajero*, May 17, 1936.

118. Nehama, *Histoire*, 2:8; 7:526.

119. Ibid., 1:8–15.

120. Ibid., 1:15–30.

121. Ibid., 1:31–38.

122. Eyal Ginio, "'Learning the Beautiful Language of Homer:' Judeo-Spanish Speaking Jews and the Greek Language and Culture between the Wars," *Jewish History* 16 (2002): 250–254.

123. *La Aksion*, February 19, 1939.

124. Isaac Emmanuel first began discussing this theme in "Un kapitolo de la istoria de Saloniko: Un movimiento mesianiko al onzen siekolo," *El Djidio* (1927): 48–50; Isaac S. Emmanuel, *Histoire des Israélites de Salonique* (Paris, 1936), 26–33.

125. *La Aksion*, March 17, 1937; *El Mesajero*, March 18, 1937.

126. Nehama, *Histoire*, 6:630–635.

127. Ibid., 7:706–710.

128. Ibid., 7:806–807.

129. Quoted in Irith Dublon-Knebel, ed., *German Foreign Office Documents on the Holocaust in Greece (1937–1944)* (Tel Aviv, 2007), 81.

130. The fifth volume appeared in 1959, and the sixth and seventh, posthumously, in 1978.

131. S. F. Chyet, "For Isaac S. Emmanuel," November 19, 1972, American Jewish Archives-Cincinnati, SC-3204.

132. Benardete, *Hispanic Culture*, 16.

133. Isaac S. Emmanuel, *Matsevot Saloniki* (Jerusalem, 1963–1968), 2:859.

134. Book of registrations of the Jewish Community of Salonica, July 19, 1925, CAHJP, Gr/Sa 30, v. 23, p. 811, entry 2950.

135. "Muestras sosietas. El 8° aniversario de la 'Shivat Sion,'" *Israel* 1, no. 4 (Sivan 5691): 3; Abraham Recanati, president of Shomre Shabbat, to the Communal Council, Av 5, 5685, CAHJP, Gr/Sa 343.

136. Isaac S. Emmanuel, "Zikhronot yeledot vebahorot," in *Avraham ha-Ivri: Kovets mukdash lamanhig vehalohem Avraham S. Rekanati* (Tel Aviv, 1958), 16–18; "[Livro de hazanim de las keiloth]," USHMM, r. 689, d. 137, pp. 40–41.

137. *La Aksion*, April 4, 1936; President Dr. N[issim] Ovadia and General Secretary O. Camhy of the Union Universelle des Communautés Sepharadites to Leon Gattegno, president of the Jewish community of Salonica, March 24, 1936, CAHJP, Gr/Sa 50.

138. The same publisher, Lipschutz, also put out the work of the Bulgarian-born writer, Saül Mézan, *De Gabirol à Abravanel: Juifs espagnols, promoteurs de la Renaissance* (Paris, 1936).

139. Emmanuel, *Histoire*, 9.

140. Isaac S. Emmanuel, *Gedole Salonki le-dorotam* (Tel Aviv, 1936).

141. Emmanuel, *Histoire*, 5. Emmanuel named the president, Leon Gattegno; the chancellor, Daout Lévy; and the secretary of the chief rabbinate, Raphael Menashe.

142. Ibid., 10.

143. Ibid., 13–14.

144. Ibid., 14.

145. Emmanuel, Lausanne, to Chief Rabbi Koretz, Salonica, November 3, 1933, USHMM, r. 752, d. 109.

146. Isaac S. Emmanuel, Breslau, to the Jewish Community of Salonica, Rahamim 25, 5684, CAHJP, Gr/Sa 41b.

147. Dr. Israel Abraham Rabin, Breslau, to Rafael Menashe, Salonica, Tevet 5, 5684, CAHJP, Gr/Sa 41b.

148. Rafael Menashe to the Communal Council, Shevat 14, 5684, CAHJP, Gr/Sa 41b.

149. Emmanuel, Lausanne, to the Jewish Community of Salonica, February 3, 1928, CAHJP, Gr/Sa 333.

150. Rabin to Menashe, Tevet 5, 5684, CAHJP, Gr/Sa 41b.

151. *El Puevlo*, November 6, 8, 9, 10, 11, and 12, 1925.

152. Isaac Emmanuel, "Un kapitulo de la istoria djudia de Saloniko. Un movimiento mesianiko al onzen siekolo," *El Djidio* (Tishri 5687): 48–50; Isaac Emmanuel, "La situasion ekonomika de la komunita djudia de Saloniko en el primer kuarto del diesochen siekolo," *El Djidio* (Pesah 5688): 7–9.

153. I. S. Emmanuel, "Saloniker Grabschriften aus dem 16 und 17 Jahrhundert," *Monatsschrift für Geschichte und Wissenschaft des Judentums* 6 (1930): 421–429.

154. Eulogy by Isaac Jerusalmi, Cincinnati, October 18, 1972 (personal communication, May 7, 2012).

155. *El Mesajero*, April 21, 1937.

156. Isaac S. Emmanuel, "Orijen de la komunita djudia de Saloniko," *El Djidio* (Pessah 5691): 12–14.

157. Emmanuel, *Histoire*, 83 ff.

158. Ibid., 14–15.

159. *Actualités*, April 12, 1942.

160. Emmanuel, Cincinnati, to Abraham Recanati, Tel Aviv, September 4, 1969, IEA.

161. "Last Will and Testament of Isaac S. Emmanuel," May 10, 1972, Hamilton County Court of Common Pleas, Cincinnati, case 1900298877.

162. Michael Molho, *Kontribusion ala Istoria de Saloniko* (Saloniko, 1932), xii.

163. *Homenaje a Don Michael Molho ofrecido por un núcleo de amigos y simpatizantes* (Buenos Aires, 1961), 62.

164. Michael Molho, *Traditions and Customs of the Sephardic Jews of Salonica*, trans. A. Zara; ed. R. Bedford (New York, 2006), xi–xix; *Homenaje a Don Michael Molho*. On Salomon Molho, see *La Epoka*, March 22, 1894 and January 1, 1897.

165. Molho to the Superior Commission of the Jewish Schools of Salonica, December 4, 1929 and June 15, 1938, CAHJP, Gr/Sa 157. See his certifications in the Jewish communal registry, "Chertifikatos," May 7, 1929–November 25, 1929, CAHJP, Gr/Sa 32, v. 30, entries 1498–1499.

166. Molho, *Traditions and Customs*, xiii.

167. Michael Molho to the Jewish Community of Kavalla, and replies, July 3, 14, 20, 23, and 28, 1929, CAHJP, Gr/Kavalla.

168. Letter from Molho to the Superior Commission of the Jewish Schools of Salonica, December 4, 1929 (French), CAHJP, Gr/Sa 157; "Prochesos verbales de la komision superiora de instruksion," December 10, 1929, BZI, 1719, v. 3, p. 139.

169. "Prochesos verbales de la komision superiora de instruksion," November 4, 1930, BZI, 1719, v. 3, p. 189.

170. Molho to the Jewish Community of Kavalla, July 14, 1929, CAHJP, Gr/Kavalla.

171. Molho, Salonica, to Henry Besso, New York, May 20, 1934, HBA, b. 32, f. 4.

172. Molho to Besso, October 25, 1935, HBA, b. 32, f. 4.

173. Molho, *Kontribusion*, xvii.

174. Ibid., iv–vii.

175. Ibid., viii.

176. Ibid., viii–xiii.

177. Ibid., xiv.

178. Ibid., xii–xiii.

179. Ibid., xiv–xv.

180. Ibid., xv.

181. "[Livro de hazanim de las keiloth]," USHMM, r. 689, d. 137, pp. 30–31; declaration of Michael Molho, May 8, 1935, USHMM, r. 689, d. 137, p. 190; cf. David Altabé, "The Portuguese Jews of Salonica," in *Studies on the History of Portuguese Jews*, ed. I. J. Katz and M. M. Serels (New York, 2000), 119–124, esp. 123; Manuel Franco, "The Twentieth-Century Portuguese Jews from Salonika: 'Oriental Jews of Portuguese Origin,'" in *Borders and Boundaries in and around Dutch Jewish History*, ed. J. Frishman et al. (Amsterdam, 2011), 111–123.

182. *Homenaje a Don Michael Molho*, 6.

183. Molho, *Kontribusion*, 83–85.

184. He emphasized the key role played by his rabbinical ancestors. Michael Molho, "Maranos del Portugal en Saloniko," and "Komo djuzgavan muestros rabanim," *Israel* (September 1934): 13, 17. For a folktale about Molho's great-great grandfather, see: "The

Sanctification of God's Name," in *Folktales of the Jews: Volume 1: Tales from the Sephardic Dispersion*, ed. D. Ben-Amos (Philadelphia, 2006), 45–51.

185. Molho, Salonica, to Nehama, Athens, October 17, 1941, FMBTN, f. 44.2, doc. 47.

186. *El Puevlo*, December 21, 1932.

187. Mérodach, "La istoria de los djidios de Saloniko. Kale konchentrar los esforsos," *La Nasion* 1, no. 3 (January 1932): 7. By the end of the decade, Molho's *Kontribusion* was valued at twenty-five drachmes, one of the less expensive Judeo-Spanish booklets on the market; letter from M. J. Covo to the president of the Communal Council with attachment, "Lista de livros en Judéo-espagnol del Señor Isaac Florentin," October 25, 1939, CAHJP, Gr/Sa 373.

188. Livros, "Kontribusion," 5.

189. Michael Molho, *Be-veth ha-Almin shel Yehudei Saloniki* (Salonica, 1932).

190. Mercado J. Covo, "Au Lecteur," in *Be-veth ha-Almin shel Yehudei Saloniki* (Salonica, 1932), 3:i–iv.

191. *Jewish Chronicle*, January 6, 1933.

192. It was also a struggle. *Jewish Quarterly Review* delayed two years before publishing the review. Henry V. Besso, New York, to Molho, Salonica, October 3, 1935, HBA, b. 32, f. 4.

193. Henry V. Besso, "Contribution to the History of Salonica," *Jewish Quarterly Review* 26, no. 2 (October 1935): 159–161.

194. Besso, New York, to Molho, Salonica, December 25, 1933, HBA, b. 32, f. 4.

195. Molho, Salonica, to Besso, New York, [November 3, 1933], HBA, b. 32, f. 4.

196. It is no wonder that, in addition to occupying himself with the Judeo-Spanish folklore of Salonica, Besso also undertook an extensive research project on Sephardic literature of eighteenth-century Amsterdam. Besso, New York, to Molho, Salonica, November 17, 1934, HBA, b. 32, f. 4.

197. Esther Benbassa and Aron Rodrigue, *Sephardi Jewry: A History of the Judeo-Spanish Community, 14th–20th Centuries* (Berkeley, 2000), 143–150.

198. Molho, Salonica, to Besso, New York, May 20, 1934, HBA, b. 32, f. 4.

199. Michael Molho, "Jewish Marriages of Yesteryear: Quaint Customs and Rigid Rituals Marked Weddings among the Sephardic Jews of Previous Generations," *American Hebrew* 139, no. 7 (August 1936): 155, 158, 166; Michel [*sic*] S. Molho, "Matrimonios Sefardiés de Ayer," *Revista Bimestre Cubana* 46 (September 1940): 414–439.

200. Michael Molho, "Cinq elegies en Judéo-espagnol," *Bulletin Hispanique* 42, no. 3 (1940): 231–235.

201. Michael Molho, *Essai d'une monographie sur la Famille Perahia à Thessaloniki* (Thessaloniki, 1938), [7].

202. Ibid., [9]; Molho, Salonica, to Juda Perahia, Xanthi, August 3, 1937, FMBTN, f. 44.2, doc. 10; *La Aksion*, March 29 and April 4, 1938.

203. Michael Molho and Avraham Mevorah, *Estorya de Los Djudios de Kastoria* (Thessaloniki, 1939), [4].

204. *El Mesajero*, June 11 and June 26, 1937.

205. Minutes of the Communal Council, July 20, 1939, USHMM, r. 690, d. 145.

206. Minutes of the Communal Council, October 17, 1939, USHMM, r. 690, d. 145; *La Aksion*, October 29 and November 23 1939.

207. Michael Molho to the Communal Council, September 25, 1940, FMBTN, doc. 42. On Molho's correspondence, see Shmuel Refael, "El archive epistolar de Michael Molho: caracterizacíon y análisis de cartas recibidas por él entre 1945 y 1963," in *Los sefardíes ante los retos del mundo contemporáneo*, ed. P. Diaz-Mas and M. Sánchez Pérez (Madrid, 2010), 345–358.

208. I. Kampeli, "Oi Evraioi tis Thessalonikis," in *Levkoma tis Voreiou Ellados*, ed. G. Nene (Athens, 1934), 69–75; Izak I. Kampeli, *O Politismos ton Evraion* (Thessaloniki, 1937); *El Mesajero*, May 23, 1937 and June 5, 10 July 1937; *La Aksion*, October 21, 1939.

209. Michael Molho, "Historia de los Gidios de las origenes hasta nuestros dias" (Salonica, 1940), FMBTN, f. 44.1, pp. 1–2.

210. Rena Molho, *Salonica and Istanbul: Social, Political and Cultural Aspects of Jewish Life* (Istanbul, 2005), 38, 49. Evoking the phrase on another occasion, Molho (p. 166) cites *Salonique, 1850–1918: la "ville des Juifs" et le réveil des Balkans*, ed. G. Veinstein (Paris, 1992), 46; Yaron Ben-Naeh, *Jews in the Realm of the Sultans: Ottoman Jewish Society in the Seventeenth Century* (Tübingen, 2008), 2, 96; Jane Gerber, *The Jews of Spain: A History of the Sephardic Experience* (New York, 1992), 153.

211. Maria Todorova, *Imagining the Balkans* (New York, 1997); Mark Mazower, *The Balkans: A Short History* (London, 2000).

212. Yerushalmi, *Zakhor*, 86.

213. See Cohen and Stein, "Sephardic Scholarly Worlds."

214. "Mis Memorias" appeared in *La Aksion* in over sixty installments from November 1931 to April 1932. Passages also appeared in French translation in *Le Judaisme Sepharadi* (1933–1937). See Aron Rodrigue and Sarah Stein, eds., *A Jewish Voice from Ottoman Salonica: The Ladino Memoir of Sa'adi Besalel a-Levi* (Stanford, 2012). For another memoir published in the 1930s, see Rena Molho, *"Los Souvenires del Dr. Yoel": An Autobiographical Account of Educational, Professional, and Social Change in Salonika at the Turn of the 20th Century* (Istanbul, 2012).

215. *Jewish Telegraphic Agency*, October 25, 1932. A street named for Saadi a-Levi still exists today in Salonica.

216. Sam Lévy, *Les Juifs de Salonique: Quelques considérations sur les origines et le passé des Juifs de Salonique* (Salonique, 1933), 47–48.

217. Chief rabbi to the Commission of Instruction, July 17, 1935, USHMM, r. 751, d. 105.

218. David N. Myers, *Re-Inventing the Jewish Past: European Jewish Intellectuals and*

the Zionist Return to History (New York, 1995), 6, 40–41; Eyal Ginio, "The Inauguration of the Hebrew University (1925) as reflected in the contemporary Ladino press of Greece and Turkey," in *Zion and Zionism among Sephardi and Oriental Jews*, ed. W. Zeev Harvey et al. (Jerusalem, 2002), 261–274 (Hebrew).

219. Mercado Covo, "Viejas papeles, viejas kazas. Del salon de Ham Mair al Halel Vezemiroth—Saloniko djidio al 20° siekolo; Saloniko al 16° siekolo; sovre el menester de estudiar la istoria de nuestra komunita," *El Djidio* (Pessah 5688): 22–29. This was an already established phrase in previous centuries that, like "City and Mother in Israel," Covo and others revived in the twentieth century. Yaron Ben-Naeh, "'Ir ha-Torah ve-ha-Limud: Saloniki k'merkaz Torah be-meot 16–17," *Pe'amim* 80 (Summer 1999): 60–82.

220. I. S. Révah, "*Histoire des Israélites de Salonique*," *Bulletin Hispanique* 40, no. 2 (1938): 214–216.

Chapter 5

1. David M. Bunis, *Voices from Jewish Salonika* (Jerusalem, 1999), 54.

2. Michael Molho, "La Necropole Juive de Thessalonique," in *In Memoriam: Hommage aux Victimes Juives des Nazis en Grèce*, ed. M. Molho (Salonica, 1948–1953 [reprint 1988]), 3:385–386. Rena Molho gives the figure of three thousand rather than five hundred workers hired by the municipality in "Germany's Policy against the Jews of Greece: The Annihilation of the Jewish Community of Thessaloniki, 1941–1944," in *Salonica and Istanbul: Social, Political and Cultural Aspects of Jewish Life* (Istanbul, 2005), 63; Maria Vassilikou, "The Jewish Cemetery of Salonika in the Crossroads of Urban Modernisation and Anti-Semitism," *European Judaism* 33, no. 1 (Spring 2000): 118–131; Stella Salem, "The Old Jewish Cemetery of Thessaloniki," in *The Cultural Forum of the Jewish Community of Thessaloniki*, ed. L. R. Arouh and Y. L. Benmayor (Thessaloniki, [2003]), 49–59; Bernard Pierron, *Juifs et Chrétiens de la Grèce Moderne Histoire des relations intercommunautaires de 1821 à 1945* (Paris, 1996), 199–203; Paraskevas Savvaidis and Anthimos Bantelas, *Polis Panemistēmiou Polis: Ē istoria tou chōrou tēs Panepistēmioupolēs tou A. P. Th. mesa apo chartes kai topografika diagrammata* (Salonica, 2000); Michael Molho, "El Cementerio judío de Salónica, verdadero museo epigráfico, histórico y arqueológico," *Sefarad* 9, no. 1 (1949): 107–130; Michael Molho, "Dos necrópolis sobrepuestas en Salónica," *Sefarad* 22, no. 2 (1962): 376–383; Leon Saltiel, "Dehumanizing the Dead: The Destruction of Thessaloniki's Jewish Cemetery in the Light of New Sources," *Yad Vashem Studies* 42, no. 1 (2014): 1–35.

3. Carla Hesse and Thomas W. Laqueur, "Orata kai Aorata Sōmata. Ē Exaleiphē tou Evraïkou Nekrotapheiou apo tē Zōē tēs Synkronēs Thessalonikēs" [Bodies Visible and Invisible: The Erasure of the Jewish Cemetery in the Life of Modern Thessaloniki] in *Ē Paragōgē tou Koinōnikou Sōmatos* [The Social Production of the Body], ed. M. Mihailidou and A. Halika (Athens, 2005), 31–56.

4. Michael Molho to the Matanoth Laevionim, February 4 and 10, 1943, JMTh,

f. 164; Devin E. Naar, *With Their Own Words: Glimpses of Jewish Life in Thessaloniki Before the Holocaust* (Thessaloniki, 2006), 30–32.

5. Nicholas P. Stavroulakis, "The Jewish Museum of Thessaloniki—Museo Djidio di Salonik," *European Judaism* 36, no. 2 (Autumn 2003): 34–40; Mark Mazower, *Inside Hitler's Greece: The Experience of Occupation, 1941–44* (New Haven, 1993), 240. While Mazower amended this perspective in *Salonica, City of Ghosts: Christians, Muslims, and Jews, 1430–1950* (London, 2004), other scholars continue to attribute the initiative to the Germans; e.g., K. E. Fleming, *Greece—A Jewish History* (Princeton, 2008), 119.

6. Joachim Jacobs, *Houses of Life: Jewish Cemeteries of Europe* (London, 2008), 94–95.

7. Hesse and Laqueur, "Orata kai Aorata Sōmata," 34.

8. Quoted in Mazower, *Salonica, City of Ghosts*, 324.

9. *Taxydromos*, July 7, 1936.

10. Lucy Garnett, *Greece of the Hellenes* (New York, 1914), 223–226.

11. As discussed in *La Aksion*, June 21, 1931.

12. Nicholas P. Stavroulakis, *Salonika: Jews and Dervishes* (Athens, 1993), 26–28; Michael Molho, *Traditions and Customs of the Sephardic Jews of Salonica*, trans. A. Zara; ed. R. Bedford (New York, 2006), 166–194; Mazower, *Salonica, City of Ghosts*, 83.

13. Quote from A. Goff, *Macedonia: A Plea for the Primitive* (London, 1921), 171–172; *El Puevlo*, October 31, 1921; *La Aksion*, June 23, 1939; Elias Petropoulos, "Kynigoi Kraniōn" ["Skull Chasers"], *Skoliastēs* (May 1986): 33–35; Julia Phillips Cohen, *Becoming Ottomans: Sephardi Jews and Imperial Citizenship in the Modern Era* (New York, 2014), 71–73.

14. Eyal Ginio, "Expansion of the Jewish Cemetery of Salonika (1709)—An Example of an Inter-Religious Struggle over Public Space in an Ottoman City," *Pe'amim* 98–99 (Winter–Spring 2004): 319–332; Evangelos Hekimoglou, *Ta mystēria tēs Thessalonikēs* (Thessaloniki, 2001), 97–135; Evangelos Hekimoglou, *H Thessalonikē tōn periēgētōn 1430–1930* (Athens, 2008), 81–84; Aron Rodrigue and Sarah Stein, eds., *A Jewish Voice from Ottoman Salonica: The Ladino Memoir of Sa'adi Besalel a-Levi* (Stanford, 2012), 139–141.

15. "Fortouna immobilaria de la Communita," December 31, 1931, JMTh, f. 22.

16. Meropi Anastassiadou, *Salonique, 1830–1912: Une ville ottomane à l'âge des Réformes* (New York, 1997), 136–157.

17. *La Epoka*, February 6, 1891.

18. *La Epoka*, December 6, 1889.

19. *La Epoka*, August 23, 1895 and May 1, 1896; *Hesed ve-Emeth: Sosiedad por amejorar el estado del Beth Ahaim* (Salonica, 1906).

20. Molho, "La Necropole Juive de Thessalonique," 382–383; Joseph Nehama, *Histoire des Israélites de Salonique* (Paris/Salonique, 1935–1978), 7:799–800.

21. *La Epoka*, December 2, 1887 and October 19, 1888.

22. Michael Molho, *Kontribusion ala Istoria de Saloniko* (Saloniko, 1932), 28–29; Michael Molho, "El Cementerio judío," 108.

23. *El Puevlo*, November 18, 1919.

24. *El Puevlo*, March 1, 1922.

25. Sam Lévy, Lausanne, to Venizelos, Paris, August 17, 1919, AIU, b. 13; Sam Lévy, "Les cimetières juifs de Salonique," *Menorah* 18 (November 15, 1927): 281.

26. *El Puevlo*, July 1, 1929.

27. *El Puevlo*, June 10, 1929.

28. Haim R. Habib, locum tenens of the chief rabbi, and J. Cazes, president of the Jewish Community of Thessaloniki to the prime minister, December 24, 1929 and S. Gonatas, governor general of Macedonia, to the political office of the prime minister, November 21, 1931, in *Documents on the History of the Greek Jews: Records from the Historical Archives of the Ministry of Foreign Affairs*, ed. Ph. Constantopoulou and Th. Veremis (Athens, 1999), 144–146, 198; superintendent of technical services to the general director of Macedonia, February 15, 1930, GMFA, USHMM, r. 1.

29. *El Puevlo*, July 1 and October 15, 1929.

30. *El Puevlo*, November 12, 1929.

31. Superintendent of the city planning office to the governor general of Macedonia, February 13, 1930, GMFA, USHMM, r. 1.

32. *El Puevlo*, February 14 and April 11, 1929.

33. *El Puevlo*, January 15 and 16, 1930; *La Aksion*, January 15, 1930; *El Puevlo*, August 22, 1930; *La Aksion*, January 21, 1930; *El Puevlo*, February 4, April 10, June 6, and June 7, 1932.

34. *El Puevlo*, June 6, 1929.

35. *El Puevlo*, June 10, 1929.

36. Ibid.

37. Rabbi Haim Habib to the Communal Council, 7 Heshvan 5690 [November 10, 1929], JMTh, f. 57.

38. Ibid.

39. *El Puevlo*, November 7, 1929.

40. Isaac S. Emmanuel, Lausanne, to the Communal Council, Salonica, November 22, 1929, USHMM, r. 755, d. 115.

41. As quoted in *El Puevlo*, June 9 and 10, 1927.

42. Correspondence between the Jewish Community of Salonica and Jewish communities in Paris, Prague, Vienna, and Berlin, November-December 1929, CAHJP, Gr/Sa 275.

43. Greek Embassies in Bulgaria, Egypt, France, Romania, and Turkey to the Ministry of Foreign Affairs, Athens, June-August 1930, GMFA, USHMM, r. 1.

44. *La Verdad*, March 15, 1921; *American Jewish Year Book* (1921–1922): 211.

45. Avram Galante, *Histoire des Israelites de Turquie* (Istanbul, 1940), 3:32–34; Victoria Solomonidis, "The Ionian University of Smyrna, 1919–1922, 'Light of the East,'" *Kampos: Cambridge Papers in Modern Greek* 5 (1997): 81–97; consul general of Greece, Smyrna, to Greek Embassy, Ankara, July 8, 1930, GMFA, USHMM, r. 1.

46. Haim R. Habib, locum tenens of the chief rabbi, and J. Cazes, president of the Jewish Community, to the prime minister, December 24, 1929 as translated in *Documents on the History of the Greek Jews*, ed. Constantopoulou and Veremis, 144–146.

47. Ibid, 146.

48. *La Aksion*, December 17, 1929; *El Puevlo*, December 27, 1929.

49. Commission for the Defense of the Jewish Cemetery to the Communal Council, December 5, 10, and 16, 1929, CAHJP, Gr/Sa 374; *El Puevlo*, November 12 and December 23, 1929 and January 22, 1930.

50. *El Puevlo*, December 26, 1929 and January 10, 1930.

51. Minutes of meeting of the cemetery commission, December 16, 1929, CAHJP, Gr/Sa 374; I. Alsheh to the Communal Council, January 10, 1930, USHMM, r. 755, d. 115.

52. Isaac Alsheh, "Raporto sovre la kuestion del simiteryo," August 31, 1930, YIVO, RG-207, f. 18.

53. Wolf to Kaklamanos, May 16, 1930, ABDBJ, acc. 3121/E3/158/3.

54. Kaklamanos to Wolf, July 4, 1930, ABDBJ, acc. 3121/E3/158/3.

55. Wolf to A. S. Diamond and Wolf to Recanati, July 7, 1930, ABDBJ, acc. 3121/E3/158/3.

56. Alsheh, "Raporto," pp. 3–4.

57. Yannis Hamilakis, *The Nation and its Ruins: Antiquity, Archaeology, and National Imagination* (Oxford, 2007), 99–101.

58. Board of Deputies of British Jews to the Assocation Amicale des Israélites de Salonique, Paris, October 23, 1930; Recanati to the Joint Foreign Committee of the Board of Deputies of British Jews, September 4, 1930; Recanati to J. M. Rich, December 19, 1930; J. M Rich to Jacques Bigart, January 3, 1931; J. M Rich to Recanati, January 12, 1931; all in ABDBJ, acc. 3121/E3/158/3.

59. *El Puevlo*, June 23, 1929.

60. Ibid.

61. *El Puevlo*, June 10, 1929.

62. Joseph Nehama, "Loke dizen las tombas a traverso nuestro simiteryo," HBA, b. 32, f. 36.

63. David Malkiel, *Stones Speak: Hebrew Tombstones from Padua, 1529–1862* (Leiden, 2014), 49.

64. Molho, *Kontribusion*, 33–34, 76–78.

65. *El Puevlo*, November 8, 1932.

66. *El Puevlo*, October 25, 1932.

67. *El Puevlo*, December 9, 1932.

68. Isaac Samuel Brudo, Salonica, to Isaac Emmanuel, Lausanne, December 4, 1931, IEA; Joseph Nehama, Salonica, to the Alliance Israélite Universelle, Paris, December 3, 1931, AIU, Grèce, b. 14.

69. Michael Molho, *Beveit ha'almin shel Yehudei Saloniki* (Salonica, 1932) (4 parts,

approx. 160 inscriptions); Isaac Emmanuel, *Gedole Salonki le-dorotam* (Tel Aviv, 1936) (approx. 500 inscriptions). After World War II, they published more of the corpus: Isaac Emmanuel, *Matsevot Saloniki* (Jerusalem, 1963–1968) (2 volumes, 1858 inscriptions); Michael Molho, *Matsevot beit ha-almin shel Yehudei Saloniki* (Tel Aviv, 1974) (1640 inscriptions plus 465 additional names).

70. Although the chief rabbinate initially accused Emmanuel of perpetrating the desecrations, Emmanuel argued that Molho was responsible. The cemetery guard, Brudo, later confessed that Molho had paid him to commit the desecrations. We do not have access to sources that reveal Molho's side of the story. The affair does not seem to have affected Molho's standing. Isaac S. Emmanuel to Rabbi Haim Habib, November 20, 1933 and February 5, 1934; Isaac S. Emmanuel to Koretz, February 5, 1934; both CAHJP, Gr/Sa 25; Emmanuel to Shemtov Saltiel, January 7, 1934; "Confession" of Isaac Brudo to the Commission of Inquiry into the Beth Ahaim Affair, May 7, 1934; both USHMM, r. 753, d. 111.

71. *El Puevlo*, December 8, 1932.

72. Baruch Ben-Jacob, *Kahal Rofeim: Grupo de medikos djidios ke egzersaron en Saloniko dezde la ekspulsion de Espanya asta oy* (Salonica, 1932), 5; *El Puevlo*, November 28 and December 9, 1932; Michael Molho, "Médicos Sefardíes de Salónica," *Sefárdica* 12 (2001): 167–197.

73. For the Latin epigraph, in dactylic hexameter, see Molho, *Matsevot beit ha-almin*, 149–150.

74. Thessaloniki Press Bureau to the Ministry of Foreign Affairs, February 2, 1930, as translated in *Documents on the History of the Greek Jews*, ed. Constantopoulou and Veremis, 148.

75. *El Puevlo*, June 7, July 18, August 29, August 31, September 1, November 28, and November 29, 1932; *La Aksion*, August 12, 24, 29, and 31, 1932; September 1, 4, and 23, 1932.

76. Extract of minutes of the Communal Council, December 31, 1933, CAHJP, Gr/Sa 138.

77. *El Puevlo*, November 1, 1932; Orly Meron, *Jewish Entrepreneurship in Salonica, 1912–1940: An Ethnic Economy in Transition* (Portland, 2012), 70–71.

78. *Makedonia*, April 1, 1936.

79. *El Mesajero*, December 22, 1935.

80. *El Mesajero*, December 8, 1935.

81. Commander of the Department of Health to the chief rabbi, March 24, 1934; Governor general of Macedonia to the chief rabbinate, August 4, 1934; both USHMM, r. 753, d. 105.

82. *El Mesajero*, April 3, 1936.

83. *Jewish Chronicle*, July 4, 1934; Koretz to the Communal Council, December 20, 1936, CAHJP, Gr/Sa 276.

84. *El Mesajero*, December 22, 1935.

85. *La Aksion*, December 10, 1935.

86. *Makedonia*, April 1, 1936.

87. Ibid.

88. *El Mesajero*, December 26, 1935; January 1 and April 2, 1936; *Jewish Telegraphic Agency*, October 21, 1935.

89. *Jewish Telegraphic Agency*, June 23, 1936.

90. Katerina Lagos, "Hellenism and Minority Education: The Promotion of Literacy and Cultural Assimilation," paper presented at the Modern Greek Studies Association, New York University (2011), 13.

91. *La Aksion*, July 29, 1936.

92. "Praktika dioikitikis epitropis Emborikou kai Viomihanikou Epimelitiriou" [Minutes of the Administrative Board of the Chamber of Commerce and Industry of Thessaloniki], meeting of July 2, 1936 at the Offices of the Chamber of Commerce and Industry of Thessaloniki. I thank Paris Papamichos Chronakis for bringing this source to my attention.

93. *El Mesajero*, April 5 and July 25, 1936. On Krallis, see Leon Saltiel, "Professional Solidarity and the Holocaust: The Case of Thessaloniki," in *Jahrbuch für Antisemitismusforschung* 24 (2015): 229-248; esp. 238.

94. "Praktika dioikitikis epitropis Emborikou kai Viomihanikou Epimelitiriou."

95. Ibid.

96. *Taxydromos*, July 3, 1936; *Makedonia*, July 3, 1936.

97. *Makedonia*, July 3 and 8, 1936.

98. *Makedonia*, July 8, 1936.

99. Quoted in *El Mesajero*, July 8, 1936.

100. Salomon Bitti, Salonica, to Daniel Alhanati, Athens, July 4, 1936, JMTh, f. 83.

101. *El Mesajero*, June 4, 1936.

102. *Israël*, July 29, 1936.

103. Sam Lévy, Garches, to Koretz, January 15, 1936, USHMM, r. 197, d. 106. See also *El Mesajero*, August 9, 1936; Sam Lévy, "Les cimetières juifs de Salonique," *Le Judaïsme Sepharadi* 5, no. 47 (November 1936): 174–175.

104. *El Mesajero*, July 28, 1936.

105. *La Aksion*, July 26, 1936.

106. *La Aksion*,, July 29, 1936.

107. *Makedonia*, July 28, 1936.

108. *El Mesajero*, July 28, 1936.

109. *Taxydromos*, July 28, 1936; *El Mesajero*, July 29, 1936; *La Aksion*, July 26, 1936.

110. *El Mesajero*, August 4, 1936.

111. *La Aksion*, July 29, 1936.

112. *La Aksion*, July 28, 1936.

113. Minutes of the Communal Council, July 30, 1936, JMTh, f. 14.

114. Ibid.

115. *El Mesajero*, August 6, 1936.

116. Minutes of the Communal Council, July 30, 1936, JMTh, f. 14.

117. *La Aksion*, July 29, 1936; minutes of the Communal Council, July 30, 1936, JMTh, f. 14.

118. *El Mesajero*, August 6, 1936.

119. Minutes of the Communal Council, July 30, 1936, JMTh, f. 14.

120. Ibid.

121. Ibid.

122. Telegram to the Ministries of Education and Religion, Agriculture, National Economy, Finance, Assistance, and the governor general of Macedonia, [summer 1936], USHMM, r. 755, d. 115.

123. Obligatory Law 890/1937, September 29, 1937, USHMM, r. 753, d. 105.

124. Nehama, Salonica, to Halff, Paris, April 1, 1937, AIU, Grèce, b. 14.

125. *El Mesajero*, March 10, 1938.

126. Simon Rousso to Koretz, March 14, 1938, USHMM, r. 691, d. 145.

127. Minutes of the Communal Council, December 16, 1937, USHMM, r. 753, d. 111; *La Aksion*, March 8, 9, and 15, 1938; *Homenaje a Don Michael Molho ofrecido por un núcleo de amigos y simpatizantes* (Buenos Aires, 1961), 16.

128. *La Aksion*, March 15, 1938.

129. Kirimis, governor general of Macedonia, to the Jewish Community of Salonica, February 3, 1939, USHMM, r. 753, d. 105.

130. Chief rabbi and the president of the Jewish Community of Salonica to the governor general of Macedonia, February 8, 1939, USHMM, r. 753, d. 111.

131. Report by Saby Saltiel, Rafael Menashe, and Simon Russo, November 21 1939, USHMM, r. 753, d. 105.

132. Chart of destroyed graves, December 3, 1939, USHMM, r. 753, d. 105.

133. Yacoel, "The Memoir of Yomtov Yacoel," in *The Holocaust in Salonika*, ed. S. Bowman (New York, 2002), 71–77.

134. Molho to Nehama, FMBTN, December 27, 1942, 44.2.

135. *Homenaje a Don Michael Molho*, 17, 40–61.

136. *Palestine Post*, October 28, 1946; *Jewish Chronicle*, November 22, 1946 and December 6, 1946; Molho, *In Memoriam*, 3:386–388; Cecil Roth, "The Last Days of Jewish Salonica: What Happened to a 450–Year Old Civilization," *Commentary* 10, no. 1 (July 1950): 49–55; David de Sola Pool, *Portraits Etched in Stone* (New York, 1952), 54–55; Elias Petropoulos, "Kynigoi Kraniōn" ["Skull Chasers"], *Skoliastēs* (May 1986): 33–35; Michael Matsas, *The Illusion of Safety: The Story of Greek Jews During the Second World War* (New York, 1997), 38–39; Ilan Karmi, "Jewish Cemeteries in Northern Greece in the Post World War II Era," in *The Jewish Communities of Southeastern Europe*, ed. I. K. Hassiotis (Thessaloniki, 1997), 229–248, esp. 238–239; Evangelos Hekimoglou, *Hoi*

Ampelokepoi echoun historia [The Ampelokipians Have History] (Ampelokepi, 1998), 155–156; Molho, "Germany's Policy against the Jews of Greece," 63–64; Maria Kavala, "Ē Thessalonikē stē Germanikē Katochi (1941–1944): Koinōnia, Oikonomia, Diōgmos Evraïōn" [Thessaloniki under German Occupation [1941–1944]: Society, Economy, Persecution of the Jews] (PhD dissertation, University of Crete-Rethymno, 2009), 146–147, 165–166; Saltiel, "Dehumanizing the Dead."

137. Miriam Novitch, *The Passage of the Barbarians: Contribution to the History of the Deportation and Resistance of Greek Jews*, trans. P. Senior (Hull, 1989), 55–57. Many of the bones remained in situ and have surfaced periodically over the years, most recently during excavations for the incomplete metro stop beside the University of Salonica.

Conclusion

1. Cecil Roth, "The Last Days of Jewish Salonica: What Happened to a 450–Year Old Civilization," *Commentary* 10, no. 1 (July 1950): 55. On the post-war period, see Rena Molho, "La reconstruction de la communauté juive de Salonique après la Shoah," in *Salonique: Ville juive, ville ottoman, ville grecque*, ed. E. Benbassa (Paris, 2014), 117–138; Rika Benveniste, *Those Who Survived: Resistance, Deportation, Return: Thessaloniki Jews in the 1940s* (Salonica, 2014) (Greek); Yakov Schiby, *Life Once Again: The Flight of the Greek Jews to Palestine, 1945–1948* (Athens, 2010) (Greek); Bea Lewkowitz, *The Jewish Community of Salonika: History, Memory, Identity* (London, 2006).

2. Cf. Dan Miron, "The Literary Image of the Shtetl," *Jewish Social Studies* 1, no. 3 (1995): 1–43; Steven Zipperstein, *Imagining Russian Jewry: Memory, History, Identity* (Seattle, 1999).

3. Joseph Nehama, "Ce qu'était la communauté juive de Salonique a la veille de la catastrophe," in *In Memoriam: Hommage aux Victimes Juives des Nazis en Grèce*, ed. Michael Molho (Salonica, 1948–1953 [reprint 1988]), 1:41.

4. *La Vara*, March 10, 1944.

5. *La Vara*, December 13, 1946.

6. Ibid.

7. *Cahiers Sefardis*, November 5, 1946.

8. El Komitato, "Prefas," *Zikhron Saloniki: Gedulata ve-hurbana shel Yerushalayim de-Balkan*, ed. D. Recanati (Tel Aviv, 1972-1985), 1:11; cf. the preface (in French) of the earlier memorial book, *Salonique, ville-mère en Israël* (Jerusalem, 1967).

9. Isaac Brudo, Haifa, to Michael Molho, Buenos Aires, June 18, 1956, FMBTN, 43.1–CE6.

10. Olga Borovaya, "Jews of Three Colors: The Path to Modernity in the Ladino Press at the Turn of the Century," *Jewish Social Studies*, 15, no. 1 (Fall 2008): 110–130; esp. 112.

11. Isaac S. Emmanuel, *Histoire des Israélites de Salonique* (Paris, 1936), 83.

12. E. g., George Th. Mavrogordatos, *Stillborn Republic: Social Coalitions and Party Strategies in Greece, 1922–1936* (Berkeley, 1983), 226.

13. *La Verdad,* November 30 and December 1, 1920.

14. *El Derito,* December 12, 1931.

15. *La Aksion,* February 16, 1936.

16. *El Puevlo,* October 1, 1928.

17. *El Mesajero,* October 13, 1936.

18. *El Mesajero,* June 26, 1936.

19. *La Aksion,* November 6, 1938.

20. On the communist activist Alberto Moreau, see Henry Besso, Washington DC, to Joseph Nehama, Salonica, April 30, 1963, JMTh/Nehama.

21. Eliau Estroumsa and Daniel Saïas, eds., *Sidur Sha'are Tefila hova le-dafus a"y ha-hevra "Tora u-melaha"* (Salonica, 1941). While preserving all of the traditional messianic passages and aspirations for a return to Zion, the prayer book modified the prayers for the holiday of Hanukkah, generally presented as a battle between Jews and their Hellenistic overlords in ancient Jerusalem. Instead of referring to the standard *Yevanim* ("Greeks"), they substituted in *Suriim* ("Syrians"), a change that made sense considering that, in the story of the holiday, the enemies of the Maccabees were the Seleucids, a Hellenistic empire based in Syria. The switch enabled the editors to avoid presenting the holiday as one about Greek-Jewish antagonism.

22. Mark Mazower, *Salonica, City of Ghosts: Christians, Muslims, and Jews, 1430–1950* (London, 2004), 416.

23. "Greece Under Occupation," in *Greece 1940–1949: Occupation, Resistance, Civil War: A Documentary History,* trans. and ed. R. Clogg (New York, 2002), 104–116; Panteleymon Anastasakis, *The Church of Greece under Axis Occupation* (New York, 2015).

24. Andrew Apostolou, "'The Exception of Salonika': Bystanders and Collaborators in Northern Greece," *Holocaust and Genocide Studies* 14, no. 2 (Fall 2000): 165–196.

25. K. E. Fleming, *Greece—A Jewish History* (Princeton, 2008), 190–204.

26. Shlomo Venezia, *Inside the Gas Chambers: Eight Months in the Sonderkommando of Auschwitz* (Cambridge, 2009), 80.

27. Leon Perahia, *Mazal* (Thessaloniki, 1990), 84–85 (Greek).

28. Nadjary miraculously survived. Translated in "Message in a Bottle: The Buried Manuscript of a Greek Jewish Inmate of Auschwitz," in *Sephardi Lives: A Documentary History, 1700–1950,* ed. J. P. Cohen and S. A. Stein (Stanford, 2014), 285–287.

29. *La Aksion,* May 19, 1935; *El Mesajero,* April 16, 1936.

30. *La Aksion,* May 3, 1938.

31. Minutes of the Communal Council, July 17, 1938, USHMM, r. 692, d. 145.

32. Joseph Nehama, *Histoire des Israélites de Salonique* (Paris/Salonique, 1935–1978), 7:530.

33. *Jerusalem Post,* February 10, 2011.

34. Devin E. Naar, "Jerusalem of the Balkans," *Jewish Review of Books* 4, no. 1 (Spring 2013): 8–11.

INDEX

Note: Locators in italics indicate pages with illustrations.

STANFORD STUDIES IN JEWISH HISTORY AND CULTURE
Edited by David Biale and Sarah Abrevaya Stein

This series features novel approaches to examining the Jewish past in the form of innovative work that brings the field into productive dialogue with the newest scholarly concepts and methods. Open to a range of disiplinary and interdisciplinary approaches from history to cultural studies, this series publishes exceptional scholarship balanced by an accessible tone that illustrates histories of difference and addresses issues of current urgency. Books in this list push the boundaries of Jewish Studies and speak compellingly to a wide audience of scholars and students.

Naomi Seidman, *The Marriage Plot: Or, How Jews Fell in Love with Love, and with Literature*
2016

Ivan Jablonka, *A History of the Grandparents I Never Had*
2016

For a complete listing of titles in this series, visit the Stanford University Press website, www.sup.org.